COLLECTIVISATION, CONVERGENCE AND CAPITALISM

STUDIES IN POLITICAL ECONOMY
edited by John Eatwell

COLLECTIVISATION, CONVERGENCE AND CAPITALISM
Political Economy in a Divided World

MICHAEL ELLMAN

University of Amsterdam

1984

ACADEMIC PRESS
(Harcourt Brace Jovanovich, Publishers)
London   Orlando   San Diego   San Francisco
New York   Toronto   Montreal   Sydney   Tokyo

ACADEMIC PRESS INC. (LONDON) LTD.
24/28 Oval Road
London NW1

United States Edition published by
ACADEMIC PRESS INC.
(Harcourt Brace Jovanovich Inc.)
Orlando, Florida 32887

British Library Cataloguing in Publication Data

Ellman, Michael
    Collectivisation, convergence and
    capitalism.—(Studies in political economy)
    1. Economics
    I. Title   II. Series
    330.12   HB171

    ISBN 0-12-237520-3

Typeset by Rowland Phototypesetting Ltd, Bury St Edmunds, Suffolk
and printed in Great Britain by St. Edmundsbury Press
Bury St Edmunds, Suffolk

SERIES EDITOR'S PREFACE

The revival of the analytical principles of classical political economy that has gathered pace since the mid-1960s has been based on the firm foundation of a logically coherent theory of value and distribution. It was the failure to provide this foundation which for many years confined the classical approach to being, at best, a repository of useful ideas on growth and technological progress (Smith's discussion of the division of labour and Marx's dissection of the labour process being good examples), or at worst, identified with simple-minded devotion to the labour theory of value as the 'qualitative' expression of capitalist exploitation—the position to which Hilferding retreated in the face of Böhm-Bawerk's critique of Marx, so depriving the surplus approach of any quantitative significance as a theory of value and distribution. The publication of Piero Sraffa's *Production of Commodities by Means of Commodities* changed all that. Sraffa not only generalised the mathematical solutions to the surplus approach which had been advanced by Dmitriev and Bortkeiwicz, but also presented the analytical *structure* of the surplus approach with stark clarity. Moreover, Sraffa provided a critique of the neoclassical theory of the rate of profit and so of the entire neoclassical explanation of value, distribution and output—hence clearing the ground for the redevelopment of classical theory.

With the analytical core now secure, attention can be turned to the development of other facets of classical and Marxian theory and to the empirical insights which this theory provides. In stark contrast to the neoclassical approach, which reduces all economic activity to a single principle—the competitive resolution of individual attempts to maximise utility subject to the constraints of technology and endowment—classical theory is constructed from a number of analytically separable components. The core of the theory, the surplus approach to value and distribution, takes as data the size and composition of output, the technology in use (the conditions of reproduction) and the real wage (or, in some cases, the rate of profit). These data do not, however, lie outside the realm of economics (as, for example, the neoclassical economists' utility functions do). We need to provide theoretical explanations of their determination. Hence Smith, Ricardo and Marx advanced theories of the real wage and of the level of output (Say's law in the case of Ricardo), and Smith and Marx presented detailed analyses of technological change. Assembled around the core, these theories are the building blocks of a general theory of the operations of the capitalist economy. There is in all this a clear danger of constructing a disjointed *ad hoc* collage of theories and empirical generalisations. This is avoided by enveloping the entire edifice in a general characterisation of the economic system: the clear specification, that is, of the capitalist mode of production. This serves both to cement the elements of the theory together and to eliminate propositions that do not fit.

This series of books is devoted to studies which develop and extend the classical framework. Broadly, there are two jobs to be done.

First, the classical theory itself must be developed and generalised. All the elements surrounding the core analysis of value and distribution—theories of output and employment, of accumulation of technology, of the wage, of competition and so on—require reassessment and 'modernisation' in the light both of Sraffa's results and of the many changing facets of the modern capitalist system. This will involve both theoretical development *and* empirical analysis. For one of the important characteristics of classical theorising is the manner in which theory is grounded in the socio-economic data of the system under consideration. The institutional environment is an essential part of the theory.

Second, the rejection of the now discredited neoclassical theory throws open a wide range of problems in international trade, development economics, fiscal and monetary policy and so forth, into which the classical approach can provide new insights. In part these will lead to the refreshing task of debunking the policy prescriptions of orthodox theory which revolve primarily around the fundamental theorem of welfare economics and the supposed 'efficiency' of competitive markets. But there is also a positive job to be done. The reconstruction of economic theory will inevitably precipitate a reinterpretation of economic policy and problems.

Just such a reinterpretation of the problems of communism and capitalism is presented in this book. In a wide variety of practical contexts Michael Ellman demonstrates the relevance of both the theoretical critique of orthodox theory and the constructive power of classical ideas. The papers on Soviet agriculture which have transformed the approach to the study of the relationship between agriculture and industry in economic development begin from the classical conception of surplus and the analysis of its distribution—whether by the price mechanism or, as in this case, by political fiat. Similarly, the discussion of the role of the price mechanism and the relationship between markets (or the lack of them) and efficiency, distinguishes carefully the claims of orthodox general equilibrium theorists from the role which prices can play within a quite different theory of economic behaviour. All this in the context of specific institutional and political environments which, Ellman shows, are central, not only to the formation of economic policy but to economic theory *per se*.

JOHN EATWELL
Trinity College, Cambridge
June 1984

PREFACE

I wish to acknowledge my gratitude to the economics faculties of Cambridge and Amsterdam universities. In Cambridge I earned my spurs as an economist and learned how to apply economic analysis to real issues of the economic development of the state socialist countries. In Amsterdam I have found a congenial atmosphere for further reflection and writing. To my colleagues and students in both universities I am grateful.

My specific debts with respect to each chapter are recorded in the footnotes to that chapter. I am also grateful to my wife for her assistance with the editing of the whole book.

MICHAEL ELLMAN
Amsterdam
January, 1984

ACKNOWLEDGEMENTS

I am grateful to the following publications and publishers for permission to reprint articles which first appeared in their pages:

Economic Journal (Chapter 2); *Journal of Development Studies* (Chapter 3); *Internationale Spectator* (Chapters 4 and 6); *De Economist* (Chapters 5 and 11); *Slavic Review* (Chapter 7); *Economisch Statistische Berichten* (Chapter 8); *Economica* (Chapter 9); Croom and Helm (Chapter 10); *Wetenschappelijk Raad voor het Regeringsbeleid* (Chapter 12); *World Development* (Chapter 13); *ACES Bulletin* (Chapter 14); *Soviet Studies* (Chapter 15); Academic Press (Chapter 16); *Intermediair* (Chapter 17); and the *Cambridge Journal of Economics* (Chapter 18).

CONTENTS

I. INTRODUCTION*

This book collects together in one easily accessible place papers published in a variety of journals and books in two languages. They represent the fruits of my last year in Cambridge and my first six years in Amsterdam. In Amsterdam I have been not an individual researcher but the leader of a research group. To mark this, I have included in the book papers written by two of my collaborators. Chapter 9 on inflation in centrally planned economies was written by Erik Dirksen, and Chapter 14 on economic reform in China by Ruud Knaack. In addition, Chapter 15 on Polish economic statistics was written jointly with Batara Simatupang. The papers are normally reprinted as they were first published, sometimes with small alterations to remove errors or provide additional information. I have not significantly changed any of them.

The book is divided into three sections. In the first, I consider the economics of the collectivisation of agriculture in the USSR. The first paper, in particular, aroused tremendous interest when first published. The three chapters taken together provide a coherent, strikingly revisionist, and I hope correct, analysis of the issues discussed.

In the second, I consider some aspects of the Soviet economy in the Kosygin–Brezhnev period. This began with the bright hopes of economic reform and ended in stagnation. The subjects range from the 1965 economic reform via Soviet grain imports to income distribution and the existence or otherwise of suppressed inflation.

In the third, I consider some problems of political economy in a divided world. The subjects range from full employment under state

* I am grateful to Bob Davies, John Eatwell, Alex Erlich, Mark Harrison, Ruud Knaack and Alec Nove for very helpful comments on an earlier version.

socialism, via economic reform in China, investment planning, and the impact of the political upheaval of 1980 on Polish economic statistics, to the economics of energy exports.

Most of the material in the book is empirical, but there are two theoretical chapters. The first takes issue with Marx and his successors about agriculture efficiency. It is argued that the theories on this important matter developed by Marx, Engels, Kautsky, Lenin, Stalin and Mao Zedong are wrong. The second criticises the convergence theory as developed by Tinbergen and his school.

As far as the collectivisation of Soviet agriculture is concerned, the traditional Western view was that Stalin had successfully implemented the policy advocated by Preobrazhensky, of squeezing the resources for rapid industrialisation out of the peasantry. In the Introduction to a famous paper (Erlich 1950, p. 58) in which Preobrazhensky was introduced to the Western academic world, it was argued that "no other viewpoint [than Preobrazhensky's] developed during these years [the 1920s] . . . was so violently repudiated at the beginning only to be implemented ultimately on a scale surpassing anything its author had ever thought possible".* Erlich's paper and subsequent book played a very useful role in introducing Preobrazhensky, and more generally the Soviet industrialization debate of the 1920s, into the Western academic consciousness. Nevertheless, the passage just quoted requires qualification and elaboration (some of which was already present in the body of the Erlich paper) to overcome some of the misinterpretations which have come to be widely believed. In particular, it is necessary to bear in mind the following points:

1. Preobrazhensky did *not* advocate forced collectivisation. In his 1926 book he advocated the use of such instruments as taxation, price policy, railway tariffs, the banking system and the state monopoly of foreign trade. As I point out in Chapter 3, in the curious language of contemporary development economics his book might well be considered as 'neo-classical' rather than 'Marxist' because he advocated the use of the price mechanism rather than coercion.

2. Preobrazhensky was concerned not just with rapid accumulation,

---

* Another idea in this paper that requires qualification is that (p. 84) the 1930s were "years of economic warfare waged by the villages against the cities". This is a curious description of the policies of 'liquidating the kulaks as a class' and 'taking grain' and their consequences.

but with *socialist* accumulation, the development of socialist relation of production. The relations of production imposed by the Stalin faction in Soviet agriculture, and more generally in the USSR, however, can more accurately be described as 'semi-serfdom'. This is discussed in Chapter 4.

3. There was no increase in unequal exchange between agriculture and industry in the USSR during the period of rapid industrialisation. There was a huge increase in the volume of investment in the USSR after 1928. Increased unequal exchange was *not* a significant factor in this increase. For the years 1928–32, the years of the First Five Year Plan, this is argued in great detail in Chapter 2.

4. In general, squeezing the resources for industrialisation out of agriculture is not a feasible strategy. Agriculture production requires substantial inputs of industrial producer goods to agricultural production and of industrial consumer goods to the rural population. Collectivisation tends to increase the material and investment intensity of agriculture. From Stalin to Brezhnev, a significant share of Soviet investment has always been allocated to agriculture.

5. The fall in urban real wages played a major role in financing rapid industrialisation in the USSR. The heroic years of Soviet industrialisation can more accurately be analysed with the help of the slogan of "the self-exploitation of the working class" than that of "original accumulation at the expense of the peasantry".

In view of these five points, the idea that Stalin "implemented" Preobrazhensky's viewpoint is unsatisfactory. The five points themselves are argued in more detail in the five sections which follow.

A. PREOBRAZHENSKY

It is unfortunate that the four lines from the Introduction to Erlich (1950) quoted above have had more impact than the body of the paper. In section IV Erlich correctly pointed out that (p. 69), "Actually, Preobrazhensky did not advocate the applications of methods of violence against the nonsocialist small-scale producers". In the same paper Erlich accurately describes the methods Preobrazhensky did advocate, state control of foreign trade and price policy. His arguments for state control of foreign trade would be familiar to a wide variety of economists and policy makers, ranging from Schacht to Godley.

As far as price policy is concerned, Preobrazhensky argued that it had two advantages over more direct means of acquiring resources. Economically, it was more efficient. "Accumulation by appropriate price policy has advantages over other forms of direct and indirect taxation of petty economy. The most important of these is the extreme facility of collection, not a single kopek being needed for any special apparatus" (Preobrazhensky, 1965, p. 111). Politically, it would arouse the least hostility. "The way of direct taxation is the most dangerous way, leading to a break with the peasants".*

It is important to note that Preobrazhensky's ideas evolved over time. In a well known paper of 1921,† the very year the NEP was introduced, he anticipated an armed conflict between the Soviet state and the kulaks. He regarded this as unavoidable and argued in good Stalinist style that "the outcome of the struggle will depend largely on the degree of organization of the two extreme poles, but especially on the strength of the state apparatus of the proletarian dictatorship". He concluded his argument—published only shortly after NEP was introduced and at a time of serious famine and disease—by warning his readers "to prepare for everything that will ensure victory in the inevitable class battles that are to come".   In his 1924 article, "The Fundamental Law of Socialist Accumulation" (reprinted in his 1926 book *The New Economics*) the thesis about the inevitable conflict between the state and the peasantry plays a central role, but economic levers (e.g. price policy) rather than administrative methods, play the key role in resolving the conflict in the interests of socialist accumulation.

In "Economic Equilibrium in the System of the USSR" (1927) attention has shifted to the conditions for growth equilibrium. The Harrodian conclusion about the essential precariousness of dynamic equilibrium is reached. The lesson is drawn that "The sum of these contradictions shows how closely our development towards socialism is connected with the necessity—for not only political but also for econ-

---

* *Pravda* 18 January 1924, speech at the 13th Party Conference. Quoted from Erlich (1950, p. 74).

† "Perspektivy novoi ekonomicheskoi politiki", *Krasnaya nov'* 3 (September–October 1921). For a discussion of this article see. L. Szamuely, *First Models of the Socialist Economic Systems* (Budapest, 1974), pp. 104–107. For a translation of the article see E. A. Preobrazhensky, *The Crisis of Soviet Industrialization* (London and New York, 1980), pp. 3–19.

omic reasons—to make a breach in our socialist isolation and to rely in the future on the material resources of other socialist countries".

In "On the Methodology of Drawing up the General Plan and the Second Five-Year-Plan" (unpublished 1931) he criticised over-investment and pointed out the danger of an "overaccumulation crisis". His argument that "socialism is production for consumption's sake" was unacceptable during the frenzy of the Soviet Great Leap Forward and was condemned as heretical. All in all, his position in 1931 seems to have been similar to that of Rakovsky, another Left Communist intellectual, who in an article of 1930 warned against the coming Soviet economic crisis (which shook the whole economy in 1931–33) and stressed the wasteful and inefficient methods of Stalinist industrialisation.* Many of the phenomena which are well known today from the writings of Kornai, Xue Muqiao and other economic reformers in the state socialist countries, such as shortages and investment tension, were first discussed by Soviet Communists reflecting on the Civil War (e.g. Kritsman) or the First Five Year Plan (e.g. Rakovsky and, before him, Bukharin in his famous article "Notes of an Economist" published in *Pravda* in September 1928).

Although the Preobrazhensky of 1921 *can* reasonably be described as a Stalinist, this is not so of the Preobrazhensky of 1927 and 1931. Like Stalin, his ideas about economic policy evolved in the 1920s, but in the opposite direction. Historically speaking, for Preobrazhensky (as for Keynes) it is a mistake to identify him entirely with particular positions since his views changed over time. (Keynes, after all, supported deflation in 1920 to deal with the inflationary crisis.) Although he developed the theory which Stalin attempted to implement, his own attitude to Stalinist industrialisation seems to have been ambivalent, since he backed the goal of industrialisation but was unhappy with the methods used to attain it. Nevertheless, it would be a gross error to depict Preobrazhensky as a fundamental opponent of Stalinist economics. Not only did he develop the theory which Stalin attempted to implement, but he broke with Trotsky and accepted Stalin's leadership in July 1929 in response to Stalin's pro-industry and anti-kulak policies. He also participated in the 'Congress of Victors' (1934), that is the victory celebrations of those who had launched a huge industrialisation

---

* 'Na s'ezde i v strane", *Byulleten' oppozitsii* no. 25/26 (1931) p. 9–32. For a translation, with introduction by R. W. Davies, see *Critique* 13.

programme, overcome the crisis of 1931–33, and introduced semi-serfdom in the USSR.

B.   SOCIALIST ACCUMULATION

Despite the impression created by much Western academic writing, Preobrazhensky was not an academic economist interested in 'growth' but a Marxist interested in the development of socialism. The original socialist accumulation he theorised about in *The New Economics* was original *socialist* accumulation. This has recently been stressed by Millar (1978) and Filtzer (1978). As Filtzer (1978, p. 66) has correctly noted,

> It was Stalin's 'contribution' to the 'theory' of the workers' movement that progress towards socialism could be assessed independently of the nature of the production relations that were being created. Preobrazhensky, like all revolutionary communists, held the view that economic wealth and highly developed techniques make the transition to socialism possible but nothing more. Those who describe Preobrazhensky, Trotsky or other members of the Left as 'super industrialisers' are themselves victims of the most banal Stalinist propaganda. Industrialisation offered only the prerequisite for building socialism. It made the development of socialist education and the acquisition of socialist culture, which were equally important in the transition process, possible but not inevitable.

If one takes as one's starting point the refusal to identify industrialisation under state ownership of the means of production and Five Year Plans with socialism, then there arises the important question of the nature of the relations of production in the USSR and Soviet type economies. This is a topical and much discussed subject (Voslensky, 1980; Konrad and Szelenyi, 1979; Lane, 1976; Hirszowitz, 1980; Ticktin, 1973; Fehér, Heller and Márkus, 1983).

A key episode in the creation of this social system was the collectivisation of agriculture in the USSR in 1929–32. In my analysis of the economics of collectivisation considerable attention is devoted to changes in the relations of production in the USSR in 1929–32. This is because I share the view that the nature of the relations of production is of great importance and because of the dramatic changes which took place in them in the USSR in 1929–32. In Chapter 2, attention is drawn to four important changes in the relations of production in the USSR during the First Five Year Plan. These were the statisation of the trade unions, the rapid growth of forced labour, the replacement of a market relationship between town and country by a coercive relationship ('collectivisation'), and the increased differentiation between the élite and the masses. In Chapter 4 I characterise the social system in agriculture resulting from the third of these changes as 'semi-feudal'.

> The reason for this description is as follows. Work on the collective farms was enforced by coercion and paid very little. The livelihood of the farmers was gained from their private plots, the right to which depended on their performance of labour for the collective farms. The peasants were tied up to the land by the passport system.* This system was very similar to that existing in mediaeval Western Europe and in pre 1861 Russia (the serfs were emancipated in Russia in 1861) . . .
>
> The regressive nature of Soviet social relations in this period, although first tried out on agriculture, did not only affect agriculture. It was during the collectivisation campaign, liquidating the kulaks as a class and taking grain, that cadres were formed who were prepared to do anything, however loathsome and bestial, provided that Stalin ordered it. In addition, collectivisation demonstrated to Stalin that it is entirely feasible to carry out drastic social changes, liquidating multi-million strata of the population, by coercion. These two factors played a major role in the mass arrests of 1937–'38 and the creation and maintenance of the Gulag Archipelago in the USSR and the countries to which the Soviet system was exported after World War II.
>
> Solzhenitsyn's treatment of collectivisation as Stalin's greatest crime is entirely logical. The Gulag Archipelago was largely a result of the decision to adopt the coercive model of the role of agriculture in economic development. Many of the first inhabitants of the camps were farmers deported from their villages at the time of collectivisation. From the point of view of numbers employed, agriculture in the USSR in the 1930s was by far the most important branch of economy. Reliance on coercion in various construction and mining enterprises was simply a small generalisation, from a quantitative point of view, of the principle, reliance on coercion, on which the main branch of the economy was organized.

The characterisation of the relations of production in Soviet agriculture during the Stalin period as 'semi-serfdom' and of Stalinism as a whole as a generalisation of the relations of production introduced by Stalin in agriculture, is very much in the spirit of Bukharin's remark-

---

* A passport is an internal identity document. Without one it is illegal to live in a town. Up till the late 1970s, passport were issued only to towns-people and not to villagers. The Soviet passport system had much in common with the South African pass system.

ably perceptive early 1929 characterisation of Stalin's agrarian policies as "military-feudal exploitation of the peasantry".*

C. UNEQUAL EXCHANGE IN THE USSR, 1928–32

The role of unequal exchange in Soviet accumulation is analysed in Chapters 2 and 3. The main sources used are the work of the Soviet historian Barsov and the unpublished official national accounts for 1928, 1929 and 1930. The main conclusion reached is that "there is no basis whatsoever for the view that the increase in investment during the First Five Year Plan was financed by an increase in the agricultural surplus".

In a 1978 survey article, Harrison (1978, p. 80) referred to this conclusion as a "real bombshell". He went on to observe that "nearly everyone now accepts that Barsov has proved that collectivisation did not enable the extraction of an increased surplus from agriculture, and that agriculture did not finance the increase in industrial accumulation in the 1930s".

To many this seemed paradoxical. The fact that agriculture in the USSR was collectivised largely in order, as Stalin put it, to collect "tribute", is well know. It is also well known that grain procurements did rise in the First Five Year Plan and that rural living standards were extremely depressed throughout the Stalin era. Stress on these two absolutely correct facts, however, ignores the following.

First, it is entirely normal in human affairs for there to be a divergence between *intentions* and *outcomes*. Marxists expected under socialism that this divergence would disappear, since mankind would consciously determine its own future. This certainly has not happened in the USSR where the leadership has been repeatedly confronted by the unexpected outcomes of its policies, from the economic crisis of 1931–33 to the economic and social stagnation of 1979–82.

Secondly, coercion is an extremely *inefficient* method of procuring agricultural products. The nineteenth century argument—shared by both liberals and Marxists—that freedom is more productive than coercion, is often correct. As the Chinese economist Xue Muqiao (1981, pp. 109–110) has observed with respect to Chinese experience:

---

* For a discussion of this characterisation, and its significance, see Cohen (1974, pp. 320–322).

For years, underpricing of agricultural products aggravated their shortage, leading to purchases on a requisition basis or by state quotas. Even to this day, non-staple foods are being rationed in many cities. If we raise the purchasing prices of these products by a reasonable margin and ensure the supply of food grain and fodder to peasants engaged in their production, the output will rise speedily to meet market demands. Many localities were assigned compulsory production targets by official orders instead of being prompted to do things by economic means, resulting in a steady decrease in output. Sole reliance on administrative authority by those who do not know how to apply the laws of a commodity economy often backfires.

The view that peasants do not respond to economic levers and that therefore administrative methods are necessary, is entirely erroneous. Peasants do respond both to economic levers and to administrative methods. The latter is an excellent way of creating shortages and famines, the former—if properly used—of increasing output and ensuring that goods are available to those with money to buy them.

Thirdly, human suffering may not be purely 'rational', "an unavoidable part of the cost of a desirable and necessary policy of industrialization" (Carr, 1961, p. 75), but also contain an important element of waste, resulting from ignorance, inefficiency, erroneous perceptions and political choices. Of course there were major objective factors leading to the grain crisis, and industrialisation was undoubtedly a progressive policy. Any regime that rapidly increased employment in sectors producing non-wage goods (e.g. heavy industry, industrial construction, defence, administration etc.) would have generated tension in the grain balance since it would have greatly increased the demand for marketed agricultural products without increasing the supply of marketed industrial products to exchange for them. This is well known and has been much discussed. Furthermore, I share the view of Marx, Stalin and Carr that industrialisation was a progressive policy in the sense that it created the possibility of a better life for the people of the USSR. Nevertheless, it is important to give due attention to the subjective aspects of the matter, to the contribution to the difficulties faced by the Bolsheviks made by their own ideas and policies.

For example, an important cause of the grain problems of 1927–32 was the exaggeration by the party leadership of grain output and hence of potential marketed output (Wheatcroft, 1974a,b, 1977). The party leadership rejected the relatively accurate estimates of specialists and substituted spurious, but politically convenient, figures.*

Similarly, blinded by their theory of the inevitable advantages of large-scale socialist production, and the inevitable backwardness of peasant agriculture, the Bolsheviks failed to notice that Soviet agriculture in the 1920s showed remarkable vitality. As Harrison (1983) has pointed out,

> The evidence is that both yields and harvests of grain grew rather rapidly until the mid-twenties, by which time they had roughly matched the pre-revolutionary benchmark. Recovery was less marked than current Soviet data would imply. It was also uneven, being least marked in the traditional grain-surplus regions of the south and centre; producer and consumer demands, which also grew rapidly, kept the grain balance under constant tension. Meanwhile, however, the degree of agriculture's monocultural dependence upon extensive grain cultivation was diminishing, and resources previously devoted to grains were being shifted into other arable and non-arable sectors. The arable hectarage devoted to relatively input-intensive, high-yielding commodity ('industrial') crops had doubled. The country's livestock herds had recovered quickly from wartime losses and, after recovery, continued until 1928 to grow at an annual rate of 3–4 per cent compared to the sluggish prerevolutionary precedent of under one per cent. Quantitative growth in live-stock herds until 1928 was accompanied by improved milk and meat yields. These encouraging trends to some extent exacerbated the difficulties on the grain front, and in any case were sharply checked in 1928. Farm technology remained backward, and yields vulnerable to environmental fluctuations. But the picture of peasant agriculture under NEP as stagnant and unresponsive to opportunities is sharply refuted.

Blinded by their theory (criticised in chapter 13), the Bolsheviks 'saw' something entirely different and their policies were influenced by this false picture.†

---

* This was the beginning of a long history of statistical falsification. The importance of independent social organisations in reducing the distortions in official statistics is shown clearly by Polish events in 1980/82 (see Chapter 15). Another example of the way Soviet economic statistics are manipulated to convey an incorrect impression is provided by macro-economic statistics for 1979–82 (Chapter 10).

† It would, of course, be a mistake to exaggerate the importance of this kind of *economic* argument in Bolshevik decision-making. For Leninists the question of power (*kto-kogo*, i.e. who rules who) was always decisive. In a well known and much quoted passage of 1929 (*Byulleten' Oppozitsii*, 1929, no. 1–2, p. 22), Trotsky wrote of the policies advocated by Bukharin that while they might well yield fruits, they would be "capitalist fruits which at no distant stage will lead to the political downfall of Soviet power". The same point, the key role of political factors (i.e. Soviet power versus the restoration of capitalism) has also been made by the two leading historians of this period (Carr and Davies, 1969, pp. 237–246).

Another problem caused by Bolshevik theory concerns social stratification in the countryside. The rural population was undoubtedly stratified, but the Bolshevik theory of rural stratification, which transplanted the categories of industrial capitalism to small-scale agriculture, was not a very helpful tool for comprehending this (Shanin, 1972). Hence all attempts to apply the Marxist-Leninist categories to the reality of rural Russia in the 1920s produced theses and analyses which "added confusion to every argument" and were largely "mythical" (Carr and Davies, 1969 pp. 19, 25). As a result, when the crisis came, it turned out that an important element of policy was a "major miscalculation" (Carr and Davies, 1969, p. 143). In general, it was not possible to rely on the support of the rural masses in making the transition from private farming to collectivist farming. Yet again, Bolshevik theory had produced expectations at variance with reality.

Another important source of the grain problem was the relative price policy which was pursued. Anxious to supply cheap bread to the workers, state procurement prices for grain were low (compared to costs of production or to the pre-war situation) relative to other agricultural products. Hence grain procurements were discouraged and the peasants grew other crops or fed their grain to their animals (see Nove, 1969, pp. 141–142). This was not a result of 'kulak sabotage' but of the counterproductive policies of the Bolshevik.

Yet another cause of the grain problem was that during NEP the Bolsheviks created—without understanding what they were doing—the world's first peace-time 'shortage economy'.* Nowadays it is well known that the victory of state socialism in this or that country, whether it is the USSR, Cuba or Vietnam, rapidly leads to widespread shortages of all goods. The famous Hungarian Kornai (1980) has developed a whole theory about shortage economies. He has shown that shortages do not result from the mistakes of this or that bureaucrat, but are deeply rooted in the institutions of state socialism and the policies of the party leadership. The Soviet shortages of the 1920s played a major role in creating the grain problem by discouraging the peasants from marketing output. It made little sense to market output when desired goods were only sporadically, or never, available (Nove, 1969, pp. 139–140).

Blind to the economic processes at work, subscribers to erroneous

---

* The terminology is Kornai's. See J. Kornai, *Economics of Shortage* (Amsterdam 1980). In the USSR in the 1920s it was known as a 'goods famine' (*tovarnyi golod*).

theories, basing themselves on falsified statistics, and pursuing a counterproductive price policy, it is scarcely surprising that the Bolsheviks found themselves in difficulties. Hence, the view that the policies which the Bolsheviks finally implemented were "an unavoidable part of the cost of a desirable and necessary policy of industrialisation" is seen to be one-sided. Industrialisation *was* desirable and necessary. The costs of the Bolshevik industrialisation policy, however, were not all "unavoidable" since only part of the difficulties and costs was inherent in the logic of rapid industrialisation. Part of them was self-created.

It should be noted, however, that I do not endorse Millar's (1974) view that collectivisation was unnecessary, "an unmitigated economic disaster". I draw attention (Chapter 2) to its role in increasing procurements of basic wage goods and providing urban labour. In Chapter 3 I draw attention to the obvious, but important, fact that whether or not it was 'necessary' it was certainly *sufficient* as a framework for the relations between agriculture and industry which enabled a remarkably rapid process of industrialisation to proceed. To establish that collectivisation was 'unnecessary' for industrialisation would require demonstration by means of a counterfactual historical experiment *using a model that is indubitably a correct representation of the underlying economic relationships.* Although the work of Hunter (1973, 1981a,b) is interesting, the difficulties which have arisen in modelling contemporary Western economies, and the serious limitations in the accepted wisdom about Soviet economic development in the 1920s and 1930s which have been revealed by detailed empirical work by Davies and his school, indicate that the time for definitive judgement has not yet come and probably never will. Furthermore, one must give due weight to the political factors that were decisive for the Bolsheviks (see footnote p. 10). In my opinion, in the present state of ignorance, the view that the policies adopted were 'necessary' for the industrialisation of the USSR is unsatisfactory because it ignores the extent to which the grain problem of the late 1920s was self created and the extent to which the policies actually implemented after 1929 were wasteful. The view that they were 'sufficient', on the other hand is obviously true. The view that they were 'unnecessary' seems to me non-proven. Moreover, when considering their 'necessity' or otherwise one must ask necessary for what? As Wheatcroft *et al.* (1982) have pointed out, the answer to the question as to whether the policies were necessary depends partly on whether one considers the goal to be industrialisation in general, or industrialisation achieved by very high levels of investment, such as took place in the USSR after 1929. It is important to realise that from a Soviet perspective collectivisation had very important positive aspects. As I point out in the Conclusion to Chapter 4,

> The collectivisation of Soviet agriculture was successful in providing the basic wage goods, industrial crops and labour needed for rapid industrialisation. It was also successful in eliminating the social basis of an anti-Communist political movement and organising agriculture on the same basis of state control and state management ('socialism') on which industry was organised.

Much Western assessment of collectivisation is implicitly or explicitly guided by non-Soviet criteria of assessment.

D. AGRICULTURE AND ACCUMULATION

Agriculture is a sector of the economy the performance of which is dependent, *inter alia*, on inputs from industry. This was just as true for the USSR in the 1920s and 1930s as for all countries today. As Millar (1976, p. 53) has correctly noted, many writers

> have not understood that there is no such thing as a self-sufficient peasant household, and there wasn't in Russia in the 1920s. Many have a notion that agriculture receives nothing from industry but a few luxuries like a pair of trousers or sugar. But the peasants also need kerosene [paraffin], matches, soap, salt, condiments, steel for plows, milling services, and a number of other goods and services that a peasant community cannot produce, or at least can in no way produce efficiently.

To suppose that agriculture produces 'surpluses', independent of the level of industrial inputs into agriculture, which are available for appropriation in the interests of accumulation, is complete fantasy. As far as industrial producer goods are concerned, it is analogous to the view that the output of motor cars is given and independent of the level of steel and rubber inputs into the car industry. As far as industrial consumer goods are concerned, it is analogous to the view that the supply of rented accommodation is given and independent of the returns to the supplier.

Hence, the parasitical approach to agriculture which assumes that it is simply a producer of 'surpluses' is doomed to failure. It can only 'succeed' in increasing marketed output—if it does that—by reducing the food available for the rural population, both human and livestock.

It is because of the interdependent nature of agriculture and industry, the higher material and investment intensity of socialised agriculture, and the adverse development of production after collectivisation, that so much of Soviet investment has always been directed to agriculture. As Wiles (1964, pp. 269–270) long ago pointed out, it is "not true that agriculture . . . has been starved of capital . . . both the official figures and [Western recalculations] put investment in agriculture at 18–20% of all investment under Stalin, during the whole period of his rule". This has become still more true since 1965, when Brezhnev's huge agricultural investment programme has been implemented. This investment may not have been very effective, but it has certainly been large. One of the ironies of Soviet collectivisation is that, although intended largely to collect 'tribute', it actually created a need for substantial investment (e.g. in tractors) to replace the resources (e.g. horses) which had been destroyed by collectivisation.

The experience of the USSR, and of other countries which have followed the Soviet model of collectivisation, is that collectivist agriculture requires a large inflow of industrial goods for its operation. This is pointed out in Chapter 3, which extends the argument of chapter 2 to the USSR in the late 1930s and to China. Socialised agriculture, at any rate in the European CMEA countries, typically requires more investment per unit of output than private agriculture. Private farmers tend to substitute their own relatively abundant labour for purchased inputs.★ On the other hand, socialised farms, faced with the difficulties of disciplining and motivating labour, the allocation by the state of investment independent of prospective returns, a soft budget constraint, and a state which sees in investment the solution to all economic problems†, tend to substitute material inputs and investment for

---

★ For example it is not clear that the wooden plough, the rhetorical symbol for Russian agricultural backwardness, gave a lower yield per hectare than the steel plough (Simms, 1982, p. 246). It did, however, require more effort than a steel plough. Hence use of the wooden plough enabled the peasant to substitute his own labour for a purchased input.
† This is an old Marxist tradition. For example commenting on the crop failure of 1891, Plekhanov argued that what was required to prevent a repetition of such an event was "the introduction of better agricultural techniques". Actually, however, as Simms (1982) has argued, the main cause of the crop failure was a drought and drought has remained the main cause of crop failures in Russia regardless of changes in technique, ownership of the means of production etc. For fundamental metereological-

labour. Similarly, private farmers tend to use to the maximum possible extent self-produced agricultural inputs whereas socialised farms with their large scale of operations and soft budget constraint tend to rely on externally purchased inputs of industrial or foreign origin. The relatively high material intensity and investment intensity of socialised agriculture is well known from many Polish studies (Simatupang, 1981). In Polish agriculture in 1975, the average value of fixed assets per fully employed person was four times greater in the socialised sector than in the private sector. Although gross output per hectare in the socialised sector in 1976 was somewhat higher than in the private sector, net output was much lower. To suppose that agriculture can be expected to provide a huge net flow of goods for an industrialisation programme, and that this is a major rationale for collectivisation, is a fallacy. The socialisation of agriculture Soviet style can be expected to lead to a greater materials and investment intensity of agriculture.

This conclusion has been assimilated into modern thinking about non-capitalist development. For example, Fitzgerald (1982) analysing original socialist accumulation in a peripheral socialist economy (PSE) has argued that the main source of accumulation in such an economy must be international differential rent (e.g. the income derived from selling primary products such as oil on the world market). Squeezing the peasantry, in his model, cannot provide resources for accumulation and is politically harmful.

Original socialist accumulation cannot be based on squeezing agriculture. It simply is not feasible. During the course of development, agriculture supplies labour, food and non-food products (e.g. cotton, leather, flax etc.) to the urban sector, and possibly also provides some exports. It also requires, however, for its development, a stream of industrial goods both for rural consumption and for maintaining and increasing production levels. The production of commodities by means of commodities applies also to agriculture. It is true that agriculture, like other sectors of the economy, generates value added which is available for taxation or voluntary transfer. The economic rent element

---

geographical reasons Russian agriculture was and is particularly vulnerable to the weather, especially to drought (see Chapter 6). What is needed to deal with this problem is not enormous low-yielding investments in production (agriculture is a diminishing returns sector and much of Russian agricultural land is low-yielding marginal land), but adequate stocks (either of grain itself or of foreign exchange).

in this value added, however, is not normally large relative to the accumulation required, and obtaining it without reducing output is difficult. Although oppressing the peasantry is, unfortunately, entirely feasible (and historically very common) obtaining substantial net resources for accumulation in this way, is not. The attempt to do the unfeasible may have severe adverse consequences both for domestic agriculture and for the socio-political system.

E.   ORIGINAL ACCUMULATION AND THE WORKERS

In *The New Economics* Preobrazhensky assumed (p. 122) that

> from the moment of its victory the working class is transformed from being the object of exploitation into also being the subject of it. It cannot have the same attitude to its own labour power, health, work and conditions as the capitalist has. This constitutes a definite barrier to the tempo of socialist accumulation, a barrier which capitalist industry did not know in its first period of development.

This assumption was erroneous. Having established their dictatorship (a dictatorship *over* the proletariat rather than *of* the proletariat) the Bolsheviks proceeded to cut real wages, suppress working class activity and impose Taylorism in a way the capitalists would have envied. According to the Soviet historian Barsov, during the First Five Year Plan the rate of surplus value quadrupled (Chapter 2 footnote p. 46). According to Vyas (1979, p. 129), "Urban real wages fell drastically during the First Plan period, and even if a longer period is taken, to include the Second Five Year Plan, real wages fell between 1929 and 1937 by 43%."*

This does *not* mean that the peasantry did not suffer under collectivisation or that the peasants were not the main victims of the famine of 1932–34. It simply means that their suffering was not a sign that an increased net transfer of commodities from agriculture was a significant source of the increase in accumulation during the first two Five Year Plans. Rather it was a sign of the fact, which is one of the conclusions of Chapter 2, that Stalin's grain procurement system enabled agriculture

---

* Per capita income did not fall in this dramatic way because of the rise in the participation rate.

to be treated as a "residual sector which absorbed shocks (e.g. bad harvests)." When there was a bad harvest it was the peasants who starved, not because net inter-sectoral transfers had moved against them but because institutions had been created which ensured that they, rather than some other sector, were the residual sector which had to bear shocks. To put it another way,

> the conclusion to be drawn from the increased poverty of the villagers (especially the Ukrainian villagers) in 1932 as compared with 1928 is not that the contribution of agriculture to investment rose, but that out of a smaller agricultural output agriculture made such the same contribution as before, and hence there was less food available for the villagers, many of whom starved as a result.

In addition to their *economic* deprivation under state socialism, workers under state socialism also experience *cultural* deprivation. This derives from the fact that not only are all independent working class organisations emasculated and transformed into corporatist organis- ations of both workers and managers, but the authorities attempt to replace the values of actual workers by those of an imaginary 'socialist man'. The whole process has been well described by the Hungarian writer Szelenyi (1979). Under state socialism:

> the immediate producer has no more control over the product of his labour than the worker in a capitalist economy. But in state-socialist societies the cultural deprivation of the working class is probably more serious than the economic—the worker is deprived not only of the products of his labour, but also of his social identity. Curiously enough, one of the first measures of the so-called 'dictatorship of the proletariat' was the abolition of all working class organisations. The authorities outlawed not only political organisations such as parties, trade unions and youth groups, but even workers' choirs and hiking clubs. Since the working class has ultimate power in society—argued the official ideo- logues of state socialism—there is no longer any need for specifically worker organisations. The trade unions were transformed into worker– management corporations (in all East European societies managerial and engineering staff belong to the same union as worker), and the same logic was applied to 'innocent' cultural and sporting organisations or clubs.
>   Not only are the workers deprived of the opportunity to associate with their fellow workers, but their quest for identity as workers is also continuously questioned. The worker is replaced with an ideological notion, that of the proletariat—the worker who is aware of his historical mission. The worker finds himself labelled as 'petty bourgeois' or 'lumpen-proletariat' if he tries to live up to his immediate values and

aspirations, and he is accused of lacking 'proletarian consciousness'. The empirically identifiable values, aspirations and way of life of the actual physical workers are confronted with the ideals of 'socialist man', who actually and in class terms is a faceless creature devised by Soviet Marxist ideologues. If someone were to analyse carefully the ideal type of 'socialist man'—a test still to be done—he would find striking similarities with the values and tastes of the high-brow upper middle class of any advanced industrial society. 'Socialist man' should read books, listen to music, be dressed like and behave with his children as doctrinaire leftwing academics do. If a semi-skilled factory labourer in Prague does not match up to this ideal, then he should be ashamed of himself.

The dictatorship over the working class having been firmly established, real wages cut sharply and the working class culturally dispossessed, the Stalinists then launched a state-sponsored Taylorist movement ('Stakhanovism'). This was a process, much opposed by the workers, by which work norms were raised by relentless pressure from above accompanied by masses of lies in the media.

In the USSR, the dictatorship over the working class which was fully established in the early Stalin period, has remained in power. The state security organs have remained too strong for the re-emergence of independent working class organisations. The most significant proletarian uprisings up till now were the camp revolts of 1952–54 so lovingly described by Solzhenitsyn. In Poland on the other hand, where state socialism has no indigenous roots and is entirely an alien imposition, 1980 saw the emergence of a mass working class movement. Although eventually suppressed by the riot police and the army, the circumstances that gave rise to it are similar throughout the state socialist world and future attempts to create autonomous working class organisations in the state socialist countries are quite possible. In the UK, the road from deportation as a reward for trade union activity, to ennoblement and a seat in the House of Lords, was a long and difficult one. In the state socialist countries it will be no more easy.

Many people are surprised that a revolution in the name of socialism should have led to the creation of an authoritarian social and political system in which an official stratum prevents the emergence of autonomous working class organisations and rules by repression. There is absolutely nothing surprising about this. As noted above, it is quite normal in human affairs for actions to have consequences entirely at variance with the intentions of the actors. It is not for nothing that history has been defined as the study of the unintended consequences of human actions. Was the outcome of the Eighty Years War (1568–1648) in the Netherlands or the revolutionary upheaval in seventeenth century England a Kingdom of the Saints? The likely course of a socialist revolution was clearly foreseen before 1917 by Bakunin, Plekhanov, Makhaisky and Michels. Bakunin argued that if the Marxists came to power they would set up "a single state bank concentrating in its hands all commercial-industrial, agricultural and even scientific production, and divide the mass of the people into two armies, an industrial and an agricultural, under the direct command of state engineers, who will form a new privileged scientific-political class." Dealing with the objection that this new privileged stratum would really be proletarian because its members would be workers, Bakunin argued—absolutely correctly—that this was wrong since they would be "former workers, who however, as soon as they have become representatives or governors of the people, *cease to be workers* and look down on the whole common workers' world from the height of the state."* Plekhanov, concerned specifically with Russia, argued in the 1880s against the Narodnik view that it would be possible to organise a socialist revolution in the near future in backward Russia. He argued strongly against this and suggested that were a revolution in the name of socialism to be made soon the resulting regime would be unable to implement the goals of the socialist movement.† At the 1906 Fourth Party Congress, Lenin polemicised with Plekhanov about the possibility of a restoration of Asiatic despotism in Russia after the revolution. He admitted that this was possible, and argued that relative and conditional guarantees against it would be provided by the absence of a bureaucracy, standing army and police, but that the only absolute guarantee would be a socialist revolution in the West. Neither the relative nor the absolute guarantees were ever met, so there is no logical reason for a Leninist to reject the Wittfogel thesis.‡ Makhaisky (1905) applied Marxist analysis

---

* These quotations are from R. Bahro, *The Alternative in Eastern Europe* (1978), pp. 40–41.

† G. V. Plekhanov, *Sotzialism i politicheskaya borba* (Geneva 1883). This is reprinted in *Sochineniya* 3rd edn (n.d.), vol. 2. See in particular p. 81. For a translation of the key passage see M. Ellman, *Socialist Planning* (1979), p. 269.

‡ By 'the Wittfogel thesis' I understand the proposition that the October Revolution led, in the USSR and all other state socialist countries, to a restoration of Asiatic despotism, to the type of traditional despotic society characterising ancient Egypt, China, Peru, etc. See K. Wittfogel, *Oriental Despotism* (Yale, 1957). (In my opinion,

to the Marxist movement and is the father of 'new class' theories. He argued that the Social Democratic parties, apparently working class organisations based on the labour movement, are in fact dominated by the educated middle class. The privileges and status of this group spring not from ownership of the means of production but from ownership of human capital conferred by education and from ownership of high status jobs access to which is only open to those with extensive formal education. This new privileged stratum aims to replace the old bourgeoisie with its system of exploitation based on private property, with a new class of mandarins enjoying a system of exploitation based on the state. Socialism and Marxism, in this view, are simply ideologies to disguise the attempt to replace one system of exploitation by another. Similarly in his classic study *Political Parties* (1911) Michels argued that a socialist revolution would result in a "dictatorship in the hands of those leaders who have been sufficiently astute and sufficiently power- ful to grasp the sceptre of dominion in the name of socialism. . . . The socialists might conquer, but not socialism, which would perish in the moment of its adherents' triumph" (Michels, 1962, pp. 348, 355).

It would be wrong to exaggerate the originality of the analysis in Part One of this book. Prior to the publications of Barsov, Millar and Ellman, scepticism about the traditional interpretation of the econ- omics of collectivisation had been expressed by Bergon (1961, p. 257), Deutscher (1963, p. 99) and Fallenbuchl (1967). Deutscher carefully explained that although Stalin *attempted* to implement an industrial- isation policy based largely on collecting tribute from the peasants, in fact this turned out to be impossible. As a result, "The major part of industry's huge investment fund was in effect a deduction from the

---

although focusing attention on some important aspects of reality, the Wittfogel thesis is a doubtful characterisation both of traditional China etc. and of the USSR. Traditional China was not as static as Marx believed and the rapid industrialisation of the USSR is a major progressive phenomenon of a type unknown anywhere in the world prior to 1760—let alone in traditional Egypt. Furthermore, the proposition, derived from Wittfogel, that economies relying on irrigated agriculture require a stronger govern- ment and higher taxes than comparable societies without irrigated agriculture, does not seem in general to be true. Wittfogel, like Voslensky, is more an embarrassment to Marxism–Leninism, an argument couched in concepts and terminology drawn from Marxism–Leninism but with entirely different policy conclusions, than a major scientific breakthrough in the characterisation of the relations of production in Soviet- type societies.)

national wages bill. In real terms, a greatly increased working class had to subsist on a shrunken mass of consumer goods while it built new power stations, steel mills and engineering plants". Similarly, Fallenbuchl (p. 7) referred to the traditional view as "one of these myths which are often repeated but which explode when they are more carefully checked." Ishikawa (1967, chapter 4) had carefully considered, and rejected, the notion that economic development in contemporary Asian developing countries should be based on resources squeezed out of agriculture. He concluded that (1967, p. 347) "The notion that in the early stage of economic development, agriculture should provide 'funds' for industrialization does not seem relevant. . . . For accelerating overall economic development, the government must be prepared unhesitatingly to allocate the required amount of centralized funds to agriculture." Nevertheless, there can be no doubt that for most of those teaching or attending undergraduate courses on Soviet economic development or related topics, the current understanding of the development of Soviet agriculture in the 1920s and 1930s and of its contribution to industrialisation, came as a "real bombshell".

The chapters in Part Two of the book comment on some aspects of the 1965–82 period in the economic history of the USSR, the years of Kosygin and Brezhnev. Topics discussed include the factors influencing Soviet grain imports (one of the most striking features of this period), the distribution of income, and the alleged absence of inflation in centrally planned economies. The latter is important not only from a substantive but also from a methodological point of view. In several widely read and influential papers (Portes, 1977; Portes and Winter, 1977, 1978, 1980), Portes used econometric methods to argue that the traditional Sovietological view about the presence of substantial suppressed and hidden inflation in the USSR and Eastern Europe was wrong. Dirksen, using traditional Sovietological methods, showed that the traditional view was quite right. In his reply Portes (1981) expressed dissatisfaction with Dirksen's data and distaste for his results. Portes' argument that shortages and queues are not necessarily a symptom of *macro*-economic imbalance but may be a symptom of *micro*-economic imbalance, of disequilibrium relative prices, was undoubtedly correct and well worth making. Nevertheless, the Portes–Dirksen discussion showed that there is much to be said for traditional Sovietological methods when they use the data available to produce correct conclusions and little to be said for methods that produce misleading results. The chapter on the distribution of earnings under Brezhnev aroused wide interest and was commented on by Nove (1982), McAuley (1982) and Chapman (1983). Chapter 10 argues that 1979–82 was a period of economic stagnation in the USSR. This, increased social tension in the USSR, is part of the explanation of the cautious Soviet reaction to the crises in Poland and the Lebanon, and led to various policy innovations under Andropov. It also explains the discussion in the USSR under Andropov of economic reform.

Part Three opens with my Inaugural Lecture at Amsterdam University. This is about full employment under state socialism and whether we in the capitalist world could learn something from this. I feel strongly that much Western writing on the USSR today, both journalistic and academic, focuses too much on shortcomings and not enough on achievements. It is necessary to take a balanced view. The USSR today has made enormous progress relative to 1937/38 and it is foolish not to recognise this. There are many areas, ranging from the teaching of mathematics in secondary schools to the clean, safe and efficient operation of the Moscow underground (enormously superior to the filthy and dangerous New York subway) in which the USSR sets good examples which should be studied carefully. This was the purpose of the Lecture. Unfortunately, the rapid growth of unemployment in the capitalist world since it was given only emphasises its arguments. The USSR, like Japan, is an advanced industrial state from which much can be learned. To suppose that nothing positive can be learned from the USSR simply because some of the traditional objectives of the socialist movement have not been realised in that country, is rather like arguing that nothing positive can be learned from Japan because the objectives of the feminist movement have not been realised in that country.

If Chapter 11 is an exercise in reverse Sovietology, Chapters 12 and 13 are exercises in traditional Sovietology. They are concerned with investment planning and agricultural organisation.

The main methodological novelty of the paper by my collaborator Ruud Knaack on economic reform in China is the idea that there are certain general propositions about the economics of state socialism which can be applied also to China, China being treated for this purpose as just another state socialist country. This idea seems strange to many China specialists, who treat China as if it were unique. It also seems strange to those who, only a few years ago, were telling us about how different China was, about how it had resolved the notorious economic problems of Eastern Europe (Robinson, 1975, 1976; Wheelwright and McFarlane, 1971). We now know that this was erroneous and that the lessons learned from the study of the administrative economy are as relevant for China as for the USSR. Hence it is not surprising that Knaack should regard Nuti's work on East European economic reform as relevant to China or that Brus should be much studied in China after December 1978. As far as institutional changes in the Chinese economy after the death of Mao are concerned, the most significant seems to have been not in industry but in agriculture. It is the return of the household as the basic unit of agricultural production. This is discussed in Knaack (1982) Nolan (1983) and Watson (1983).

The paper on the impact of natural gas on the Dutch economy (Chapter 16) was presented at a conference in Oaxaca, Mexico in 1980. It was intended as a warning to Mexican and British economists and policy-makers that the possession of oil or gas would not be a panacea for all economic woes. A cautious depletion policy, slow growth of oil output, and support for domestic industry and agriculture were recommended. Since it was written, an increase in estimated gas reserves, and oil discoveries, have made the decline in Dutch production easier to manage. In a Comment on a paper presented at the Oaxaca conference by an economist at the Bank of Mexico, attention was drawn to the importance of disaster avoidance, the fact that in a crisis "refinancing the debt may be difficult", and that "creditors may exert an adverse effect on economic policy, e.g. by pressing for trade liberalisation" (Barker and Brailovsky, 1981, p. 257). Subsequent events have shown that these warnings were not without foundation.

The paper criticising the convergence theory (Chapter 18) has aroused widespread interest. It gave rise to a debate in the *Cambridge Journal of Economics* and has been subsequently referred to by Kerr (1983) and Kornai (1983). The latter's position is (ibid. p. 181) "identical with Ellman's in several important questions, or is near to it." It has also been supported by Garnsey (1982).

I hope enough has been said to encourage the reader to read on.

THE ECONOMICS OF THE
COLLECTIVISATION OF
AGRICULTURE IN THE USSR

II.   DID THE AGRICULTURAL SURPLUS PROVIDE THE RESOURCES FOR THE INCREASE IN INVESTMENT IN THE USSR 1928–32?*

. . . the surplus product created by the labour of the Soviet peasantry played a big role in the establishment of a mighty socialist industry. The contribution of the Soviet peasantry to the solution of this immensely important historical task was great. Nevertheless, the majority of the accumulation, necessary for carrying out socialist industrialisation, was obtained from the non-agricultural branches of the economy and was created by the working class. (Barsov, 1969, p. 137)

Data which have recently become available (Barsov, 1968, 1969; *Materialy*, 1932) make possible an analysis of the sources of the increase in investment in the USSR during the First Five Year Plan (1928–32) and the contribution to that increase of the agricultural sector. This is a subject about which there has recently been considerable discussion (Millar, 1970, 1971, 1974; Nove, 1971a, 1971b). The size of the increase in investment in the USSR during the First Five Year Plan can be seen from Table II.1.

Table II.1 shows that, measuring in 1928 prices, during the First Five Year Plan the volume of investment more than quadrupled and rose from 14·8% of the net material product in 1928 to 44·1% in 1932.

* Originally published in the *Economic Journal* December 1975. This paper has benefited greatly from discussion with James Millar, Brian Reddaway, Bob Rowthorn, Steven Wheatcroft, and others. Earlier versions were presented at seminars at the London School of Economics, Nuffield College and Glasgow University.

Table II.1[a]

Net material product[b] of the USSR in 1928–32 (milliards of 1928 roubles)

	1928	1929	1930	1931	1932
1. National income, of which:	25·0	27·4	32·4	36·4	40·1
1 (a) Consumption	21·3	22·6	23·2	22·7	22·4
1 (b) Investment	3·7	4·8	9·2	13·7	17·7
National income by sector of origin[c]					
2. Industry	7·6	9·5	12·6	15·0	17·8
3. Construction	1·9	2·3	3·3	6·0	6·0
4. Agriculture	9·4	9·1	9·1	9·0	8·3
5. Trade	3·0	3·3	3·9	4·3	5·1
6. Transport (freight)	1·1	1·3	1·5	1·6	1·9
7. Forestry	1·4	1·7	1·8	n.a.[d]	n.a.[d]
8. Other	0·8	0·7	0·9	1·2	1·0

[a] In this table, and subsequently, I have rounded off the data. This explains a number of minor discrepancies.

[b] This is 'national income' as defined in the material product system (MPS) of national income accounting. For an introduction to the Soviet system of national income accounting see Becker (1972). For a comparison of the MPS and SNA systems see Stone (1970). All the data in this paper derived from Barsov or *Materialy* (1932) are based on MPS accounting.

[c] The total national income by sector of origin differs slightly from the national income figures given in row 1. The reason for this is that row 1 is for national income *utilised* whereas the sum of rows 2–8 is national income *produced*. The difference is accounted for by losses and the foreign trade balance.

[d] In 1931 and 1932 forestry is included with 'industry' and 'other'.

Source: Barsov (1969, pp. 90–92). In Vainshtein (1969, pp. 95–99), there are some data, also derived from *Materialy* (1932), which differ in two main respects from Barsov's. First, for each of the years 1928–31 inclusive Vainshtein's estimate of national income utilised is *c.* 4% greater than Barsov's. The reason for this appears to be that Vainshtein includes "communications" (i.e. post, telegraph, telephone and wireless) and "catering" in the national income. Secondly, for each of the years 1928, 1929 and 1930 Vainshtein's estimate of agricultural output in 1928 prices is greater than Barsov's. I have used Barsov's data to ensure comparability with the figures for 1931 and 1932, for which only the Barsov data exist.

The ultimate source of rows 1, 1(a) and 1(b) is table 1(a), p. 83, of *Materialy* (1932). The figure for consumption is row 2 of the second variant and for investment is row 7 of the same table. The sum of these is the figure for national income. The ultimate source of rows 2–8 is table 1(a), p. 105, of *Materialy* (1932). The only exception is for agriculture, where the figure in Table 1(a), p. 105, of *Materialy* (1932) is the Vainshtein one, not the Barsov one. Barsov explains that his figure for agricultural output is lower because he has subtracted losses.

Clearly, measuring in 1928 prices, agriculture could not possibly have provided the resources for industrialisation in 1928–32 because by the end of the First Five Year Plan annual investment was more than double total annual agricultural output, and the increase in investment during the First Five Year Plan (i.e. the excess of investment in 1932 over investment in 1928) was substantially greater than the entire output of agriculture in any year.

The increase in investment during the First Five Year Plan required both labour and commodities. The increase in the labour force came mainly from agriculture (but partly from the previously urban unemployed and the growth of the population) and was fed on food obtained from agriculture. The increase in commodities came largely from industry and construction themselves. (Some came from overseas in exchange for agricultural and other primary exports.) During the First Five Year Plan the Soviet net material product rose by 60% and virtually all this increase was used to increase investment.

In order to analyse more closely the role of agriculture, and its relationship to industry, during this period, consider the data set out in Tables II.2, II.3 and II.4.

The main features of Table II.2 are the big increases in grain, potatoes, vegetables, cotton and flax fibre, and the big declines in meat, eggs, milk and sugar. The marketed output of basic wage goods (bread, potatoes and cabbage) rose sharply. The marketed output of livestock products fell significantly.* In view of the importance of grain in this period some data on it are set out in Table II.3.

I suggest that seven conclusions follow from Table II.3. First, this period saw a sharp increase in procurements of grain both absolutely and as proportions of gross marketed output and of the harvest. Secondly, there was a large increase in net marketed output of grain both absolutely and as a proportion of the harvest. Thirdly, there was a big increase in exports of grain after collectivisation. Fourthly, there was an increase in urban grain supplies per worker in 1929 and 1930,

---

* As Kahan has correctly noted: "Within the earlier period of development of the collective farms the composition of both gross and marketable output underwent a substantial change. The share of crop output increased and the share of livestock output decreased. Within the crop category, except for increased output of some industrial crops and increased share of wheat among the grains, a shift from higher value products to lower value products took place. In terms of delivery of the marketable output of grains and increasing the output of most industrial crops (such as cotton and sugar beets), the collective farms have fulfilled their functions within the realm of possibilities. They contributed to an increase of about three times in the volume of marketings from 1928 to 1961." (Kahan, 1964, p. 261, one footnote omitted.)

Table II.2

Marketed output of agriculture[a] by product in 1928–32 (millions of long tons)

	1928	1929	1930	1931	1932
Grain (gross)	15·7	19·5	22·6	23·7	19·4
Grain (net)	8·3	10·2	17·9	18·8	13·7
Sunflower seed oil	1·4	1·2	0·8	1·4	0·6
Flax seed	0·3	0·4	0·25	0·3	0·27
Hemp seed	0·13	0·13	0·07	0·06	0·05
Raw cotton	0·7	0·9	1·1	1·3	1·2
Flax fibre	0·16	0·25	0·19	0·26	0·29
Hemp fibre	0·12	0·15	0·12	0·08	0·04
Sugarbeet	9·4	5·9	13·2	10·4	6·1
Tobacco	0·03	0·03	0·04	0·06	0·05
Makhorka	0·7	0·8	0·9	1·3	0·8
Potatoes	4·1	5·5	8·8	9·1	8·4
Vegetables	1·1	1·5	2·5	3·2	2·3
Meat (deadweight)	1·7	1·7	1·2	1·1	0·8
Milk	5·9	5·9	5·4	4·8	3·2[b]
Eggs (milliards)	4·7	4·1	2·8	1·8	1·3
Hides, large (millions)	13·7	16·7	16·7	14·3	11·9
Hides and skins, small (millions)	31·4	33·3	37·6	42·4	31·5
Wool	0·04	0·045	0·05	0·05	0·04

[a] Measurement of inter-sectoral flows naturally depends on how the 'sectors' are defined. For the definitions used in this paper see the Appendix. 'Marketed output of agriculture' means products produced by agriculture and sold to the non-rural population or abroad. Output sold by one farmer to another or to rural non-agriculture is excluded. The figures are gross, i.e. they include agricultural products processed in the towns and subsequently purchased by persons included in the agricultural sector. The only exception is grain. Because of the importance of this product, and the availability of data, its marketed output is shown both gross and net (i.e. excluding grain either ground into flour in the towns and then repurchased by persons included in the agricultural sector or delivered to grain deficit rural areas).

[b] This figure differs from the one given by Barsov. The reason for this is that Barsov's total is not the sum of its constituents. Breakdowns by constituents are only given for 1932, and milk seems to be the only commodity for which there is such a discrepancy (see the table facing p. 112 of Barsov, 1969). I have added the constituents rather than used Barsov's total, because the latter is implausible. On p. 104 of Barsov (1969) there is yet another figure, 3·7, for this item.

Source: Barsov (1968, p. 70; 1969, p. 103 and table facing p. 112).

followed by a sharp decline. Fifthly, after collectivisation the burden of bad harvests fell primarily on agriculture. It was the harvest retained by agriculture, not exports or urban grain supplies, which fell sharply in 1931, the worst harvest of the period. Sixthly, the success of the state in raising net marketed output both absolutely and as a proportion of the

Table II.3

USSR grain balance for 1928–32 (millions of long tons)

	1928	1929	1930	1931	1932
1. Harvest	73·1	71·7	77·2	69·5	69·6
2. Gross marketed output, of which:	15·7	19·5	22·6	23·7	19·4
2(a). Procurements by the state	10·8	16·1	22·1	22·8	18·5
3. Net marketed output, of which:	8·3	10·2	17·9	18·8	13·7
3(a). Exports	0·1	0·3	4·8	5·1	1·7
4. Imports	0·3	0·1	0·1	0·0	0·2
5. Urban supplies (3 + 4 − 3a)	8·5	10·0	13·2	13·7	12·2
6. Urban grain supply per worker[a]	0·88	0·95	1·0	0·79	0·58
7. Harvest retained by agriculture	64·8	61·5	59·3	50·7	55·9

[a] This row consists of row 5 divided by the number of workers in each year. For the latter I used the figures for the total of 'workers and employees' less those engaged in agriculture (e.g. state farms) given in *Trud* (1968, pp. 23 and 24). The figures in row 6 are a very rough and imperfect measure of welfare because they ignore (1) losses, industrial use of grain and consumption by urban livestock, (2) the shift from wheat to rye which took place in this period, (3) changes in the ratio of workers to dependents. Sources: *Materialy* (1932, pp. 312–19, Table 2), and Clarke (1972, *passim*).

Table II.4

Industrial goods delivered to agriculture in 1928–32 (1928 retail prices, milliards of roubles)

	1928	1929	1930	1931	1932
1. Consumer goods received by the agricultural population:[a]					
(a) purchased in state and co-operative retail trade[b]	3·0	3·8	4·3	3·4	3·2
(b) purchased on the private market[c]	0·4	0·2	0·1	0·2	0·1
(c) total (a + b)	3·4	4·1	4·4	3·7	3·3
2. Producer goods received by agriculture (i.e. implements, machines and equipment)[d]	0·6	0·7	0·9	1·4	1·4
3. Total industrial goods delivered to agriculture (1c + 2)	4·0	4·8	5·3	5·2	4·8

[a] Bread products are excluded as are services (for further details see Appendix).
[b] This includes both rural retail trade and that proportion of urban retail trade accounted for by the peasantry. Data on the former are in published statistics, data on the latter, compiled by Narkomfin, are in the archives of the Central Statistical Administration. Both are in current prices. Barsov transformed them into constant price data by using an index of state and co-operative retail trade prices.

Table II.4 Notes – *cont.*

c For the private market, data on turnover in current prices is in the archives of the Central Statistical Administration. It was transformed into constant price data by Barsov using an index of private trade prices. For 1930–32 the underlying current price data are only approximate, relying on peasant family expenditure surveys or simply on expert estimates.

d Because of lack of data, a number of construction products used for building by agricultural enterprises, and for housing by the agricultural population, are excluded, as, for the same reason, are the industrial products (e.g. fuel) which form part of the current inputs of agriculture.

Source: Barsov (1968, p. 75; (1969), pp. 118–119).

harvest, after collectivisation, and in turning agriculture into a residual sector, had as its mirror image the catastrophic fall in livestock numbers in 1929–32 and the famine of 1932/3 (which both mainly resulted from the shortfall in the harvest retained by agriculture). Seventhly, 1929–32 naturally falls into two periods. In the first, 1929–30, the average harvest and urban grain supplies per worker were above the 1928 levels. In the second, 1931–32 the average harvest and urban grain per worker were below the 1928 levels, and both urban and rural living standards fell sharply.

Table II.4 shows clearly the large increase in the flow of producer goods to agriculture in 1928–32* (a disproportionately large share of these producer goods went to the state farms and to the machine and tractor stations).† It also shows that the First Five Year Plan was *not* marked by a sharp fall in the volume of industrial consumer goods bought by agriculture. The volume of industrial consumer goods bought by agriculture rose by about 30% from 1928 to 1930 and then fell back, reaching a level in 1932 marginally below that of 1928. The large structural shifts shown in Table II.4 and, especially, Table II.2, also reveal that propositions about inter-sectoral flows in 1928–32 are very sensitive to the weights used to construct the sectoral indices. Nevertheless, it is interesting to summarise the data in Tables II.2 and II.4, and this is done in Table II.5.

---

* The magnitude of state investment in agriculture after collectivisation was emphasised in Wiles (1962, p. 270).

† This does not mean that there was substantial net investment in agriculture in 1928–32. Simultaneously with substantial net investment by the state there was very large disinvestment by the rural population, so that, for example, despite the delivery of tractors to the countryside the traction power (including animals) available to agriculture fell sharply. In 1928 there was 1 h.p. for every 3·63 hectares of land sown to grain, and in 1932 1 h.p. for every 6·02 hectares (Barsov, 1969, pp. 85–86).

Table II.5

Inter-sectoral flows in aggregate terms, as seen from the village,[a] 1928–32

	1928	1929	1930	1931	1932
1. Volume index of marketed output of agriculture[b]	100	110[c]	128[c]	132	102
2. Volume index of industrial goods sold to agriculture	100	122[c]	135[c]	130	121
3. Relative aggregate flows ((1) ÷ (2) × 100)	100	90	95	101	84

[a] The weights used to construct row 1 are average *producer* prices of 1928/9, and for row 2, 1928 *retail* prices (i.e. including indirect taxes and distribution charges). This, together with ([b]), explains the description 'as seen from the village'.

[b] These figures are gross, with the exception of grain which is net. They refer to the products listed in Table II.2, which comprise not quite all (95% in 1928) of marketed agricultural output.

[c] For 1929 and 1930 Barsov gives alternative figures for both row 1 and row 2. For row 1 he gives 124 and 130 and for row 2 112 and 128 (Barsov, 1969, p. 130). (In Barsov, 1968, p. 77, he gives not 112 but 121, presumably a misprint.)

No explanation is given of the difference for row 2. It may be that the figures in the text are for 'Industry', while the alternative figures are for 'the industrial sphere'.

For row 1 the difference is only significant for 1929, and Barsov explains it by the fact that in the calendar year 1929 grain was collected both from the 1929 harvest and from the 1928 harvest. Hence it follows that the figures in row 1 of Table II.5 refer to the marketed output of each harvest regardless of which calendar year it was procured in.

I have preferred the figures in the text to the alternative ones on grounds of comparability. For 1931 and 1932 there is only one set of figures, and it seemed desirable that those for 1929 and 1930 should be comparable with them.

Source: Barsov (1969, p. 123).

Table II.5 makes it clear that, using the weights explained above, 1928–32 was *not* characterised by an increase in the volume of agricultural goods delivered to the towns related to the volume of industrial goods delivered to the agricultural sector. Considered from the standpoint of relative inter-sectoral flows, agriculture was much better off in 1932, better off in 1929 and 1930, and worse off only in 1931 (and then only marginally) than in 1928.

The prices at which these inter-sectoral flows took place are shown in Table II.6.

The traditional view was that collectivisation, with its compulsory procurements at low prices, turned the terms of trade against agriculture. Table II.6 shows, however, that in each of the years 1930–32, the first three years of collectivisation, the terms of trade of agriculture were *more* favourable than in 1928, the last pre-collectivisation year. The

Table II.6

The terms of trade between agriculture and industry, as seen from the village,
1928–32

	1928	1929	1930	1931	1932
Agricultural goods					
1. Plan procurements price index	c. 90	111	116	119	109
2. Decentralised procurements price index	—	—	—	—	354
3. Free market price index[a]	n.a.	233	525	815	3006
4. Weighted producer price index[b]	100[c]	117	180	199	314
Industrial goods					
5. State and co-operative trade rural retail price index	97	99	107	130	285
6. Private trade retail price index	125	139	218	393	846
7. Producer goods price index	100	100	100	100	108
8. Weighted consumer price index[d]	100[c]	101	110	171	241
Terms of trade (i.e. (4) ÷ (8) × 100)	100	116	164	116	130

[a] In 1930, 1931 and the first half of 1932, the free market was a black market.
[b] The weights were derived by Barsov from his working of the "approximate" data available in the archives of the Central Statistical Administration (Barsov, 1969, p. 101). For example, for 1932 Barsov estimates that the sale of agricultural products realised 12·6 milliard (1932) roubles, of which centralised procurements realised 3·8, decentralised procurements 1·3, and free market sales 7·5 (Barsov, 1968, p. 73). For 1931 Barsov's data imply that free market sales were c. 11% of the total volume of marketed agricultural output, which seems quite possible.
[c] 1927/28.
[d] The weights were derived by Barsov from data in the archives of the Central Statistical Administration.
Source: Barsov (1969, pp. 108, 112, 115 and 123).

terms of trade did move in favour of the state sector, in the sense that procurement prices remained virtually static while the rural retail prices of goods produced by state industry rose sharply, as one would expect on the traditional view. Simultaneously, however, the terms of trade of agriculture also improved because the quantities of agricultural products sold on the free market, together with the huge price rise on that market, were more than sufficient to counterbalance the stability of procurement prices.* (The benefits of the high free market prices accrued to the private sector of agriculture, i.e. peasants who had not

---

* This had earlier been pointed out in Malafeev (1964, pp. 130–131). Malafeev also provides data by product which are reproduced in the table on the next page.

yet been collectivised, regions where agriculture had not yet been fully collectivised, e.g. Central Asia and Transcaucasia, and those collective farmers who had a marketable surplus from the output of their private plots. Naturally, this helped to weaken the collective farms.)

It is clear from Table II.6 that the answer to the question 'how did the terms of trade move in the USSR during the First Five Year Plan?' depends crucially on how the 'sectors' are defined. If one does as Barsov does, and divides the economy into two sectors, 'agriculture' and 'the industrial sphere', then, on his data, the terms of trade moved in favour of agriculture.* It is, however, possible to divide the economy into three sectors: 'agriculture' defined as in Barsov, the 'state sector' which obtains agricultural products at procurement prices and sells industrial products to agriculture, and a 'proletarian sector' which sells its labour power to the state and buys agricultural products at a weighted average of ration and free market prices. With this classification, comparing 1932 with 1928, the terms of trade both of agriculture and of the state improve, while those of the 'proletarian sector' deteriorate.

The data in Table II.6 also make it clear that during the First Five Year Plan the USSR experienced a rapid inflation, led by the free-market price of food products. As Maynard (1963, p. 237) correctly noted:

The quantity of industrial products which it is possible to buy at co-operative retail prices by the sale of agricultural products

	At plan procurement prices			At free market prices		
	1929	*1930*	*1931*	*1929*	*1930*	*1931*
Metres of cotton cloth for						
1 centner of rye	14·7	17·3	11·7	78·5	119·7	126·9
10 eggs	1·0	1·3	0·9	2·0	4·9	6·3
Pairs of boots for						
1 centner of rye	0·335	0·132	0·174	1·52	2·22	1·88
10 eggs	0·020	0·023	0·013	0·09	0·09	0·094

Source: Malafeev (1964, p. 130).

---

* Use of the word 'trade' may give the reader a misleading idea of the nature of some of these transactions. For a description of how state procurements were organised in this period see Lewin (1974).

the enormous rise in prices which took place in Soviet Russia in the 1930s was the consequence of the failure of agricultural output to rise in the early stages of rapid industrial growth. Severe excess demand for food and other agricultural products was therefore produced, causing their prices to rise steeply: in consequence, costs of production in industry were affected.

In part, the redistribution of the national income in the USSR in 1928–32 was effected in a way analogous to the redistribution of the national income in the United Kingdom in World War I as described by Keynes in *How to Pay for the War*. A rapid inflation cut real wages and enabled the state to redistribute resources towards non-consumption. According to one estimate (Vyas, 1974, p. 7.15) average real wages fell by 49% between 1928 and 1932.*

In order to consider the role in this period not just of 'agriculture' but also of the 'agricultural surplus', it is necessary to define precisely what is meant by the latter. Following Millar (1970, pp. 83–84), consider an economy divided into two sectors: agriculture (sector 1) and industry (sector 2). Its social accounts can be arranged as follows:

$$O_1 = C_{11} + C_{12} + I_{11} + I_{12}, \tag{1}$$

$$O_2 = C_{21} + C_{22} + I_{21} + I_{22}, \tag{2}$$

where O_1 is the output of agriculture, O_2 is the output of industry, C_{ij} is the consumption of the output of the ith sector in the jth sector, and I_{ij} is the investment of the ith sector in the jth sector.

Three kinds of agricultural surplus can now be defined: the agricultural export surplus, the net agricultural surplus, and the net agricultural industrialisation surplus. The agricultural export surplus $(B_1) \equiv (C_{12} + I_{12}) - (C_{21} + I_{21})$. It is simply the visible export surplus of 'agriculture', conceived of as a country trading with another country

---

* This estimate is based on 1928 weights and a particular estimate of the share of manufactured consumer goods consumed in the industrial sphere. Using 1937 weights and the same estimate it drops to 39%, and using both 1937 weights and a different estimate of the share of manufactured consumer goods consumed in the towns it drops to 17%. The use of 1928 weights rather than 1937 ones seemed appropriate because 1928 was the first of the five years under consideration, whereas 1937 was five years after the last year of the period. The estimate used of the share of manufactured consumer goods consumed in the towns seemed the most plausible.

known as 'industry'. The net agricultural surplus (which following Millar, who introduced the concept, will be denoted N_1) $\equiv B_1 + I_{11} + I_{21}$. The net agricultural surplus measures agriculture's net contribution to net investment in the economy as a whole.* The 'net agricultural industrialisation surplus' $(P_1) \equiv N_1 - I_{11} = B_1 + I_{21}$. It measures agriculture's net contribution to the net resources which industry has available for investment in the economy as a whole. Assuming that the two-sector model does not do too much violence to the reality of the period, that the flows are measured in appropriate prices, that one is concerned with agriculture's contribution to commodity flows (as opposed to labour flows), and that one is concerned with the Keynesian problem of determining the sector of origin of net investment rather than the Marxist problem of determining the changes in social relations which made possible this investment, then these concepts can be used to measure agriculture's contribution to investment during this period.† The data Barsov provides can be used to measure each of these three concepts in three different units, and this is done in Tables II.7, II.8 and II.9.

Three interesting conclusions follow from Table II.7. First, the net agricultural surplus measured in 1913 world market prices was positive and significant throughout the First Five Year Plan.‡ This is what one

---

* This can most easily be seen by summing the net agricultural surplus and the net industrial surplus:

$$N_1 + N_2 = B_1 + I_{11} + I_{21} + B_2 + I_{12} + I_{22}$$
$$= I_{11} + I_{21} + I_{12} + I_{22},$$

i.e. the 'net agricultural surplus' and the 'net industrial surplus' measure net investment by sector of origin.

† Some problems arising from the data used are considered in the Appendix.

‡ The inference about the net agricultural surplus which Millar drew from Table II.7 is that "If 1913 price relatives are . . . used to weight the flows to and from agriculture, the net agricultural surplus is indeed positive, and increases somewhat between 1928 and 1931. However, it is quantitatively small in each year including 1928, and the 1932 level is less than in 1928" (Millar, 1971, p. 383). This, as Millar has agreed in correspondence, contains two mistakes. First, it refers to the agricultural export surplus, not the net agricultural surplus. Secondly "quantitatively small" is a misleading description of the net agricultural surplus. Two thousand eight hundred million 1913 roubles, the average net agricultural surplus for 1928–32, is almost double industrial investment in the USSR in 1928 and about a fifth of Soviet national income in 1928.

Table II.7

Agricultural surplus in 1928–32 in 1913 world market prices (milliards of roubles)

	1928	1929	1930	1931	1932
1. Marketed output of agriculture[a] (i.e. $C_{12} + I_{12}$)	3·3	3·7	4·2	4·4	3·4
2. Industrial goods delivered to agriculture[b] (i.e. $C_{21} + I_{21}$)	1·5	1·8	2·0	1·9	1·8
3. Agricultural export surplus (1 − 2, i.e. B_1)	1·8	1·9	2·3	2·5	1·6
4. Industrial producer goods delivered to agriculture[c] (i.e. I_{21})	0·2	0·2	0·3	0·5	0·5
5. Agricultural goods invested in agricultures[d] (i.e. I_{11})	1·1	0·1	0·2	0·3	0·2
6. Net agricultural surplus (3 + 4 + 5, i.e. $B_1 + I_{11} + I_{21}$)	3·2	2·3	2·8	3·2	2·3
7. Net agricultural industrialisation surplus (6 − 5 or 3 + 4, i.e. $N_1 − I_{11}$ or $B_1 + I_{21}$)	2·0	2·2	2·6	2·9	2·1

[a] This is in producer prices and is gross for all products other than grain, which is net.

[b] This is row 3 of Table II.4 converted into 1913 world market prices.

[c] This is row 2 of Table II.4 converted into 1913 world market prices. The 1928 retail prices were converted into 1913 world market prices by dividing them by 3·1:

$$\frac{\text{1928 Soviet industrial prices}}{\text{1913 world market prices}} = 3·1 \text{ (see Barsov, 1968, p. 66).}$$

This method of calculation is rather a crude one, because the 3·1 is a ratio of *wholesale* prices, whereas the figures in Table II.4 are *retail* prices.

[d] Row 5 was calculated as follows. In 1928, 1·2 milliard roubles of agricultural products, in 1928 prices, were invested in the national economy (Barsov, 1969, p. 90). Assume that all these products were invested in agriculture. Then investment of agricultural goods in agriculture in 1913 world market prices was $1·2 × 0·94 = 1·1$ milliard roubles. (World agriculture prices of 1913 = 0·94 × Russian agricultural prices of 1928. Barsov (1968, p. 66.) Similarly for the other years. (For 1930 Barsov's figure of −0·2 is a misprint for +0·2.)

It may seem difficult to reconcile positive numbers in row 5 for 1930, 1931 and 1932 with the fact of a major diminution in the number of livestock in these years. One explanation is that according to the method used by TsUNKhU in compiling *Materialy* (1932) the fall in livestock numbers was a 'loss' rather than a 'disinvestment', i.e. it reduced 'output' but not 'investment'. For example, in 1930, 70% of the fall in livestock numbers was treated in this way (Barsov, 1969, p. 135). In addition, the assumption that $I_{12} = 0$ in all years is obviously a source of error. Even in 1928, $I_{12} = \frac{1}{10}(I_{11} + I_{12})$ (Barsov, 1969, pp. 61, 90).

Source: Rows 1–3 are taken from Barsov (1968, p. 78).

would expect on the traditional interpretation. Secondly, there was *not*, at any rate in 1930–32, a big increase as a result of collectivisation.★ Hence it follows that agriculture did *not* finance the increase in investment during the First Five Year Plan if all the flows are measured in 1913 world market prices. This *is* contrary to the traditional interpretation. Thirdly, the agricultural export surplus was much greater in 1913 than in any of the years 1928–32. Barsov (1968, p. 78) estimates it at *c.* 3·3 milliard roubles (in 1913 world market prices) in 1913, which is about 35% greater than in 1931. If these figures are accurate† they indicate that "original accumulation at the expense of the peasants" reached its peak in the Stolypin era. In 1928 industry obtained the agricultural export surplus through the price mechanism, the terms of trade between industry and agriculture in the USSR in 1928 being much less favourable to agriculture than the world market prices of 1913.‡

Table II.8 shows that, measured in 1928 prices, agriculture ran a trade deficit with industry throughout 1928–32 and that the deficit was greater at the end of the First Five Year Plan than at the beginning. Measured in 1928 prices, the net agricultural surplus was small before collectivisation (4% of national income in 1928) and fell to negligible levels (*c.* 0·5% of national income on average in 1930–32) as a result of collectivisation! Measured in 1928 prices, the net agricultural industrialisation surplus was negative throughout the First Five Year Plan (except in 1931 when it was very slightly positive)! These are indeed findings which appear dramatically at variance with the traditional view.

★ If one takes into account the fact that the positive values for I_{11} in 1929, 1930, 1931 and 1932 are probably an illusion (see the second paragraph of note *d* to Table 7 above) then the fall in the net agricultural surplus during the First Five Year Plan is striking, and Millar's argument strengthened. Even if one prefers the alternative concept of the 'net agricultural industrialisation surplus' to measure the agricultural surplus, comparing 1932 with 1928 there is no increase in the agricultural surplus. Although this measure does show a substantial increase in 1929–31 it is much less than the increase in investment.

† They largely reflect the difference between the relative prices of industrial goods and agricultural goods on the world market, and in Russia, in 1913 (1913 was a good harvest year for Russia).

‡ In 1928 Soviet industrial prices were about three times 1913 world market prices of industrial goods, whereas agricultural prices were only about 10% above 1913 world market prices.

Table II.8

Agricultural surplus in 1928–32 in 1928 prices (milliards of roubles)

	1928	1929	1930	1931	1932
1. Marketed output of agriculture[a]	3·2	3·5	4·0	4·2	3·2
2. Industrial deliveries to agriculture[b]	4·0	4·8	5·3	5·2	4·8
3. Agricultural export surplus (1 − 2)	−0·8	−1·3	−1·3	−1·0	−1·6
4. Industrial producer goods delivered to agriculture[c]	0·6	0·7	0·9	1·4	1·4
5. Agricultural goods invested in agriculture[d]	1·2	0·1	0·2	0·3	0·3
6. Net agricultural surplus (3 + 4 + 5)	1·0	−0·5	−0·2	0·7	0·1
7. Net agricultural industrialisation surplus (6 − 5, i.e. 3 + 4)	−0·2	−0·6	−0·4	0·4	−0·2

[a] These figures are in producer prices and are gross for all products except grain which is net. They are the figures in Table II.2 aggregated by means of 1928 prices.
[b] This is row 3 of Table II.4.
[c] This is row 2 of Table II.4.
[d] This is row 5 of Table II.7 multiplied by $\frac{100}{94}$, with an adjustment to avoid a rounding error.
Source: Barsov (1969, table facing p. 112).

Tables II.7 and II.8 show that there was an agricultural export *surplus* throughout the First Five Year Plan if 1913 world market prices are used to measure the intersectoral flows, but an agricultural export *deficit* if 1928 Soviet prices are used. The fact that the sign of the net inter-sectoral flow varies according to whether 1913 world market or 1928 Soviet prices are used is simply a result of the fact that the prices of industrial goods relative to those of agricultural goods were much higher in the USSR than on the world market in 1913. Similarly in the United Kingdom in 1954/5–1969/70, because the relative price of agricultural products fell (as a result of differential rates of labour productivity growth), the use of final year relative prices to measure agricultural output at the end of the period produces a substantially lower figure than the use of first year relative prices (Wagstaff, 1972). Both of these historical phenomena, as also the well known Gerschenkron effect, are simply examples of the so-called index number problem.

It is important to note that the more successful the Soviet state was in 1928 in applying the policy recommended by Preobrazhensky of raising the relative price of industrial goods, the smaller the agricultural export surplus measured in 1928 prices would have been. A negative agricultural export surplus for 1928–32 measured in 1928 prices might be not an indication of a negative contribution by agriculture to net investment, as Millar argues, but an indication that the authorities were *successfully* pursuing "a price policy consciously calculated so as to alienate a *certain* part of the surplus product of private economy".* The significance of the sign of the *ex post* accounting figures for the agricultural export surplus depends on whether, and to what extent, the prices which actually prevailed in 1928 were more favourable to industry than those which would have prevailed if the Soviet government had continued the "enrich yourselves" policy.

Hence it can be seen that the weight Millar attached to the measurement of the surplus in 1928 prices is unfounded. Given that it is suspected by many that 1928 prices were manipulated so as to extract a surplus via the price mechanism, the use of 1928 prices to investigate the existence of a surplus is unsatisfactory. What is required for an analysis of this problem is a measure of value which is independent of the prices which actually ruled in 1928.

Barsov based his conclusions first (in his article) on measurements in 1913 world market prices, and subsequently (in his book) on measurements in (Marxian) values. His procedure in the latter case is to take the 1928 prices and transform them into Marxian values by adjusting them for the different quantities of labour embodied in different goods. On this basis the agricultural surplus is as set out in Table II.9.

The reason why these value calculations show an agricultural export surplus throughout the First Five Year Plan, unlike calculations in unadjusted 1928 prices, is that Barsov considers that the market prices of 1928 overstate the labour embodied in industrial goods relative to the labour embodied in agricultural goods, which implies that in 1928, either deliberately or by chance, the outcome of the policies of the price-fixing organs was 'a price policy . . . calculated so as to alienate a *certain* part of the surplus product of private economy".

---

* Preobrazhensky (1965, p. 110). Millar of course is aware of this possibility. In his theoretical analysis he emphasises the importance of measuring the intersectoral flows in 'appropriate prices'. When drawing inferences from the Barsov data, however, he does not discuss this possibility.

Table II.9

Agricultural surplus in 1928–32 in Marxian values (milliards of labour-adjusted roubles.[a])

	1928	1929	1930	1931	1932
1. Marketed output of agriculture	2·9	3·2	3·6	3·8	2·9
2. Industrial deliveries to agriculture	1·7	2·0	2·2	1·9	1·8
3. Agricultural export surplus (1 − 2)	1·2	1·2	1·4	1·9	1·1
4. Industrial producer goods delivered to agriculture	0·3	0·3	0·4	0·5	0·5
5. Agricultural goods invested in agriculture	1·2	0·1	0·2	0·3	0·3
6. Net agricultural surplus (3 + 4 + 5)	2·7	1·6	2·0	2·7	1·9
7. Net agricultural industrialisation surplus (6 − 5, i.e. 3 + 4)	1·5	1·5	1·8	2·4	1·6

[a] These are 1928 roubles, adjusted for the quantities of labour embodied in different goods. In effect the figures are amounts of labour time. 1 labour adjusted rouble is the average amount of labour time embodied in 1 rouble's worth of commodities in 1928. Sources and methods:

(1) Row 1 consists of row 1 of Table II.8 adjusted by Barsov's conversion coefficient (Barsov, 1969, p. 49) of 0·9 ($\frac{1000}{1171}$ = 0·9).

(2) Row 2 consists of row 2 of Table II.8 adjusted by Barsov's conversion coefficient (2·4 for 1928–30, 2·7 for 1931 and 1932 (Barsov, 1969, pp. 49 and 128)). Barsov's data on labour productivity differ from those of American researchers such as Hodgman (1954, p. 113) and Galenson (1955, pp. 236–237). The differences are explained by differences in estimates of output and differences in weighting. I have used the Barsov data rather than alternative data because in Tables II.9 and II.10 I am not offering independent estimates of the national accounts in (Marxian) values, but simply rearranging the Barsov data to make clear certain things which are explicit or implicit in his analysis.

(3) Row 4 consists of row 4 of Table II.8 adjusted by 2·4 and 2·7, the Barsov conversion coefficients.

(4) Row 5 consists of row 5 of Table II.8 adjusted by 0·9, Barsov's conversion coefficient.

(5) The figures in Table II.9 differ from those in the corresponding table in Barsov (1969, pp. 130–131), table 12. This is because:

(a) For marketed output of agriculture I have used the figures in the table facing page 112 of Barsov (1969) rather than those on pages 60–61. The reason for this is the implicit treatment of the value added by the industrial sphere to grain returned to agriculture if the data on pages 60–61 are used (see Appendix).

(b) For industrial deliveries to agriculture I have used the trade data in Table II.4 above, for the reason given in (a).

Table II.9 attempts to answer the question 'to what extent did intersectoral flows in the USSR during the First Five Year Plan depart from the principle of equivalent exchange?' It is the basis for Barsov's view that resources *were* extracted from agriculture throughout the

First Five Year Plan, but that the amount of unequal exchange was *not* increased by collectivisation.* Millar (1974, p. 752) appears to consider that Barsov's measurement in terms of Marxian values is an attempt to measure "the extent to which income created in agriculture and non-agriculture was allocated to the 'rightful' claimants". This shows a misunderstanding of Marx's labour theory of value, which is not a moralistic theory of what *ought* to happen, but a descriptive theory of the allocation of labour power, the human contribution to production, the purpose of which is to reveal the social relations of which the allocation of labour is a crucial part. Barsov's attempt to measure who did the work which was embodied in the increase in accumulation of the First Five Year Plan, that is, on whom the burden of accumulation fell, is a very useful one because it helps to illuminate the relations of production in 1928–32.

Barsov uses his value calculations to corroborate the conclusion reached in his 1968 article, based on calculations in 1913 world market prices, that the increase in accumulation during the First Five Year Plan was not financed by an increase in unequal exchange with agriculture. His value calculations can also be used, however, to show the sources of the increase in accumulation in 1928–32, and this is done in Table II.10.

Table II.10 shows that in 1929–32 (the years of the Soviet Great Leap Forward) the industrial sphere not only provided the resources to offset the decline in accumulation originating in agriculture, but also provided the whole of the increase in accumulation.† The increase in absolute surplus value in the industrial sphere resulting from the increase in the urban labour force accounted for 30% of the increase in accumulation, and the increase in relative surplus value for 101%. The

---

* The reader of Millar (1974), especially pp. 759–760, may not appreciate the fact that although Barsov rejects the view that collectivisation increased the amount of unequal exchange, he nevertheless adheres to the traditional view that there was unequal exchange throughout the First Five Year Plan.

† In order to avoid misunderstanding it is necessary to bear in mind the following: the large contribution to the increase in accumulation made by persons working the industrial sphere who moved from agriculture during this period is treated as a contribution to accumulation by the industrial sphere because they made their contribution in the industrial sphere. It is of course true that if agriculture had not contributed those people to the industrial sphere the increase in accumulation which in fact took place would have been impossible.

Table II.10[a]
Sources of accumulation in 1928–32 (Marxian values[b])

	1928	1929	1930	1931	1932	1929–32[c]
1. The value of accumulation in the national economy[d] (milliards)	2·3	2·0[e]	3·8	5·1	6·6	17·5
2. The increase in the net agricultural surplus as a proportion of the increase in accumulation	—	—[f]	22%	54%	−53%	−31%
3. The increase in accumulation in the national economy resulting from an increase in surplus value in the industrial sphere (100% − (2)).	—	—	78%	46%	153%	131%
4. Proportion of increase in accumulation resulting from the increase in *absolute* surplus value in the industrial sphere[g]	—	—	17%	31%	27%	30%
5. Proportion of increase in accumulation resulting from increase in *relative* surplus value in the industrial sphere (i.e. the fall in real wages) (3 − 4)	—	—	61%	15%	126%	101%

[a] The theoretical model underlying Table II.10, together with a fuller version of the table, are being prepared for separate publication.

[b] As in Table II.9 (Marxian) values are measured in Barsov's unit for them, labour adjusted roubles.

[c] 1928, rather than 1927, has been taken as the base year partly because there are no data for 1927 fully comparable with those for 1928, and partly because 1928 was the last fully pre-collectivisation year.

[d] This is row 1b of Table II.1 adjusted by Barsov's conversion coefficients. For 1928 this is 1·6 (Barsov, 1969, p. 66 − $\frac{4477}{2849}$ — 1·6), for 1929 and 1930, 2·4, and for 1931 and ∶ 1932, 2·7 (see note 2 to Table II.9).

^{e} The reason for this decline is that, in values, the increase in accumulation in industry and construction was more than offset by the decline in accumulation in agriculture.

^{f} There was no increase in accumulation in 1929.

^{g} This is the surplus produced in the industrial sphere in 1928 (1·02—see Barsov, 1969, pp. 65–6) adjusted by the increases in employment in 1929–32 and expressed as percentages of the increments in row 1.

source of the increase in accumulation in 1929–32 was the surplus obtained from the employment of additional workers in the urban sector at real wages less than those enjoyed by employed workers in 1928 plus the surplus obtained by reducing the real wages of those who had been employed in 1928. As Barsov (1968, p. 82) put it: "The chief burden lay on the shoulders of the working class."* In *The New Economics* (1965 edn, p. 122) Preobrazhensky discussed such methods of original socialist accumulation as taxation, price policy, railway tariffs, the banking system and the state monopoly of foreign trade. He assumed, however, that

> from the moment of its victory the working class is transformed from being the object of exploitation into being also the subject of it. It cannot have the same attitude to its own labour power, health, work and conditions as the capitalist has. This constitutes a definite barrier to the tempo of socialist accumulation, a barrier which capitalist industry did not know in its first period of development.

It appears that this assumption was invalid (at any rate with respect to real wages in 1928–32).† In view of the limitations of the data and the crudity of the methods of calculation employed, the figures in Table II.10 should be treated as illustrative rather than precise. The broad picture, however, seems accurate.

The table shows the great importance for accumulation in 1928–32 of

---

* By this he means not that the chief contribution was made by those who were employed workers in 1928, but that the chief contribution came from those working in the industrial sphere for part or all of 1928–32, and not from those who remained in agriculture. Some of those working in the industrial sphere for part or all of 1928–32 had been employed workers in 1928, but many had been either urban unemployed or villagers in 1928 and might not be classified as part of the 'working class' by some sociologists. Barsov's position contrasts with the traditional view that the main contribution was made by those who *remained* in agriculture.

† It was not invalid with respect to the length of the working day and opportunities for improving qualifications.

four important changes in the relations of production. First, the changed relationship between the workers, the trade unions and the state. In 1928 the unions were still concerned with the short-run interests of their members. By 1932 they were primarily concerned with contributing to industrialisation and facilitating increases in productivity. The transition from trade unionism to production mindedness had been made. Without this it would have been impossible to quadruple the rate of surplus value in four years.* Secondly, the rapid growth of forced labour.† This was important not only directly, but also indirectly, because it contributed to disciplining the free workers, like unemployment under capitalism.‡ Thirdly, the replacement of a market relationship between town and country by a coercive relationship ('collectivisation'). It was the application of force which enabled the state to raise net marketed output of grain so sharply. In addition, the substitution of coercion for the market created, in the well-known words of Marx's analysis of original accumulation, one of "those moments when great masses of men are suddenly and forcibly torn from their means of subsistence and hurled as free and 'unattached' proletarians on the labour market" (Marx, 1961 edn, p. 716). Between 1928 and 1932 the urban labour force rose from under 10 million to more than 21 million. Most of the new workers came from the villages. They would scarcely have moved to the towns when real wages there were falling so fast had not coercion made conditions in the villages even worse. As Swianiewicz (1965, p. 114) pointed out: "during the First Five Year Plan it [the movement of labour from the villages to the towns] was the result of the dramatic worsening of life and security of much of the peasantry [caused by collectivisation]". "The effect of dekulakization was that the tendency of the peasants to stay in their native villages during collectivisation was broken down, and hundreds of thousands of them, terror stricken and pressed by hunger, went to

---

* According to Barsov (1969, pp. 69, 128) the rate of surplus value in the industrial sphere rose from 27% in 1928 to 110% in 1932. Looked at from the standpoint of contemporary developing countries one can say that in the USSR accumulation was not hindered by a labour aristocracy which consumed resources which might otherwise have been accumulated. (For a discussion of the contemporary situation see Turner (1972).)
† For a good analysis of this see Swianiewicz (1965). The increase in forced labour is one institutional form which the increase in the rate of surplus value took.
‡ This was pointed out by Deutscher (1950, p. 92).

the towns in search of food and employment. This was particularly so in the Ukraine" (p. 121). For example, "The deportation of part of the prosperous peasantry to forced-labour camps induced many others to fly from their native villages and to seek for some means of existence in industrial centres; and this assisted the process of mobilizing labour for industrialization" (p. 209). Fourthly, the increased differentiation between the élite and the masses, between those who directed the process of accumulation and those who contributed to it, between the 'officers' and 'men' of the army of socialist construction.*

Table II.10 also shows the sharp variations in the sources of accumulation between the years of this four-year period, and hence the danger of generalising about 'the sources of Soviet accumulation' or 'Soviet industrialisation strategy' in the absence of calculations of the type set out in Table II.10 for a longer run of years. Data for this are not yet available.

CONCLUSIONS

1. Measuring in 1928 Soviet prices, during the First Five Year Plan the volume of investment more than quadrupled, and rose from c. 15% of the national income (as measured by the Soviet accounting system) in 1928 to c. 44% in 1932. This increase in investment required both labour and commodities. The increase in the labour force came mainly from agriculture and was fed on food obtained from agriculture. The increase in commodities came largely from industry and construction themselves.

2. Agriculture made an essential contribution to the development of the Soviet economy during the First Five Year Plan. It (a) provided the industrial sphere with a greatly increased supply of basic wage goods (bread, potatoes and cabbage), (b) provided the industrial sphere with a large addition to its labour force,† (c) provided substantial

---

* The introduction of bread rationing and 'closed' shops (i.e. shops open only to those working in specified organisations) appears to have coincided (Carr-Davies, 1969, p. 703), both taking place in the autumn of 1928.

† Millar (1974, fn. 19) believes that "as an economic rationale for collectivization, the mobilisation-of-labour argument is without force". The reasons for this are that "in the first place, there is no evidence that the supply of labour was deficient prior to the

exports, (d) contributed to import substitution (by increasing output of cotton and tea – Kahan, 1964, p. 262; Barsov, 1969, p. 104), and (e) was transformed into a residual sector which absorbed shocks (e.g. bad harvests).*

3. The fall in agricultural output, and in the number of livestock, during the First Five Year Plan, were serious setbacks to Soviet economic development. They led to a famine, a sharp fall in real wages, and a rapid inflation.

4. The sign and size of the agricultural surplus in 1928–32 depend crucially on how it is defined and which units are used to measure it. In particular:

    (a) Measured in 1913 world market prices, the net agricultural surplus (i.e. agriculture's net contribution to net investment in the economy as a whole) was positive throughout the First Five Year Plan, but the 1929–32 average was below the 1928 level.

    (b) Measured in 1928 Soviet prices the net agricultural surplus was lower in each of the years 1929–32 than in 1928.

    (c) Measured in Marxian values the net agricultural surplus was positive throughout the First Five Year Plan, but the 1929–32 average was below the 1928 level.

    (d) It follows from (a), (b) and (c) above, together with the very large increase in investment in 1929–32, that there is no basis whatsoever for the view that the increase in investment during the

---

initiation of collectivisation. In the second place it is clear that collectivization encouraged an excessive off-farm flow of labour". In this connection it is necessary to note:

    (a) Of course there was no urban labour deficiency *prior* to collectivisation (indeed there was widespread and serious unemployment) but from 1930 onwards (when the unemployed had been absorbed) there was a rapidly increasing need for urban labour which could only be met by agriculture.

    (b) Without collectivisation it is difficult to conceive of a large scale movement of labour to the towns at a time when living conditions there were falling dramatically.

    (c) The off-farm flow of labour may have been 'excessive' given the level of labour productivity in agriculture, the assumption that there was no disguised unemployment in agriculture, and the aim of increasing agricultural output. It was not, however, 'excessive' given the aim of rapidly raising industrial output, the assumption of disguised unemployment in agriculture, and the view that the way to raise labour productivity in agriculture was to industrialise.

---

* This was pointed out to me by Francis Seton. The point has also been made by Kahan (1964, p. 259).

First Five Year Plan was financed by an increase in the agricultural surplus.*

5. Comparing 1932 with 1928, collectivisation did *not* increase the net agricultural surplus (measured in 1913 world market prices, 1928 Soviet prices or Marxian values), nor did it turn the terms of trade between agriculture and industry in favour of industry, nor did it increase agricultural output. It did, however, increase procurements of grain, potatoes and vegetables, thus facilitating an increase in urban employment and exports, swing the terms of trade between agriculture and the state in favour of the state, and facilitate the rapid increase in the urban labour force (by depressing rural living conditions).

In this period collectivisation appears as a process which enabled the state to increase its inflow of grain, potatoes and vegetables and its stock of urban labour, at the expense of livestock and the rural and urban human population.†

6. The agricultural and industrial sectors are interdependent. Neglect of this can lead to a parasitical attempt to 'extract a surplus' as opposed to a policy aimed at raising output and productivity in both sectors.

7. From a Keynesian point of view, the sources of the increase in investment in 1928–32 were (a) the utilisation of previously wasted resources (e.g. unemployed labour), (b) the increase in the urban labour force, (c) the increase in the volume of basic wage goods marketed by agriculture, (d) the fall in urban real wages, (e) imports (both of machines and of skilled labour), and (f) the increase in the output of industry and construction during the First Five Year Plan. The two key mechanisms for obtaining the additional investment resources were

---

* This conclusion is unaffected if one of the other two definitions of 'agricultural surplus' used in the paper is preferred. Moreover, even if subsequent research shows that some alterations are needed to Table II.4 (see Appendix), the magnitude of the adjustments which preliminary research suggests may be necessary would not affect this conclusion.

† As Swianiewicz (1965, p. 91) argued, collectivisation "succeeded in reducing the share falling to the village in the distribution of grain, in arresting a tendency towards a reduction in the area sown, and in preventing the rise in the village of any organised political movement defending the interests of the peasantry—and to this extent it can be considered a success. But it was not able to bring about an expansion of agricultural production to a degree corresponding to the growing demand, and to this extent it was a failure."

collectivisation (which made possible the increase in the volume of basic wage goods marketed by agriculture and the increase in the urban labour force) and the rapid inflation (which facilitated the fall in urban real wages).

8. From a Marxist point of view, the origin of the huge increase in accumulation during the First Five Year Plan was (a) an increase in absolute surplus value resulting from the increase in the urban labour force (30%), and (b) an increase in relative surplus value resulting from the fall in real wages (101%), less (c) a decrease in unequal exchange with agriculture (−31%). The four key mechanisms for obtaining the additional accumulation were: the transition of the unions from trade unionism to production mindedness, the rapid growth of forced labour, the replacement of a market relationship between agriculture and the industrial sphere by a coercive relationship, and the increased differentiation between the élite and the masses.*

9. Much traditional teaching of the economic history of this period suffers from six weaknesses. First, perhaps because statistics were lacking, excessive attention has been paid to the pre-collectivisation discussion of theoretical possibilities, at the expense of an analysis of the post-collectivisation outcome.† Secondly, there has been a tendency to confuse marketed output of grain, which did increase sharply in 1928–32, with marketed agricultural output as a whole, which did not. Thirdly, there has been a tendency to assume that the delivery of industrial goods to agriculture in 1928–32 was negligible. Fourthly, insufficient attention has been paid to the evolution of real wages in 1928–32. Fifthly, not enough attention has been paid to the *improvement* (from the point of view of agriculture) in the terms of trade between agriculture and industry during the First Five Year Plan, caused by the high prices for food products on the free market. Sixthly, the undoubted suffering of the peasants caused by collectivisation has often been treated as a source of investment.‡

---

* Conclusion (8) is, of course, the 'transformed' version of conclusion (7).

† In analysis of the theoretical discussion, much more attention should have been paid to Trotsky's idea of original socialist accumulation by means of the self-exploitation of the working class (Trotsky, 1927, 1923).

‡ In my view the conclusion to be drawn from the increased poverty of the villagers (especially the Ukranian villagers) in 1932 as compared with 1928 is not that the contribution of agriculture to investment rose, but that out of a smaller agricultural output agriculture made much the same contribution as before, and hence there was less food available for the villagers, many of whom starved as a result.

10. The data now available make possible a significant step forward in our knowledge of the economic history of the USSR during the First Five Year Plan. In particular, they greatly add to our knowledge of material product flows in 1928–30. Account must be taken, however, of the limitations of the data, some of which are considered in the Appendix. Moreover, great care should be exercised in generalising on the basis of the experience of 1928–32. These were exceptionally turbulent years. In addition, because it is such a short span of years it may be distorted by random harvest effects. In particular, the fact that the analysis terminates with the exceptional year 1932 may lead to misleading inferences being drawn. Further work is required, both to evaluate and use fully *Materialy* (1932) and to extend our knowledge of the period after 1932. Such work would provide a firmer statistical basis for the analysis of Soviet economic development from the beginning of the First Five Year Plan to the commencement of the Great Patriotic War than is now available, and enable better grounded conclusions to be drawn.

APPENDIX: THE DATA

1. The chief underlying statistical source for this paper is *Materialy* (1932). This is a 381-page book of national income statistics for the USSR for 1928–30 compiled by the official central statistical organisation. It contains two introductory essays, 224 pages of statistical tables and 61 pages explaining the sources, methods and definitions used in compiling them. Furthermore, it is not an isolated work but the fruit of a tradition of calculating national economic balances – for example, the well-known one for 1923/4. Hence it can be considered an authoritative and generally reliable source. Nevertheless it has its limitations both from the point of view of actual numbers and of methodology. As the authors themselves point out (p. 9):

> We cannot treat the present work as absolutely complete either in the field of methodology or in the field of the empirical study of the economy. It is only a first attempt, which was rendered extremely difficult by the deficiency of statistical data and by the absence of solutions to many theoretical questions of the economy of the transitional period . . . For all these reasons the present work does not purport to be definitive either from a statistical or methodological point of view.

The account of how the grain output figures for 1930 (p. 248) and livestock output figures for 1928–30 (p. 250) were obtained makes clear their limitations. For an English translation of *Materialy* (1932) see Davies & Wheatcroft (1985).

2. The statistics for this period relate to 'agriculture', the 'agricultural sphere', the 'rural population', 'industry' and the 'industrial sphere'. 'Agriculture' consists of the productive enterprises which produced the products listed in Table II.2 (together with a few others) and the population engaged in, or dependent upon, agricultural occupations, plus domestic production and the population engaged in it. Agriculture, together with rural non-agricultural activities such as rural construction, forestry, fishing and hunting, form the 'agricultural sphere'. The agricultural sphere together with persons living in the countryside engaged in essentially urban sectors (industry, transport and trade) form the 'rural population'. 'Industry' consists of large and small industry (and the population engaged in, or dependent upon, industry). The 'industrial sphere' (this is my terminology—Barsov refers to it as the 'non-agricultural sphere') consists of industry, construction, trade and transport (freight). Barsov's data and analysis (and following him that of this paper) mainly refers to the relationship between 'agriculture' and the 'industrial sphere', defined as explained above. This introduces two sources of error. First, it excludes transactions between rural non-agricultural activities on the one hand and both agriculture and the industrial sphere on the other. The reason for this is the absence of data for rural non-agricultural activities for 1931 and 1932. (*Materialy* (1932) contains such data for 1928–30 but the sources used by Barsov for 1931 and 1932 do not.) There is no reason to suppose that were the requisite data to be available it would vitiate the conclusions reached by Barsov and by this paper. Secondly, it excludes services. The reason for this is that according to the methodology used in *Materialy* (1932) the national income consists of material products only and hence detailed data about services is not necessary for national income accounts. This means that if agriculture were a net consumer of services in this period (as it probably was) then all Barsov's (and my) calculations of agricultural surpluses *exaggerate* the contribution of agriculture to investment because resources consumed by providers of services to agriculture were *not* available for investment. (Millar (1974, pp. 755 and 759) has made an attempt to allow for services. *Some* data on the latter are in *Materialy*, 1932.)

3. In order to measure the 'agricultural surplus' given that the figures presented in the paper for marketed output of agriculture use the *net* figure for grain, it is desirable to subtract from the gross figure for industrial goods delivered to agriculture bread products valued at agricultural *producer* prices. Otherwise value added (e.g. by transport and grinding) to grain by the industrial sphere would appear as investment resources originating in agriculture. Barsov is aware of this. Therefore, although I have not found an explicit statement to this effect, I assume that Table II.4, row 1 (and consequently the subsequent tables which use the Table II.4 data), excludes bread products valued at agricultural *producer* prices. (Millar (1974), Table 1, row D, subtracts bread products at *retail* prices and accordingly his row N *exaggerates* the agricultural surplus. On the other hand, the trade statistics which underlie my Table II.4 may also be a source of error.)

4. Table II.4 is derived from published and unpublished *trade* statistics. Their reliability requires separate investigation. They appear to differ from the data on pages 60–61 of Barsov (1969), which are derived from *Materialy* (1932). Since Table II.4 is used for all the calculations of surpluses, errors here would affect them.

III. ON A MISTAKE OF PREOBRAZHENSKY AND STALIN*

Most writing on the economic significance of the Soviet collectivisation of agriculture has tended to assume that, whatever the human costs associated with it, it was at any rate successful in increasing the net transfer of commodities from agriculture to industry. Hence, collectivisation in other countries may be expected to do the same. Recent empirical work on quantitative developments in both Soviet and Chinese agricultural-industrial relationships, has thrown serious doubt on the validity of this assumption. The paper surveys the new evidence and relates it to a major argument put forward to justify collectivisation.

According to a famous book by the Bolshevik Preobrazhensky (1926), before a self-sustaining process of socialist accumulation could proceed in the USSR, a period of initial accumulation at the expense of the non-socialist sector of the economy (predominantly agriculture) would be necessary. Building on this argument, Stalin explained to the Central Committee of the Communist Party in July 1928 that the resources for Soviet industrialisation would have to be taken partly from the peasantry, which would be obliged to pay a 'tribute' to finance industrialisation.† It seems clear that a major reason for the collectivisation of Soviet

---

* Originally published in *The Journal of Development Studies*, **14**, no. 3, April 1978.
   This is a revised version of a paper circulated at the Conference 'Soviet Economic Development in the 1930s' held at the Centre for Russian and East European Studies. University of Birmingham, in May 1977. I am grateful to Bob Davies, Donald Filtzer, Bob Lewis, Michael Lipton and Alec Nove for helpful criticism.
† In the interest of historical accuracy it is necessary to note the following.
   Preobrazhensky did *not* advocate forced collectivisation. In his 1926 book he advocated the use of such instruments as taxation, price policy, railway tariffs, the

agriculture was precisely to establish an institutional framework suitable for collecting tribute from the peasantry.

Recent empirical work (Barsov 1968, 1969; Millar 1974, Ellman 1975) has established that, during the First Five Year Plan (1928–32) there was no increase in the net transfer of commodities to industry. In some quarters doubt has been expressed about the representativeness of the years 1928–32. In view of this it is interesting to consider a longer period, and this is done in Table III.1.

The table corroborates the view (p. 39) "that 'original accumulation at the expense of the peasants' reached its peak in the Stolypin era". It also shows that the increase in investment in the USSR in the First Five Year Plan was *not* a result of increased unequal exchange (because the amount of unequal exchange in 1932 was about the same as in 1928). It also shows that the amount of unequal exchange in the late 1930s was *less* than it had been a decade earlier, i.e. before collectivisation. Hence it would appear that for the USSR in 1928–38 the view that collectivisation enables the net transfer of commodities from agriculture to be increased is wrong. An important argument for collectivisation appears to be fallacious.

This does not mean that collectivisation had no functional results for Soviet industrialisation. It *did* stimulate an increase in the urban labour force. (The use of coercion to create a labour force was what Bukharin in his *Economics of the Transition Period* had mainly meant by 'original socialist accumulation'.) It also led to an increase in the marketed output of basic wage goods. Hence it seems reasonable to assert that

---

banking system and the state monopoly of foreign trade. In the curious language of contemporary development economics his book might well be considered as 'neo-classical' rather than 'Marxist' because he advocated the use of the price mechanism rather than coercion. Preobrazhensky developed his ideas further in a 1927 paper in *Vestnik Kommunisticheskoi Akademii* No. 22 and in an unpublished but much criticised paper of 1931 or 1932.

Similarly, Stalin did not, in the speech referred to, advocate with enthusiasm exclusive and long-term reliance on squeezing the peasantry as the source of resources for Soviet industrialisation. He discussed two sources of accumulation, the working class and the peasantry, and stressed the regrettable and temporary nature of the 'tribute' which the peasantry would have to pay.

Nevertheless, agriculture was collectivised in order to collect tribute, and the importance of original accumulation at the expense of the non-socialist sector had been argued by Preobrazhensky.

Table III.1

Unequal exchange between agriculture and industry in the USSR at selected dates (millions of labour adjusted roubles)ᵃ

	1913	1923/4	1928	1929	1930	1931	1932	1937	1938
1. Marketed output of agricultureᵇ	5539	1956	3710	4581	4815	4882	3781	3458	3530
2. Consumer and producer goods obtained by agriculture from industry	1717	606	1836	2060	2358	2107	1950	2144	2152
3. Unequal exchange (i.e. 1–2)	3822	1350	1874	2521	2457	2776	1831	1314	1377
4. Coefficient of equivalentness (i.e. 1/2)	3·22	3·22	2·02	2·22	2·04	2·31	1·94	1·61	1·64
5. Unequal exchange as a proportion of agricultural output (%)	36·3	17·0	18·8	27·7	27·5	31·1	21·7	15·7	16·7

ᵃ This is the unit in which Barsov measures (Marxian) values. 1 labour adjusted rouble is the average amount of labour time embodied in 1 rouble's worth of commodities in 1928. It may seem odd that the figures in row 1 for 1937 and 1938 compared with 1932, and in row 2 for 1937 and 1938 compared with 1930, should show declines. The reason for this is that the figures are in labour time, not units of output. There is no reason to suppose that there would be a fundamental qualitative alteration in the situation depicted in the table if the unit of measurement were prices or quantities.

ᵇ 'Marketed output of agriculture' means products produced by agriculture and sold to the non-rural population or abroad. It excludes output sold by one farmer to another or to rural non-agriculture.

Source: Barsov (1974, p. 96). Barsov himself states that the precise figures should only be considered as approximations. Nevertheless, his work is based on detailed analysis of a wealth of published and unpublished statistics, some of high quality, and has to be taken seriously. The statistical sources used by Barsov for the compilation of the table are, for 1913 the calculations of Strumilin, Vainshtein and Dichter; for 1923/4 the official balances for that year published in 1926; for 1928–30 the unpublished official material product balances compiled in 1932; for 1931 and 1932 archival material; for 1937 and 1938 the unpublished official material product balances compiled in 1939. The 1928–30 balances are much in advance of the national income accounts available for other countries for this period, and form a landmark in the international history of social accounting. An English translation of them is forthcoming.

collectivisation was a sufficient condition for agriculture to provide major resources (wage goods and labour) for Soviet industrialisation.

Was the Soviet experience unique, or is it corroborated by the experience of the other state socialist countries? According to a recent and very useful summary of the evidence for China (Paine, 1976, pp. 285, 295),

> although data problems preclude any firm conclusions about the absolute magnitude of the intersectoral resources transfer in any particular year, the direction of the transfer (i.e. a steady shift *in favour* of agriculture) during the first half of the 1950s is clear in *relative* terms from both the financial and real standpoints.

As far as the policies pursued since the end of the economic crisis 1959–61 are concerned: "Whether or not these policies merely reduced the extent of agriculture's net contribution to accumulation in the rest of the economy or turned it into a net deficit sector is not clear." In other words, Chinese experience, like Soviet experience, indicates that the argument for collectivisation based on its alleged efficacy in increasing the net transfer of commodities from agriculture to industry is wrong.

CONCLUSION

An important argument for collectivising agriculture put forward by Stalin and subsequently widely repeated, based on an earlier argument by Preobrazhensky, is that collectivisation enables the net transfer of commodities from agriculture to industry to be increased. The evidence, both for the USSR and China, indicates that this argument is erroneous.

IV. FIFTY YEARS OF COLLECTIVISED SOVIET AGRICULTURE, 1929–79*

In the capitalist countries industrialisation was usually effected, in the main, by robbing other countries, by robbing colonies or defeated countries, or with the help of substantial and more or less enslaving loans from abroad. . . .

One respect in which our country differs from the capitalist countries is that it cannot and must not engage in colonial robbery, or the plundering of other countries in general. That way, therefore, is closed to us.

What then remains? Only one thing, and that is to develop industry, to industrialise the country with the help of *internal* accumulations. . . .

But what are the chief sources of these accumulations? As I have said, there are only two such sources: firstly, the working class, which creates values and advances our industry: and secondly the peasantry.

The way matters stand with respect to the peasantry in this respect is as follows: it not only pays the state the usual taxes, direct and indirect; it also *overpays* in the relatively high prices for manufactured goods—that is in the first place, and it is more or less *underpaid* in the prices for agricultural produce—that is in the second place.

This is an additional tax levied on the peasantry for the sake of promoting industry, which caters for the whole country, the peasantry included. It is something in the nature of a 'tribute', of a supertax, which we are compelled to levy for the time being in order to preserve and accelerate our present rate of industrial development, in order to ensure an industry for the whole country. . . .

It is an unpalatable business, there is no denying. But we should not be Bolsheviks if we slurred over it and closed our eyes to the fact that,

---

* This article was first published (in Dutch) in the *Internationale Spectator* for October 1979. It was one of a number of articles for the general reader to mark the fiftieth anniversary of the beginning of the collectivisation of agriculture in the USSR.

unfortunately our industry and our country cannot at present dispense with this additional tax on the peasantry. (J. V. Stalin, July 1928)

. . . in a number of places there are interruptions in the supply to the population of meat and other livestock products. (L. I. Brezhnev, September 1976)

The history of Soviet agriculture in the past fifty years can conveniently be considered in two periods, 1929–53 and 1954–79. The first period is that of Stalin's rule, the second is that of Khrushchev and Brezhnev.

A.   1929–53: SEMI-SERFDOM AND RAPID INDUSTRIALISATION

The main purpose of collectivising agriculture was to ensure that it supplied industry with the resources for rapid industrialisation. Two subsidiary purposes were to eliminate the social basis of an anti-Communist political movement and to organise agriculture on the same basis of state control and state management ('socialism') on which the rest of the economy was based.

Collectivised Soviet agriculture achieved the following with respect to Stalin's goals. It supplied the state with sufficient basic wage goods (grain, potatoes and cabbage) and industrial crops (e.g. cotton) and labour to enable a very rapid process of industrialisation to take place. The kulaks were liquidated as a class and since then active political opposition in the countryside has not been a political threat to Soviet power. Agriculture has been organised on the basis of state control and state management, with one difference, partly formal and partly real. The difference is that most of Soviet agriculture in this period was run, not by state enterprises as in industry, but by nominally cooperative enterprises, the collective farms. This did have some real effects, all of which were detrimental to their members. For example, collective farmers were not entitled to wages or social security benefits. On the other hand, it was partly formal, since the state had as much control over the collective farms as it needed. *De facto*, collective farm chairmen were appointed by the relevant party committee and the state obtained the necessary marketed output by the compulsory delivery quotas and the payments exacted by the Machine and Tractor Stations for their services.

Nevertheless, despite these three important achievements, collectivised Soviet agriculture in this period suffered from two grave problems, one social and the other productive.

The social problem was that the relations of production in agriculture were regressive. In the chapter on agriculture in my book *Socialist Planning* (1979) I have described the relations of production in Soviet agriculture in this period as 'quasi-feudal'. Similarly, the Medvedev brothers in their biography of Khrushchev (1977) refer to it as 'semi-feudal' and the situation of the peasantry as that of 'semi-serfdom'. The reason for this description is as follows. Work on the collective farms was enforced by coercion and paid very little. The livelihood of the farmers was gained from their private plots, the right to which depended on their performance of labour for the collective farm. The peasants were tied to the land by the passport system. This system was very similar to that existing in mediaeval Western Europe and in pre 1861 Russia (the serfs were emancipated in Russia in 1861).

Lewin, in his contribution to Tucker (1977) has described the Stalin system as a hybrid of Marxism and Tsarism. From Marxism it drew the emphasis on the progressive nature of rapid industrialisation, economies of scale, large-scale investment as the way to raise productivity, the usefulness of coercion in creating a new mode of production, and the backwardness of peasant agriculture. From Tsarism it drew the practice of organising agriculture in collective units for tax collection purposes, tying the rural population to the soil, the absence of civil liberties for the peasants, and the treatment of the peasants as an estate fundamentally worse off than the ruling élite or the mass of the urban population. A by-product of this hybrid of Marxism and Tsarism was the Soviet practice of describing regressive social forms with progressive sounding terminology. For a long time this confused many outside observers.

The regressive nature of Soviet social relations in this period, although first tried out on agriculture, did not only affect agriculture. It was during the collectivisation campaign, liquidating the kulaks as a class and taking grain, that cadres were formed who were prepared to do anything, however loathsome and bestial, provided Stalin ordered it. In addition, collectivisation demonstrated to Stalin that it is entirely feasible to carry out drastic social changes, liquidating multi-million strata of the population, by coercion. These two factors played a major role in the mass arrests of 1937–38 and the creation and maintenance of the Gulag Archipelago in the USSR and the countries to which the Soviet system was exported after World War II.

Solzhenitsyn's treatment of collectivisation as Stalin's greatest crime is entirely logical. The Gulag Archipelago was largely a result of the decision to adopt the coercive model of the role of agriculture in economic development. Many of the first inhabitants of the camps were farmers deported from their villages at the time of collectivisation. From the point of view of numbers employed, agriculture in the USSR in the 1930s was by far the most important branch of economy. Reliance on coercion in various construction and mining enterprises was simply a small generalisation, from a quantitative point of view, of the principle, reliance on coercion, on which the main branch of the economy was organised.

The productive problem of collectivised Soviet agriculture in this period was that semi-serfdom is a poor way of raising efficiency and stimulating economic growth. Grain production in the USSR in 1953, the year Stalin died, was below the 1913 level, and grain production per head much below it. In 1953 meat production per head was also below the 1913 level. The stock of both cattle and sheep were below the 1928 level and the *per capita* stock of pigs also below it. The entire Soviet population (except for a tiny élite) was only just above subsistence level, food was difficult to obtain, expensive, of poor quality and (together with drink) totally dominated the budget of urban families. Furthermore, because of the poor level of output, high prices on the free (collective farm) market, and the need to provide state investment for agriculture, collectivisation did not lead to an increased net transfer of resources from agriculture to industry. The Preobrazhensky–Stalin theory about financing industrialization by levying a 'tribute' on the peasantry turned out to be a mistake. Collectivisation did ensure that agriculture provided certain essential inputs for the industrialisation programme, but it did not ensure an increased net inter-sectoral flow of commodities. A substantial part of the cost of the Soviet industrialization programme was borne by the urban population. Urban real wages fell sharply during the First Five Year Plan and did not permanently exceed their 1928 levels till the mid 1950s.

B. 1954–79: SECOND EMANCIPATION AND RAPID AGRICULTURAL GROWTH

In this period, the situation in Soviet agriculture radically changed, with numerous important reforms. These came in two main waves, a Khrushchev wave of reforms in 1953–58 and a Brezhnev wave after 1964.

In 1953–58 Khrushchev encouraged the private plot, substantially raised procurement prices, reduced agricultural taxes, enormously increased the sown area and abolished the Machine and Tractor Stations. Unfortunately, Khrushchev was not consistent in his progressive policies. For example, in his later years in office he re-introduced restrictions on the private plot. In addition, in traditional Soviet fashion he often used, or caused to be used, counterproductive administrative methods. A classic example of this is the 1959–60 fiasco of Ryazan methods.

In 1957 Khrushchev launched an entirely unfeasible campaign to overtake the USA in meat and milk production in three or four years (i.e. by 1960 or 1961). (This absurd pronouncement was an important reason why the 'anti-Party group' tried to remove Khrushchev from office.) The first secretary of the Ryazan party committee, seeking to win fame and favour for himself, committed his region to more than double meat production in 1959. A conference of the regional activists in agriculture committed it to even more grandiose targets. On December 16 1959 a letter appeared in all the leading Soviet newspapers announcing the achievement of the targets. How had this been done? Quite simply. The animals which had been slaughtered included also milk cows and breeding stock. Thousands of cows and pigs were obtained from the private plots of collective farmers and others by pressure. Officials from the Ryazan region travelled to other regions to buy up cattle which appeared in the statistics as "produced by Ryazan". Workers were made to buy meat in the shops and resell it to the state which counted it as "procurements". The result of this "triumph" was that agriculture in the region was on the point of collapse. At the end of 1960 a special delegation from the Central Committee went to investigate. The Ryazan first secretary shot himself.

Khrushchev was removed from office partly because of the inadequacy of his agricultural policies (as exemplified by the bad harvest of 1963 and the resulting need for substantial grain imports), and Brezhnev has pursued a more consistent policy. Procurement prices have been raised again, private plots encouraged, something akin to a wage system introduced in Soviet collective farms, the pension system for collective farmers much improved, passports have been issued to villagers and enormous investments made in agriculture.

The enormous increase in the real income of the rural population in 1953–79, the issue to them of passports (which in principle means that they are no longer tied to the soil and have the same status as the urban population instead of being a separate estate), the extension to them of a virtual wage system and of social security, taken together, can reasonably be described as a 'second emancipation'. (The first emancipation, of course, was in 1861, when serfdom was abolished. The need for a second emancipation was created, as explained above, by the regressive Stalinist policies.) The second emancipation was enormously significant for the USSR as a whole and for the rual population in particular and marked a major social advance for the USSR. As one would expect, the virtual abandonment of coercion in agriculture was accompanied by the closing of the camps and release of their inmates (in 1954–57) and withdrawal of the tying of urban workers to their place of work (in 1956).

In addition to this major social advance, Soviet agriculture in this period has also seen a major economic advance. Output has increased significantly. The USSR has ceased to be a country threatened by famine and with a population only just above subsistence level. It has become a country in which the *per capita* consumption of food has increased significantly over many years and in which the average diet has greatly improved. This is a major achievement of Soviet power and a significant gain for the people of the USSR (see Chapters 6 and 13).

Despite these two very important achievements, Soviet agriculture in 1954–79 was still plagued by four serious problems. They concerned its low initial level, costs, distribution, and year-to-year fluctuations.

The social and productive level of Soviet agriculture at the time of Stalin's death was very low. Hence even after a quarter of a century of progress and growth, numerous problems and difficulties remain.

Soviet agriculture is a high cost agriculture, requiring massive inputs of labour, land and investment. Labour and land productivity are still low today, although they have increased significantly in this period (especially labour productivity). The return on investment in Soviet agriculture was, and is, low. The high costs of Soviet agriculture have two main causes, one natural, the other social.

The natural problem faced by Soviet agriculture is that only a small part of the country has the combination of soil, temperature and precipitation necessary for low cost agriculture. The USSR has by far the world's largest and best soil resources. Nevertheless, in general where the soil is excellent the rainfall is inadequate, and where the rainfall is (barely) adequate the soil is usually poor. Only about 1% of Soviet farmland (mainly the eastern coast of the Black Sea) receives 28 inches or more precipitation a year. Much of the western United States and practically all the area east of Nebraska receive more than 28 inches. Hence vast areas of the USSR are too dry for normal agriculture.

The social problem is that administrative methods of organising the economy ('socialist planning') cause especially serious inefficiencies in agriculture. Two examples of this are production for plan rather than for use, and the organisation of labour.

Production for plan rather than for use is a well known problem of the administrative economy ('socialist planning') (see Ellman, 1973, pp. 51–53). It is particularly serious in agriculture since individual farms, unlike major heavy industrial or military plants, do not have the political influence necessary to ensure that their needs are met. (In fact their position is so weak that substantial resources allocated to agriculture are used for other purposes, and the collective and state farms are obliged by the higher bodies to assign some of their financial and material resources to urban organizations*.) The significance of this problem can be seen by looking at the immense mechanisation programme that has been pursued under Brezhnev.

The Ninth Five Year Plan (1971–75) provided that 28% of total productive investment in agriculture should be devoted to increasing its machine park. During the Eighth and Ninth Five Year Plans (1966–75) the Soviet collective and state farms received more than three million tractors, 900 000 combine harvesters, 1 800 000 trucks and special-purpose vehicles, and milliards of roubles worth of other farm machinery. The power per worker ratio in agriculture doubled. Not only did the number of machines increase, but also their quality. For example,

---

* See the decree trying to overcome this situation in *Sobranie postanovlenii Pravitel'stva SSSR* 1978, no. 19, pp. 379–80.

among the tractors the proportion of wheeled (rather than caterpillar) ones has greatly increased.

Nevertheless, the present situation with respect to mechanisation is far from satisfactory. Much auxiliary agricultural work is still not mechanised. Of the necessary machines, some are not produced at all, and others in insufficient quantity. Many machines are of poor quality. The main reasons for the low efficiency of the Soviet agricultural machinery park appear to be the conflict of interest between the farms and the factories, the conflict of interest between the farms and *Sel'khoztekhnika* (the organisation responsible for supplying goods to the farms), the limited opportunities for the farms to determine what kind of machinery is produced, the low degree of specialisation in production, the delivery of machines in knocked down form, the lack of complementary machines, and the apathetic attitude of the work force.

Farms have only a very limited opportunity to determine the production programmes of the factories. They send in indents (*zayavki*) with their requirements, but naturally these list only goods in production. Furthermore, the indents of agriculture are on average only satisfied 60 to 70% (Sergeev 1972, p. 246). The production programmes of the factories are actually determined by themselves and by various higher bodies. This problem is simply one aspect of a general problem confronting the administrative economy, to enable the consumer to determine what is produced. As Brezhnev observed in his speech at the 25th Party Congress

> It is important not only to remember that the end purpose of production is to satisfy various social requirements but also to draw practical conclusions from this. One of them is unquestionably to give the consumer, whether this concerns primary or other materials, machines, equipment or consumer goods, broader possibilities for influencing production. In this respect many elements of the economic mechanism must be basically improved.

It is well known that in the administrative economy labour morale, enthusiasm and interest in the work done, are poor (Ellman, 1979, pp. 171–173). This is particularly important in agriculture, because of the difficulties of supervising labour in this sector. This results from the sequential nature of agricultural work, the fact that it is spatially scattered, the heterogeneous nature of the resources (e.g. fields of different quality) and the erratic and seasonal nature of the natural inputs (e.g. precipitation and temperature). Two examples of the resulting problems are the apathetic attitude of the labour force to the repair of agricultural machinery, and the chequered history of the link (*zveno*).

Although the *production* of agricultural machinery in the USSR (in terms of numbers) compares well with that of the United States, the *availability* does not. This largely results from the poor maintenance of the Soviet agricultural machinery park. An American specialist on Soviet agriculture has described how he took a Soviet agricultural specialist to visit a farm in New York operated by one man with the part-time help of his teenage son. When the Soviet visitor saw all the well-kept equipment, he wanted to know how many repair men were in the work force. The farmer smiled and explained that he made routine maintenance and minor repairs on the spot, and his son helped him after school during the winter to make major overhauls and major repairs. He got spare parts from the local farm machinery dealer. The Soviet specialist found this hard to believe and kept looking round for more workmen (Shaffer, 1977, p. 34). A well motivated farmer does not need an army of repair men to keep farm machinery in good repair.

Because of the difficulty of supervising agricultural labour, it has often been suggested in Soviet discussion that labour be organised in small groups which are assigned particular means of production (land and machinery), left to organise production themselves, and divide up the output (or a proportion of it) among themselves. This is the so-called link (*zveno*) system, the most autonomous variant of which is the normless link. There have been numerous experiments on these lines, which have produced good economic results. Nevertheless, normless links remain exceptional. In fact, one of their chief organisers, Ivan Khudenko, died in prison. Why has this type of labour organisation been suppressed? The reason seems to be that the dominant group in the USSR wishes to preserve the essence of Soviet society, organisation of everything in accordance with instructions from above, and is strongly opposed to permitting lower level initiative and autonomy regardless of the resulting losses in efficiency. Lower level initiative and autonomy, if permitted, would make a whole army of supervisors unnecessary. As a supporter of normless links has noted: "Just think of all those who keep an eye on the ploughman's work: the accountant, the manager, the team leader, the representative of people's control, the village Soviet, the agronomist, the political agitator, the journalist and even the quality control officer."* Naturally all these people do not want to become redundant.

It is quite natural, in view of the above analysis, that one of the main success stories of Soviet agriculture (in terms of gross output, if not of value added or fodder inputs) has been that of intensive poultry production, a variant of agri-business often known as 'factory farming'. The intensive production of chickens and eggs has made considerable progress in recent years in the USSR. Production in this sector is organised just as in factories. Production depends mainly on adequate fodder and machinery and other modern inputs. The necessary labour, which is spatially concentrated, can be supervised relatively easily.

Throughout this period, and still today, the Soviet government was unable to organise for all its citizens a continuous supply of basic foods. (This was no problem for those with access to the closed distribution system†.) Shortages, queues, and the need to devote substantial time to obtaining groceries, have been permanent features of the Soviet scene, especially in provincial towns. (In the USSR the availability of goods is much better in Moscow, Leningrad, Riga and Tbilisi than in small and medium towns). The problems with the availability of food in the USSR have two main causes, one concerned with the distribution sector and the other concerned with price policy.

The processing and distribution sectors in the USSR are relatively poorly developed, and this is one explanation of the poor availability of food. To some extent this is a deliberate policy by a government which stresses the crucial importance in economic growth of manufacturing industry and strives to minimise the allocation of labour and investment to 'non-productive' sectors such as distribution. It is indicative of Soviet economic priorities that a recent Soviet writer on consumption treated the home delivery of bread and milk, which are quite common in the advance capitalist countries, as desirable but something which in the USSR would only be organised in the distant future (Anchishkin, 1977, p. 100).

The retail price policy pursued in the USSR is incompatible with the

---

* *Novyi Mir* 1969, no. 4, p. 159. In 1983, after four bad harvests, a US grain embargo and serious food shortages, an official campaign in favour of normless links was launched.

† In the USSR there is a special 'closed' distribution system for the élite, access to which depends on holding high official position.

universal availability of quality food, in particular of meat products. State retail prices of food have been kept constant for many years in the USSR. This has had three effects. First, the people of the USSR have been spared (at any rate in state trade) the massive food price increases that have taken place in the capitalist world. In this respect the stability of the Soviet economy has been much greater, and the dissatisfaction of the population much less, than in the capitalist countries. Secondly, meat subsidies (the difference between the cost of meat products to the state and their retail price) have become a significant item in the national accounts. In 1969 planned consumer subsidies on meat were 2% of the net material product, and by 1975 had reached 5% of the net material product. Thirdly, there has been a chronic situation of market tension in recent years. Naturally, if prices are fixed below the supply and demand equilibrium levels, there will be shortages, queues and difficulties in obtaining products. In the USSR meat has a high income elasticity of demand and money incomes are rising. Hence, even if meat output rises (which it has been doing except after bad harvests) rising prices may be necessary to preserve equilibrium in the market. The importance of this is shown by the behaviour of prices on the free (collective farm) market. In 1968–77, food prices on the collective farm markets rose, on average, for the country as a whole, at 3·4% p.a., and in Moscow, with its higher incomes and relatively poor agricultural resources, by 5·9% p.a. (Severin, 1979).

It is rather striking that at present the two great powers are suffering from the shortage of a basic commodity. In the USA it is petrol and in the USSR meat. In both cases the shortages could be ended by raising prices, but in both countries this is thought politically unacceptable. In recent years Hungary has shown the importance of price increases in preserving equilibrium on the market. Nevertheless, up till now, the adverse experience of Poland, where price increases for meat have twice in seven years generated nation-wide strikes and riots, has up till now had the bigger influence on Soviet policy-making.

The sharp annual fluctuations in Soviet agricultural output, especially grain output, are a serious problem for the USSR. They are largely caused by the weather (see Chapter 6). Bad harvests have an adverse effect on the livestock sector (and, given the price policy pursued, on the availability of meat in the towns) and on the balance of payments.

When Soviet agriculture was first collectivised, its main organisational forms were the collective farms, their members' private plots, the machine and tractor stations, and the state farms. Since then, the machine and tractor stations have been abolished (in 1958) and the collective farms have been increasingly merged and also transformed into state farms. In 1940 there were 237 000 collective farms in the USSR, and they basically correspond to the traditional villages. The average collective farm was composed of just 81 households. The state farms were only a small sector of agriculture. There were only about 4000 state farms with about 6% of the rural labour force. At the end of 1977 there were only 27 000 collective farms with an average of 483 households. A process of amalgamation had replaced the old, small, collectives by much larger units. At the same time the number, and importance of the state farms had grown. By 1977, there were about 20 000 state farms employing almost half of the rural labour force.

In June 1976 a Central Committee decree 'On the further development of specialization and concentration of agricultural production based on inter-farm cooperation and agro-industrial integration' was published.* It compared the current process of agricultural concentration with the collectivisation of agriculture four and a half decades earlier.

> Under collectivisation small individual peasant farms with their primitive means of production cooperated; the current process of agricultural concentration is characterised primarily by the unification of the efforts of collective and state farms with the aim of creating big enterprises of an industrial type with large volumes of marketed output, the deepening of specialization of all farms, the creation of development of new forms of inter-farm links, radical changes in the structure and character of production.

---

* *Economicheskaya gazeta* 1976, no. 24. The term 'agro-industrial integration' normally refers to two phenomena: first, the creation of agricultural enterprises using industrial type methods of production, e.g. intensive livestock (poultry, cattle) production; secondly, vertical integration, for example of the growing of crops with their processing. The advantage of both types of integration is the cost cutting which it can bring about.

Inter-farm (generally inter-collective farm) cooperation is mainly concerned with the establishment of specialised enterprises (usually construction enterprises) by several farms. The aim is to gain the economies of scale resulting from concentration and specialisation. For example, it was hoped that the specialised inter-farm livestock and poultry enterprises would have lower costs than traditional agricultural enterprises. In addition, the intercollective farm construction enterprises are often able to use local building materials, thus avoiding any call on state resources.

One result of the huge state investment in agriculture in recent years has been a reduction in the differences between collective and state farms and a decline in the importance of the former. Some data on this were given above. The gap between the income and consumption levels of the collective farmers and state employees has been reduced. Social differences between the village and the town have also been reduced, as the new passport regulations show. More and more industrial output and investment have gone to the collective farms. Many collective farms are now part of inter-farm enterprises. It seems likely that the future will see a continued decline in the number and importance of the collective farms (as they are merged and transformed into state farms) and a continued reduction in the economic and social differences between the urban and rural population. (This is a traditional Communist objective.)

C. CONCLUSION

The collectivisation of Soviet agriculture was successful in providing the basic wage goods, industrial crops and labour needed for rapid industrialisation. It was also successful in eliminating the social basis of an anti-Communist political movement and organising agriculture on the same basis of state control and state management ('socialism') on which industry was organised. Collectivisation also created a semi-feudal social system and had an adverse effect on the output and availability of food.

Since Stalin's death (1953) a second emancipation of the rural population has taken place. At the same time a significant, and sustained, increase in food production has taken place. The diet of the Soviet population has greatly improved, and living standards, both rural and urban, grown substantially. Nevertheless, Soviet agriculture continues to experience a number of important problems. These are its costs, poor availability of food, and severe year-to-year output fluctuations. The high costs result from the adverse natural conditions and the fact that agriculture suffers particularly severely from the general problems of the administrative economy (e.g. production for plan rather than for use, and poor labour morale). The poor availability of food primarily results from a combination of a stable state retail price policy, increases in money incomes and a high income elasticity of demand for food, especially meat. The low priority of the distribution sector is also a factor. The year-to-year output fluctuations are caused by the weather.

The old, one-village, collective farms have largely disappeared. By a process of amalgamation and transformation they have been replaced by a much smaller number of large collective farms and a growing number of state farms. The economic and social differences between the collective farmers and the state-employed sections of the population have been declining in recent years. In the 1980s and 1990s, it seems likely that Soviet agriculture will increasingly be organised by large state farms, using capital intensive methods, together with private plots.* The collective farms will have served their purpose and be seen to have been a successful transitional form between private and state ownership.

---

* Private plots are, and will remain for the foreseeable future, an important part of Soviet agriculture. See for example, Broekmeyer (1978). Both the state and the private sectors are likely to survive the withering away of the collective farm sector. (In 1980–81, in response to the stagnation of meat output in the late 1970s, the US grain embargo, and the upheaval in Poland, the private sector was once more officially encouraged. Indeed, in his speech at the 26th Congress (1981), Brezhnev devoted a whole paragraph to the importance of the private sector.)

THE SOVIET ECONOMY UNDER
KOSYGIN AND BREZHNEV

V. SEVEN THESES ON KOSYGINISM*

In September 1965 A. N. Kosygin, Chairman of the Council of Ministers of the USSR, outlined a programme of economic reform the declared intention of which was to complement the quantitative achievements of the Soviet economy by qualitative ones, to raise substantially the efficiency of Soviet industry. (These reforms were intended to complement the reform in agriculture announced by L. I. Brezhnev in March 1965.) An important feature of the programme was a reform of the planning system including changes in the planning of profit and in enterprise incentives. Much Western comment focused on this aspect of the reform rather than on other aspects (e.g. the reintroduction of the economic ministries which had been broken up by the 1957 reform) and treated it as corroboration of the thesis that a necessary condition for an efficient economy is profit-based inequality. The economic reform was implemented in 1966–69, and subsequently substantially modified.† In the Eighth Five Year Plan the main focus of

---

* Originally published in *De Economist* (1977) **125**, no. 1.
† The chronology is as follows:

September 1965	Reform announced
1966–70	Eighth Five Year Plan
1966–69	Reform implemented
1967	New price lists introduced
December 1969	Central Committee meeting discusses shortcomings of the economy
1971–75	Ninth Five Year Plan
June 1971	Decree issued on new method of calculating incentive funds in Ninth Five Year Plan
1973	Central Committees decree on reorganising industry into Associations. Statute of the Association published.
1973–80	Reorganisation of industry into Associations
1976–80	Tenth Five Year Plan

attention in the field of reorganising planning and management was expanding the role of economic levers and increasing the independence of enterprises. In the Ninth Five Year Plan it was improving central planning, industrialising agriculture, placing greater reliance on foreign trade and reorganising industrial management.

The purpose of this chapter is, on the basis of this experience, to assert seven theses about the reform and survey the evidence corroborating these theses. The theses are as follows:

1. The Kosygin reform consisted of seven changes in planning which were intended to raise allocative efficiency and change the distribution of income. Their efficiency in the former was largely frustrated by a whole series of unforeseen problems (and they were subsequently modified and in part reversed), but they did succeed in the latter (which in turn led to problems, which resulted in further policy modifications).

2. The convergence theory is harmful as a guide to understanding developments in the USSR. Whereas what has actually taken place in the USSR is a number of detailed changes in the planning system, adherents of this theory, blinded by their preconceptions, 'saw' a further example of convergence between socialism and capitalism.

3. The neo-classical theory of the firm* is unhelpful as a guide to understanding the evolution of Soviet planning.† It is easy to construct a theory of the output maximising enterprise analogous to that of the profit maximising enterprise.‡ This, however, throws no light on the behaviour of Soviet enterprises or on the course of the reform.§

---

* I have in mind the analysis set out, for example, in Samuelson (1948) especially chapter 4, or in Henderson and Quandt (1958).

† For a more general argument along these lines see Kornai (1971).

‡ See for example Ames (1965).

§ In a recent paper Domar (1974) discusses how the maximisation of a weighted average of profits and sales could lead a manager to choose a socially optimal output point. In this connection the following observations are relevant:

(a) the aim of the reform was to motivate enterprises to adopt taut plans. The interesting questions surely are, was this successful? If not, why not? Is it desirable for enterprises to adopt taut plans?

(b) Domar assumes, in accordance with the neo-classical tradition, that the marginal cost and marginal revenue schedules are known, that calculating the optimum from the data is trivial, and that the problem is to motivate the manager to pick the optimal point. In fact some of the data may be unknown, part of the problem is to motivate the

4. The socialism/capitalism dichotomy is unhelpful for understanding the evolution of Soviet planning. Soviet planning evolves under the influence of the scientific-technical revolution, the competition of the two systems, its own achievements, and the internal economic and social problems of the USSR. No light whatsoever is thrown on this evolution by analysis in terms of, either 'the building of communism' or 'the restoration of capitalism'.

5. Much of the Soviet writing of the early 1960s associated with the reform, such as that of E. G. Liberman,* gave an extremely superficial analysis of the problems of the administrative economy.†

6. Kosyginism provides one more example of the fact that many economic changes which are defended on the ground that they contribute to improving efficiency are in fact largely concerned with distribution.

7. The Soviet economic reform can only be fully understood as a social phenomenon. It was one aspect of the reaction in the USSR in the early 1960s against the type of society which had developed in 1929–52. Its subsequent modification and in part reversal reflected the modification and partial reversal after 1965 of the sociopolitical programme implicit in the decisions of the XX and XXII Party Congresses.

---

manager to improve the 'data' (e.g. to cut costs), and calculating an optimum may be difficult or impossible or pointless.

(c) It is ironical that by the time Domar's article, explaining how a maximand consisting of a weighted average of sales and profits could lead to the optimum, had appeared, the reform had been modified in a number of respects to overcome the limitations of incremental sales and profitability.

(d) Because he makes all the conventional neo-classical assumptions Domar avoids all the interesting and important questions raised by the evolution of the reform. These include, the risk averting behaviour of managers, the distinction between enterprises and managers, and the importance of sociopolitical issues such as distribution.

---

* As Selucky has correctly noted, "The influence and importance of the proposals formulated by Liberman (particularly in his article published in *Pravda* on September 9, 1962), were greatly over-rated in the West. Although he did suggest the use of the profit criterion, he by no means intended that directive planning should be abolished. He merely meant that profit should be seen as a target of the central plan" (1972, p. 116). Cf. also Treml (1968).

† It is noteworthy that in his 1970 book E. G. Liberman gives considerable weight to the theory of the optimally functioning socialist economy developed by the Soviet mathematical economists.

The use of the category 'profit', the use of material incentives, the formation of enterprise incentive funds, and the profit motive, were *not* innovations introduced into the Soviet economy by the reform. The first three were not innovations because they had existed for many years. The latter was not an innovation because it was not introduced.

The innovations which were introduced by the reform which were concerned with the issues stressed in Western comment affected seven things:

(1) the distribution of profitability rates;
(2) the allocation of profit;
(3) production for use rather than for plan;
(4) the type of behaviour which the enterprise incentive funds were designed to encourage;
(5) the identity of the fund-forming indices;*
(6) the size of the enterprise incentive funds;
(7) the role of the enterprise in maintaining and expanding the capital stock.

A.   THE DISTRIBUTION OF PROFITABILITY RATES

Prior to the reform there was a very wide dispersion of profitability, by industry, enterprise and product, with about 20% of all industrial enterprises and some entire industries (such as coal mining) loss-making. Part of the reform was a revision of the price lists which was intended, *inter alia*, to reduce the dispersion of profitability rates and to reduce the number of loss making enterprises. It was successful in this.

B.   THE ALLOCATION OF PROFIT

Since 1950 profit has increased dramatically, not only absolutely but also as a proportion of the income of the state budget. Whereas in 1950 payments by state enterprises out of their profits were only 9% of the

---

* By a 'fund-forming index' is meant an index, such as gross output, labour productivity or profit, the value of which (possibly together with certain other factors) determines the size of the enterprise incentive funds.

income of the state budget and only about a sixth of turnover tax, in 1965 they were 30% of the income of the state budget and 80% of turnover tax. By 1970 they were 35% of the income of the state budget and greater than turnover tax. Payments by state enterprises out of their profits, rather than turnover tax, had become the chief item of revenue in the state budget. The reform introduced three changes into the allocation of enterprise profits. First, it introduced two new forms of payment from profits to the state budget, payment for the use of fixed and circulating capital, and fixed or rent payments. Secondly the procedure was introduced by which bank interest is paid out of profit rather than included in costs. Thirdly the former enterprise fund was replaced by three new material incentive funds.

The introduction of a system of payment for capital was intended to prevent enterprises applying for investment goods and investment funds when their prospective return is below their opportunity cost, and to prevent them hoarding fixed and circulating capital when the return on them is below their opportunity cost. This measure had been introduced a decade and a half earlier in Yugoslavia, and was a feature of economic reform throughout Eastern Europe. How effective has it been in raising efficiency? According to a Soviet survey of Eastern European experience "The practice of utilising payments for capital both in the USSR and in the other socialist countries does not yet allow us to answer the question what role it has played in improving their utilisation" (Koz'bor and Chevkassov, 1969, p. 31).

The introduction of fixed or rent payments was intended to provide an incentive for the efficient use of natural resources and to eliminate those differences in profitability between enterprises which are caused by factors outside the control of the enterprises (e.g. newer equipment in one plant than another). The introduction of fixed payments in manufacturing industry encountered the well known problem of individual norms (Ellman, 1971, pp. 146–147) and hence it would probably be preferable to eliminate quasi rents by a profits tax.* The introduction of rent payments, for example in the oil and natural gas industries, was not effective in improving efficiency. The method of calculating rent payments was per ton of output rather than for the use of particular deposits. Hence this reform of financial planning provided no economic

---

* This has been argued, for example, by Sitnin (1969, p. 166).

incentive to end such wastes as the burning off of natural gas produced as a by product at oilfields. (Ellman, 1973, p. 117; Kozyrev, 1972, pp. 122–131).* The introduction of rent or fixed payments did enable the dispersion of profitability rates to be reduced.

The change in the allocation of profit which the reform brought about can be seen from Table V.1.

A feature of Table V.1 is the sharp increase in the proportion of profit paid into the economic incentive funds. A major feature of the reform was the replacement of the former enterprise fund by three new economic incentive funds, the material incentive fund which is used to pay cash bonuses, the sociocultural fund (which is used to finance equipment for canteens and kindergartens, passes to rest homes and sanatoria and the building and repair of housing and children's holiday camps) and the production development fund. This feature of the reform embodied innovations 4–7 in the list on p. 78.

C.   PRODUCTION FOR USE RATHER THAN FOR PLAN

A characteristic feature of the administrative economy is the use of productive capacity to produce goods which are less useful to consumers than other goods which could be, but are not being, produced. This arises because enterprises are primarily concerned with plan fulfilment,

---

* An economist who read a draft of this chapter enquired:
(a) why do enterprises burn gas which could be sold at a profit? and
(b) why are enterprises not instructed to make use of it by the planners?

The answer to (a) appears to be both administrative and economic. If enterprises use their own initiative, to sell gas which is not in their sales plan, they may face criminal penalties as in the case referred to in footnote p. 82, for doing something not in the plan. In addition, any profit so received would simply increase the free remainder of profit, which is paid to the state, and would not bring any economic benefits to the enterprise. (For an explanation of 'free remainder of profit' see footnote p. 81.)

The answer to (b) appears to be twofold. First, the planners cannot ensure the efficient allocation of resources by specific central decisions because they lack the knowledge and time necessary for this. (This proposition, indeed, is the starting point of proposals such as the introduction of rent payments as guides to efficient decision making). Secondly, the planners cannot ensure the efficient allocation of resources by exhortation because if such exhortation were listened to the economy would cease to be a planned one in the Soviet sense, i.e. an economy in which all economic activity is supposed to proceed in accordance with specific instructions from above.

the planners do not know precisely what is required, and the consumers (who may be productive organisations such as industrial enterprises, or private individuals) do not have any possibility of influencing production. It is well known that in the USSR in the early 1960s the divergence of the output of consumer goods from requirements was a much discussed problem.

In principle there are a number of measures which can be taken to deal with this type of problem. The plan indices can be altered so as to make enterprises more responsive to requirements, the knowledge available to the planners about requirements can be improved, the opportunities for consumers to influence production planning can be enlarged, or the type of behaviour expected of enterprises can be altered. An important aspect of the reform was that action was taken on all four of these fronts. Sales replaced output as the main quantitative plan index (this is discussed further in Section E), extensive research was undertaken into consumer demand, the planning process was

Table V.1

The allocation of the profit of industrial enterprises before and after the reform (in %)

	1965	1970
Total profit	100	100
of which		
paid into state budget	71	62
of which		
deductions from profit	71	4
payment for fixed and circulating capital	—	17
rent or fixed payments	—	5
free remainder of profit*	—	35
remaining at the disposal of the enterprise	29	40
of which		
paid into the economic incentive funds	6	14
used to finance investment	9	14
used for other purposes	14	10

Source: *Narodnoe khozyaistvo SSSR v 1974g*, Moscow, 1975, p. 740.

* Under the reform residual profits went to the state. 'Free remainder of profit' is a residual payment to the state budget which consists of that part of profit which is not retained by an enterprise and which is not paid into the state budget under a specific head, such as payments for capital and rent payments.

altered so as to reduce the role of higher administrative bodies and increase the role of consumers in the determination of output programmes, and the type of behaviour by enterprises which the authorities aimed to encourage was altered (this is discussed in Section D below).

Already in 1964, as an experiment, the planning process was altered for two clothing plants, the Bolshevichka in Moscow and the Mayak in Gorky, which were switched over to production on the basis of orders from the retail trade. A similar system was introduced throughout light industry by the reform. This brought production more into line with requirements (see Ellman, 1973, p. 53). Nevertheless experience shows that "It would be a mistake to suppose that the introduction of a system of orders automatically provides for the establishment of the necessary economic links between trade and industry, directed at the full satisfaction of the demand of purchasers" (Sarychev, 1970, p. 201). The reasons why consumer goods enterprises are still not producing in accordance with requirements appear to be as follows. First, the system of determining output programmes adopted by the September (1965) Plenum (see the decree of the CC and the Council of Ministers of 4 October 1965 No. 729) was a compromise between production for plan and production for use and was a retreat from the full Bolshevichka-Mayak experiment. The official, reformed, procedure for drawing up production plans for an enterprise is as follows. To begin with, an aggregated plan is determined for the enterprise. Then, on the basis of this plan and of the orders from customers respecting assortment and other details, the enterprise draws up contracts with its customers, after which the plan must be approved by the higher administrative bodies and issued as obligatory indices to the enterprise. Secondly, manufacturers still have difficulties in obtaining the necessary materials (most producer goods are still rationed). Thirdly, the permanent sellers' market persists. Fourthly, the wholesale price system is such that the assortment pattern required by consumers is often not the most profitable assortment. Fifthly the behaviour required of enterprise management is still obedience to instructions from above rather than the use of initiative to meet social needs.*

It is important to realise that the problem of bringing production into

---

* For a cautionary tale of what happens to managers who forget this, see the court case quoted in Ellman (1973, p. 48).

line with requirements exists not just for consumer goods but also for producer goods. It was largely for this reason that in the 1960s many Soviet economists urged the transition from the rationing of producer goods to wholesale trade. In his speech at the September (1965) Plenum Kosygin declared that it was intended to "develop wider connections between producer enterprises and consumer enterprises. It is essential gradually to make the transition to wholesale trade in separate types of materials and equipment." A number of experiments and small steps were made in this direction, but nevertheless the overwhelming bulk of turnover in materials is still allocated rather than traded.

The need for production to be in line with requirements is still officially recognised, but within a few years of the reform the emphasis switched from measures which can be described as 'a greater role for market relations' to measures which can be described as 'improvements of central planning'. For example, the way in which the traditional system of drawing up production and distribution plans hindered the co-ordination of production and requirements was widely discussed in the USSR in the early 1960s and the conclusion often drawn that what was needed was the general transition to the determination of current production programmes on the basis of orders received and the linking of producing and consuming enterprises by wholesale trade.* The most important changes in the planning system which were actually implemented, however, were concerned with improving the information available to the planners and the techniques for processing it. For example, in some of the chief administrations of Gossnab the error generating indent system of determining requirements was replaced by more up-to-date methods and programming techniques used for calculating production schedules and attachment plans (see Ellman, Fitz, pp. 36–37 and 72–75).

The reasons for this shift of emphasis appear to have been primarily political rather than technical. Experience in Yugoslavia and Czechoslovakia made it increasingly plain that reforms advocated under the banner of 'rising efficiency' were largely concerned with reducing the role of the state in economic life and changing the distribution of income. Given that the Soviet state is committed to major military and investment programmes, wishes to avoid potentially dangerous public

---

* See for example the *Izvestiya* article translated in full on pp. 101–105 of Ellman (1971).

wrangles between national republics for investment funds on Yugoslav lines, and to preserve a social order in which obedience to one's superiors is a major virtue, the shift of emphasis between the September (1965) and the December (1969) Plena is understandable.

D.   TYPE OF BEHAVIOUR

For the analysis of the change in behaviour which the reform of the enterprise incentive funds was designed to effect, it is helpful to distinguish between two types of incentive system:

(a) incentive aimed at encouraging plan fulfilment and overfulfilment, and

(b) incentive aimed at encouraging taut plans.

The system of incentives for plan fulfilment and overfulfilment can be expressed as follows:

$$B = a + b(Q_a - Q_p) \qquad \text{when } Q_a \geq Q_p$$
$$B = 0 \qquad \qquad \qquad \text{when } Q_a < Q_p \qquad (1)$$
$$a,b > 0$$

where B is the value of the bonus, Q_p is the planned value of the bonus forming index, and Q_a is the actual value of the bonus forming index. This type of incentive system is intended to provide an incentive both for plan fulfilment ($a > 0$) and for plan overfulfilment [$B = f(Q_a - Q_p)$, $f' > 0$]. What this type of incentive system actually does is to provide incentives both for enterprises to adopt plans which are less than the maximum possible (so-called 'slack' plans) and to attain values of plan fulfilment which are less than the maximum possible.

The reason why there is an incentive for enterprises to adopt slack plans is because the incentive formula provides a penalty for underfulfilment (absence of bonus). A risk-averting enterprise is naturally tempted to reduce this risk by trying to obtain a low plan which is unlikely to be underfulfilled. The reason why the enterprise has an incentive to attain only a low level of plan overfulfilment is that Q_p in period $t + 1$ is generally Q_a in period t plus a small percentage increase (this is known as 'planning from the achieved level'). One way of averting the risk of a high Q_p in $t + 1$ is to avoid a high Q_a in t.

The system of incentives for taut plans (i.e. plans which are for the maximum possible) can be written as follows:

$$B = aQ_p + ka(Q_a - Q_p) \quad a, k > 0$$
$$\text{If } Q_a > Q_p \quad 0 < k < 1 \qquad\qquad (2)$$
$$\text{If } Q_a < Q_p \qquad k > 1$$

The first term of the expression is intended to provide an incentive to adopt a high plan, the second an incentive to overfulfil the plan.*

A feature of the reform was a shift from the first type of incentive system to the second, which was intended to motivate enterprises to aim at taut plans. Despite this, slack plans have remained common. As a Deputy Chairman of Gosplan noted in 1973, the provision of material incentives for the adoption of taut plans "did not give the desired results" (Bachurin, 1973, p. 61). The main reasons for this seem to be, the administrative uncertainty which characterises the Soviet economy, the system of incentives for managerial personnel, and the risk-averting behaviour of Soviet managers.

Although a number of writers have argued that a major advantage of socialist planning is that it eliminates the uncertainty which characterises the capitalist mode of production, it is in fact well known to those familiar with the functioning of the economies of the European socialist states, that for any enterprise, the plan for the following year, the final version of the plan for the current year, and the timely arrival of inputs ordered through the supply system, are all uncertain. A major source of this uncertainty is, as I have shown elsewhere (Ellman, 1973, chapter 1), the fact that the techniques used for the compilation of current plans—material balances and input-output—are unable to ensure their consistency and hence repeated alterations to the plans during the planned period are necessary for the economy to function adequately. When a *Pravda* correspondent enquired of the chief accountant of an enterprise working under the reformed system why enterprises were still adopting slack plans, he was shown by way of reply a letter from Rosglavkhlopkoprom of the Ministry of Light Industry of the RSFSR received on 27 December raising the annual profits plan (of the year about to end) by 275 thousand troubles.† A slack plan provides the

---

* For further details see Ellman (1973, pp. 43–44).
† B. Kuz'michev, *Pravda*, 3 June 1968.

enterprise with a buffer to absorb any increase in the plan or breakdown in supply during the planned period.

Despite the fact that the method by which, in 1966–71, the enterprise incentive funds were formed, was intended to provide an incentive for adopting taut plans, the formula by which managerial bonuses were determined was still based on the old principle of incentives for plan fulfilment and overfulfilment. This contrast can be seen clearly by comparing the formula for determining the material incentive fund with the formula for determining managerial bonuses. The formula for determining the material incentive fund was

$$MIF_a = [a\Delta S_p + ka(\Delta S_a - \Delta S_p) + bP_p + kb(P_a - P_p)]\frac{WF}{100}$$

where MIF_a is the actual material incentive fund, a, b and k are positive constants, ΔS_p is the planned increase in sales, ΔS_a is the actual increase in sales, P_p is the planned level of profitability, P_a is the actual level of profitability, and WF is the wage fund.

The formula for determining managerial bonuses was

$$B_{Man} = k[a + b(\Delta S_a - \Delta S_p) + c(P_a - P_p)]\frac{WF_{Man}}{100}$$

Where B_{Man} is the managerial bonus fund, a, b, c and k are positive constants, and WF_{Man} is the managerial wage fund.†

It is clear that whereas the formula for determining the enterprise's material incentive funds is a formula of type (2), the formula for determining the current bonuses paid to managerial personnel* is of type (1). This has naturally had the traditional effects (to provide

---

* For a fuller account of the rules for determining current managerial bonuses see Ellman (1971, p. 149).

† The managerial personnel comprise the director, chief engineer, deputy director, chief economist, head of the planning and economic department, chief accountant, head of the department of technical control, and the head office officials.

The bonuses paid to the remainder of the engineering-technical personnel and employees (see footnote p. 93) may be for fulfillment and overfulfillment of the plan for the fund-forming indices of the enterprise, but they may be related to other enterprise indices or to shop indices.

incentives both for the adoption of slack plans and the attainment of low values of plan overfulfilment).*

Bearing in mind that it is the bonuses actually paid to people, rather than the sums entered in an enterprise's accounts, that provide a material incentive, it is scarcely surprising that the reform did not lead the enterprises to adopt taut plans. One way of dealing with this difficulty would have been to form the current managerial bonuses on the same basis as the enterprise incentive funds themselves, that is to allow managerial personnel to receive current bonuses if the plan were underfulfilled, provided that the plan was a high one relative to the extent of underfulfilment. In the course of a discussion of this point in a *Pravda* article a Gosplan official rejected this proposal on the revealing ground that it would contradict the directive character of the plan and weaken plan discipline. Rather than recognise that enterprise management has considerable room to manoeuvre within the framework of the plan and attempt to guide the enterprise in a socially rational direction by the use of economic levers, he preferred to "strengthen plan discipline."†

This formulation reveals a major contradiction in the formulation and implementation of the reform. An important aspect of the reform was the attempt to encourage enterprise management to use its initiative during the process of plan formulation and implementation and to steer these initiatives in a socially rational direction by the use of economic levers (prices, profit, material incentives). On the other hand, the attitude that the function of enterprise management, like all other inferiors, is to carry out instructions, remained deeply entrenched. Hence the system actually implemented was a compromise, in which institutional changes designed to encourage enterprise management to use its initiative were effected (e.g. the material incentive fund was created, and formed on a new basis) but they were prevented from having their desired effect by the retention of aspects of the former system of economic administration (the view that inferiors should carry

---

* The current bonuses paid to managerial personnel are not the only bonuses still related to plan fulfilment and overfulfilment. Bonuses for inter-enterprise socialist competition are formed similarly. In addition, the bonuses paid to workers out of the wages fund are also often for plan fulfilment and overfulfilment. Furthermore, the judgment of inferiors by superiors throughout the hierarchy of economic adminis-tration is still often related to plan fulfilment and overfulfilment.

† *Pravda*, 14 January 1969, article by Ivanchenko.

out orders and the formula for determining current managerial bonuses which gives effect to this view).

Notwithstanding numerous models in which the behaviour of social-ist enterprise management is assumed to be bonus maximisation, careful study of Soviet experience suggests that perhaps a more reveal-ing assumption is that of risk aversion. It is easy to see that for risk-averting enterprise management even under the reform plan underfulfilment and an increase in the plan are asymmetrical. The loss from each 1% of underfulfilment (reprimands, inspection by higher bodies, loss of managerial bonuses, reduction in the enterprise incen-tive funds) is much greater than the gain from each 1% by which the plan is increased (30% or more of the marginal increments to the enterprise incentive funds and marginal increments to the managerial bonuses). Hence risk aversion is another reason why the new system failed to lead to the universal adoption of taut plans.

Although, for reasons given above, slack plans remain common, fragmentary evidence suggests that the reform may have had the effect of reducing the extent of plan overfulfilment (see Naidenov and Radina, 1974; Kovalev and Lapeta, 1971, pp. 24–25).

It is important to note that a taut plan may well be inefficient. It may provide for the inefficient use of inputs, be at an inefficient scale of output, use an inefficient technology, or produce goods which make a smaller contribution to the national economy than some alternative outputs.* To aim at taut plans only makes sense as a heuristic device in an economy in which it is assumed that efficiency is ensured by the planning system (e.g. by the system of norms used in planning material requirements) and that the only source of inefficiency is the bargaining process by which enterprise plans are drawn up.

The fact that the traditional incentive system actually provides incentives for the adoption of slack plans, and the need for profit related incentives which would provide an incentive for taut plans, was argued by E. G. Liberman in his 1950 book and was widely repeated by Western commentators in the 1950s and 1960s. Both as a diagnosis and as a prescription, it is a very superficial analysis of the causes of inefficiency in Soviet industry. In Hungary an alternative diagnosis,

---

* For a discussion of the relationship between tautness and efficiency see Poltorygin (1979); Bor and Poltorygin (1969).

that the administrative economy formed an integrated economic mechanism, with characteristic advantages and disadvantages, and that if it were desired to overcome the disadvantages what was required was an alternative economic mechanism, was formulated in the 1950s (Kornai, 1959), and implemented from 1968 (the NEM). In the USSR it is noteworthy that, in line with the diagnosis offered at the December (1969) Plenum of the Central Committee, the main focus of efforts to raise efficiency has shifted substantially. During the Eighth Five Year Plan the main stress in raising efficiency was on the economic reform, but during the Ninth Five Year Plan it was on the introduction of management information and control systems, foreign trade and the development of associations.

In view of the problems encountered by the attempt to provide incentives for taut plans Ya. G. Liberman (1968) argued that instead of motivating the adoption of taut plans, enterprise incentives ought to be concerned with motivating the attainment of high results (i.e. the bonus system should be of the type $B = aQ_a$). This suggestion implied the abolition of current planning. The authorities, however, wished to retain current planning, and the system announced in 1971 and in effect from 1972 was a system which combines incentives for adopting a taut plan with incentives for plan fulfilment and overfulfilment. Because the former is a feature of the reform and the latter a feature of the traditional system, the current system of enterprise incentives can be considered a partial retreat from the reform, aiming as it does to motivate both types of behaviour.★

The system decreed in 1971 is as follows. In the five year plan of each enterprise or association there is a plan for its incentive funds. If the relevant annual section of the enterprise five year plan is fulfilled, the enterprise receives the level of incentive funds provided for in the annual section of the five year plan, and if it is over/under-fulfilled it adds/subtracts an additional amount. This is clearly an example of incentives for plan fulfilment and overfulfilment. In addition, however, if the enterprise adopts an annual plan greater than in the relevant annual section of its five year plan its incentive funds are increased, the amount of the increase depending on the extent to which the enterprise

---

★ As Adam (1973) correctly noted, "the latest five-year plan (for 1971–1975) represents a 'recentralization' of planning and a return to several features of the incentive system that had existed prior to 1965."

raises its plan and the extent of overfulfilment. This is an example of incentives for adopting a taut plan. Moreover, the existence of enterprise five year plans, an innovation of the Ninth Five Year Plan, removes one of the reasons (uncertainty about the value of the plan for the following year) for aiming at slack plans. Some small changes in the system for determining the material incentive fund were introduced during the Ninth Five Year Plan.*

E. THE IDENTITY OF THE FUND-FORMING INDICES

The traditional bonus-forming index was gross output, the limitations of which, such as the implicit incentive for expensive methods of producing expensive products, are notorious. The reform replaced the former system by two new fund-forming indices, incremental sales and profitability. Incremental sales was introduced as a fund-forming index as a proxy for the volume of consumer satisfaction resulting from the work of an enterprise. The switch from gross output to sales was largely ineffective because in the permanent sellers' market which characterises the Soviet economy the two indices are very similar from an economic point of view.† Such a switch in indices without a corresponding change in the functioning of the economy (from a sellers' market to a buyers' market) was, in part, another reflection of the very superficial analysis of the causes of inefficiency in Soviet industry on which the reform was based. Profitability was introduced as a fund-forming index (and redefined for this purpose) because it was regarded as a measure of efficiency, an idea which seems to have come from the official investment criterion. The use of profitability was not very helpful, both because of the price system (i.e. the wide dispersion of profitability rates, even after the 1967 price reform) and because of the perverse implicit investment criterion (Ellman, 1973, p. 141).

The limitations of these two indices were widely discussed in the USSR, and the new system which applied from January 1, 1972

---

* For discussions of the post 1971 system see pp. 31–33 of Schroeder (1973), Vasil'eva (1973) and Weitzman (1975). For the system of forming the enterprise incentive funds in force from 1974 see *Finansy SSSR*, 1975, No. 6, pp. 75–85.

† The limitation of incremental sales as a fund-forming index have been pointed out by a number of writers. See for example Selucky (1972, p. 125) and Kovalev and Lapeta (1971, pp. 29–30).

introduced a number of changes. As far as the identity of the fund-forming indices is concerned, the most important changes were as follows. First, at the stage of plan compilation, incremental sales was, in general, replaced by incremental gross output—or commodity output (*tovarnaya produktsiya*)—i.e. in this respect the 1965 reform was reversed. This is not the first time gross output has survived an attempt to dethrone it. In 1959 it was 'replaced' by cost reduction.

The specific reason for this reversal was that sales are, naturally, measured in the prices actually ruling in the year concerned, whereas the Five Year Plan, of which the planning of the incentive funds is now a part, is calculated in conventional, fixed prices (first 1967 prices and then 1973 prices). Accordingly the quantitative index to which it is simple to relate the material incentive funds when compiling the plan is output and not sales. Nevertheless, the quantitative index to which actual output is related (for the purpose of assessing plan fulfilment) remains incremental sales.

Secondly, the profitability index used in calculating the enterprise incentive funds for the enterprise five year plan was changed, in general, from net profitability (*raschetnaya rentabel'nost'*) to gross profitability (*obshchaya rentabel'nost'*). The difference between the two is that the former, but not the latter, excludes payment for capital, fixed or rent payments and interest on bank credit. The reason for this change is that these items are often difficult to plan five years forward. The result of this change, of course, was greatly to undermine the usefulness of payment for capital, fixed or rent payments and interest on bank credit as guides to efficiency because they no longer affect the profitability index which is used for fund-forming.

Thirdly, labour productivity was introduced as an additional fund-forming index. In addition it was stated that the size of the incentive funds would also depend on indices reflecting the technical level of output, e.g. the proportion of high quality output.

Fourthly, for the production development fund the system of fund-forming indices was abolished and replaced by simple deduction from profit (together of course with depreciation and receipts from the sale of superfluous equipment).

Fifthly, permission was given for experiments with alternative fund-forming indices, such as speedy running in of new capacity and increase of capacity, which have been used at the Volga car plant and the West Siberian Railway, and cost reduction.

In order to overcome one of the limitations on sales as an index (the division of output into profitable and unprofitable) from 1975 the procedure was introduced whereby in calculating the incentive funds, assessing the results of socialist competition, and also in paying bonuses, one of the most important conditions became the fulfilment of the contractual obligations to deliver specific products at specific times.

In the middle of the 1970s renewed discussion was taking place in the USSR about the merits and demerits of various indices for evaluating the work of enterprises and associations. Further changes can be expected.

These developments can be regarded as official recognition that the two fund-forming indices introduced by the reform are quite unable, by themselves, to ensure efficiency.

F.   THE SIZE OF THE FUNDS

In connection with socialist incentive systems, much has been said, and written, on the topic of moral versus material incentives. The analysis above of the type of behaviour which incentives aim to motivate, and the identity of the bonus-forming indices, could have been concerned, at any rate in principle, with either moral on material incentives. In the USSR, for example, moral incentives have traditionally been intended to motivate behaviour of type (1). Hence in a book on incentives the Soviet economist Bazarova (1968) noted that in cases of plan underfulfilment "the moral consequences are far from being unimportant. The enterprise which has not fulfilled its plan is responsible to the ministry or chief administration, to the regional (or district) committee of the party, to those shops and workers who did fulfill their obligations" (p. 138). Similarly a *Pravda* journalist, in an article on the weakness of the reform referred to the fact that "It is no secret that the following idea is still firmly implanted in the consciousness of many managers: 110% means honour, a banner, a bonus, a place in the Presidium; but 99% means scowls, reproaches and a stern talk in the district committee."*

Nevertheless, the reform *was* largely concerned with *material* incentives. A major innovation introduced by the reform concerned the size

---

* B. Kuz'michev, *Pravda*, 3 June 1968.

of the enterprise incentive funds, which was greatly increased by the reform, as is shown in Table V.2. Whereas in 1965, the last year before the reform, the utilised economic incentive funds of industrial enterprise were only 1·4% of the value of industrial output, by 1970 they had quintupled as a proportion of industrial output and were almost eight times larger in absolute terms.

Of that part of the incentive funds used for cash bonuses (the material incentive fund), the predominant part goes to the engineering technical personnel.* In enterprises which transferred to the new system in 1966, the average pay of employees was 10·3% higher, of engineering-technical personnel 8·2% higher and of workers only 4·1% higher than in 1965. Similarly in the fourth quarter of 1967 bonuses paid out of profits were only 3·3% of the wages of workers, but 22% of those of engineering-technical personnel and 20% of those employees (Ellman, 1973, pp. 139–140).

The very substantial increase in the size of the economic incentive funds should be seen as part of the reaction against Khrushchev's policies, in this case the egalitarian incomes policy of the late 1950s and early 1960s (Yanowitch, 1963, pp. 683–697). In 1959–65 the average monthly wage of workers rose by 15·7 roubles and of engineering-technical personnel by only 10·5 roubles. In some branches of industry foremen were receiving lower wages than the men they were supervising. The

Table V.2

Utilised economic incentive funds of industrial enterprise

	1960	*1965*	*1970*	*1965 as % of 1960*	*1970 as % of 1965*
1. Millions of roubles	1037	1363	10 313	131	757
2. % of industrial output	1·4	1·4	7·0	100	500

Source: *Narodnoe Khozyaistvo SSSR v 1965 g*, Moscow, 1966, p. 775 and
   Narodnoe Khozyaistvo SSSR v 1972, Moscow, 1973, pp. 532 and 720.

---

* In the USSR industrial personnel are divided into three categories, 'workers', i.e. manual workers, 'employees', i.e. white collar workers such as clerks in the accounts department, and 'engineering-technical personnel' i.e. engineering and technical personnel with a higher or secondary technical education.

small share of the material incentive fund going to the workers during the transitional period (1966–69) was widely recognised as a weakness of the reform. The 1971 decree specifically stated that the proportion of the material incentive fund going to the workers should be increased. This should be seen as one of a number of measures (raising the minimum wage to 70 roubles a month, introducing transfer payments for low incomes families, raising minimum pension levels) aimed at improving the position of the lower paid adopted in the wake of the 1968 events in Czechoslovakia, the December (1969) Plenum and the December 1970 events in Poland.

The introduction of the material incentive fund, and its rapid increase in size, was part of a process by which the share of result-related payments in total wages rose significantly, and should be seen as part of an attempt to raise the rate of growth of labour productivity by the use of material incentives. The development of this policy in the 1960s can be seen from the data in Table V.3. The partial retreat from the reform which characterised the Ninth Five Year Plan was also reflected in a renewed stress on moral incentives, on mobilising the masses. One form of such mobilisation was socialist competition. Another was the adoption of counter plans. (A counter plan is a revised plan worked out on the initiative of the enterprise collective on the basis of uncovering and using additional productive possibilities of the plant and people of an enterprise.) These are often combined, socialist competition being concerned with the adoption and fulfillment of counter plans. Counter plans provide mainly for an increase in output, a widening of the assortment, a raising of quality and an increase in the rate of growth of labour productivity. The widespread adoption of

Table V.3
Sources of wages paid to industrial workers
(all industries, in %)

	1961	1971
1. Payments according to the wage scales (tariffs)	73·2	61·2
2. Payments for overfulfilling piece work norms	7·6	11·6
3. Bonuses from wages fund	7·4	11·0
4. Bonuses from the material incentive fund	—	5·2
5. Result related wage payments (2 + 3 + 4)	15·0	27·8
6. Other	11·8	11·0

Source: *Sotsialistichskii Trud*, 1973, No. 4, p. 89.

counter plans revived a practice which had been important during the First Five Year Plan. The pioneers in the ninth plan were the workers in the Ivanovo textile trade.

G. THE ROLE OF THE ENTERPRISE IN
MAINTAINING AND EXPANDING THE CAPITAL STOCK

An important feature of the reform was a great increase in the resources at the disposition of the enterprises for decentralised investment. This was done by creating a new enterprise incentive fund, the production development fund, financed from depreciation, the sale of superfluous equipment and profit (via the fund forming indices), the resources available to which were much greater than those available from the former enterprise fund. The intention was that once the reform was implemented one fifth of all industrial investment would be financed from this source. It was hoped that giving a greater role in investment to the enterprise would raise the efficiency of investment because the enterprises would know better than the central planners the most efficient ways to modernise and expand existing enterprises.

This change encountered some teething troubles, for example the difficulty of obtaining investment goods for decentralised investment in an economy in which they are rationed. Nevertheless by the early 1970s it had been implemented and was generally considered to have played a useful role in raising the efficiency of investment.

In September 1972, however, at an expanded meeting of Gosplan held to consider the 1973 plan, in the course of a discussion of investment planning, Kosygin argued that

> The question of construction financed out of decentralised investment requires special consideration. At the present time enterprises dispose of significant sums for the expansion of capacity, the modernisation of equipment and other purposes connected with improving production. How are these sums utilised? In 1971 the plan for decentralised investment was fulfilled 128%, which amounted to 14·7 thousand million roubles as against 11·5 thousand million in the plan. The overwhelming bulk of these resources were utilised correctly and efficiently. Large sums, however, were spent not on industrial buildings and not on housing and improving conditions for the workers, but on the construction of administrative buildings and other objects which are scarcely of primary importance. Such expenditures are impermissable. Discipline

here must be strict. The USSR Gosnab and its local organs must not permit the use of substantial resources for this kind of construction.*

In accordance with this argument, in the plan for 1973 the share of decentralised investment in total investment was cut sharply.† This should be seen partly as a response to particular examples of waste of the type referred to by Kosygin, and partly as another of the partial reversals of the 1965 reform which characterised the early 1970s.

H.   CONCLUSION

The experience of the Soviet economic reform announced in September 1965, introduced in 1966–69, and surveyed in this chapter, corroborates the theses asserted at the beginning of the chapter.

---

* *Planovoe khozyaistvo*, 1972, No. 11, pp. 6–7.
† Attention has been drawn to this by Bush (1973) p. 43.

VI. SOVIET GRAIN IMPORTS AND THE WEATHER*

A. INTRODUCTION

In recent years considerable concern has been expressed in various quarters about the effects of possible changes in the climate on the world economy. For example, in 1974 the CIA published a paper which pointed out that a cooling trend in the northern hemisphere, which was being forecast by a number of climatologists, would have a severe adverse effect on the world's poor, substantially increase the death rate from malnutrition and related diseases in many third world countries, adversely effect the rich food importing countries and greatly improve the power of the United States.†

In view of the apparently freakish weather in a number of countries in recent years, and the widespread fears that this might be associated with

---

* Originally published, in Dutch, in *Internationale Spectator*, October 1978. The paper was written as a contribution to the study "Drought and Man: the 1972 Case History". This is one of three studies which comprised the International Federation of Institutes of Advanced Study (IFIAS) research programme on "The impact of climatic change on the character and quality of human life". The views expressed in the paper are those of the author alone. The problem, and the way to approach it, were suggested to me by Dr R. Garcia, Senior Study Author of the "Drought and Man" study. I am grateful to the participants in the September 1977 IFIAS Workshop for helpful comment and additional material, to Erik Dirksen for research assistance, to Professor K. E. Wädekin for helpful criticism and to Mr S. Wheatcroft for permission to use some of his work on the effect of climate on Soviet grain output. It is intended that an expanded English language version of the paper be published also as Annex 1 of Vol. 1, *Nature Pleads Not Guilty*, the forthcoming final report of the IFIAS project.
† CIA, *Potential implications of trends in world population, food production, and climate* (Washington DC, 1974).

adverse climatological trends, various studies are underway throughout the world to analyse the relationship between the weather and the world economy. This chapter, which concerns the relationship between the weather in the USSR and Soviet grain imports in 1972–73, is part of a wider case study of the effects of the weather on the world economy in 1972. The year 1972 was selected for special examination because of the coincidence of the Sahelian drought, the failure of the Indian monsoon, and the drought and short growing season in the USSR. The USSR was selected for special examination in order to examine the links between its bad weather, its massive grain imports and the big increase in world grain prices in 1972–73 which so destabilised the world economy.

During the 1970s the USSR was a substantial grain importer, as Table VI.1 shows. In the seven years 1970–76, which included two bad harvests (1972 and 1975), the USSR was a net grain exporter in two, a substantial net grain importer in four, and in approximate grain trade balance in one. The table also shows that the main Soviet grain imports in this period were in two pairs of years (1972–73 and 1975–76). In each case they were a response to a poor harvest in the first of the years in the pair (1972 and 1975).[*]

Soviet grain exports go mainly to five countries, namely Poland, GDR, Czechoslovakia, Cuba and North Korea. It may be wondered why the USSR exports grain in years in which it is a net importer. The reasons appear to be as follows. First, the five chief recipients of Soviet grain exports are all countries with whom the USSR has close political links. To reduce exports to them might have undesirable political consequences. Secondly, because of the USSR's reserves of gold and

Table VI.1
Soviet grain imports and exports (millions of tonnes)

	1970	1971	1972	1973	1974	1975	1976
Imports	2·2	3·5	15·5	23·9	7·1	15·9	20·6
Exports	5·7	8·6	4·6	4·9	7·0	3·6	1·5
Balance	+3·5	+5·1	−10·9	−19·0	−0·1	−12·3	−19·1

Sources: The annual *Vneshnyaya torgovlya SSSR* for the years 1970–76 (Moscow, 1971–77).

---

[*] It seems very likely that this pattern will be repeated in 1977–78.

foreign exchange, and its high credit rating, it is much easier for the USSR to finance grain imports than it is for countries such as Cuba and North Korea. Thirdly, the chief recipients of Soviet grain exports receive it under long-term trade agreements. These cannot normally be abrogated easily.

Coinciding with the big Soviet net grain imports of 1972 and 1973 was a massive rise in world grain prices. This is often blamed on Soviet buying. It should be noted, however, that the internal factors determining world grain prices are current demand, current supply *and stocks*. A major factor in explaining the jump in world grain prices in 1972–73 was the (successful) policy of the chief exporting countries in reducing stocks (so as to save them financing costs and avoid depressing the world market).*

The importance of this can be seen from the contrasting experiences of 1965–66 and 1972–73. In 1965–66 world stocks of wheat and coarse grains were reduced by some 35 million tons, or 25%, because of a poor harvest in the USSR and a threatened famine in India. In 1972–73 stocks fell by some 44 million tons, or almost 30%, mainly because of unusually large imports by the Soviet Union. The observable effect on prices and world trade in the first instance was negligible. In the second, however, prices rose dramatically and normal patterns of world trade were threatened with disruption. An important factor in these different outcomes was the state of world grain stocks. World grain stocks (as a percentage of current consumption) at the *beginning* of the 1972–73 agricultural shock were not much larger than at the *end* of the 1965–66 shock (Trezise, 1976). This reduction in stocks was the result of government policies of reducing the acreage sown to grain pursued in North America in the intervening years.

In addition, part of the explanation of the rise in world grain prices in 1972–73 was clearly external to the grain trade (because it coincided with a spectacular boom in virtually all commodity prices) and was

---

* This has been widely noted. For example, Kaldor has written that "Many people are also convinced that if the United States had shown greater readiness to carry stocks of grain (instead of trying by all means to eliminate its huge surpluses by giving away wheat under PL 480 provisions and by reducing output through acreage restrictions) the sharp rise in food prices following upon the large grain purchases by the USSR, which unhinged the stability of the world price level far more than anything else, could have been avoided." (Kaldor, 1976, p. 713.)

caused by factors affecting the world economy as a whole in that period. Such factors include simultaneous expansionary policies in a number of industrial countries leading to a sharp increase in world effective demand and the collapse of the capitalist world monetary system. When the external factors were not present, a big increase in Soviet grain imports (as in 1975–76 and 1977–78) was not associated with a jump in world grain prices.

B.   WEATHER CONDITIONS

The big Soviet net grain imports of 1972, 1973, 1975 and 1976 largely reflected bad weather in two years (1972 and 1975) combined with certain Soviet Government policies (see below). As far as the weather is concerned, most of the major grain-growing areas in the USSR suffer from marginal climatic conditions. This is a commonplace of economic geographies of the USSR. Over most of the grain growing regions, the growing season is short (because the land is so far north) and the precipitation inadequate. Furthermore, the weather in the USSR and particularly in the major agricultural production areas fluctuates substantially from year to year and significantly more than in other major world agricultural production areas. Basically this is a result of the combination of a highly continental weather pattern with the occasional blocking in the seasonal path of depressions, which together produce the well known *sukhovei*, dry hot East winds which blow from Central Asia across the Volga, North Caucusus and the Ukraine. This combination of marginal conditions and sharp weather fluctuations ensures that Soviet grain output fluctuates sharply from year to year in accordance with changes in the weather.*

The impact of the weather in Russia on the size of the harvest was already known long before the collectivisation of Russian agriculture. Well known studies are those by Fortunatov (1893), Brounov (from the late 1890s), Chetverikov (1920s) and Oboukhov (1920s). Before 1914 Russia was internationally recognised as being a pioneer in developing

---

* The material in this chapter concerning the influence of the weather on Soviet harvests is borrowed from a study which S. Wheatcroft is preparing on the productivity of Soviet agriculture in the 1920s and 1930s. I am grateful to Mr Wheatcroft for permission to use this material.

"the first comprehensive approach to the weather crop problem which extended over a large geographical area" (Sanderson, 1954, p. 188).

Until very recently, however, very little attention was paid, either in the USSR or the West, to the use of weather data to explain fluctuations in Soviet harvests since 1929 (when the collectivisation of agriculture was initiated). The reasons for this are quite simple. In the USSR, for many years the orthodox view was that under socialism the advantages of socialism would vastly outweigh 'mere' natural conditions. "There are no fortresses which Bolsheviks cannot storm" was a well known Stalinist slogan. Hence bad harvests were blamed not on the weather but on 'wreckers', 'kulak saboteurs' etc.* Rather than admit that agriculture was not doing well and analysing the causes of this, the Soviet government started publishing spurious output statistics (so-called biological yield) and relying on quacks (such as Lysenko).

In the West, little attention was paid to the effects of the weather on Soviet harvests since this interpretation conflicted with propaganda needs. If each poor harvest showed 'the failure of socialist agriculture' why bother about the effects of the weather? It is noteworthy that the United States Central Intelligence Agency has recently published a report in which the weather is used to explain away much of the *success* of Soviet agriculture in recent years.†

C. OUTPUT

Soviet grain output statistics in the third quarter of the twentieth century are characterised by two things: first, a strong upward trend; secondly, very sharp year to year fluctuations. The first of these phenomena appears to be caused by a huge increase in modern inputs (e.g. chemical fertilisers and machinery), an increase in the sown area, and an improvement in the economic position of the farmers (whose real incomes have increased enormously in this period). The second is

---

* The widespread view (energetically propagated by the Soviet writer Sholokhov) that the fall in Soviet livestock numbers in the First Five Year Plan was entirely due to kulak sabotage, appears to be a political myth. It neglects the role of the decline in available animal feed in this period.

† *USSR: the impact of recent climate change on grain production* Research Aid, (CIA, Washington DC, 1976).

mainly caused by the weather. Some data on the trend and on fluctuations are set out in Tables VI.2 and VI.3.

Table VI.2 shows clearly the high trend rate of growth of Soviet grain output over this twenty-five year period. This impressive achievement is not confined to grain, but applies to other types of agricultural production as well.

Table VI.2

The trend in Soviet grain output (five year averages, bunker output in millions of tonnes [a])

	1951–55	1956–60	1961–65	1966–70	1971–75
Soviet grain output (annual average)	88·5	121·5	130·3	167·6	181·6

[a] These statistics are not comparable with those for many other countries. The published Soviet statistics refer to 'bunker' output. Most other countries (but not China prior to 1960 and possibly not China since 1960—see Sinha (1975, p. 204)) measure 'barn' output. The former exceeds the latter because it includes some moisture content of the grain; thrash and dirt admixtures; and losses during transport, handling and preliminary storage. The average relationship between bunker output and barn output is not known. Scattered evidence suggests that an average deduction of 20% from bunker output may give a rough estimate of the barn output (see K. E. Wädekin, 'Soviet harvest losses and estimates barn yield of grain in 1975", *Radio Liberty Research Bulletin*, April 21 1976). Wädekin has also suggested (On the calculation of Soviet grain losses, *Radio Liberty Research Bulletin* April 5 1978) that the often applied deduction of 15% to make Soviet grain output statistics comparable with those of Western countries, may be accurate as an average for some years, but for individual years the necessary deduction may range from 28% (as in 1977) to 8%.

Whether measuring in bunker output distorts the trend, does not appear to be known.

Source: *Narodnoe khozyaistvo SSSR v 1975 g*, Moscow, 1976, pp. 310–311.

Table VI.3

Fluctuations in Soviet grain output[a] (annual bunker output, millions of tonnes)

	1970	1971	1972	1973	1974	1975	1976
USSR grain output	186·8	181·2	168·2	222·5	195·7	140·1	223·8

[a] Professor Wädekin has suggested (in correspondence with the author) that the percentage of losses tends to increase in years of very good harvests and to decrease with poor harvests. This is because of the shortage of harvesters and the protracted period of harvesting when the harvest is very good. If correct, this means that measuring bunker output rather than barn output magnifies the year to year fluctuations of Soviet grain output.

Sources: *Narodnoe khozyaistvo SSSR v 1975g*, Moscow, 1976, p. 311; *SSSR v tsifrakh v 1976 godu*, Moscow, 1977, p. 120.

Table VI.3 shows clearly the sharp year to year fluctuations, caused by the weather, to which Soviet agriculture is prone. In the bad year of 1972, bunker output was 7% less than in the previous year and 24% less than in the exceptionally good following year. In the other bad year of 1975, bunker output was 28% less than in the previous year. It should be noted that the drop in Soviet bunker grain output in 1972 was quite small in percentage terms. It was much less than that of 1975, and also less than that of 1967, 1965, 1963, 1959, 1957, 1953 and 1951.

Soviet agriculture in the third quarter of the twentieth century was a successful agriculture. According to US specialists (Millar, 1977), in the quarter century 1951–75, total output grew at not less than 3·4% p.a. The population in this period grew at only 1·4% p.a., so that *per capita* output grew at *c*. 2% p.a. This was a very satisfactory performance, and one much better than that of many other countries. For example, although there is considerable uncertainty about both population and output data for China, a well known US specialist on the Chinese economy has estimated that there has probably been no appreciable rise in *per capita* grain output in that country in the whole period since the recovery of the economy in 1952 to the mid seventies (Eckstein, 1977, p. 212). Besides this *quantitative* improvement, there was also a *qualitative* improvement, with a significant increase in the output of high quality products. Considered historically, the most important achievement of post-Stalin agricultural policy has been to eliminate famines in the USSR. Famines were endemic in Tsarist Russia. The USSR has experienced two major peace-time famines, in 1921–22 and 1932–34. In addition, throughout 1932–53 malnutrition was an important factor contributing to mortality in the USSR. As a result of the progress of the Soviet economy since the end of the Great Patriotic War, it seems entirely likely that there will never again be a famine in the USSR (save only in the wake of nuclear war). This is an achievement of fundamental importance in a country traditionally prone to famines.

Nevertheless, Soviet agriculture in the third quarter of the twentieth century suffered from four problems. First, its very low initial level (largely resulting from the policies pursued in the previous quarter century). Secondly, the fact that it was a high cost agriculture, requiring massive inputs of land, labour and investment. Thirdly, output, especially of grain, fluctuated sharply from year to year due to weather conditions. Fourthly, the investment, labour and price policies pursued in the processing and distribution sector were not favourable to the general availability of good quality food.

D.   TRADE POLICY AND GRAIN USE

Bad harvests are a *necessary* condition for the USSR to enter the world grain market as a major importer. They are not, however, *sufficient*. In order to explain the Soviet imports it is necessary to consider also the policies of the Soviet Government with respect to international trade and grain use.

As far as international trade is concerned, it is well known that the USSR seeks a rapid expansion of it. It naturally wishes, however, to trade on favourable terms. Obviously one reason for the big grain imports of 1972 and 1973 in response to the modest decline in output in 1972 was the very favourable terms (with respect both to price and to credit) at which the USSR was able to buy grain. The author has no knowledge of the reasons for this state of affairs, so advantageous for the USSR. It is outside the scope of this chapter to speculate on the causes of these favourable terms (e.g. the advantages of the state monopoly of foreign trade, the ignorance of US traders and of the US Government, desire to promote *détente*, purchase of conciliatory policy in Vietnam, desire of Republican Administration to benefit US farmers, etc.). It is sufficient to note that the quantity of grain bought was undoubtedly influenced by the favourable terms on which it was available.

In the period 1965–1975 the Soviet government pursued a policy of rapidly expanding the output of meat. Table VI.4 clearly shows the rapid increase in 1965–75 in meat output (especially poultry—largely reared by intensive methods) in the USSR. The result of this is that when the harvest fails, if the meat output increase policy is not to be jeopardised, substantial grain imports (or stock reductions) are necessary so as to provide feed for the animals. The data for 1973 and 1976 show that, even with massive grain imports, a poor harvest in one year normally leads to a fall in meat output (mainly pork) in the following year as a result of fodder shortages.

In 1931 when there was a bad harvest, the USSR was a net *exporter* of grain to pay for machinery imports, despite shortages of basic cereals for human consumption. In 1963 when there was a bad harvest the USSR imported grain, partly to ensure that there would be an adequate supply of basic cereals for the human population and partly to ensure adequate feed for the greatly expanded livestock population. In the 1970s when there were bad harvests the USSR imported grain to ensure that the animals would be fed so that the human population would have enough meat (as is done by West European countries). This change in policy over the year reflects the success of the government's industrialisation policy and its increasing attention to popular welfare, i.e. its increasing short-term consumer orientation. This is manifested not only by its foreign trade policy but also by its investment policy. Since the mid 1960s, the USSR has been investing in agriculture on an enormous scale. Hence, although it is common in the West to criticise the USSR for its big grain imports of 1972 and 1973 (either because it indicates an inefficient agricultural system or because it disrupted the world economy) one might just as well praise the USSR for devoting much more attention in the 1970s than previously to the immediate living standards of the population.

The reader may well ask why the Soviet government adopted this policy of increasing meat output. Is it not aware of the currently fashionable doctrine that animals are an extremely inefficient way of converting cereals to protein and that a more cereal based diet throughout the world would be more in the interests of the world economy? In the USSR the pro-meat policy is explained with reference to the scientific norms for the consumption of various food products. (The

Table VI.4

Meat production in the USSR (millions of tonnes)[a]

	1940	1965	1970	1971	1972	1973	1974	1975	1976
Total	1·5	5·2	7·1	8·2	8·7	8·3	9·4	9·9	8·4
of which									
Beef and veal	0·9	2·4	3·5	3·7	3·9	3·9	4·4	4·5	4·4
Mutton	0·2	0·4	0·4	0·4	0·4	0·4	0·4	0·4	0·4
Pork	0·4	1·8	2·2	2·9	3·2	2·8	3·1	3·3	2·1
Poultry	0·1	0·2	0·4	0·4	0·5	0·5	0·6	0·7	0·7
Other kinds of meat and category 1 offal	0·1	0·5	0·7	0·8	0·8	0·8	0·8	0·9	0·8

[a] Columns may not add to totals because of rounding.

Sources: *Narodnoe khozyaistvo SSSR v 1975 g*, Moscow, 1976, p. 229; *Narodnoe khozyaistvo SSSR za 60 let*, Moscow, 1977, p. 259.

method of norms is the basic method of consumption planning in the USSR.) Some data on these norms are set out in Table VI.5.

Table VI.5 shows clearly the logic of the meat output expansion of the late 1960s and early 1970s. In 1970, whereas the actual Soviet consumption of bread was 124% of the norm, and of potatoes 134%, that of meat and meat products was only 59%. Hence the policy of improving the diet by reducing the share in it of bread and potatoes and expanding that of meat (and also other livestock products such as milk and eggs).

Where do these norms come from? In the Soviet literature they are treated as 'scientific' norms derived from the findings of nutritional science. (They are compiled by the Academy of Medical Sciences.) It is obvious, however, that a major role is played by the international demonstration effect.

E.   CONCLUSIONS

The causal chain running from bad crop weather in the USSR in 1972, leading to a bad harvest in the USSR in 1972, leading to big Soviet grain imports in 1972 and 1973, leading to an explosion in world grain prices in 1972/73 is a weak one and overlaid with other factors.

First, the fall in world grain stock levels (resulting from the policy of

Table VI.5
Actual and normative food consumption in the USSR (kg/head/year)

Food	Norm	1970 actual	1970 as % of norm
Bread (in terms of flour), groats, macaroni products	120	149	124
Potatoes	97	130	134
Vegetables and melons	146	83	57
Sugar	37	39	106
Vegetable oil and margarine	7	7	93
Meat and meat products	82	48	59
Fish and fish products	18	15	85
Milk and milk products	434	307	71
Eggs	17	9	53

Note: The figures have been rounded. This explains some minor discrepancies.
Source: P. Weitzman, "Soviet Long Term Consumption Planning: Distribution according to Rational Need", *Soviet Studies*, July 1974.

the grain exporting countries) and factors external to the grain trade (the world boom and the collapse of the Bretton Woods monetary system) played an important part in raising world grain prices.

Secondly, poor weather was only one, and not the main, cause of the big Soviet grain imports of 1972 and 1973. In 1972 the weather in the USSR *was* unusual. In the European part of the USSR it was hot and dry, and in the Asiatic part of the USSR (especially Kazakhstan and Siberia) cool and wet (Katz, 1973). Nevertheless, the weather was not so bad from an agricultural point of view. Measured by the percentage fall in grain output compared to the previous year,[*] the weather in the USSR was much better in 1972 than in 1975, and better than in 1967, 1965, 1963, 1959, 1957, 1953 and 1951. This finding is confirmed by direct measurement of the weather, which indicates that in 1969–74, and especially in 1970–73, Soviet weather was particularly *favourable* for grain production.[†] This favourable weather appears to have been just one aspect of a climatic fluctuation effecting the entire Northern Hemisphere in this period. Other aspects were the Sahelian drought and failures of the Indian monsoon. Non-weather factors influencing Soviet grain imports in 1972 and 1973 were the very favourable terms on which the grain was available and the policy of the Soviet government of building up livestock numbers in order to improve the people's diet.

This case study suggests the following hypothesis about the effect of climatic change on human society. While climatic change clearly has important effects on human society, the main factors affecting the development of human society at the present time are not external (such as weather) but internal (e.g. economic, social and political).[‡]

---

[*] This is only an indirect way of measuring the weather, and may seem rather arbitrary. It should be noted, however, that so-called 'direct' methods involve weighting different kinds of weather factors (e.g. precipitation, wind and temperature) over different regions and different months. Furthermore, it is not so arbitrary, given that it is the weather induced fluctuations in grain output that we are interested in.

[†] *USSR: the impact of recent climate change on grain production* Research Aid, (CIA, Washington DC, 1976) passim.

[‡] Similarly, A. K. Sen (1977) has shown that the Bengal famine of 1943 was not primarily caused by a weather induced failure of production, but by economic and social factors effecting demand and distribution. In the same vein, Dando (1976) has argued that in the millenium 971–1970 Russian famines were predominantly man-made, not natural, disasters.

VII. THE DISTRIBUTION OF EARNINGS UNDER BREZHNEV*

A characteristic feature of the 1970s is also the increase in the differentiation of wages as one of the means of strengthening the principle of material incentives. (*Problemy raspredeleniia i rost narodnogo blagosostoyaniya*, Moscow, 1979, p. 120)

It is well known that the USSR experienced a significant reduction in the inequality of earnings after 1956. It seems to be less well known that the dispersion of the earnings of workers and employees reached its most egalitarian level in 1968 and that inequality of the earnings of workers and employees increased between 1968 and 1976.† Tabular and graphic representations of the dynamics of the dispersion of earnings in the USSR are set out in Table VII.1 and Fig. 7.1.

Table VII.1 and Fig. 7.1 show that the inequality of the earnings of both industrial workers and workers and employees reached a low point in 1968 (associated with the increase in the minimum wage to 60 roubles per month) and has since increased. For workers and employees, by 1976 it had roughly regained the interpolated 1965 level.‡

---

* First published in *Slavic Review*, December 1980.
† For example, Jerry Hough gives the impression that the post-Stalin reduction of the inequality of the earnings of workers and employees continued into the mid-1970s (see Hough, 1976, p. 12). This has been quoted by popular writers. Albert Szymanski, for example, argues in his recent book that the trend toward earnings equalisation has continued since the 1940s (1979, pp. 60–61). He bases his study partly on Hough. Only data up to 1970 are considered in McAuley (1979).
‡ A. S. Rzhanitsyna anticipated that inequalities of earnings would diminish during 1976–80 (Rzhanitsyna, 1979, p. 123). The reasons for this were the increase in the

Table VII.1

Earnings inequality in the USSR (decile ratio[a])

Year	Industrial workers	All workers and employees
1924	4·47	—
1927	3·60	—
1930	3·33	—
1934	3·16	—
1946[b]	5·43	7·24
1956	3·36	4·44
1959	3·31	4·21
1961	2·82	4·02
1964	2·67	3·69
1966	2·78	3·26
1968	2·50	2·83
1972	2·63	3·10
1976	—	3·35[c]

[a] The decile ratio is the ratio of the highest earnings in the bottom 90% of earnings to the highest earnings in the bottom 10% of earnings.

[b] Alastair McAuley considers that in view of the unreliability of the data "the purported distribution of earnings for this year should be treated with suspicion" (see McAuley, 1979, p. 219). Rabkina and Rimashevskaia themselves point out that the data for 1946 are not fully comparable with that for the other years for two reasons. First, the 1946 study did not distinguish between industrial workers and all those employed in industry, and "therefore the figure of 5·43 was determined . . . on the basis of indirect data" (see Rabkina and Rimashevskaya, 1978, p. 21, note 5). Second, the coverage was different.

[c] Another source gives 3·46 (see *Portrebnosti, dokhody, potreblenie*, Moscow, 1979, p. 95).

Source: Rabkina and Rimashevskaya (1978, p. 20).

It is important to note that the data in Table VII.1 and Fig. 7.1 throw no direct light on the distribution of welfare between persons. The latter depends on the distribution of tertiary incomes between house-

---

minimum wage to 70 roubles per month (which took place during 1976–77), the improvement of the relative position of workers in the traditionally low-paid service sectors, and the improvement in the relative incomes of collective farmers.

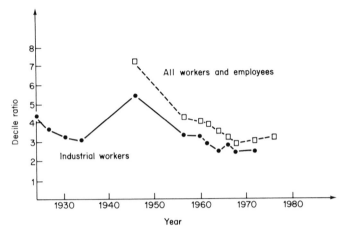

Fig. 7.1 Earnings inequality in the USSR.

holds, adjusted by differences in household composition.* The data in Table VII.1 and Fig. 7.1, however, only cover part of the primary income distribution (collective farmers, non-earners, transfer payments, and benefits in kind, are all excluded). The importance of family circumstances and of secondary income distribution are illustrated by the data from a survey in Kostroma set out in Table VII.2.

Table VII.2 shows, as one would expect, that the percentage of well-paid individuals in poor households is much lower than the percentage of well-paid individuals in well-off households. It also shows, however, that 16% of the earners in well-off households are low paid and that only 33% of the earners in well-off households are well paid. In fact, of the total number of well-paid individuals, only 35% were in the well-off families. On the whole, the differentiation of

---

* The 'primary income distribution' is the distribution of gross earnings and property income. The 'secondary income distribution' is the primary income distribution corrected for taxes and transfer payments. The 'tertiary income distribution' is the secondary income distribution corrected for income in kind from the state (for example, subsidised housing and free medical care). McAuley (1979) distinguishes between 'earnings' and 'income'. His A1, A2, A4, B2, and B3 correspond to the primary income distribution, the same (less taxes and plus A3) correspond to the secondary income distribution, and the latter (plus C2 [including housing]) corresponds to the tertiary income distribution.

Table VII.2

Relationship between earnings and per capita
family income in Kostroma in the mid-1970s (in %)

Incomes	Earnings		
	Low paid	Average paid	Well paid
Poor	61	37	2
Average	41	47	12
Well off	16	51	33

Source: *Potrebnosti, dokhody, potreblenie,* Moscow, 1979, p. 106.

families by income in the USSR in the 1970s seems to have exceeded the differentiation of earners by earnings, with important regional differences.*

CONCLUSION

The post-Stalin decline in the inequality of the earnings of workers and employees in the USSR (as measured by the decile ratio) came to an end (possibly temporary) in 1968. Between 1968 and 1976 the inequality of the earnings of workers and employees in the USSR (as measured by the decile ratio) increased, in 1976 reaching approximately the 1965 level. No direct conclusions can be drawn from this for the Soviet distribution of welfare between persons.

* See *Portrebnosti, dokhody, potreblenie,* Moscow, 1979, p. 106.

VIII. INCOME DISTRIBUTION IN
THE USSR*

the quality of the data on living standards collected, processed and summarised by the statistical organs is far from meeting requirements, which significantly reduces their usefulness for economic analysis. (*Differentsirovannyi balans dokhodov i potrebleniya naseleniya* Moscow, 1977, p. 39)

"among families with high per capita incomes single people and couples without children predominate (comprising 50–70%). (Ibid, p. 97)

A. INCOME DISTRIBUTION AND OFFICIAL DOCTRINE

According to Marxism-Leninism, income distribution is not an *end* of policy but a *means*, a method of raising labour productivity and increasing production. In the words of a phrase of Lenin's which is repeatedly quoted in Soviet sources, "distribution is a method, an instrument, a means, for increasing production". Egalitarianism has been officially condemned since a famous speech of Stalin's in 1931, and the main stress of official policy since then has been on 'material incentives', on the need to provide material rewards for hard work and improving qualifications. Hence, Soviet people generally disbelieve accounts of Western progressive income tax systems. If they are convinced that what they are hearing is true they tend to ask, "But does this not undermine the principle of material incentives? How can labour productivity in your country grow?" To use the current US termin-

* This is a slightly revised version of an article first published, in Dutch, in *Economisch Statistische Berichten*, 26 August 1981.

ology, Stalin was an early adherent of 'supply side economics' and present day Reaganites and Communists are united in believing in supply side economics. Mr Brezhnev would entirely agree with Mrs Thatcher about the harmfulness of high marginal tax rates on earned income.

Currently the Marxist-Leninist view about income distribution is that egalitarianism is harmful because it has an adverse effect on production, but that excessive differentiation is also to be opposed and reduced. The advantage with respect to income distribution, according to this view, of socialism over capitalism, is that under socialism there is no private ownership of the means of production and hence there is (virtually) no income from property. It is state ownership of the means of production which, according to Marxism-Leninism, constitutes a qualitative difference between capitalism and socialism and constitutes the qualitative superiority of the latter. Although there are, of course, high and low earnings in the USSR, this in the Marxist-Leninist view is no criticism of the USSR since such differentials are necessary to stimulate labour productivity and reward the most productive members of society. Only petty bourgeois egalitarians and Maoists, it is argued, could think otherwise.

It is also the Marxist-Leninist view that in the long run, as productivity rises and goods become abundant, there will be a transition from distribution according to work to distribution according to need. Already, according to the official view, there are significant areas of distribution according to need, such as free or heavily subsidised goods and services (e.g. education, housing, medical care) and transfer payments. As productivity rises, goods become abundant, and work becomes a basic human need rather than a necessity, they can be expanded.

From a Marxist-Leninist point of view, the policies of levelling earnings traditionally advocated by West European socialist parties are harmful and misguided. They are harmful because they have an adverse effect on the work enthusiasm of the skilled workers and key managerial personnel. They are misguided since they divert attention from the main issue, the ownership of the means of production, to a side issue, the distribution of earnings. Hence in the USSR there is nothing similar to the British supplementary benefit programme so as not to weaken the effect of the economic whip in maintaining and increasing the participation rate. Instead there is a full employment policy which provides security of employment for all and a steadily increasing volume of employment, enormous training and education programmes to ensure the development of human talent, steadily increasing minimum wages and average wages, and a slowly improving system of transfer payments (e.g. old age pensions and payments to multi-child households with *per capita* incomes below the poverty line).

B.   INCOME DISTRIBUTION AND EQUALITY

In a non-market economy the distribution of money income gives only very limited information about 'equality' as understood in Western Europe. There are three reasons for this.

First, there are very important *power* inequalities arising from the non-market nature of the economy. To reduce the role of market relations and increase the role of administrative methods means, as far as inequality is concerned, to increase the importance of stratification by power relative to stratification by income and wealth. Obviously in the Gulag there were enormous inequalities between prisoners and guards, but they were not primarily income inequalities! As I have observed elsewhere,

> As far as the distribution of power is concerned, it would seem that the result of the combination [in the state socialist countries] of a permanent dictatorship with the absence of independent social organisations, is inequalities of power much greater than in liberal democratic capitalist countries. The inequality between those who organised, and those whose lives were transformed by, collectivisation and the Gulag Archipelago in the USSR; collectivisation, the Great Leap Forward and the Great Proletarian Cultural Revolution in China; and sending down the entire urban population in Cambodia; were all enormous (Ellman, 1979, p. 268).

An analogous source of non-income inequalities in capitalist countries is inequalities of wealth. In a non-market economy of the Soviet type, to neglect power differences in an assessment of inequality would be as absurd as to neglect wealth differences in assessing inequality in the UK.

Secondly, there are important areas of consumption access to which is not determined by money income. These are of two kinds, goods which also exist in market economies, and goods which only exist in non-market economies. An example of the first kind is provided by housing. Although there is a kind of market in co-operative flats in Soviet towns, the best dwellings are allocated to those holding high office as a non-monetary perk. Similarly, there are special shops which supply high quality goods, which otherwise would be difficult to obtain or unobtainable in the USSR, to top people in accordance with their jobs. Similarly travel to capitalist countries is not something which one can simply walk into a travel agency and buy, but something which is only possible with the agreement of the relevant party and KGB organisations.

Because important areas of consumption are determined by bureaucratic position and not by income, a policy of subsidies for basic goods and services may turn into a policy of increasing inequality, of taxing the badly off to subsidise the well off. As the Hungarian sociologist Szelenyi noted in a classic study of the sociology of housing distribution in Hungary (1972), "Rent subsidies thus turned into wage supplements increasing the differences between low and high incomes . . . the administrative system of housing distribution proved to be disfunctional, that is it led to a result which differed from its declared aim." This problem can be overcome either by making greater use of charges, and more generally of the market mechanism, for publicly provided services (which in East European practice is associated with so-called economic reform) or by bringing the actual distribution of housing and medical care into line with the principle of distribution according to need.

The classic example of an important consumption good which does not exist in a non-market economy concerns information. In the USSR, of course, there exist no domestic newspapers which provide extensive foreign news coverage such as *The Financial Times*, *Le Monde* etc. At the same time access to Western newspapers and books is very limited. Nevertheless, there are some people whose position in the bureaucratic hierarchy requires them to know what is going on abroad (e.g. editors, ideological officials, foreign ministry officials, research workers in specialised institutes, officials in the Central Committee apparatus etc.). Hence for them there are special TASS bulletins (graded, naturally, on the need to know principle) with accurate information. Similarly, in all important libraries there are special sections (with politically sensitive or foreign books) only accessible to those with special permission to use them.

Thirdly, it is entirely possible to increase equality, in a statistical sense, by 'levelling down'. For instance, it is broadly true (although there are some important exceptions such as owner-occupied housing and savings bank deposits) that wealth is equally divided in the USSR. This, however, does not mean that everyone is well off, but that everyone is badly off (all means of production belong to the state). Similarly, it may well be that the Pol Pot regime in Kampuchea increased statistical equality, but this was notoriously a case of levelling down rather than levelling up. Increasing equality of wealth by abolishing private ownership of wealth, or increasing equality of income by reducing everyone to subsistence level, are both perfectly possible. They are not, however, very attractive. Nor are they what is usually understood as 'equality' by West Europeans, although statistically they undoubtedly qualify for this label.

C. DATA PROBLEMS

The data currently available on the Soviet income distribution are very poor. They basically consist of reconstructions by Western specialists (such as Wiles (1974) and McAuley (1979)) of censored Soviet publications derived from the data of the Soviet Central Statistical Administration. This introduces two main sources of error: first, errors in the underlying CSA data; secondly, errors introduced by the censorship process.

The underlying CSA data are based on sample surveys of the employed population for 1958, 1966 and possibly also for 1972. The samples taken were not fully representative (for example the 1958 and 1967 surveys excluded the agricultural population). Furthermore, the concept of 'income' employed was a restrictive one which excluded income in kind and fringe benefits. Hence the CSA data for the urban population are an inaccurate estimate of the secondary income distribution.* For the collective farmers, the data available to the CSA are based on family budget sample surveys. These are known to be unrepresentative. Hence it can be seen that the data available to the CSA are not very reliable.

---

* It is customary to distinguish between the 'primary', 'secondary' and 'tertiary' income distributions. For a brief definition of these terms see the first footnote on page 110.

Poor as they are, the data available to the CSA are a lot better than that available to Westerners interested in the subject. The reason is that the CSA does not publish, neither in its annual statistical handbook, nor in its monthly journal, nor in other publications, any details about Soviet income distribution. Instead, various Soviet specialists, using the CSA data, have published bits of information derived from it, such as measures of dispersion (e.g. the decile ratio) and graphs of the whole distribution with the numbers removed. These publications, of course, are subject to pre-publication censorship (like everything else published in the USSR). The censors strive to eliminate entirely statistics the publication of which is thought to be harmful for the USSR (e.g. the infant mortality figures for the 1970s). The censors also try to see that the published figures are calculated in such a way that they present the situation in the USSR in a favourable light. This applies, for example, to the figures for coal output, grain output, and retail prices, which are all non-comparable with apparently similar data for other countries. The censorship also stands guard over the official, but falsified, version of certain events (e.g. the number of deaths during the siege of Leningrad).

In addition to the information about income distribution derived from the sample surveys of the employed population, which is the ultimate source of Western estimates of the Soviet income indistribution, there appears also to be unpublished information available to Soviet specialists derived from the balance of money incomes and expenditure of the population (Osipov, 1972, p. 78). The balance of money incomes and expenditures of the population is an important planning instrument. A component of the system of material balances, it is used, *inter alia*, to try and preserve overall balance in the availability of consumer goods and the purchasing power of the population. These data give estimates of inequality in the USSR which are greater than those in the published Soviet literature. The reasons for this discrepancy are unclear. One possibility is that the populations considered are different. According to Osipov, the highest paid groups are party and state officials, army officers, managers and scientific research workers. It is possible that these groups are excluded from the 'state employees' data for the earnings distribution of whom are presented by McAuley. This would mean that McAuley's estimates of earnings inequality only includes workers, employees and ordinary engineering-technical personnel and excludes the highest earners. Another possibility is that the 'earnings' concept is different. Osipov's 'gross wages fund' may include non-cash earnings such as housing subsidies and educational, medical and holiday subsidies. Since these are probably more unequally distributed than money incomes this would have a considerable influence.

It is entirely normal for statistics gathered for different purposes to give different pictures of reality. For example, in Western countries, statistics on 'unemployment' derived from the social security system usually differ substantially from those derived from census data. In this case the reason is that there are normally many people in Western countries who would like jobs but are not eligible for unemployment benefits. What is unusual about the case of Soviet income distribution is *not* the existence of such discrepancies. It is that only part of the relevant data is published, and that the data which (from an egalitarian point of view) reflects unfavourably on the USSR, is unpublished.

It is hard to disagree with Korzec's view (1978) that as a result of the deficiencies in the data, while it is possible to make some definite statements about the Soviet income distribution, it is impossible to give a clear overall picture because of data limitations.

D.   THE ABSOLUTE INCOME LEVEL

In considering the absolute income level, two levels are particularly important, the subsistence level and the poverty level.

1.   *The Subsistence Level*

The subsistence level is that level of income below which people die of hunger and cold and or diseases resulting from malnutrition or cold. The extent to which people in a particular country fall below the subsistence level is a very important characteristic of its income distribution.

During the Lenin–Stalin period, significant numbers of people in the USSR fell below the subsistence level on several occasions, notably 1921/22, 1932/34, 1941/43 and 1946/47. Indeed it seems likely that in the whole period 1930–53 Soviet people were dying from food deficiency diseases. In the 1930s the USSR experienced major epidemics largely arising from food shortages. These catastrophes resulted from war (in 1941–43), or the aftermath of war (in 1921–22), drought (in 1921–22, 1932–34 and 1946–47), the state taking grain needed by the rural population (in 1932–34), the low levels of agricultural output and productivity and Soviet agricultural policies.

Hence it can be seen that the claim by some Western writers (e.g. Adler-Karlsson, 1976) that state socialism is superior to capitalism in the provision of *essentials* requires, to say the least, to be modified in view of the repeated failures of the USSR in the Lenin–Stalin period (and also of China in 1960–62) to provide all the population with the most basic essential of all, sufficient food to prevent starvation.

In the Krushchev–Brezhnev period there was a considerable growth of agricultural output. In addition in the 1970s the USSR imported fodder on a large scale. Hence,

> The USSR has ceased to be a country threatened by famine and with a population only just above the subsistence level. It has become a country in which the *per capita* consumption of food has increased significantly over many years and in which the average diet has greatly improved. This is a major achievement of Soviet power and a significant gain for the people of the USSR (chapter 4, p. 63).

Although *shortages* of food products, *queues* for food products and *de facto rationing*, are common in the USSR at the present time (in the wake of the stagnation of meat output in the late 1970s, the bad harvests in 1979, 1980 and 1981 and the refusal to increase state retail prices to supply and demand balancing levels), the whole population is now well above subsistence level.

The successful agricultural policies of Krushchev and Brezhnev, which have substantially raised agricultural output, their successful foreign policies, which have avoided a major war, and the increase in world market prices of oil, natural gas and gold, which have enabled the USSR to finance large-scale fodder imports, have led to this favourable result.

2. The Poverty Level

'Poverty' is always a relative and culture-bound concept. What is 'poverty' in London might seem quite attractive in Calcutta. In the United States, half a million families below the 'poverty' line own two or more cars. Poverty levels for the USSR have been calculated by Soviet specialists. These, together with Soviet data on income distribution, enable one to say what proportion of the Soviet population at various times fell below the 'poverty' level as defined by Soviet specialists for Soviet conditions. This has been done by McAuley.

It turns out that in 1960, only two decades ago, the average *per capita* income in the USSR was only about 80% of the poverty level! This means that in 1960 the average person in the USSR was living in poverty. Since then the situation has improved substantially. By 1974 the average income was *c.* 140% of the poverty level. As far as the rural population is concerned, as late as 1965 the overwhelming majority of members of collective farm households were in poverty. It was only in the late 1960s that the average income of members of collective farm households reached the poverty level. Overall, in the late 1960s *c.* 40% of the Soviet population were still in poverty. At the present time poverty in the USSR increasingly results from an adverse earner/dependent ratio within a family rather than low earnings per earner, a phenomenon that will sound familiar to the Child Poverty Action Group.

E.   RELATIVE INCOMES

1.   *The Dynamics of Earnings Inequalities*

As far as the evolution of Soviet earnings inequality over time is concerned, the basic information is as set out in Table VIII.1.

It is important to note that the data in Table VIII.1 throw no direct light on the distribution of welfare between persons. The latter depends on the distribution of tertiary income between households, adjusted by differences in household composition. The data in Table VIII.1, however, only cover part of the primary income distribution (collective farmers, non-earners, transfer payments and benefits in kind, are all excluded).

The overall picture shown by Table VIII.1 is of a situation in which earnings inequalities increased sharply in the Stalin period, were reduced sharply in the Krushchev period, and have increased somewhat in the Brezhnev period. At the present time there are some large income inequalities in the USSR by West European standards. For example, senior army officers, high party officials, successful writers,

Table VIII.1

Earnings inequality in the USSR (decile ratio)[a]

Year	Industrial workers	All workers and employees
1924	4·47	n.a.
1927	3·60	n.a.
1930	3·33	n.a.
1934	3·16	n.a.
1946[b]	5·43	7.24
1956	3·36	4·44
1959	3·31	4·21
1961	2·82	4·02
1964	2·67	3·69
1966	2·78	3·26
1968	2·50	2·83
1972	2·63	3·10
1976	n.a.	3·35[c]

a The decile ratio is the ratio of the highest earnings in the bottom 90% of earnings to the highest earnings in the bottom 10% of earnings.

[b] For 1946, McAuley considers that in view of the unreliability of the data, "the purported distribution of earnings for this year should be treated with suspicion" (1979, p. 219). Rabkina and Rimashevskaya themselves point out that the data for 1946 are not fully comparable with those for other years for two reasons. First, the 1946 study did not distinguish between industrial workers and all those employed in industry, and "therefore the figure of 5·43 was determined . . . on the basis of indirect data" (p. 21 note 5). Secondly, the coverage was different.

[c] For 1976, another source gives 3·46 (not 3·35). See *Potrebnosti, dokhody, potreblenie*, Moscow, 1979, p. 95.

Source: Rabkina and Rimashevskaya (1978, p. 20).

members of the Academy of Sciences, diplomats, and managers of large heavy industrial concerns often have an income of 10 times or more the minimum wage (70 roubles a month). These are large disparities in a country in which many people receive less than the minimum wage (e.g. some collective farmers and old age pensioners). In addition, as explained above, the tertiary income distribution works to *increase* absolute inequalities.

2. *International Comparisons*

As far as international comparisons are concerned, the following points are particularly important.

First, property income does exist in the USSR in the form of interest on savings bank deposits, imputed rent from owner occupied housing, and rent from housing (e.g. rooms let during the summer in holiday resorts). Nevertheless, it seems likely that it is a much less significant aspect of the income distribution and of social stratification than in the UK or the USA.

Secondly, the relative incomes of different groups are strikingly different from the situation in the capitalist world. Whereas in the latter the free professionals are traditionally high earners, in the USSR medical doctors (except for senior medical administrators) are traditionally a low paid group. (Many of them are women which makes it easier to exploit them.) On the other hand, some groups of manual workers, e.g. coal miners and bus drivers, are rather well paid, with incomes in excess of those of most university graduates.

Thirdly, private ownership of housing, i.e. owner-occupation, primarily occurs among the lower income groups rather than the higher. The reason for this is that the majority of the houses in private ownership are traditional style houses without running water and central heating. The high income groups live predominantly in modern flats with good facilities and low rents which are the property of the state.

Fourthly, there is no redistributive income tax in the USSR. The maximum marginal rate of income tax in the USSR is 13%. Most Soviet government revenue is collected through indirect taxation. This falls particularly heavily on goods which loom large in the household budgets of low income families, e.g. vodka.

Fifthly, although international comparisons are often made, it seems likely that data limitations undermine their relevance for the USSR (see above). Nevertheless, it is noteworthy that all the studies in the literature show that the state socialist countries have a more equal distribution of income than similar capitalist countries.

3. *Sexual Inequality*

Throughout the world employed women earn less than men. This is so in the advanced capitalist countries, in the third world, and also in the economically advanced central European state socialist economies. It is also so in the USSR. There are no official overall Soviet statistics of the relative earnings of men and women (because of the awkward picture they would show) but a variety of sample surveys have been taken and reported in the specialist Soviet literature (see McAuley, 1981, chapter 2). These all show earnings inequalities similar to those in Western Europe. Although women occupy a variety of interesting and satisfying jobs in the USSR, most Soviet women are engaged in unskilled work, low level jobs and traditional 'feminine' occupations. Soviet women work primarily to earn enough to support a family (this is normally impossible on only one income) and their jobs are often monotonous and exhausting.

4. Regional Inequality

The Soviet Union is a very large state, with substantial differences in natural conditions and levels of economic development between its regions. Whereas in Estonia the level of economic and cultural development is similar to that of Finland, in Turkmenia it is closer to that of Iran or Afghanistan. Georgia has a climate which provides very good conditions for agriculture, whereas much of the USSR is in the permafrost zone. Some data on inter-republican income differences are set out in Tables VIII.2 and VIII.3.

The two tables show that there exist significant differences between average incomes in the different republics. Important factors causing them are differences in participation rates between republics and the high productivity of private plots in the Baltic republics. It should be noted, however, that these differences are low by international standards. Furthermore, one should not draw exaggerated conclusions from the data in Tables VIII.2 and VIII.3. One should be extremely wary, for example, of concluding from the data in Table VIII.3 that rural living standards are higher in the RSFSR than in Georgia. That would be to ignore differences in the weather and in the availability of goods between republics and also in the fact that women's domestic labour brings substantial benefits to the other members of their household. Similarly, despite the relatively low *per capita* incomes in Central Asia depicted in Tables VIII.2 and VIII.3, the 1960s saw substantial *immigration* of Russians to Central Asia in search of sunshine, fruit and vegetables. There are important aspects of living standards which are not captured by income statistics!

Table VIII.2
Average per capita *tertiary income of state employee households in 1970 (in % of USSR)*

Estonia	122·8
Latvia	116·5
Lithuania	107·6
RSFSR	104·4
USSR	100.0
Ukraine	99·5
Moldavia	96·9
Byelorussia	95·2
Armenia	90·3
Georgia	89·0
Kazakhstan	86·6
Uzbekistan	82·3
Turkmenia	80·1
Tadjikstan	78·8
Kirkizia	78·2
Azerbaijan	72·1

Source: McAuley (1979, p. 139). (Strictly speaking, the 'income' measured in this table is not tertiary income since it takes no account of direct taxes and housing subsidies.)

5. *Urban–Rural Inequality*

There are still substantial income inequalities in the USSR between urban and rural areas. Some relevant data are set out in Table VIII.4. It shows clearly the improvement in the relative position of the collective farm households that took place in the 1960s. Nevertheless, even as late as 1965, the overwhelming majority of people in collective farm households had incomes below the poverty level. The relatively unfavourable position of the collective farm households in the early 1960s resulted from the legacy of the semi-feudal relations of production in agriculture established by Stalin and the low levels of productivity in agriculture.

An interesting aspect of the interaction of republican and rural–urban inequalities is that in the three Baltic republics, since the mid 1960s *per capita* incomes have been *higher* in collective farms households than in state employee households, mainly as a result of the high productivity of the private plots of Baltic collective farmers.

Table VIII.3

Average per capita *tertiary income of collective farm households in 1970 (in % of USSR)*

Estonia	215·7
Latvia	171·8
Lithuania	158·1
Kazakhstan	116·7
RSFSR	115·1
USSR	100·0
Byelorussia	99·6
Georgia	97·6
Turkmenistan	95·0
Moldavia	88·5
Armenia	80·3
Uzbekistan	72·8
Kirgizia	71·4
Azerbaijan	61·8
Tadjikstan	57·7

Source: McAuley (1979, p. 128). (Strictly speaking, the 'income' measured in this table is not tertiary income since it excludes direct taxes and the imputed rents of owner occupied housing.)

Table VIII.4

Average per capita *tertiary income of collective farm households as % of that of state employee households*

1960	1965	1970	1974
69·6	80·5	83·4	83·2

Source: McAuley (1979, p. 29). The income concept ('total income'—direct taxes) is not quite the same as 'tertiary income' since it fails to include either the imputed rent of owner occupied housing or the difference between actual and free market rents.

6. The Élite

The published data used by Western specialists such as McAuley naturally contain no information about the Soviet élite. The existence of this group, and the size and nature of its privileges, are subjects which are very sensitive in the USSR and hence the censorship prevents information on this subject appearing in open sources. Nevertheless, there is some information about this topic, stemming from the writings of Western academics such as Matthews (1978) and emigrants such as Voslensky (1980).

Matthews investigated the question of whether there existed in the USSR an élite with real incomes significantly above the average. His investigation is summed up in Table VIII.5. This shows an élite group of 0·2% of the employed population with incomes much above the average. The extent to which the élite is turning (or has already turned) into a hereditary group, whether or not it should be described as a 'class', and the relationship between the élite and the *nomenklatura*, are at the centre of contemporary polemics. It should be noted that in terms of living standards, wealth, and independence from the state, the Soviet élite is worse off than the US élite.

Table VIII.5
Élite occupational groups in the USSR in 1970[a]

	Thousands	%
Party officials	95	38
State, Komsomol and trade union officials	60	24
The intelligentsia[b]	43	17
Enterprise managers	22	9
The military, police, diplomatic service	30	12
Total	250	100

[a] Persons earning 450 roubles a month or more and having access to substantial non-cash benefits. (Average wages in the USSR in 1970 were 122 roubles per month.)
[b] i.e. academicians, heads of higher educational institutions, institutes, faculties and laboratories; head doctors; senior legal officials; editors and senior journalists; leaders in arts and artistic bureaucracy.
Source: *Survey* vol. 21, no. 3, p. 13.

7. Active and Inactive

The Soviet Union has an extensive system of transfer payments, old age pensions, sickness benefits, maternity benefits, invalidity benefits etc. Considered from a British perspective, perhaps the main features of the Soviet social security system are the (virtual) absence of anything corresponding to supplementary benefit (so as not to weaken the economic whip), the absence of unemployment benefits (the state provides jobs for workers, not money for shirkers, as Mrs Thatcher would put it), the absence of a general child benefit system, the significant proportion of people of pensionable age without pensions (probably mainly because they do not have the work record necessary for a pension), and the low level of payments such as pensions and child benefits relative to money earnings. In the USSR, to be economically inactive is financially unattractive. Nevertheless, compared to a US worker, the financial position of an ill Soviet worker is quite good. He gets free hospital treatment, and when he comes back to work has waiting for him the nest egg made up of the sickness benefit paid to him while he was ill. In addition, the chance of a Soviet worker being declared redundant is negligible.

8. *Family Circumstances*

The second of the two quotations which head this chapter draws attention to the very important fact that in the contemporary USSR family circumstances are of very great importance in determining differences in *per capita* income. High *per capita* incomes are predominantly found in households of single people and childless couples, low *per capita* incomes in households with dependents (e.g. children or retired people).

In the European state socialist countries as a whole, differences in the level of earnings account for only a small proportion of differences in *per capita* incomes. The main causes of differences in *per capita* incomes are differences in the dependency ratio. Households with a high earner but an adverse dependency ratio have low *per capita* incomes, and households with low earners but a favourable dependency ratio have high *per capita* incomes.

9. *The Black Market*

In the USSR there exists a significant black market which naturally affects the income distribution in a way extremely difficult to capture in income distribution statistics. This is also true for Britain. In Britain, the black economy is caused mainly by the tax and social security systems, in the USSR by the inability of the state economy to provide all the consumer goods and services wanted by the population. The black market in the USSR works to redistribute income in favour of those with goods (e.g. those stolen from state enterprises or produced in underground workshops) or services (e.g. building craftsmen, doctors) to sell for which there is a substantial demand. It is one of the factors, along with special shops for top people only and the system for the distribution of housing and medical care, which undermine the meaning of the published statistics on the income distribution.

F.   CONCLUSIONS

1. According to the official doctrine of the USSR, Marxism-Leninism, the levelling of earnings, such as is often advocated by West European socialist parties, is harmful and misguided.

2. Stalin was an early adherent of 'supply side economics' and present day Reaganites and Communists are united in believing in supply side economics.

3. In the USSR, money income differences only throw a very limited light on 'equality', because of the importance of power inequalities and the allocation of consumption goods on the basis of bureaucratic position rather than money income. This is particularly important in the fields of 'free' or heavily subsidised consumption, such as housing and medical care, where non-market methods produce results at variance with their declared aims and a greater use of the market mechanism would produce greater equality.

4. The data currently available on the Soviet income distribution are very poor.

5. Since the Great October Socialist Revolution, the income levels of large numbers of Soviet people have several times fallen below the subsistence level. The last time this happened was in 1946–47.

6. Poverty remains a serious problem in the USSR. It increasingly results from an adverse dependency ratio per household.

7. Soviet earnings inequalities (for state employees) rose sharply under Stalin, fell under Khrushchev and increased somewhat under Brezhnev.

8. There are significant differences between the situation in the USSR and that in the capitalist world. Property income is much less significant in the USSR. Some professional groups (e.g. doctors) are

relatively badly paid in the USSR, and some manual groups (e.g. coal miners) are relatively well paid in the USSR. Data limitations make the meaning of the overall interpersonal distribution between the USSR and other countries problematic. For what it is worth, all such studies in the literature show a more equal distribution of income in state socialist than in comparable capitalist ones.

9. Soviet women earn significantly less than men, as in Western Europe.

10. There are significant differences in income levels between the Soviet republics.

11. Income levels of state employee households always have been and still are (except in the Baltic republics) higher than those of collective farm households. As late as the mid 1960s, the majority of those in collective farm households were below the poverty line.

12. There exists a small élite in the USSR, with incomes much above the average and with access to substantial non-monetary benefits (e.g. second houses).

13. In the USSR, to be economically inactive is often financially unattractive. The system of transfer payments in the USSR is poorly developed compared to the welfare states of North-West Europe.

14. The dependency ratio is a major factor determining differences in per capita incomes in the USSR. If it were desired to reduce income inequality in the USSR, the main methods would be to introduce a general and generous child benefit system, to raise and extend to all retired people old age pensions and to make greater use of charges and more generally of the market mechanism for housing and medical care. An alternative to the latter which would achieve the same result, would be to bring their actual allocation into line with the principle of distribution according to need.

IX. THE CONTROL OF INFLATION? ERRORS IN THE INTERPRETATION OF CPE DATA*

Conventional wisdom has it that there is in Eastern Europe, especially in the USSR, a significant amount of repressed inflation. Although until recently official price statistics showed hardly any open inflation, there are some indicators that are alleged to indicate repressed inflation. In this connection the widespread shortages, the ratio of collective farm market prices (CFM prices) to state retail prices, the volume of personal savings accounts and an indicator developed by Holzman (1960) are often cited.† Using these indicators, Bronson and Severin (1966, p. 516) come to the conclusion that in the USSR during the early 1960s inflationary pressures were growing. In the same vein Schroeder and Severin (1976, p. 631) constructed an alternative price index for the USSR that slowly but steadily rises over the period 1955–75. This price index, it was assumed, is more accurate than the official Soviet retail price index, whose deficiencies are analysed by Bornstein (1972).

Portes (1977) argued that in the centrally planned economies (CPEs) little serious 'hidden' or repressed inflation can be demonstrated. One

---

* Originally published in *Economica*, August 1981. A reply by Portes was published in the same number. The author is grateful to Michael Ellman and the referee for helpful comments.
† Holzman's measure, which takes into account the volume of sales in each market, "presents the ratios of the excess money spent in the collective farm market due to higher prices to the sum of state sales plus collective farm market sales valued at state prices. In other words, letting P_s, P_k, Q_s, Q_k represent the prices and quantities on state and collective farm markets respectively, our ratio is: $100\{Q_k(P_k - P_s)/P_s(Q_s + Q_k)\}$" (Holzman, 1960, p. 170). (This is only a true indicator of inflation if $\Delta P_s = 0$.)

of his arguments is that savings behaviour is often misinterpreted (Portes and Winter, 1978). Another argument was that many of the phenomena could be explained micro-economically in terms of the disequilibrium relative prices of particular goods. (This argument is supported by Pickersgill, 1977.) A third argument was that there was no evidence of suppressed inflation in the behaviour of CFM prices. Although the first two arguments seem fundamentally correct, this third argument is erroneous, at any rate for Poland and the USSR since 1971.

Portes (1977, p. 121) gives a table for two CPEs, Hungary and Poland, which purports to show that behaviour of CFM food prices and state retail food prices is consistent with macro-economic equilibrium on the consumption goods market for all but a few brief periods during the years 1955–75. Examination of the data for Poland, however, gives a widening gap between state retail and free market prices for the years 1971–75, a fact that must have been noted by Portes, for he stated (1977, p. 110) that in Poland in the period 1972–75 there was some evidence of repressed inflation. Portes also uses a table (p. 121), published by Garvy (1977),[*] in which Holzman's indicator shows that between 1955 and 1971 repressed inflation in the USSR has fallen.

The weakness of Portes' argument is as follows.

1. In his econometric work with Winter (Portes and Winter, 1977, 1978) he stated that: "any final judgment on the question of repressed inflation, that began this investigation, must await the disequilibrium estimation for which this paper and Portes and Winter (1977) provide a basis" (Portes and Winter, 1978, p. 17). This disequilibrium estimate having not yet been published, it seems somewhat premature already to draw conclusions from it.

2. His work is based on research on data of Czechoslovakia, GDR, Hungary and Poland. From this he infers conclusions regarding all CPEs, including the USSR, while most other work is concerned with data on the USSR alone.

3. It is possible now to show that Holzman's indicator for the USSR since 1971 is rising again. This, together with rising CFM prices, indicates increasing repressed inflation in the USSR in the 1970s.

---

[*] According to Portes (1977, p. 121), this table was published in G. Garvy, "Stabilization Policy and Monetary Equilibrium", *CESES* (1975), but it was reprinted in Garvy (1977, p. 180).

In a recent article Severin (1979) has provided some new evidence on CFM prices. Her data are set out in Table IX.1. The table shows that the behaviour of CFM prices in the USSR since 1955 can conveniently be divided into four periods. Up to 1959, the period of Khrushchev's successful agricultural policies, CFM prices declined. In 1960–64, the period of Khrushchev's unsuccessful agricultural policies, CFM prices

Table IX.1

USSR: Index of all-union collective farm market prices, 1955–77, 1955 weights (1970 = 100)[a]

Year	
1955	91·1
1956	82·6
1957	80·0
1958	83·4
1959	81·7
1960	82·6
1961	86·9
1962	93·7
1963	97·9
1964	100·5
1965	92·8
1966	88·5
1967	88·5
1968	89·4
1969	97·0
1970	100·0
1971	99·7
1972	103·4
1973	106·1
1974	105·5
1975	113·5
1976	118·9
1977	120·9

[a] Since 1968 the Soviet annual statistical handbook has omitted direct data on CFM prices, probably because of the embarrassing picture they would reveal.

Source: Severin (1979, p. 27).

increased. In 1965–71, the period of Brezhnev's successful agricultural policies, CFM prices were stable. Since 1972, CFM prices have once more risen. Hence it can be seen that Portes' (1977) omission of any mention of the behaviour of Soviet CFM prices since 1971 in a discussion of inflation in CPEs is seriously misleading.

Using the methodology described in Holzman (1960, p. 170) and in Severin (1979, p. 33), Holzman's indicator of suppressed inflation in the USSR can be calculated for the period up to 1982 (Table IX.2). We see from this table that Portes' picture of a continuously falling Holzman indicator is wrong for the period since 1971. Both CFM prices and Holzman's indicator have risen significantly since 1971. Especially during the years 1975–81 inflationary pressures have risen. In addition,

Table IX.2
Index of Holzman's indicator of inflationary pressures for the USSR (1955 = 100)

Year	Index (1955 = 100)
1971[a]	22
1972	23
1973	25
1974	23
1975	27
1976	30
1977	30
1978	34
1979	34
1980	37
1981	40
1982	40

[a] Garvy gives for 1971 an index of 23, but the difference with the above index for 1971 is probably due to revised data in subsequent Soviet annual handbooks.

Source: Calculated according to the Holzman method from data in the statistical annual *Narodnoe khozyaistvo SSSR* for various years.

the official state retail price indices for Poland, Hungary, Romania and Czechoslovakia for 1978 and 1979 show significant increases. Furthermore, an important aspect of the Polish economic crisis of 1979–82 was a massive inflation.

According to Portes (1977), there are stable retail prices and an absence of repressed inflation in the CPEs. From this 'fact' he draws dramatic reverse Sovietological conclusions. Closer scrutiny of the data, in particular for recent years, suggests that the 'fact' is wrong, and hence the conclusions unwarranted.

X. DID SOVIET ECONOMIC GROWTH
END IN 1978?*

What happened to the national income [of Hungary] in 1974? At current
prices it showed an increase of 4·7 per cent, while at comparable prices
the growth became already 7 per cent ('Statistical Yearbook 1974',
Budapest, 1975, pp. 73–4). Instead of 'deflation', 'inflation' of the index
occurred. What was the real growth? In my opinion it was at most 1–2 per
cent in 1974. And this would have been good to know at that time. (A.
Bródy, 1980, p. 196)

The purpose of this chapter is to assess the macro-economic performance of the Soviet economy in 1979–82. Many people have the idea,
carefully fostered by certain Soviet official statistics, that during the
current world economic crisis the USSR has continued growing, albeit
at slower rates than in the past. In this chapter Soviet statistics on the
performance of the economy in 1979–82 will be critically assessed in
order to establish whether or not this is true. The chapter has a tentative
character and its conclusions should not be treated as definitely proven.

The Soviet official statistics for the growth of national income are set
out in Table X.1

Casual inspection of Table X.1 shows two important things. First,
prior to 1982, the implicit NMP price deflator is very low and indicates a
rate of inflation of under 1½% p.a. As a statement about the Soviet price

* I am grateful to J. Cooper, C. Davis, P. Hanson, M. Kaser, R. Knaack and K. E.
Wädekin for helpful comments on, and discussion of, a draft of this chapter. It was first
published in J. Drewnowski (ed.) (1982) *Crisis in the East European Economy*, chapter 6,
London. For an earlier comment on the worsening economic situation in the USSR see
my article, "Economic Crisis in the USSR", *Critique*, vol. 12.

Table X.1

Annual rates of growth of Soviet net material product[a] according to Soviet official statistics[b] (in % p.a.)

Year	NMP produced		NMP used[c]	
	Current prices	Comparable prices	Current prices	Comparable prices
1975	2·6	4·5	4·0	4
1976	6·2	5·3	5·5	5
1977	5·2	4·5	4·3	3·5
1978	5·1	4·8	5·3	4
1979	3·4	2·5	2·9	2
1980	4·9	3·5	4·9	3·8
1981	4·3	3·3	4·4	3·2
1982	7·5	3·9	7·2	3·5

[a] 'Net material product' is the Western term for what in the USSR is referred to as 'national income'. It is calculated according to the MPS (material product system) method rather than the SNA (system of national accounts) method used in the West and therefore is not comparable with 'national income' as calculated in the West. It is roughly true that GDP = NMP + non-material services (e.g. education) + depreciation + rent. An alternative formulation is that it is roughly true that NMP = GDP − (non-material services + depreciation + rent).

[b] The figures are taken from, or derived from, the statistical handbooks *Narodnoe khozyaistvo SSSR* and *SSSR v tsifrakh* for various years. The data given each year in these handbooks for the most recent year are provisional and sometimes subsequently altered. In general I have used the later, rather than the earlier data, on the assumption that the former incorporates further information and hence is more accurate. The only exception is that where the most recent handbooks only enable the figures to be calculated with a large rounding error and the earlier handbooks give, or enable to be calculated, a more precise figure, then the earlier handbooks have been used.

[c] According to official explanations, the difference between NMP produced and NMP used is caused by losses and the foreign trade balance. The foreign trade balance which adds to or subtracts from NMP produced to yield NMP used, is valued in import prices for an import surplus and in export prices for an export surplus. See M. Kaser (1961), "A Survey of the National Accounts of Eastern Europe", *Income and Wealth*, vol. IX, p. 162.

level in 1975–81 this is suspicious. (Particularly suspicious is the *c.* 2% implicit *fall* in the price level of the NMP produced in 1975.) It seems possible that some kind of statistical trickery is going on to produce this result, as is in fact implied by the Hungarian economist Bródy in the quotation which heads this chapter. Already ten years ago, Becker (1972, p. 109) suggested that "The implicit price deflator of NMP may be downwards biased". Since then, inflationary pressures in the USSR have greatly increased and, for the period from 1975 onwards, Becker's cautious "may be" can be replaced by the more robust "is obviously". Not only Hungarian and US economists are in the sceptical camp. In his well-known study of the national income of the USSR, Vainshtein (1969, pp. 133–137) rejected the idea that in 1958–67 the NMP used in comparable prices grew faster than the NMP in current prices (i.e. that the Soviet price level fell in 1958–67) as is shown in official statistics. He suggested that this ignored some significant open and hidden* price increases.

Secondly, the figures for 1979 and for the four-year period 1979–82 show a sharp deterioration compared with 1978 and the four-year period 1975–8. In 1979, NMP used in comparable prices grew, according to Table X.1, at only half the rate of 1978 or the average for 1975–8. In the four years 1979–82, NMP used in comparable prices grew, according to Table X.1, at only about three-quarters of the rate in the previous four years.

The two factors considered above, taken together, suggest that from the standpoint of economic growth, 1979 was the beginning of a period in which performance deteriorated sharply compared to previous years.

Should the information that NMP used in comparable prices rose by 3·1% per annum in 1979–82 be accepted, or is it affected by bias in the NMP implicit price deflator? The views of Bródy, Becker and

---

* It is customary to distinguish between open, suppressed (or repressed) and hidden inflation. Open inflation, the sort of inflation normal in the West, is an ordinary rise in prices. Suppressed inflation is an excess of demand over supply which is not reflected in official price increases (because prices are controlled by the state) but in increased shortages, lengthening queues, a growing black market, an increasing divergence between the official retail prices and actual transactions prices (including bribes, etc.) and growing subsidies. Hidden inflation is an increase in prices which does not show up in the official index because of statistical trickery, e.g. the introduction of 'new' goods which differ from the old only by means of their higher prices, etc. (A pioneer in the field of hidden inflation was the UK during World War II. It was imperative for the government to massage the index since wages were tied to it. In this way wage drift could be combated.)

Vainshtein have already been cited. More recently, the Soviet economist Volkonsky (1981, p. 98, italics added) has more or less repeated the argument of Schroeder (1972, pp. 307–312):

> In our statistics price indices are calculated from a fixed list of goods. Such indices in fact reflect only price changes resulting from changes in the official prices for particular goods. *With fixed price lists, however, it is possible for a significant growth in the indices for a group of prices and for the general level of prices to take place*, as a result of alterations in the volumes of output of the different goods within a group, as a result of the introduction of new goods, as a result of quality changes etc. Such a "hidden" growth of prices is not insignificant both from the point of view of the efficiency of the planned management of production and also from the standpoint of the psychology of consumers.

The arguments put forward by Becker, Bródy, Vainshtein, Schroeder and Volkonsky suggest that all the official figures for Soviet macro-economic magnitudes in comparable prices are biased upwards due to deficiencies in the ways that the price indices are calculated. Hence the official figures for the level of NMP used in comparable prices in the years 1979, 1980, 1981 and 1982 are probably too high. There is an additional factor, however, which suggests that the degree of exaggeration is rising over time and that the 'law of equal cheating'[*] does not apply in 1979–82. In this period inflationary tension in the USSR rose sharply relative to the early 1970s. Both open and suppressed inflation increased. Hence in 1979–82, in all probability, not only the official figures for the level of NMP used in comparable prices, but also for the rate of growth of NMP used in comparable prices, are biased upwards.

Open price increase in state retail trade in the USSR have taken place on a number of occasions in recent years, eg 5 January 1977, 1 March 1978, 1 July 1979 and 15 September 1981. The first price increases affected carpets, silk fabrics, cut glass, taxi fares, etc. The second affected petrol, spare parts for cars, coffee and jewellery. The third affected cars, jewellery, food served in restaurants and cafés in the

---

[*] The 'law of equal cheating' is the proposition that, although at any given time Soviet macro-economic output statistics contain a considerable amount of padding, this does not affect measures of the rate of growth since the proportion of padding is probably constant over time. See Nove (1977, p. 352).

evening, carpets, beer drunk in beer halls etc, furs and furniture. The last affected jewellery, cut glass, carpets, furs, leather goods, china, high quality woollen and downy shawls, some suites of furniture, petrol, boats, alcoholic drinks and tobacco goods. Although most of the goods in these lists can be regarded as luxury goods rather than necessities, their combined effect was no doubt significant. This applies in particular to the large price increases for alcoholic drinks and tobacco goods (officially 17–27% on average) in September 1981 which is bound to have hit living standards sharply. Further price increases, especially for alcoholic drinks, took place in 1982. Not only have state retail prices risen significantly in recent years, but so have the prices of a wide range of producer goods, mostly notably as part of the general revision of the price lists which came into effect on 1 January 1982. This increased, for example, the average price of coal by 42%, that of natural gas by 45%, that of ferrous metal products by 20%, industrial timber by 40% etc.

The increase in suppressed inflation is shown by the following. First, since 1974 prices at the collective farm markets have been rising continuously (Severin, 1979, p. 27).* Hence there has been a steady increase in the Holzman indicator of suppressed inflation (see previous chapter).† Secondly, shortages worsened in the late 1970s and queues lengthened. For this there is abundant first-hand ('anecdotal') evidence. Thirdly, by the end of 1981, rationing of meat and dairy products was widespread in the USSR. This resulted from the combination of stagnant output, a significant increase in money incomes, high income elasticities of demand for these products, and the attempt to prevent state retail prices rising too much. The latter was no doubt partly a response to fear of a possible spread of the 'Polish disease'. Fourthly, the agricultural subsidies have been increasing significantly. These appear to have risen from about 19 billion roubles in 1978 (4·6% of NMP used) to 25 billion roubles (5·6% of NMP used) in 1980 and 33 billion roubles (7% of NMP used) in 1981.‡

In a shortage economy it would be useful and sensible to collect and

---

* Severin only gives data up to 1977, but these prices continued to rise in 1978–82.
† Table IX.2 p. 133 shows that the Holzman indicator rose from 23 in 1974 to 40 in 1982.
‡ See *Finansy SSSR*, 1982, no. 1, p. 25; *Sotsialisticheskaya industriya*, 3 July 1981; and *Argumenty i fakty*, 1981, no. 16. The 33 billion roubles are for food subsidies alone. There are also some input subsidies.

publish statistics on shortages, just as in a market economy it is useful and sensible to collect and publish statistics on unemployment. This has been forcefully argued by the Hungarian economist Kornai (1980, vol. A, p. 46) who has observed that, "A long time passed before the systematic observation and measurement of unemployment was introduced in every capitalist country. In socialist countries the shortage problem has become topical. Sooner or later the systematic measurement of shortage indicators will be organized." The same point has been argued in a Soviet book (*Planovyi*, 1981, p. 185) sponsored by the Central Economic Mathematical Institute of the USSR Academy of Sciences (TSEMI).

> At the present time the study of unsatisfied demand is conducted in a clearly unsatisfactory way. The task consists of replacing the episodic recording of unsatisfied demand by the regular supply of these data to the state statistical agencies. The need has arisen to work out special forms for recording unsatisfied demand and to determine scientific methods for the summarising of the data received.

Although, unfortunately, at the present time published Soviet statistics are deficient in indices of shortages, it is to be hoped that in due course the advice of Kornai and TSEMI will be followed and that it will not be necessary to rely on the crude indices used in the previous paragraph.

In the late 1970s the social indicators movement spread to the USSR (*Sovershenstvovanie*, 1979; *Pokazateli*, 1980). Hence in the Eleventh Five Year Plan (1981–85) the section on raising living standards of the previous five year plans was transformed into a plan for social development. Accordingly, it would be in keeping with contemporary ideas, both Western and Soviet, about the assessment of Soviet development in 1979–82, to look not only at economic but also at social indicators. One important social indicator is the extent and importance of shortages and queues. Shortages and queues, of course, are a normal feature of the Soviet economy. Indeed, the Hungarian economist Kornai in his famous work *Economics of Shortage* has developed a whole economic theory about them. As he has noted (1980, vol. A, p. 134), "The instantaneous intensity of shortage fluctuates round its normal value, and from time to time may grow particularly severe, which may lead to the sharpening of social and economic tensions". 1979–82 was one such period in the USSR. A particularly important shortage is that of housing. In 1979–82 the existing severe housing shortage worsened. This can be demonstrated as follows. A standard measure of the housing shortage is the relationship between the number of households and the number of dwellings. For the USSR, official data on household numbers for non-census years are not published. Following Morton (1979, p. 799), however, one can use the number of marriages as a proxy for the increase in household numbers. This is an imperfect measure since it excludes both deaths (which reduce the housing shortage) and any (actual or potential) decline in the average size of households and demolition (which increase it). Nevertheless, in the absence of direct data on household numbers for non-census years it is not too bad a proxy. Morton himself showed that the housing shortage, measured this way, declined in every year between 1961 and 1968, but steadily increased between 1969 and 1977. Data for 1978–82 are now available, and these show that the number of flats completed has continued to be much below the number of marriages. In addition, it is well known that the Soviet mortality situation, notably infant mortality, deteriorated in the early 1970s (Davis and Feshbach, 1980). Although the tighter censorship prevents one from determining precisely what happened to the age-specific death rates in 1979–82, it should be noted that the crude death rate for the population as a whole rose significantly in both 1979 and 1980 (*Narkhoz.*, 1980, p. 31). Most of this increase was probably accounted for by the ageing of the population. Some of it, however, may well have resulted from a worsening of the age-specific death rates, data on which are no longer published.

That the inclusion of social indicators is an assessment of the development of the USSR should worsen the USSR's position relative to the OECD countries would not be entirely surprising. The UN's Economic Commission for Europe has recently carried out a study (*Economic Bulletin for Europe*, vol. 31, no. 2, New York, 1980), in which conventional measures of GDP and NMP were replaced by a synthetic index based both on industrial inputs (e.g. steel consumption) and welfare data (e.g. housing space and conditions). This kind of calculation has three advantages for inter-system comparisons of economic growth. First, it removes distortions caused by the differences between the MPS and SNA methods (both systems are measured in the same way). Secondly, it removes distortions caused by the biased price deflators used in the CMEA countries. Thirdly, it removes the artificial advantage which measuring only 'productive' indices and ignoring welfare indicators confers on countries which adopt 'rushed' growth rather than 'harmonious' growth (to use Kornai's terminology). When

applied to the USSR and the UK in 1951–73 it led to a sharp reduction in the difference between the two countries in the *per capita*
rate of macro-economic growth (although the difference remained
substantial).

Given that the official summary macro-economic data in prices are
unreliable, it is interesting to present some physical output data to get a
picture of what happened to the Soviet economy in 1979–82. This is
done in Table X.2.

Table X.2 shows a slow but continuous growth of electricity output,
stagnation in the car industry, in housing construction and in iron ore
and coal mining, a slow and declining rate of growth of oil output, a
modest decline in the timber sector, fast growth in natural gas output, a
volume of railway freight that in 1982 was still below the 1978 level, four
bad harvests and stagnation in the livestock sector. Summarising,
Soviet official statistics in physical terms for 1979–82 give the following
picture of what happened to the Soviet economy in 1979–82. This is
stagnation. In housing construction there was stagnation. In fuel and
raw materials production the situation varied from fast growth via slow
growth to stagnation and slow decline. In agriculture the situation
varied between sharp decline and stagnation. Railway freight transport
formed a national economic bottleneck. Since in 1979–82 the population grew at almost 1% p.a., the *per capita* picture was still worse.

The reason for this depressing* situation was the combination of four
bad harvests with a secular trend, extending over more than 30 years,
for the rate of growth to fall steadily. The secular trend for Soviet
growth to decline is a well known phenomenon which has been
discussed recently by Hanson (1981), Brus (1981) and Bergson (1981).
It can be seen clearly from the data presented in Table X.3.

Table X.3 shows clearly that the rate of growth of Soviet net material
product has been falling continuously for 30 years with the exception of
a relatively favourable period in the late 1960s.

It is important to note that although the Soviet growth experience in
1979–82 compares unfavourably both with the Soviet past and with
economically successful countries such as Japan, it compares quite well
with a number of countries. In Poland, the NMP produced fell by about

---

* According to the Party Programme adopted at the Twenty-second Congress (1961),
in 1980 the Soviet NMP would be in the range 720–750 billion roubles. In fact it was
only 458·5 (NMP produced, current prices), i.e. only about 63% of the target.

Table X.2
Soviet economy 1979–82, selected physical data

Year	Electricity output (billions of kWh)	Car output (millions)	No. of flats built[a] (millions)	Oil output including condensate (million tonnes)	Iron ore output (million tonnes)	Timber output (million m³)	Natural gas output (million m³)	Coal output[b] (million tonnes)	Railway freight[c] (million tonnes)	Grain output[d] (bunker output million tonnes)	Meat output[e] (million tonnes)	Whole milk production[f] (million tonnes)	Rate of growth of population (in % p.a.)
1978	1202	1·3	2·1	572	246	284	347	664	3776	237	9·6	24·8	0·9
1979	1238	1·3	1·9	586	242	273	379	658	3688	179	9·6	25·0	0·8
1980	1295	1·3	2·1	603	245	278	406	653	3728	189	9·2	25·3	0·8
1981	1325	1·3	2	609	242	274	434	638	3746	n.a.[g]	9·3	25·7	0·8
1982	1367	1·3	2	613	244	270	467	647	3725	n.a.	9·3	26·4	0·9

[a] The number of flats built in the USSR peaked in 1959 and in 1982 was about one quarter below that level.

[b] This is the net, or so-called *tovarnyi*, output.

[c] For a good discussion of the economics of Soviet railway freight see V. Selyunin, "Nerv Ekonomiki", *Druzhba Narodov*, (1981), no. II.

[d] Soviet grain output statistics measure 'bunker' output rather than 'barn' output. The former exceeds the latter because it includes some moisture content of grain, trash and dirt admixtures, and losses during transport, handling and preliminary storage.

[e] Includes offal. The figures in the table are for industrially processed meat, not for total gross output. The latter also fell in 1978–82.

[f] i.e. kefir, sour cream (*smetana*), milk products and milk, calculated in milk equivalent. The figures in the table are for industrially processed milk, not for total gross output. In 1978–81 the latter declined by 6%. The reason why the output of industrially processed milk could rise at the same time that total gross output fell is that in this period the extent of marketing and processing of Soviet agricultural production rose.

[g] This is another example of the deterioration of Soviet statistical reporting in recent years. No figure is given in the plan fulfilment report for grain output. Instead there is the following revealing sentence, "State grain resources will provide in full for the supply to the population of bread and bread products". Soviet grain imports in 1981 were very large.

Sources: *Narodnoe khozyaistvo SSSR* various years.

Table X.3

*Annual average rates of growth of Soviet net
material product at comparable prices
according to Soviet official statistics*[a]

Year	NMP produced at comparable prices
1951–55	11
1956–60	9
1961–65	7
1966–70	8
1971–75	6
1976–80	4

[a] Figures have been rounded to nearest whole number.
Source: *Narodnoe Khozyaistvo SSSR*, various years.

2% in 1979, 4% in 1980 and 13% in 1981. In the UK, GDP (output measure) rose by about 2% in 1979, but fell by about 3% in 1980 and about 3% in 1981. In the UK, manufacturing was a real disaster area, corresponding to grain in the USSR. In the two years 1980 and 1981 UK manufacturing output fell by about 14%. By Polish or British standards, the USSR's growth performance was good in 1979–82. The USSR also maintained full employment.

CONCLUSION

Soviet official statistics make it difficult to form a clear picture of the macro-economic development of the Soviet economy in 1979–82 because of the worsening upward bias resulting from an unsatisfactory price deflator. The available data indicate that it is improbable that there was any significant increase in *per capita* national income in 1979–82. In addition, certain social indicators, e.g. shortages and queues (in particular for meat, dairy products and housing) and the crude death rate, deteriorated.* Hence, it seems reasonable to charac-

---

* In 1981 and 1982 the crude death rate improved (*Narkhoz* 1982 p. 30) but in 1982 was still above the 1978 level.

terise the period 1979–82 as one of economic and social stagnation. Soviet *per capita* economic growth does seem to have come to a halt, possibly temporary, in 1978. The stagnation was caused by a combination of the long-term tendency for the rate of economic growth to decline, with four bad harvests. This picture is a provisional one and may require revision, either upwards or downwards, as more data become available.*

The Soviet stagnation of 1979–82 compares adversely with the Soviet past and with the experience of an economically successful country such as Japan but compares favourably with the experience in the same period of countries such as Poland and the UK.

---

* From the statistical handbook for 1982, it can be seen that, even according to official statistics, in 1982 average real incomes per head were static and average real wages fell by 1%. (This partly reflects a fall in consumption as a share of the national income in 1982.)

POLITICAL ECONOMY IN A
DIVIDED WORLD—
STATE SOCIALISM

XI. FULL EMPLOYMENT—LESSONS FROM STATE SOCIALISM*

The institutional framework of a social system is a basic element of its economic dynamics (Kalecki, 1970).

Today capitalism is only one of several economic systems. . . . If it is true that the centralized command economies can guarantee full employment, the free market economies cannot afford the luxury of mass unemployment. . . . (Halm, 1960).

A. INTRODUCTION

In the post World War II period, a (largely) new branch of economics grew up. It was often called 'Sovietology'. Like all serious branches of economics, it arose in response to a new economic problem—the existence on our planet of durable rival economic systems, each claiming to be superior. Unfortunately, the labels used to describe these systems often themselves reflect a prior political evaluation which prejudges the outcome of studies in this area. For this reason in my writings (e.g. Ellman, 1979) I use the terms 'capitalist' and 'state socialist' economies. This is intended to be a real type terminology which does not prejudge the outcome of research into the properties of the systems.

Sovietology originally concerned itself with establishing precise data

* Originally published in *De Economist*, 1979, no. 4. This is the full text of an inaugural lecture given by the author as Professor of the economics of centrally planned economies of the University of Amsterdam on 12 February 1979. The author is grateful to W. Brus, J. van den Doel, W. Driehuis, P. Hanson and A. Nove for helpful comments and discussion.

about the Soviet economy, e.g. in agriculture (e.g. Jasny, 1949) and national income (e.g. Bergson, 1961). The information collected and assessed in these studies tended to be accurate and valuable. Indeed, at the twentieth congress of the Soviet Communist Party in 1956, the Soviet leader Mikoyan, in the course of his criticism of the state of Soviet economics adversely compared the number of Soviet economists working on the Soviet economy with the number of American economists working in this field! In addition to this empirical work, Sovietology engaged in the criticism and attempted refutation of the Marxist-Leninist claim that state socialism represented a higher mode of production than capitalism (Wiles, 1962; Grossman, 1967; Bergson, 1968). The general drift of its arguments was that the problems of the state socialist countries (a misallocating price system, production for plan rather than for use, shortages and queues for consumer goods, the double burden of paid work and housework on women, the technology gap) showed the great merits of capitalism and the problems arising from the elimination of the price mechanism and private ownership. The negative features of state socialism, so carefully described and analysed by Sovietology, were used to justify the status quo in the West and embarrass critics of Western society. On a more theoretical level, the economic discussions taking place in the state socialist countries were used as evidence of the essential soundness of the theories taught (and much criticised in certain quarters) in the West (e.g. Campbell, 1961).

Recently, two new trends have emerged within Sovietology, one theoretical and the other empirical. The first (e.g. Montias, 1976) aims to construct a general theory of economic systems with which to discuss and compare the properties of actual real economies. The aim is to replace the existing one-sided theoretical models hitherto used for this purpose (neo-classical general equilibrium theory and Marxism-Leninism) which originated in the nineteenth century by a neutral theoretical apparatus derived from contemporary work on systems theory and economic processes. This development followed a decade of intensive criticism of neo-classical general equilibrium theory (e.g. Pasinetti, 1965; Kornai, 1971; Loasby, 1976) and general recognition of its limitations. It also paralleled the criticism, within political Sovietology, of the totalitarianism paradigm and its replacement by ideas drawn from contemporary political science and sociology (e.g. Fleron, 1969; Hough, 1969; Skilling, 1971; Lane, 1976; Hough, 1977).

The second new trend within Sovietology, known as 'reverse Sovietology (Markowski, forthcoming), aims to consider whether there might be anything in the experience of the state socialist countries from which we in the capitalist world could learn something positive. Reverse Sovietology does not deny the existence and importance of the negative findings of the experience of state socialism. Nor, more generally, does it deny the existence and importance of the negative phenomena described by political Sovietology and much emphasised in the Western media. It simply considers whether, in addition to all these negative lessons, there might not be some positive lessons to be learned from the experience of state socialism. Is our economic system really so perfect that we cannot learn anything from the experience of the other economic system?

A classic example of reverse Sovietology in action concerns the price system. Traditional Sovietology concentrated on the perfectly correct fact that *relative* prices under state socialism are often such as to generate substantial misallocation of resources. Reverse Sovietology accepts this, but investigates the question of whether anything useful can be learned from the behaviour of the *absolute* price level (Portes, 1977, 1978). Might not an investigation of how some countries control inflation be useful for generating policy ideas about how to reduce inflation without wasting substantial resources in unemployment and idle capacity?

This chapter will discuss another example of reverse Sovietology, the state socialist experience with full employment.* The experience with respect to employment of a group of countries with radically different economic institutions from ours is interesting both in itself and as a possible source of ideas for resolving our difficulties.

It is one of the proud boasts of the state socialist countries that they have eliminated unemployment. Unemployment, along with inflation and job insecurity, are, it is argued in the state socialist countries, social evils inseparable from capitalism and easily avoided with state ownership of the means of production and national economic planning. This claim raises a number of issues, namely:

---

* For a traditional Sovietological discussion of this topic see Mesa-Lago (1968). See also Bornstein (1978).

1. What is 'full employment'?
2. Does it exist under state socialism?
3. If the answer to 2 is affirmative, how is it achieved and maintained?
4. How should the resulting state of affairs be evaluated?
5. What lessons, if any, has this got for employment policy in the capitalist world?

B. WHAT IS 'FULL EMPLOYMENT'?

In recent years the measurement and concept of 'employment' have been much discussed (Sen, 1975; Worswick, 1976; Mouly, 1977). This results both from the re-emergence of unemployment as a serious economic problem in the advanced capitalist countries and from the recognition of important differences between the situation in those countries and in many Third World countries. In addition to all the problems relating to the concepts of 'employment' and 'unemployment' resulting from differences in economic structure, when comparing economic systems it is most important to note that the concepts of 'employment' and 'unemployment' are system- and class-related. They relate primarily to market economies and wage and salary earners. This can easily be seen by considering other economic systems, e.g. one based entirely on peasant agriculture. Here there is neither 'employment' nor 'unemployment.' There is no 'employment' since society is not divided into employers and workers. Everyone works for his own household. There is no 'unemployment' since a rise in the labour force relative to the means of production leads either to the performance of more work (e.g. the intensification of agriculture) or to spreading the given work over more people. Hence there arises the question, is 'unemployment' specific to capitalism, or is it a universal feature of industrial societies?

Sen has suggested that 'employment' has three aspects. First, it has an income aspect, that is it gives an income to the employed. Secondly, it has a production aspect, that is it yields an output. Thirdly, it has a recognition aspect, that is it gives the employed person recognition of being engaged in a worthwhile activity. For the purpose of our present discussion it is possible to define full employment as a situation in which all those who desire it are engaged in an activity which possesses all three attributes.

C. DOES FULL EMPLOYMENT EXIST UNDER STATE SOCIALISM?

There are six basic types of unemployment under state socialism, transitional, frictional, structural, seasonal, political and disguised. Each will be considered briefly below.

Transitional unemployment is a normal feature of the early years of state socialism in countries with a large agricultural sector, low productivity in agriculture and significant real income differences between the urban employed and the rural population. For example, the USSR in the 1920s and China in the 1950s both experienced large-scale unemployment. The reason for this, in both cases, was the large-scale influx of peasants into the towns. The rate of this influx was much in excess of the growth of jobs in the towns. Both countries dealt with the problem by the use of administrative measures. In the USSR from 1930 to the late 1970s, the Soviet authorities prevented the excess rural population from causing unemployment by administrative controls over the outflow of labour from the villages, i.e. depriving villagers of internal passports.* This reflected, and enhanced, the position of the rural population as second-class citizens.

In China, urban unemployment resulting from the influx of peasants into the towns was a very serious problem in the 1950s. The main method of dealing with it is by the household registration system (Whyte, 1977) and 'sending down' or *xiaxiang* and *xiafang* (Bernstein, 1977). Household registration books are legally required for all residents of Chinese cities. To this extent the system is similar to the Dutch population register (*bevolkingsregister*). The crucial difference is that an application to be registered in a city may be refused by the relevant Chinese officials and normally is in the case of arrivals from the countryside. 'Sending down' (*xiaxiang* and *xiafang*) means that people, such as those leaving school or recent arrivals, are rounded up and sent back to the countryside.† This has the great advantage of saving on urban food demands and hence on the marketed output of agriculture.

---

* Even with passports, Soviet citizens cannot choose freely where to live. Certain cities, e.g. Moscow, are 'closed', i.e. permission to live in them is not normally granted.

† This is analogous to the repatriation of immigrant workers from the industrialised West European countries when the demand for their labour fell.

Once the unemployed are back in their villages, the responsibility for feeding them rests primarily on themselves, their families and their production teams. In their villages the former unemployed have both an obligation to work and a right to share in the output of their private plot and of their team. Sending down was also used, after the victory of state socialism in South Vietnam, in Laos and Cambodia to reduce the unproductive urban populations in those countries. In Cambodia it was used on a particularly large scale. The use of sending down has enabled China and Cambodia to avoid the bloated urban agglomerations and shanty towns that are common in Third World countries. In China these measures seem to have had some success in reducing the urban unemployment from the high figures of the 1950s. By 1971 the authorities claimed that full employment had been reached. In 1978 the existence and importance of urban unemployment was once more officially recognised. At the same time sending down came in for public and official criticism. This reflected the reduced reliance on administrative measures after the 11th Congress.

Frictional unemployment, in the sense of workers who are unemployed for short period between jobs, is a normal phenomenon in all countries where workers are free to change jobs. Although direction of labour is common under state socialism (e.g. China, the USSR in 1940–56) at the present time the freedom of urban workers to change their jobs is normal in the CMEA countries. Hence there arises a phenomenon which in advanced capitalist countries would be included in the measured 'unemployment'. How significant is this quantitatively? Needless to say, there are no Soviet statistics on unemployment, frictional or otherwise, since unemployment has been 'abolished'. Mesa-Lago (1968, pp. 120–128) has estimated frictional unemployment among industrial workers in the USSR at about 2–3%. On the other hand, Wiles (1972) estimated it at about 1·3%. Both calculations are inferences from unreliable data and have considerable margins of error. Because of this, and because the underlying data appear to differ significantly between years (and also between sectors of the economy and between regions) neither should be quoted as the authoritative estimate of frictional unemployment in the USSR.* Comparing fric-

---

* Mesa-Lago calculated two figures, one based on total labour turnover and the other based only on lags between jobs. The former exceeds the latter because of turnover due to retirement, military service, official or organised transfers, and study. For the former

tional unemployment in the USA and USSR, Wiles argued that the great advantage of the latter, even when there is full employment in the USA, is not the absence of frictional unemployment in the USSR but the fact that its average duration is under half of that in the USA. This is a significant and important advantage of state socialism.

Structural unemployment arises from some structural mismatch between the supply and demand for labour. Examples include the problem of finding sufficient jobs for women in coal mining towns and the problem of finding jobs for sociology graduates. Structural unemployment can conveniently be split into two parts, geographical and skill. By structural unemployment (geographical) is meant some regional mismatch in the supply and demand for labour. By structural unemployment (skill) is meant some mismatch between the skills supplied and required. How are these problems dealt with in the state socialist countries?

Regional employment policy in the state socialist countries has both socio-political and economic aspects. First, it is an aspect of the Leninist nationalities policy. The latter is concerned, not with ensuring purely 'formal' political freedom for formerly subject nationalities but with their rapid social and economic development. Secondly, it is concerned with the efficient utilisation of natural resources. Hence, Soviet regional policy combines both large-scale industrial investment and rapid expansion of social services such as education and medical care in densely populated formerly backward areas, such as Central Asia, and large-scale natural resource development in sparsely populated Siberia. The enormous expansion of urban employment opportunities in Soviet Central Asia during the period of Soviet power is a major achievement of Soviet power.

One would expect that in a market economy the labour force would have to adjust to the availability of jobs, but that in a socialist planned economy the supply of jobs would be adjusted to the availability of labour. In an empirical study Pryor (1973, pp. 290–297) corroborated this expectation. He found that regional differences in the proportion of the population engaged in mining and manufacturing showed an

---

he calculated a figure of 3·3% and for the latter 2·1%. Wiles used a lower figure (20 working days) for the average period between jobs than Mesa-Lago (27 working days). In addition, Wiles used a lower figure (*c.* 1/5) for the ratio of labour turnover to total employment than Mesa-Lago (*c.* 1/3).

approximately equal tendency to diminish in the post World War II period in the state socialist and capitalist countries, but that in the former this was associated with jobs moving to where the people were, and in the latter with the reverse. There are problems with the data used for this exercise, but this is an interesting, if provisional, finding.

On the whole, the example of Soviet Central Asia and Pryor's statistical study suggest that it is reasonable to assert that regional policy is more successful in the state socialist countries than in the capitalist ones in adapting the supply of jobs to the availability of labour. A major reason for this is the different implementation methods used in the two systems. In the capitalist world, regional policy is largely concerned with the provision by the state of financial incentives to private industry. The effectiveness of this depends on how well the incentive system is designed, the responsiveness of private industry, and the general economic environment. In the state socialist world, regional policy is concerned with the direct provision by the state of the necessary investment and the organisation by the state of expanded social services.

The main method used to prevent structural unemployment (skill) in the state socialist countries is that of manpower planning. Manpower planning is an integral part of socialist planning on a par with materials planning and investment planning. It is intended to ensure that the requirements of the national economy for particular skills, now and in the future, are met by an adequate supply of these skills. The number of places provided in technical schools, adult education courses, higher educational institutes and universities is determined by the estimated needs of the national economy. In Dutch terminology, this is a system of student stops in every subject and all educational institutions, with competitive exams (and also 'influence' of various kinds) rather than the drawing of lots, to choose between students. It is combined with a guarantee of a job for all new graduates (via the allocation of new graduates for the first three years of their working life). Such a system is unattractive both to the Dutch student movement and to neo-classical economists. It is unattractive to the student movement because of the restrictions on student choice it implies. It is unattractive to neo-classical economists because of the fallibility of planners' forecasts and substitutability between skills. Both types of criticism have a certain validity, but nevertheless, as practised in the state socialist countries, manpower planning does seem to play a useful role in adapting the labour force to the needs of the national economy.

Seasonal unemployment arises when some branches of economic activity are possible only at certain times of the year. Its size depends (apart from social organisation) on the proportion of the labour force engaged in such activities (e.g. farming, forestry, construction, fishing etc.) and the climate. In countries where a large proportion of the labour force is engaged in agriculture (e.g. China) or the climate in much of the country is very severe (e.g. the USSR) this is a serious potential problem. The state socialist countries tackle this problem in a variety of ways.

In China, for example, great efforts have been made to use off-season farm labour for labour-intensive rural infrastructure activities (Nickum, 1978). These include the construction of water control and irrigation systems, land terracing, afforestation, road building, the construction of schools, hospitals, other public buildings and housing. Since the labourers on these projects are usually paid in work points* issued by their normal production teams and construction machinery is conspicuous by its absence, the cost to the state is zero or very little. The advantage of this system is that otherwise underemployed villagers produce useful output at zero or very little state opportunity cost. The disadvantages are that arduous work is performed during time which may well have considerable private opportunity costs for the labourers (e.g. in terms of leisure or household activities), that it may have an adverse effect on agricultural output (if some of the labour is not really surplus or if the resulting reduction in food and cash payments per work point has disincentive effects), and that the output may be useless (like the Pyramids of ancient Egypt) or harmful (e.g. badly planned irrigation projects).

Similarly, the Cuban revolution is proud of having rapidly eliminated seasonal unemployment in rural areas. This was a serious scourge of pre-revolutionary Cuba. Even a hostile writer has noted that "There is no doubt about the validity of this claim" (Mesa-Lago, 1968, p. 427). A very important factor in this achievement, however, seems to have been the fall in agricultural labour productivity brought about by the policies

---

* A work point is a claim against the output of a team. This system approximately corresponds to the labour day system on Soviet collective farms under Stalin and Khrushchev.

of the revolutionary government. While it is, of course, always possible to eliminate unemployment by reducing productivity, this is not a very attractive road to follow, as the Cubans subsequently realised.

Political unemployment arises as a result of the political disapproval by the state of certain individuals or groups. This is obvious for emigration applicants, political opponents, 'trouble-makers' etc. The labour movement has always condemned the black lists operated in the capitalist world by individual employers and groups of employers. In a one-employer state with restrictions on self-employment and the impossibility of emigration, the matter is still more serious. A quantitatively significant example is provided by the prolonged existence in the USSR of substantial rural underemployment. A feature of the Soviet manpower scene in the Stalin period, and to a lesser extent in the 1950s and 1960s, was the existence and prevalence of rural underemployment. A major cause of this was political. The Bolsheviks viewed the countryside as a source of tribute and possible political enemies and neglected the welfare of the rural population. Hence, after 1929 the newly organised collective farms and their members were forbidden to undertake the handicraft activities traditional in Russian villages, especially during the farming off-season. This is not an inevitable feature of state socialism, as experience in China and in Hungary under the NEM has shown.

Disguised unemployment arises when some part of the employed population, although receiving an income and recognition, are not making a positive contribution to output. According to a widespread view in the Netherlands, the state socialist countries have not 'solved' the unemployment problem, they have simply 'disguised' the unemployment by ordering factories and offices to employ people who are in fact redundant. This is a burden on the real incomes of those who would anyway be employed, is very inefficient, and the main explanation of full employment under state socialism. This problem does exist and is a burden on the real incomes of those who would be employed in any case. On the other hand, it does not seem to cause dynamic inefficiency. Although the absolute level of labour productivity in the state socialist countries is not high, the rate of growth of labour productivity has been in the international mainstream (Gomulka, 1971), i.e. there have been no obvious signs of dynamic inefficiency. Furthermore, much of the popular Dutch discussion ignores the recognition component of employment and the fact that rationality criteria for a capitalist firm and a socialist state differ. For a socialist state (like a peasant family) it is rational to employ labour till its marginal product is zero, whereas for a capitalist firm it is only rational to employ labour till its marginal product equals the wage rate. For a capitalist firm, but not for a socialist state, the cost of maintaining the unemployed is an 'externality'. In addition, disguised unemployment in the form of labour-hoarding by employers or informal work-sharing by employees, is of course normal also under capitalism, as, e.g. in the UK. In fact, if any country is suffering from disguised unemployment it is the Netherlands, with its low participation rate, high proportions of 'unfit for work' and 'ill' people and government make-work schemes. Moreover, stress on the existence of disguised unemployment neglects the policies outlined in Section D below.

Despite transitional, frictional, structural, seasonal, political and disguised unemployment, it seems to me to be reasonable to describe the situation normally existing in the state socialist countries as 'full employment'. 'Full employment', of course, is a conventional rather than precise concept. If, in the capitalist world 'full employment' exists when unemployment as measured in the country concerned is only, say 3%, then the situation normally existing in the state socialist countries can, in my opinion, reasonably be described as 'full employment'. This is because of the steadily rising employment levels, the high participation rates, the (almost) universal job security, the absence of cyclical unemployment, the large number of vacancies and the desperate search for personnel by many enterprises. The prospect of suddenly losing one's job because of the vagaries of the conjunctural situation, competition from other firms, new products or overseas, which is a permanent source of worry and anxiety for much of the labour force under capitalism, simply does not exist under state socialism. The employment situation in the two systems differs qualitatively. As Hanson (forthcoming) has put it,

> There is, I believe, one important respect in which the Soviet economic system is more humane than our own: provided you do not wish to emigrate or to disseminate unorthodox ideas, it offers almost total job security. A Soviet employee can virtually rule out the possibility that he will ever be made redundant. He may be sacked or demoted for gross indiscipline or on political grounds, but he cannot be fired for being an embarrassment to the profit and loss accounts. Insofar as one can consider this feature of the system on its own, it is obviously attractive.

D. HOW IS IT ACHIEVED AND MAINTAINED?

How is permanent full employment under state socialism achieved? It is convenient to discuss the causal factors under two heads, the restricted role of the law of value,* and direct control by the state over aggregate distribution. In this context, the restricted role of the law of value has five aspects, rationality criteria, large investment programmes, the choice of techniques, the expansion of the quaternary sector† and administrative control over the influx of rural labour.

As was pointed out above, in principle the appropriate *rationality criteria* for a capitalist firm and a socialist state differ. This is familiar from the literature on choice of techniques in less developed countries and on cost-benefit analysis. A capitalist firm is interested in its survival and profits. Costs borne by society as a whole are 'externalities'. A socialist state is concerned (or ought to be) with social costs and benefits. Hence it may be entirely rational for the socialist state, but not for a capitalist enterprise, to employ workers whose marginal product is below their wage. To borrow an example from my colleague van den Doel, whereas it makes no sense for a capitalist firm to organise door-to-door milk deliveries if this is loss-making, for a full-employment-oriented state it would make excellent sense if the loss were less than or equal to the unemployment benefit saved. For a balanced discussion of this point it is important to note that because of the complexity of the decision-making process, even under state socialism decision-making is inevitably dispersed and many of the decision-making units in practice ignore externalities and act like textbook capitalist firms.

The *large investment programmes* pursued over decades in all the state socialist countries are an important factor in raising employment in them. These investment programmes are pursued for national economic reasons and quite independently of the short run profitability of particular plants. (This is why they can be considered an aspect of 'the restricted role of the law of value'.) The new plants have provided jobs for large numbers of workers. Rapid accumulation in order to catch up

---

* In this context, the 'law of value' means atomistic decision-making in an economy co-ordinated by the market mechanism.

† The 'quaternary sector' is a phrase used in Dutch discussion to describe publicly provided services such as education, medical care and law and order.

with and overtake the most advanced capitalist countries is a permanent feature of state socialism. That this should play a major role in maintaining full employment is in complete accord with Keynesian theory. In the *General Theory*, Keynes wrote that "I conceive, therefore, that a somewhat comprehensive socialisation of investment will prove the only means of securing an approximation to full employment." How large are the investment programmes under state socialism? Some data on this question is set out in Table XI.1. Although, as explained in the note, the data in Table XI.1 are not directly comparable with that for the capitalist world, they are indicative of an enormous investment effort, maintained over decades, which in the capitalist world is probably matched only by Japan in the 1950s and 1960s.

Table XI.1
Gross investment as a proportion of the net material product (in %)

Country	1966–70	1971–75	Plan 1976–80
Bulgaria	35·1	35·1	30–32
Czechoslovakia	31·1	33·7	31–33
GDR	27·6	28·7	29·1
Hungary	32·9	35·9	36·5
Poland	25·3	36·4	31·1–31·3
Romania	28·8	34·1	33–34
Soviet Union	27·0	29·9	29·5–30·1

Note: The figures in this table are analogous to, but different from, those for gross investment as a share of the national income of capitalist countries. The differences arise from two causes, which normally work in opposite directions. First, the prices of investment goods are normally relatively cheaper than consumption goods in the state socialist countries. Secondly, net material product is calculated differently from national income.
Source: *Economic survey of Europe in 1976*. Part II. (UN ECE 1977).

The analytical and practical issues arising from these large investment programmes and the conditions necessary for their implementation are fundamental issues which cannot be properly considered in the time available here. I have devoted 40 pages of *Socialist Planning* (Cambridge, 1979) to these questions, and anyone interested can consult that work.

It is obvious that *the choice of techniques* to be embodied in the investment programmes plays a major role in determining the extent to which they will contribute to raising employment. This is a particularly topical issue at a time when it is widely feared that technical progress in the West may take on a labour-saving form so that large investment programmes may simply reduce the volume of employment. As far as the state socialist countries are concerned, the view of economists such as Kalecki (1972) and Joan Robinson (1977) is that where choices exist, a socialist state should make choices different from those made by capitalist firms. Whereas one would expect a capitalist firm to maximise profits, a socialist state should aim at maximising employment and output.

In practice, the USSR has traditionally adopted what have come to be known as 'labour-intensive variants of capital-intensive techniques'. This means that investment has tended to take the form of the construction of large modern plants, often imported from the West or scaled-up versions of Western plants, in which the basic production technology is highly mechanised but in which many auxiliary processes, e.g. materials handling, are not highly mechanised and are labour-intensive. This dualism had the advantage of combining modern technology with some saving of scarce investment resources.

From this point of view, an interesting development in Maoist China was the development of small-scale rural industry. This often made use of indigenous technology. Surveying the experience with it, I argued (Ellman, 1979, p. 102) that

> The main advantage of the rural small-scale sector is that it can use resources which have a zero state opportunity cost to produce goods useful for agriculture. It can also play a useful role in adapting labour to industry. The main disadvantages seem to be that productivity is low and quality often low also. On the whole it seems to be a justified but temporary expedient under conditions of extreme scarcity of resources, which facilitates a more efficient allocation of resources than would otherwise have taken place.

The theoretical arguments of Kalecki and Joan Robinson and the two practical examples which have just been given indicate that the technology embodied in new investment and hence the employment effect associated with it is not purely exogenous but has an important policy component.

The fact that the employment effect of investment depends on the volume of investment and the choice of techniques embodied in it is obvious from the analysis of any growth model.★ What the study of state socialism adds to the analysis of growth models is the observation that, if entrepreneurs are unwilling to invest in sufficient volume and in appropriate techniques, then the state can do the job.

The *expansion of the quaternary sector* has played an important role in maintaining full employment in the state socialist countries. I have in mind services such as education, medical care and scientific research.

The effectiveness of the three policies discussed above can easily be seen by looking at the data about the Soviet labour force set out in Table XI.2.

I suggest that four interesting conclusions follow from the Soviet

Table XI.2
State employment in the USSR (in millions)

Year	Total[a]	In-dustry	Agri-cul-ture[b]	Con-struc-tion	Trans-port	Edu-cation and culture	Trade	Med-ical care	Science
1951	40·4	15·3	3·4	3·3	4·1	3·3	3·4	2·1	0·7
1956	51·9	19·7	6·0	4·5	5·2	4·1	3·8	2·7	1·1
1961	65·9	23·8	7·5	6·5	6·5	5·2	5·0	3·7	2·0
1966	79·7	28·5	8·9	7·5	7·4	6·9	6·3	4·4	2·7
1971	92·8	32·0	9·5	9·5	8·2	8·3	7·8	5·2	3·3
1976	104·2	34·8	10·8	10·7	9·4	9·3	9·0	5·9	3·9

[a] The total is greater than the sum of the subheadings given because I have omitted some sectors (e.g. forestry, communications).
[b] This column excludes non-state (i.e. collective farm) employment in agriculture. This (together with the policy of expanding the state sector of agriculture) explains why it grows over time.
Sources: *Soviet Economic Prospects for the Seventies*, JEC US Congress, Washington DC, 1973, pp. 508–509; *Narodnoe khozyaistvo SSSR za 60 let*, Moscow, 1977, p. 463.

★ For example, Furth *et al.* (1978) is their study of Marx's theory of unemployment conclude that "The main social problem in connection with innovation is not whether there is expulsion of labour, but what are the chances of re-employing labourers in time and in sufficient numbers. This depends on the level of capital accumulation and on the capital-saving character of technical change in general and for each technique. Those techniques which are both labour-saving and capital-saving are characterized by a tendency to expel labour, but may directly or indirectly lead to the re-employment of labourers. However, this possibility will only be realized if entrepreneurs are willing to invest."

employment data. First, the USSR has been very successful in expanding employment. In the twenty-five years 1951–76 state employment
increased more than 150%. Second, there is an absence of cyclical
unemployment in the USSR. In every year of this period employment
was greater than in the previous year. Third, there are no signs in the
USSR of the much-discussed 'de-industrialisation' which haunts the
UK and the Netherlands. Industrial employment in the USSR has
steadily increased throughout this period. Fourth, employment in the
quaternary sector (education and culture, medical care and science)
has increased both absolutely and relatively. On the whole, the table is
evidence of the success of the three policies discussed above, i.e. large
investment programmes, suitable choice of technique and expansion of
the quaternary sector. In fact, at the present time, when the capitalist
world is suffering from an unemployment problem, the USSR and her
allies in Eastern Europe are suffering from a labour shortage.

Administrative control over the influx of rural labour is very important in
countries such as the USSR and China. It was discussed above under
the heading 'transitional unemployment'.

Direct control by the state over aggregate distribution is a major
feature of state socialism (Brus, 1977) and of great importance. Whereas
under capitalism important chunks of expenditure (investment, consumption, exports) are partly determined by exogenous factors, under
state socialism these are all (more or less) under the control of the state.
This has numerous important consequences. For example, whereas
under capitalism an increase in savings may have the adverse effects
discussed by Keynesian economics, under state socialism it simply
means that retail prices can be lower than they would otherwise have
been. As far as full employment policy is concerned, direct control by
the state over aggregate distribution has three aspects. They are the
rational low wage policy, the absence of the demand constraint, and
direct control over the size of the labour force.

The *'rational low wage policy'* (this is the official Chinese terminology)
is an important part of the explanation of permanent full employment
under state socialism. By a 'rational low wage policy' is meant a
deliberate policy of keeping down real wages per worker so as to spread
the available wages fund over as many workers as possible and hence to
maximise employment and output. It is normal in the state socialist
countries, especially in the early stages of industrialisation, for the rate
of growth of real wages to be kept well below the rate of growth of labour

productivity. This limits the demand for wage goods and contains urban–rural inequalities. Limiting the demand for wage goods enables a given marketed output of agriculture to provide employment for the maximum number of workers. In addition, it enables industry to increase the share of its output devoted to accumulation. Both these factors contribute to raising the growth rate of employment and output. To operate a rational low wage policy requires a government which pursues an economic policy with a long time horizon and prevents active working class opposition (e.g. by ensuring that the trade unions function as transmission belts for government economic policy and by using sufficient repression). Examples of the rational low wage policy are the fact that in the USSR the level of real wages per worker did not permanently exceed the 1928 level till the mid-1950s,* and that in China real wages appear to have been about the same in the mid-1970s as they were in 1957.

Under state socialism, a rational low wage policy may encounter two problems. First, it may have an adverse effect on labour productivity. This seems to have happened, for example, in the USSR in the early 1930s and in China in 1958–77. Secondly, it may be impossible to implement because of working class opposition. This was an important factor in Poland in 1956–60 and in the early 1970s. The Polish government in those periods had come to power largely as a result of working class opposition to the previous low growth of real wages and wished to appease the workers. Similarly, in China the wage increase of 1977 came after prolonged industrial unrest. These two problems are important and suggest that it is a mistake to imagine that independent trade unions are the only barrier to a rational low wage policy.

The *absence of the demand constraint* is an important factor explaining full employment under state socialism. The state can use its control over aggregate distribution to ensure that unemployment due to lack of effective demand does not exist. It can do this because the state monopoly of foreign trade, conservative monetary and fiscal policy, and state control of prices, prevent international developments causing unemployment or full employment causing runaway inflation. On the other hand, the state socialist countries do experience unemployment or

---

* To a considerable extent, of course, this was caused not by the rational low wage policy but by the Great Patriotic War.

irrational use of labour, arising through lack of supplies. Examples are the decline in employment in Chinese industry in the wake of the Great Leap Forward and the permanent under-utilisation of labour in the USSR resulting from the wasteful supply system.* This illustrates the general proposition that a basic difference between capitalism and state socialism is that in the former growth is normally demand-constrained and in the latter supply-constrained. It is important to note that the elimination of the demand constraint is likely to have a dramatic effect on the working of all parts of the economy (Kornai, 1971, chapter 19).

Direct control over the size of the labour force is another important factor explaining full employment under state socialism. I have in mind in particular the choice of the retirement age and of the length of the educational period. In the USSR and China retirement age is 60 for men and 55 for women, both of which are early by international standards. In addition, in all the state socialist countries education has been enormously increased and extended. Similarly, hours of work compare favourably with those in capitalist countries at comparable levels of development.

E.   EVALUATION

Westerners often evaluate state socialism by reference to the absence of unfavourable aspects of their own social system, such as unemployment. This naturally produces a favourable impression. People in the state socialist countries often protest that this is an absurd procedure which produces a distorted picture. As a character in Zinoviev (1978, p. 133) observes, what is absent from a society is less interesting than what is present. "The characteristic of a snake is not that it does not have legs, but that it slides." In this vein I wish to draw attention to four aspects of full employment policy, state-socialist style, which enable it to be set in its context.

Despite free medical services (except for medicines which have to be paid for) the Soviet death rate has been steadily rising since 1964. The infant mortality rate and virtually all the age-specific death rates have

---

* According to one estimate (*Khozyaistvennaya* 1968), 25% of all Soviet working time is lost through difficulties with the supply system.

also been rising in the past decade. The causes of this phenomenon are unclear. It seems possible (Davis, 1978) that one reason for rising mortality among small children (between birth and three years) is the increasing proportion left in day-care institutions where they are very vulnerable to infections, while the mother takes on paid employment.

A feature of the transition from traditional capitalism to modern capitalism is the growth of income maintenance for the unemployed. In most state socialist countries, since 'unemployment has been abolished' such schemes are lacking. This can have a serious adverse effect on workers classified by management as 'trouble-makers' and 'agitators'. In fact, for a Soviet worker, the alternative to employment is not receiving unemployment benefits but prosecution under the 'anti-parasite' laws. It is a long time since unemployment was treated as a criminal offence in Western Europe.

A feature of full employment, state-socialist style, is the wasteful use of labour. It is not easy here to distinguish clearly between cause and effect, but it is obvious that a considerable fraction of the employment in the USSR results from inefficiency and that to a considerable extent this is the cause of the labour shortage that so concerns the authorities at the present time. One example was given above, that of the waste of labour caused by the inefficient supply system. Another concerns the long construction and running in periods for new industrial plants and the waste of resources on incomplete projects which have long worried the authorities in the state socialist countries, especially the USSR. Although bad for efficiency, this is no doubt good for employment in construction!

A striking feature of the East European employment scene which is likely to be unexpected and disturbing for Dutch trade unionists and socialists is the widespread dissatisfaction with it both by workers and managers. One of the features of the 1970s has been production co-operation agreements between firms in the capitalist and state socialist worlds. According to a study of such agreements between US firms and Poland and Romania (Hayden, 1976), in the latter two countries "worker morale and initiative [are] close to non-existent". The account of how the US capitalist corporation Clark Equipment Company, as part of its technology transfer agreement with the Polish concern Bumar Union for the manufacture of heavy duty planetary reduction axles, had to instill pride of achievement into the indifferent Polish workers by appealing to their patriotism (Hayden, 1976, p. 49) is deeply ironical. If these accounts are typical, they would seem to suggest that, at any rate in Poland and Romania, worker motivation, morale and pride in work compare unfavourably with that normal under capitalism.*

To describe accurately worker attitudes and behaviour in the state socialist world, and the causes thereof, is quite impossible in the space available here. I have raised the matter only to emphasise that the experience of state socialism clearly shows that full employment, security of employment, state ownership of the means of production and national economic planning are not sufficient conditions for the achievement of the historic aspirations of the labour movement. State socialism, like all other economic systems, has both achievements and problems.

The managerial dissatisfaction with the existing system is easy to understand. The traditional capitalist methods of maintaining labour discipline (unemployment, substantial income inequalities) have been abandoned. The Stalinist methods (open coercion) have also been abandoned. Efficiency, flexibility and worker interest in the job to be done, are only to be observed in the newspapers. Hence the nostalgia for traditional capitalist methods of maintaining labour discipline so marked among East European managers and their spokesmen.

F. LESSONS FOR FULL EMPLOYMENT POLICY IN THE CAPITALIST WORLD

I suggest that ten lessons can usefully be drawn for full employment policy in the capitalist world from the experiences of the state socialist countries.

First, full employment policies have an important political component. Unemployment is not simply a technical problem to be solved by accumulating and applying technical knowledge. In his famous 1943 paper 'Political aspects of full employment,' Kalecki argued that the discovery of the theory of effective demand would not lead to permanent full employment because of the existence and importance under

---

* I do not wish to suggest that this situation is caused by full employment. For a discussion of what does cause it see Ellman (1979, pp. 171–173).

capitalism of social groups who do not want full employment. These may range from employers and pensioners who get 'boom tired' because of rising inflation and improvements in the bargaining position of labour, via a central bank which gives priority to currency stability, to a well-organised labour aristocracy which defends its own interests at the expense of a poorly organised lumpen proletariat of women, immigrants, young people, etc. The existence of full employment and security of employment under state socialism partly reflects the virtual absence of such groups and partly reflects the fact that full employment and security of employment play a significant part in legitimising the social system and present political arrangements of state socialism. A striking feature of macro-economic policy in the capitalist world in recent years has been the use of unemployment as an instrument of economic policy, as a means of controlling inflation. This has partly reflected the political weakness of those groups that suffer from unemployment.

Second, to a considerable extent, economic policies possess significant complementarities and cannot be successfully implemented in isolation. This may mean that policies which work well in conjunction with other policies, may be complete failures if used in isolation. This has been much discussed in the Sovietological literature in connection with economic reform in Eastern Europe. As the distinguished Hungarian economist Kornai (1959, p. 225) long ago explained "One cannot exchange a cog in an integrated, functioning machine for another one of quite a different type. The latter may be new, but will obstruct the working of the machine nevertheless."

A good example of the significance of this concerns the rational low wage policy. This has long been widely advocated in the UK under the name 'incomes policy'. Elsewhere I have argued, on reverse Sovietological grounds, that "to suppose that incomes policy in the UK can be maintained permanently without major institutional and policy changes seems to the author a profound illusion." I suggested that necessary conditions for a permanent incomes policy would probably be price control, steady growth of real incomes, full employment, a proletarian government and a non-permissive approach to breaches of labour discipline.* It is easy to see that a rational low wages policy *on its own* is likely to lead to unemployment when it is used (because there is

---

* See Ellman (1979, pp. 182–188) and Ellman (1980a).

no policy to ensure that the resources saved are used to stimulate exports, investment or the quaternary sector), a wages explosion when it comes to an end, and to the trade unions being blamed for phenomena caused not by them but by the economic order in terms of which their behaviour is entirely rational (Tarling and Wilkinson, 1977; Rowthorn, 1965).

Third, some unemployment is probably inevitable in any industrial society. In particular, to suppose that state ownership of the means of production and national economic planning, by themselves, are sufficient to eliminate unemployment is an illusion.

Fourth, the 'unemployment problem' as experienced in the capitalist world is, to a considerable extent, system- or order-related. That is, it derives from some properties specific to our economic order. Other economies, with different institutional arrangements, do not suffer from it. I thus arrive from the empirical side, from the side of reverse Sovietology, at the same conclusion which Driehuis and Van den Doel (1979) arrive at from the theoretical side.

Fifth, the stress on lack of effective demand as one of the causes of unemployment in the Netherlands (e.g. *Rapport*, 1978) is corroborated by the experience of the state socialist countries. In the state socialist countries it is precisely the absence of the demand constraint that is, as argued in Section C, one of the causes of the permanent full employment.

Sixth, a rational low wage policy has been advocated for the Netherlands by a number of economists (van den Doel *et al.*, 1976). The idea is to enable state employment to be expanded without worsening the balance of payments or inflation. Reverse Sovietology can say two things about this proposal. On the one hand, as part of a suitable package of policies it can play an important role in ensuring full employment. To this extent the idea has much to commend it. On the other hand, under capitalism it may encounter three economic problems and one political problem. First, it may have an adverse effect on domestically generated effective demand. (The importance of this depends on the ratio of foreign trade to national income, and the extent to which the policy is complemented by policies to expand exports, investment and quaternary employment). This is not a problem under state socialism, where, because of direct state control over aggregate distribution the state always generates at least as much demand as is necessary and where economic problems mainly occur on the supply side. Second, removal of the incentive provided by falling quasi-rents on old machines might have an adverse effect on technical progress, innovation and investment. Under state socialism, where technical progress and investment are, in principle, decided by the planners and do not depend on the expectations of firms about future quasi-rents, this is not a significant problem. Third, as explained above, the rational low wage policy is only one aspect of a whole package of policies and it is far from clear that it can be applied on its own in a different economic system. In this connection, it is necessary to note that Dutch macro-economic discussion is more sophisticated than the British one since Dutch economists who advocate a rational low wage policy advocate it as part of a package which includes an expansion of the quaternary sector and of investment.* The political problem that a rational low wage policy might encounter in the Netherlands is that democracy encourages a short-term rather than a long-term view of decision-making (van den Doel, 1979, p. 119).

Seventh, those economists in this country who advocate expanding the quaternary sector are arguing for a policy that is entirely feasible and which can play a useful role in ensuring full employment. It is, however, necessary to note that if those people who would have been employed anyway do not regard the additional services as part of their income, then increased public sector employment will generate higher inflation than would otherwise have been the case (this is familiar from discussion of the negative balanced budget multiplier).

Eighth, those economists who have stressed the need for an expansion of investment as an employment-created policy are obviously right. Under capitalism, however, there is an important institutional problem which does not arise under state socialism, that of persuading firms to

---

* One of the attractions for an economist coming to work in the Netherlands is the sophisticated level of macro-economic discussion here. For example, whereas the negative balanced budget multiplier was first discussed to my knowledge in the English language literature in Rowthorn (1977), where it was treated as if it were some kind of discovery, it had already been widely discussed in the Netherlands for several years. Similarly, the work which has been done here on distinguishing between types of unemployment and the way their relative importance varies between countries and over time (Driehuis, 1977) is of great importance from both analytical and policy perspectives. Furthermore, the critique (Driehuis and van der Zwan, 1978) of excessive reliance on econometric models in policy formulation is of interest and relevance for many countries. Similarly, advocates of incomes policy in the Netherlands always advocate it together with policies to ensure that the resources saved are actually utilised.

undertake investment which may be socially rational but which may not be rational for them.

Ninth, the experience of state socialism throws some light on the rival merits of income maintenance for the unemployed (as practised in the capitalist world) and job creation (as practised in the state socialist world). For someone who is only unemployed for a short period between jobs, the capitalist system of income maintenance is clearly desirable and superior to the practice of the state socialist world. On the other hand, for the long-term unemployed, the state socialist emphasis on job creation, by investment and expansion of the quaternary sector, has much to be said for it.

Tenth, reduction of the retirement age and extension of education, which are traditional proposals of the trade unions in the Netherlands and elsewhere for dealing with unemployment, can indeed be part of a successful strategy for maintaining full employment. Of course, for those who enjoy their jobs and do not want to retire, *compulsory* early retirement is a serious burden ('ageism').

G.   CONCLUSIONS

1. It is not true, as far as employment problems are concerned, that the state socialist countries are some kind of paradise where such problems are non-existent. There can be massive transitional unemployment. In addition, there may be frictional, structural, seasonal, political and disguised unemployment. Income maintenance for the unemployed is normally poorly developed. The use of criminal proceedings against the unemployed is not attractive. Nor is rising infant mortality associated with increasing female employment. Nor is unemployment arising from political discrimination. Nor is full employment resulting from direction of labour and low productivity in agriculture. Full employment may be associated with low labour morale, inflexibility and difficulties of adaptation. Hence, the removal of the discipline provided by unemployment may seem undesirable to managers in a society in which new relations of production have not been fully developed. More generally, Marxists should realise that the standard contrast between problem-ridden capitalism and problem-free socialism is a complete illusion. There are different economic systems, each with characteristic achievements and problems. Each can fruitfully

learn from the other, but to make the transition from one to another is to exchange one set of problems for another.

2. Nevertheless, it is broadly true to say that the participation rate in the state socialist countries is higher than in comparable capitalist countries, that the employed population enjoys permanent security of employment, that there is no cyclical unemployment, and that after the transitional stage there is no 'unemployment problem'.

3. The main measures causing this state of affairs are the restricted role of the law of value and the direct control by the state of aggregate distribution. The former includes rationality criteria, large investment programmes, the choice of techniques, the expansion of the quaternary sector and administrative control over the influx of rural labour. The latter includes the rational low wage policy, the absence of the demand constraint and direct control over the size of the labour force.

4. Ten policy lessons for the capitalist world can be drawn from the experience of state socialism. These are set out in Section F above.

5. In some important respects state socialism is superior to capitalism. This applies in particular to full employment policy and specifically to the duration of frictional unemployment, regional employment, security of employment, the non-utilisation of unemployment as a policy instrument and the emphasis on job creation.*

---

* In some important respects, of course, capitalism is superior to state socialism. For a comparison of the two systems from the standpoint of a large number of criteria see Ellman (1979, chapter 10).

XII. INVESTMENT PLANNING IN THE STATE SOCIALIST COUNTRIES AND ITS RELEVANCE FOR REINDUSTRIALISATION*

In Keynesian macroeconomics and in the economic policy of capitalist states (if conceived in the Keynesian spirit) the main worry is how investment is to be stimulated when entrepreneurs do not have enough willingness to invest, and how the state can be directed towards more investment activity. Mainly because investment is not sufficient there is not enough aggregate demand. This problem is unknown in the socialist economy. Investment intentions need never be stimulated, since there is permanent self-stimulation. (J. Kornai, 1980 vol. A p. 202)

It should be borne in mind that institutionalisation can hinder, as much as it can stimulate, the innovation process . . . The creation of all kinds of committees, about which the White Paper [on structural change and economic growth] has much to say, is more likely to stimulate bureaucratisation than innovation. Functionaries who talk about innovation are generally not the ones who bring it about! (M. Brouwer and H. de Jong, 1978, pp. 268–269)

---

* Originally published in *Sectorstructuurbeleid: Mogelijkheden en beperkingen* (The Hague, 1980).

I am grateful to J. de Beus, W. Brus, J. Cooper, C. Davis, J. van den Doel, P. Hanson, P. Hare, H. de Jong, R. Knaack, J. Kornai and G. Reuten for helpful comments and discussion. I am also grateful to J. Cooper, C. Davis, P. Hare and J. Kornai for permission to refer to their unpublished work.

A. PROBLEM BACKGROUND

For many years economic thought in the West has been dominated by a mixture of neo-classical and Keynesian ideas. Hence it is no surprise that economic policy has been dominated by a mixture of faith in the price-market mechanism and faith in demand management. The price-market mechanism has been relied on as an efficient user of the information available to society, as a valuable feedback mechanism and as a motivational force. Demand management has been relied on to attain and maintain full employment. Recent events have greatly shaken this faith. The resulting reaction has taken two forms. On the one hand, many people have gone back to the old faith in a government of rules and not of men (Friedman 1969, 1975, 1977). On the other hand, many people have become interested in 'the supply side', 'structural policy', 'investment planning', a 'controlled economy' (Klein, 1978; *Selectieve groei*, 1976; *Sectornota*, 1979; Hafkamp and Reuten, 1980; Kawakami, 1979). In this connection the questions arise, how does investment planning work in the state socialist countries and can we learn anything from this experience?

A description of investment planning in state socialist countries can be found in many sources (Berri, 1977, chapter 8; Ellman, 1979b, chapter 5; Nove, 1977, chapter 6) and will not be repeated here. Nor do I wish to repeat here the lessons for Dutch economic policy which I derived in the previous chapter from the state socialist experience with planning for full employment. I will simply pick out some important issues.

To avoid confusion, it is important to note that in this chapter by 'investment planning' is understood a situation in which the state has replaced business firms as the originator and implementor of investment projects. Agencies of the state decide, or attempt to decide, the share of investment in the national income, the sectoral and temporal allocation of that investment, and the technical form of the investment. The chapter is not concerned with other usages of the term 'investment planning', e.g. the use of this term to describe state sponsored cartelisation. The purpose of the chapter is twofold: first, to provide accurate information about investment planning, enabling its achievements and problems to be clearly seen; secondly, to relate that information to Dutch policy discussion.

B. DATA ON SHARE OF INVESTMENT IN THE NATIONAL INCOME

The state socialist countries normally maintain a share of investment in the national income which is high by international standards. Some data on this are set out in Table XII.1.

To convert the data in Table XII.1 into figures comparable with Western figures for the share of investment in national income is a tricky and controversial problem (Vainshtein, 1967; Osiatynski, 1973; Kýn, 1974; Lee, 1979). Nevertheless, it is clear that the shares of investment in the national income in the European CMEA countries are very high by international standards.*

C. EVALUATION OF SHARE OF INVESTMENT IN THE NATIONAL INCOME

According to many authors, e.g. Cornwall (1977), investment plays a major role in stimulating economic growth. Also it contributes to employment (Ellman, 1979a). Perhaps the most positive evaluation of these high shares of investment is that given by Horvat.

According to the Yugoslav economist Horvat, the high shares of investment in the national income of state socialist countries are optimal, and a significant advantage of this economic system. His argument (Horvat, 1958, 1965) is based on three assumptions. First, that the objective of economic policy is to maximise the rate of growth. Secondly, that the marginal productivity of investment is a diminishing function of the share of investment in the national income. Thirdly, that the marginal productivity of investment reaches zero well before the share of investment in the national income reaches 50%, because an economy has a maximum absorptive capacity. "The easiest way to use this concept is to conceive the economy as a gigantic productive capacity capable of being expanded at a certain *maximum* rate, also at a lower rate, but *not at a higher* rate. Any additional inputs (investment) would

---

* According to CIA estimates, in 1977 gross investment as a percentage of the GNP was 30·2% in the USSR, compared with 15·8% in the USA, 21·8% in the Netherlands, and 31·2% in Japan (*CIA Handbook of Economic Statistics 1979*, Washington DC 1979, pp. 29, 62).

Table XII.1

Ratio of gross fixed investment to net material product for European CMEA countries (in %)

	1976	*1977*	*1978*
Bulgaria	36·9	39·7	36·5
Czechoslovakia	33·6	34·1	34·3
GDR	31·4	31·8	31·5
Hungary	36·0	38·2	38·3
Poland	39·0	38·8	38·0
Romania	38·3	39·2	42·4
USSR	29·7	29·3	29·4

Note: The figures in Table XII.1 are analogous to, but different from, those for gross investment in relation to the national income of capitalist countries. The difference arises from two causes, which normally work in opposite directions. First, the prices of investment goods are normally relatively cheaper than consumption goods in the state socialist countries. Secondly, net material product is calculated differently from national income.

Source: *Economic Survey of Europe in 1978*, Part 1 (UN Economic Commission for Europe, New York 1979), p. 132. These figures are taken from the official statistics of the countries concerned. They differ from the figures for the accumulation fund as a percentage of the national income to be found in these official statistics (see for example *Statisticheskii ezhegodnik stran-chlenov soveta ekonomicheskoi vzaimopomoshchi 1978*, Moscow 1978, table 18, p. 42). Two reasons for this difference are, the difference between 'fixed investment' and 'accumulation', and the difference between 'gross' and 'net'.

not produce *additions* to but *reductions* of output". The idea is that, above a certain point, the technical and social problems caused by the reorganisation of production to accommodate the investment, are such that the marginal product of the investment is negative.

Skill and knowledge will always be increasing, but the physiological substratum and social habits impose quite definite limits to the *speed* of the change. The increase of production requires continual readaptation of the whole social structure. This may not be evident in a slowly expanding economy. Yet, suppose that the rate of growth is 10%. Then in a generation of two twelve-year periods output would increase 10 times. Our children would have to manipulate an output 100 times as great, and our grandchildren 1000 times as great. An underdeveloped and poor country of today would after only seventy years manipulate an annual social income of some $100,000 *per head of the population*—do not these figures sound startling? Obviously there is a physical limit to the rate of expansion to which society is able to adapt itself.*

Given these assumptions, the problem of planning the optimal share of investment can be illustrated by Fig. 12.1. The figure depicts a situation in which, when the share of investment is low, the return on marginal investment is high. As the share rises the return falls. When the absorptive capacity of the economy is reached, the maximum rational share of investment (A) is reached.

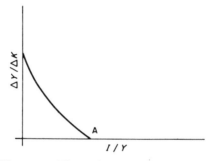

Fig. 12.1.   The optimal share of investment.

Accordingly, for any economy, the problem of finding the optimal share of investment resolves itself into the empirical question of finding out what the maximum absorptive capacity of that economy is. According to Horvat, his criterion "produces a share of investment in national income of about 35% . . . if recent experience and national income statistics may be trusted."†

D.   INVESTMENT TENSION

On the other hand, the high share of investment also has important negative features. It has a significant opportunity cost, in terms of consumption foregone. This can have important political conse-

---

* For a similar argument by the Polish economist Kalecki, see his paper in *Gospodarka planowa*, 1958, vol. XIII, no. 1.
† A valuable feature of the Horvat approach is that its direct attention to the possibility of wasteful over-investment (investment which is in excess of A). It seems that this situation has often occurred in the CMEA countries.

quences. In addition, the simple identification of investment as *the* growth inducing factor seems too simple, as the Hungarian economist Jánossy (1971) has argued. Moreover, to invest right up to A (on Fig. 12.1) means to make many investments that offer only small returns, despite rising real incomes over time and diminishing marginal utility of income.

Because of the high shares of investment in the state socialist countries, these countries are normally characterised by 'investment tension'. This means, shortages of the materials and people required for investment projects, excessive construction and running in periods for new plants, waste of resources in incomplete investment projects and perpetual pressure for more people, goods and foreign exchange to be allocated to the investment sector.

A theoretical discussion of investment tension can be found in Chapters 9 and 10 of Kornai (1980). Practical examples are abundant in the empirical literature about the state socialist countries. A Polish example is given in Table XII.2.

Similarly, a study (Hanson and Hill, 1979) of the experience of UK exporters of turnkey chemical plants to the USSR, produced similar

Table XII.2
Construction periods in Poland

	Capitalist countries	During the 3 year plan (1946–49)[a]	During the 6 year plan (1950–55)[b]
Coal mine of 5000 tons capacity per day	8–10[c]	—	13–15
Electric thermal power station of 200–300 MW	c 2[d]	—	4–5
Quality steel mill of medium size	2–3[e]	—	over 7
Canned meat factories, slaughter houses	—	0·75–1·00	3–4

[a] The three year plan was a rehabilitation plan similar to those throughout Europe after World War II. On its formulation and implementation the Socialist Party had considerable influence.
[b] The six year plan was Poland's first Soviet-style plan.
[c] UK and FRG.
[d] Western Europe.
[e] Western Europe. (A similar mill was built in pre World War II Poland in two years.)
Source: Zielinski (1973, p. 5).

results. It showed that from the contract to the completion stage (this excludes the delays caused by lengthy negotiations over the contract) typically took about double the time in the USSR that it would in Western Europe.

Despite innumerable speeches by political leaders, endless official decrees, improvements in planning techniques, stress on the need to raise efficiency and have intensive growth (i.e. growth based on raising productivity rather than merely the massive application of inputs), and economic reforms, such as the Kosygin economic reform of the 1960s in the USSR, this situation has continued down to the present. For example, in the USSR in 1965–75, i.e. the decade following the Kosygin reform, the volume of unfinished construction rose not only absolutely but also *relatively*, i.e. as a proportion of investment in the year (Bychek and Chistyakov, 1977, p. 112).

Elsewhere I have argued (Ellman 1979a, p. 21) that "the 'unemployment problem' as experienced in the capitalist world is, to a considerable extent, system or order-related. That is, it derives from some properties specific to our economic order. Other economies, with different institutional arrangements, do not suffer from it". In exactly the same way, investment tension is system or order-related. It cannot be changed by speeches of top political leaders or a change in personnel, but reflects deeply rooted properties of the economic mechanism. Even the transition to the New Economic Mechanism in Hungary was not very effective in dealing with it (Soós, 1978).

Hence, investment planning, which writers not familiar with the reality of the state socialist countries often regard as *the* advantage of state socialism, is often treated by writers familiar with the state socialist countries as a particularly troublesome, difficult and inefficient area of planning, as a "planners' nightmare" (Hare, 1979). In fact, economists in the state socialist countries often wonder whether investment in their countries can reasonably be regarded as 'planned' at all. The reasons for this at first sight odd position are, the divergence between plans and outcomes, e.g. with respect to costs, time taken to complete projects and investment cycles, the inertia of decision making (i.e. planning from the achieved level), and the number of 'unplanned' projects started (i.e. projects not in the original plan but embarked on later, often against the will of the central planning office).

These phenomena are not accidental results of the stupidity of this or that official, but an inevitable result of replacing economic rationality by bureaucratic rationality. Investment tension has two main economic results. First, it reduces efficiency (Xue Muqiao, 1981, p. 199). Secondly, it slows down technical progress. As far as the first is concerned, the Hungarian economist Bauer (1978, p. 257) has noted that

> The fact that more investment projects are simultaneously in progress than enabled by the investment potential of the economy results in prolongation of construction periods and delays in completions. The most important consequence is a higher share of accumulation fund tied up in the stock of unfinished investment than necessary and therefore one per cent of growth of fixed capital requires more accumulation than otherwise.

As far as the second is concerned, Bauer (1978, p. 257) has observed that

> The prolonged completion of investment projects is unfavourable for technological development, too, since the new capacities may embody in essence the technology available at the time of projecting. This technology—both product design and knowhow—may become obsolete if its operationalization is delayed.

E.   INVESTMENT PLANNING AND THE DISTRIBUTION OF INCOME AND WEALTH

The fact that in the state socialist countries control of investment is in the hands of the state has important consequences for the distribution of income and wealth. One of the arguments for an unequal distribution of income and wealth is that it is necessary in order to ensure finance for investment, where investment is in the hands of private firms. Similarly, the capital market is a major factor generating inequality of income and wealth between persons (Thurow, 1976). With state planning and financing of all investment, both this need for inequality, and the institutions which generate it, disappear. On the other hand, those who hold senior posts in the state apparatus, in societies in which investment is determined by the state, normally use their position to obtain important material benefits (Matthews, 1978). It seems likely, however, that élite consumption in the state socialist countries, as a proportion of total consumption, is smaller than in comparable capitalist countries.

F. INVESTMENT PLANNING AND REGIONAL POLICY

Regional economic policy in the state socialist countries has both socio-political and economic aspects. First, it is an aspect of the Leninist nationalities policy. The latter is concerned, not with ensuring purely 'formal' political freedom for formerly subject nationalities but with their rapid social and economic development. Secondly, it is concerned with the efficient utilisation of natural resources. Hence, Soviet regional policy combines both large-scale industrial investment and rapid expansion of social services such as education and medical care in densely populated formerly backward areas, such as Central Asia, with large-scale natural resource development in sparsely populated Siberia. The enormous expansion of urban employment opportunities in Soviet Central Asia during the period of Soviet power is a major achievement of Soviet power.

One would expect that in a market economy the labour force would have to adjust to the availability of jobs, but that it is a socialist planned economy the supply of jobs would be adjusted to the availability of labour. In an empirical study, Pryor (1973, pp. 290–297) corroborated this expectation. He found that regional differences in the proportion of the population engaged in mining and manufacturing showed an approximately equal tendency to diminish in the post World War II period in the state socialist and capitalist countries. In the former, however, this was associated with jobs moving to where the people were, and in the latter with the reverse. There are problems with the data used for this exercise, but this is an interesting, if provisional, finding.

On the whole, the example of Soviet Central Asia and Pryor's statistical study suggest that it is reasonable to assert that regional policy is more successful in the state socialist countries than in the capitalist ones in adapting the supply of jobs to the availability of labour. A major reason for this is the different implementation methods used in the two systems. In the capitalist world, regional policy is largely concerned with the provision by the state of financial incentives to private industry. The effectiveness of this depends on how well the incentive system is designed, the responsiveness of private industry, and the general economic environment. In the state socialist world, regional policy is concerned with the direct provision by the state of the necessary investment and the organisation by the state of expanded social services.

G. INVESTMENT PLANNING AND EXTERNALITIES

It is often asserted that a major advantage of investment planning is that it enables externalities to be internalised. That is to say, that whereas private business firms, because of the importance of external effects, are bound to make socially irrational decisions, the state can overcome this tendency. This is a familiar argument of economists in the Pigovian and Marxist traditions. It also plays a prominent role in the thought of West European Social Democratic parties.

This line of argument has been criticised both theoretically and empirically. On the theoretical level, authors associated with the 'new political economy' have emphasised the characteristic wastes and inefficiencies of the political and bureaucratic processes. Similarly, in Ellman (1978) I argued that the traditional Marxist-Leninist model in which a central authority takes rational decisions on behalf of society, suffers from fundamental defects of a decision-making–theoretical kind. On the empirical level, the Soviet, East European and Chinese press are full of examples of lack of co-ordination, of failures by decision-makers to take account of the whole picture. Important factors explaining these problems are the partial ignorance of the planners, the fact that decision-making is inevitably split between entities which pursue their own interests, bureaucratic rivalries between decision-making organisations, neglect by technocratic decision makers of *costs* and *markets*, and the bureaucratic suppression of initiatives from below. Two interesting examples of the latter are the chequered history in Soviet agriculture of the 'link' (*zveno*) and the demise of the consulting firms set up by young Soviet scientists and engineers in the reformist era of the 1960s. The former was discussed in Chapter 4 above, pp. 66–67.

As for the second example, this has been described in Broekmeyer (1976, pp. 80–81), Löwenhardt (1975) and Cooper (1979, pp. 26–27). In Novosibirsk in 1967 a group of young graduates established, under the auspices of the Komsomol (Communist Youth League) a firm called Fakel which was intended to bridge the gulf between science and industry. Novosibirsk is the seat of the Siberian branch of the Academy of Sciences, and this initiative had much in common with the science-based firms established in the USA in the vicinity of MIT and other centres of scientific research. Similar firms were set up in other Soviet cities. These gave good economic results. Nevertheless, within a few years, both Fakel and most of the other similar firms had disappeared. They had no official legal status and attracted strong opposition from financial and credit agencies, which regarded them as actual or potential sources of abuse of state financial control. They simply did not fit into the Soviet economic system, a system based on obedience to instructions from above and not initiatives from below.

In view of all these theoretical and empirical arguments, it is entirely understandable that in a recent Dutch Labour Party (PvdA) discussion paper over economics (PK, 1979, p. 33) the authors write that the sort of planning they advocate should be free of petrifaction and bureaucratisation. Otherwise, they argue, it might lead to a still greater gulf between production and social needs than the free play of market forces. The authors hope to overcome this potential problem by combining planning with democracy. This repetition of Mannheim neglects the possibility that such a set up might simply combine the absence of the merits of market decisions (attention to costs and markets, and innovation), the problems of bureaucratisation, and the problems of democratic decision-making (short sightedness, lengthy time taken to reach a decision and high cost of decision-making).

H.   PLAN FORMULATION AND PLAN IMPLEMENTATION

Economists, and others, who advocate investment planning, often exaggerate the importance of plan *formulation* at the expense of plan *implementation*. This ignores the divergence between *intentions* and *results*. Such a divergence is normal in all human affairs, and in the field of investment planning creates two risks.

First, there is the danger—widespread throughout the world—of purely paper planning. A good example of this is the British National Plan of the mid 1960s. All the work on this was concerned with the calculations which underlay it and obtaining the approval for it of the social partners. Since there was no policy in it to overcome the chief bottleneck hindering its realisation (the difficult balance of payments situation) and no institutions obliged to fulfil it, it rapidly lost all contact with reality.

Secondly, instead of the state imposing social rationality on private firms, as desired by its advocates, planning may turn into a process by which private firms impose their wishes on the state and obtain from the state financial benefits (e.g. subsidies). As De Jong (1979) has reported,

> At a recent symposium on industrial restructuring in Amsterdam, the dominating influence of the business world on Government policy (rather than the other way round) was formulated by De la Pierre (Paris), Gribben (London) and Caves (Harvard). The English experience was that when firms and the state want the same thing, then it is possible to achieve results, but that when there are contradictions the state has to withdraw and its plans are not implementable.

Even in Japan, "the ability of MITI to get its way is limited when its goals clash with the interests of business firms or other government agencies".

An essential feature of planning theory in the state socialist countries is the unity of plan *formulation* and plan *implementation*. This is displayed, for example, in the basic Soviet planning principle of *adresnost'*, which means that to every plan target there should correspond an organisation (or address) responsible for *implementing* it. This is intended to ensure that the plans are more than the inaccurate forecasts known as 'plans' in many capitalist countries. Similarly, this basic principle of the unity of plan formulation and plan implementation also plays a major role in the theory of the optimally functioning socialist economy (SOFE) which has been worked out by the Soviet school of mathematical economists. This theory stresses the need simultaneously to improve the way the plans are drawn up and the way they are implemented.

It might be thought that since there are no strong institutions (such as private firms and independent trade unions) in the state socialist countries opposed to directive planning, and the need for the unity of plan formulation and implementation is recognised in theory, economic life would be a process in which the plans were implemented. It turns out, however, that in many respects the outcome normally diverges substantially from the plan. Well known examples of this are the volume of unplanned economic activity, and the discrepancy between plan and outcome, for agriculture and for industry, and for long-term, five-year and annual plans. Two interesting examples of such divergences are investment cycles and long-term planning.

Many people have traditionally contrasted investment planning, a smooth socially rational process for ensuring that production is in accordance with social needs, with the irrational cyclical capitalist investment process. Experience has shown, however, that socialist investment too is prone to cycles (Ellman, 1979b, pp. 143–147). The causes of this unexpected phenomenon have given rise to a wide international discussion. Two important factors seem to be the political process and the bargaining process by which plans are drawn up.

Long-term plans play an important role in socialist planning theory. They are intended to determine the strategy of economic development and provide the framework within which the five-year and annual plans can provide more operational guidance for the economy. The practice is entirely different. There have been seven attempts in the USSR to compile a long-term plan. None of them have had any practical influence on the management of the economy. A similar situation exists elsewhere, e.g. in Hungary (Friss, 1971). The most recent example of the sad fate of Soviet long-term plans concerns the 1976–90 Fifteen Year plan. It was never finished and never officially adopted. The reason for this dismal record is the inevitable partial ignorance of the planners. After a short time it always becomes obvious that the main current problems are not those considered by the plan. Although useless the long-term plans are costly, for two reasons. First, their compilation involves a large effort. Secondly, the compilation of long-term plans encourages the idea that since all relevant data have already been processed at the centre, the duty of everyone else in the economy is simply to carry out instructions. This may simply result in wasteful and socially irrational responses to the changing situation because subordinates are barred from socially rational responses and the centre lacks the information.

I.   ENVIRONMENT COMPATIBLE INVESTMENTS AND PUBLIC SECTOR INVESTMENTS

It is sometimes suggested in Dutch discussion that the kind of investment planning desirable in this country is that which stimulates environment compatible investment (e.g. in energy saving) and public sector investment (e.g. housing, town planning, medical care, water control and land reclamation, roads, railways, telecommunications etc.). When resources would otherwise be wasted and the resulting objects are useful, this is obviously a socially rational policy (although it may not be easy to combine with anti-inflationary policies). It should be noted, however, that such a kind of investment planning has little in common with investment planning as practised in the state socialist countries.

As far as the environment is concerned, in recent years increasing efforts have been devoted to planning it in the state socialist countries. In the 1970s a central body for environmental questions, the State Committee on hydrometeriology and control of the environment, was established in the USSR. Similarly, the Soviet Tenth Five Year Plan (1976–80) included for the first time a section on safeguarding the environment. Nevertheless, pollution is a serious and growing problem in the USSR (Singleton, 1976; Komarov, 1978). Important reasons for this include the enormous industrialisation programme pursued over more than five decades, the stress on quantitative fulfilment of planned output targets, the complexity of the decision-making process, the costs of environmental protection, the absence of independent social organisations and the censorship. Some striking examples of the importance of these factors, and their results, have been given by Komarov (1978, pp. 137–138).

One large chemical factory in the Krasnoyarsk region, producing polyethylene film, had become by 1975 an excellent example of how to turn 'waste' into useful products. From its very beginning in 1968 the factory poured into the atmosphere huge quantities of fluorine. Over a radius of several kilometers the taiga shrivelled up. From the very beginning the factory engineers understood that the optimal way of protecting the atmosphere was to retain the fluorine and sell it to other enterprises where fluorine is a scarce raw material. To put this simple and in all respects beneficial idea into practice required more than five years. Forcing it through numerous higher agencies cost its enthusiasts heart attacks. Meanwhile, thousands of hectares of taiga perished. In the factory everyone smiled ironically and said, 'If we were a private firm, the owner would have sold the fluorine from the very first day'. More likely, the owner, worrying about both his own profits and compliance with environmental protection laws, would have introduced changes already at the design stage.

In this case the matter was complicated by the fact that the production of fluorine and polyethylene are controlled by different chief administrations of the Ministry for the chemical industry. That they agreed in principle that utilisation of the fluorine was necessary and rational, and that they are located on adjacent floors of the same Ministerial building, made no difference. Every chief administration must first of all do what it was created to do, i.e. fulfil the output plan for a certain product. The solution of any problem not falling within this task takes years.

Things drag on even longer when different ministries are involved. The end of the struggles about the full utilisation of the resources of the Kar-Bogaz-Gol bay on the Caspian sea or the apatite-nepheline ore of the Kola peninsular, are not yet in sight. The "waste" which is dumped at the Khibinsky mines contains much nepheline, a valuable material for the aluminium industry. The Ministry of non-ferrous metals, however, does not want to spend millions on the construction of a concentrating mill. This would worsen the plan indices of the whole ministry for several years. Nor does the chemical ministry want to do it. A plant for the processing of dumps constructed by it would not make a favourable impact on any of the chief plan indices. Why should the Ministry build it? For a eulogistic newspaper article? That is an insignificant incentive in comparison with an expenditure of millions and the risk of losing one's job in the event of not fulfilling the plan. While discussions have dragged on for a decade, the aluminium raw material is not simply stored up. For some reason or other, it is poured into Lake Imandra!

As far as stimulating public sector investment is concerned, it should be noted that investment planning as practised in the state socialist countries is primarily concerned with the so-called productive sector of the economy (industry and mining, agriculture, construction and freight transport). The so-called non-productive sector (e.g. housing, medical care and education) has traditionally been treated as of secondary importance. One example of this is that the pay of people working in these sectors has traditionally been relatively low. In view of its shortage, low quality and unequal distribution (Morton, 1979; Szelenyi, 1972), the Soviet housing system is clearly no model for a developed country. Similarly, in view of its poor quality (Knaus, 1980), declining effectiveness (Davis and Feshbach, 1980) and unequal distribution (Davis, 1979, pp. 169–180) the Soviet medical system is clearly no model for a developed country either. Investment in these 'non-productive' sectors has been economised on, not stimulated.

J.   REINDUSTRIALISATION

It is sometimes suggested in Dutch discussion that what the country needs is a state directed process of reindustrialisation. In recent years it has suffered from deindustrialisation, with declining employment in industry. What is needed, it is argued, is a process of state supported and encouraged industrialisation as in the years following World War

II. In this connection, people wonder whether the experience of socialist planning has anything to offer.

The state socialist countries have undoubtedly implemented rapid industrialisation programmes. Furthermore, they do not suffer from deindustrialisation, inadequate investment, inadequate inputs for R and D, the priority of finance over industry or the use of unemployment as a policy variable. Nevertheless, I am doubtful whether detailed lessons for domestic consumption can be drawn from this record, for three reasons.

First, the costs of this achievement have been high. These costs (high share of investment in the national income, extensive waste and inefficiency, creation of a suction or shortage economy) have been considerable and would probably be unacceptable in this country.

Secondly, the institutions of these countries are very different from those of this country. The state socialist countries lack private business firms, a capital market, independent trade unions and extensive feedback mechanisms (see Section O).

Thirdly, the "structure determining factors" (de Jong, 1980) for the Netherlands are very different from those of the USSR. In the USSR, the military need for a strong central government, immense domestic resources, a socially and technically backward agriculture, an authoritarian political system and deep-rooted bureaucratic traditions, are structure determining factors. In the Netherlands, on the other hand, the crossroads position of the country and its balance between individual freedom and social solidarity, are structure determining. It is noteworthy that another small country, with a population of the same order of magnitude as this country, which shares the crossroads position of the Netherlands and whose attitude to individual freedom is more Central European than East European (i.e. Hungary), although a member of CMEA, has remodelled its institutions to reduce the role of planning and expand the role of market relations.

Soviet-type investment planning evolved in response to the pressing demands of rapid industrialisation in the specific conditions of the USSR in the 1930s. It subsequently became institutionalised and was then diffused to other countries with little regard for their specific needs. This system is now in many respects dysfunctional even in the USSR and attempts are being made in that country, so far vainly, to adapt it to new circumstances. Therefore one would not expect to be able to transplant the experience to a country with a very different problem, reindustrialisation, and with very different structure determining factors.

In view of these fundamental considerations, it seems more sensible when thinking about how to manage a reindustrialisation programme in this country, to look at a country which is also dependent on foreign trade and whose institutions are more similar to the Netherlands. A good example of such a country might be Japan (or South Korea).

K.   THE COMPLEMENTARITY OF ECONOMIC POLICIES

Writers in the tradition of the Tinbergian theory of the optimal economic regime sometimes imagine that it should be possible to construct in this country an *optimal* economic order which would combine the advantages of market, bureaucratic and democratic decision-making. For example, Driehuis and van den Doel (1979) have recently advocated "democratic imperative planning". In this way it is hoped to gain the advantages of all three methods of decision-making. In connection with this repetition of Mannheim it is appropriate to make three reservations.

First, it is important to pay attention to the normal discrepancy between *intentions* and *results* (see Section H).

Secondly, the freedom of manoeuvre of any government is normally severely *constrained*, most fundamentally by the structure determining factors discussed in Section J. It may not be feasible, because of the constraints, for a small and foreign trade dependent country, to act in the way indicated by abstract, universally valid, arguments.

Thirdly, an important lesson of the CMEA experience with economic reform is the *complementarity* of economic control mechanisms. As Kornai (1979b, pp. 17–18) has observed:

> The tradition of economics has accustomed us to the concept that everything can and must be "optimised". It is therefore understandable that the idea arose that an "optimum economic system" must be designed, combining the best possible "rules of the game" and the best operating control mechanisms. Those setting this aim envisage something like a visit to a supermarket. On the shelves are to be found the various components of the mechanism, incorporating the advantageous qualities of all systems. On one shelf, there is full employment as it has been realised in Eastern Europe. On another, there is the high degree of workshop organisation and discipline, like in a West German or Swiss

factory. On a third shelf, economic growth free of recession, on a fourth price stability, on a fifth, rapid adjustment of production to demands on the foreign market. The system designer has nothing to do but push along his trolley and collect these "optimum components", and then compose from them at home the "optimum system".

But that is a naive, wishful day-dream. History does not provide such supermarkets in which we can make our choice as we like. Every real economic system constitutes an organic whole. This may contain good and bad, and more or less in fixed proportions. The choice of system lies only among various "package deals". It is not possible to pick out from the different "packages" the components we like and to leave what we dislike.

An example of the importance of these complementarities is full employment policy. Full employment is a major achievement of state socialism. It is combined, however, with major problems of labour inflexibility, work morale and lack of effort and interest by workers. It may sound strange in the Netherlands, but it is an important fact that in 1978–79 there took place extensive public and press discussions both in Poland and China about the poor level of work effort and the difficulty of combining security of employment and full employment with adequate effort. For many economists and administrators in the state socialist world, security of employment and full employment, while recognised to be achievements from a social point of view, are considered to be serious problems from an efficiency point of view. Adequate effort can always be obtained by sufficient incentives, negative (e.g. threat of dismissal) as well as positive (e.g. financial reward). Full employment can always be obtained by state socialist policies and institutions. How to combine the two is an unresolved problem.

L. TECHNICAL PROGRESS

It is widely recognised that a major function of Government economic policy in Western countries should be to stimulate and guide technical progress. Recently considerable attention has been devoted to this subject in this country (*Innovatienota*, 1979; *Innovatie*, 1979). What is the experience of the state socialist countries with respect to technical progress?

The state socialist countries have experienced rapid technical progress over long periods of time. They have shown rates of growth of labour productivity and changes in assortment that compare very well with those of the leading industrial country of the nineteenth century (the UK) and of the twentieth century (the USA). On the other hand, this has required very high rates of investment (by international standards) and has not been unique in the post World War II world. They have tended to copy, rather than originate, new technology. In the 1960s and 1970s they had great trouble in modernising the product mix of existing plants, and more generally, in reducing the technology gap between themselves and the leading industrial countries. Furthermore, they have shared the world-wide decline in growth rates in the late 1970s.

In recent years much has been written about the effects of central planning of technical progress (Kornai, 1971; Sutton, 1973; Hanson, 1976; Berliner, 1976; Slama and Vogel, 1977; Fleron, 1977; Perakh, 1977). One of the most striking findings to emerge from this research (Amann, 1977) is that, despite the great emphasis placed in Soviet planning on technical progress, the technological gap between the USSR and the leading capitalist countries is substantial and has not diminished in the past 15–20 years.

In what ways does central planning hinder technical progress? Factors hindering innovation include, the hostility of the authorities to unrestricted intercourse with the capitalist world and especially to the free movement of people,* the state monopoly of foreign trade, the risk-averting behaviour generated by the system, the centralisation of initiatives and accompanying lack of competition, the emphasis on economies of scale even where this conflicts with rapid changes in assortment, the separation of research from development, the stress on cutting costs of the producers of equipment rather than on service to customers, and the emphasis at all levels of the economic hierarchy on quantitative plan fulfilment.

An important factor hindering innovation is the policy of centralisation of initiatives. Each industry has a Ministry which is responsible for adopting the latest ideas, incorporating them in its investment plan and

---

* The importance of the free movement of people for stimulating innovation has been noted by Heertje (1979, p. 21). He has drawn attention to "the policy conclusion that fostering the mobility of technically highly qualified employees is an instrument that positively influences the diffusion of technical knowledge". The reverse is also true. For a discussion of this point in the Soviet context see Broekmeyer (1976, pp. 93–102).

imposing a unified technical policy on its industry. Each Ministry has a research institute which is responsible for stimulating technical progress in the industry or a branch of it. Complaints are frequent (see for example Bek, 1971) that innovation is hindered by the monopoly position of the major R and D organisations. Examples of technical conservatism at the R and D stage in the USSR include the fact that alternatives to the home grown SKB process for the manufacture of synthetic rubber were almost ignored, and that processes for the manufacture of alloy and quality steel other than electric-slag remelting received inadequate attention (Amann, 1977). It is noteworthy that in the military field, where innovation is particularly important to the Soviet Government, competition is encouraged. For example, in the Stalin period Tupolev and Myasishchev headed design teams that competed in the design of bombers, and Yakovlev and Mikoyan teams that competed in the design of fighters.

Hillege (1979, pp. 133–134) has described the swing in the emphasis of studies of innovation in the West after about 1965 from "technology push" to "demand pull". The most recent studies have shown that "successful innovation depends heavily on the extent to which the selection of innovations is open to market signals". Soviet experience confirms this by emphasising how innovation is hampered by neglect of market considerations. The Soviet economic mechanism plays a major role in hindering technical progress by the stress it places on supply, rather than demand. In a demand-constrained economy (such as a capitalist economy normally is) competition between firms to satisfy customers is an important factor stimulating technical progress. In a supply-constrained economy (such as the state socialist economies normally are) obtaining supplies and plan fulfilment are dominant considerations, and customers have to make do with what they are allocated.

Motivational factors are very important in innovation. The labour market and the capital market provide incentives under capitalism. Under state socialism, however, the dominant motivation in the white economy* seems to be risk aversion.

---

* By the "white economy" is meant the legal economy, as opposed to the illegal or "black" economy. For an elaboration and discussion of this schema in the Soviet context see A. Katsenelinboigen, Coloured markets in the Soviet Union, *Soviet Studies*, January 1977.

A graphic example of the problems created for innovation by the Soviet planning system is provided by the sad story of Tulachermet (Cooper, 1979, pp. 24–25). In order to overcome the barrier between research and development that earlier experience had shown to be a barrier to innovation, in recent years a number of special organisations, known as 'science-production associations' or, from their Russian initials, NPOs, have been created. Their distinguishing feature is that they combine research, development and production. Such an organisation has been created in the iron and steel industry and is known as 'Tulachermet'. Since its formation in 1974 this NPO has achieved an outstanding record in the rapid creation of progressive new metallurgical processes, including several world firsts patented abroad. Yet despite its record, many of its developments remain as individual semi-industrial and trial installations within the confines of the NPO, and are only slowly being introduced at other enterprises of the ministry. Its director general has noted that, "It used to be projects that gathered dust on the archive shelf; now it is bits of iron" (*Pravda*, 6 March 1977). One of the reasons for this state of affairs is that the ministry of the iron and steel industry plans on the basis that the research-production cycle for new processes in the industry is a minimum of ten years: Tulachermet has reduced it to a mere one or two years. Thus a new process created after the approval of the current five year plan has to wait its turn until the following plan before the appropriate equipment for an industrial application can be made by the heavy engineering industry.

M. LINKS WITH THE WORLD ECONOMY

Importing know-how from overseas has always played a major role in stimulating technical progress in the state socialist countries. In the 1920s various branches of the Soviet economy were opened up to Western firms as concessions, entire plants were built by Western firms in the First Five Year Plan, and the import of entire plants has continued in the 1960s and 1970s. Similarly, in recent years the USSR has reached R and D co-operation agreements with numerous Western firms.

Another approach to the import of technology is firm-to-firm industrial co-operation. This goes beyond mere one-off purchase of machines and licenses to long-run technological, production and marketing co-operation. A leading role in firm to firm industrial co-operation has been played by Poland and Hungary.

Yet another approach to the import of technology (and the earning of foreign currency) is the creation, on the territories of the state socialist countries (or in third countries), of joint venture enterprises with investment and management participation by Western firms. This approach was initiated in Yugoslavia and Romania, and followed by Hungary, Poland, China, Vietnam and Bulgaria.

A prominent role in all these forms of economic development has been played by multinational companies. As Heertje (1979, p. 21) has quite rightly observed, the multinationals "are preeminently suitable for achieving the rapid diffusion of know-how relating to new processes and new products". In view of this it is entirely understandable that recent years have seen the establishment of socialist multinationals (officially known as 'socialist common enterprises'). For a discussion of them see Zurawicki (1979, Chapter 4).

The above-mentioned facts indicate the importance for technical progress of openness to the world economy, and the usefulness of the multinationals.

N.   INSTITUTIONAL REQUIREMENTS FOR INVESTMENT PLANNING

The institutional arrangements of the state socialist countries are very different from those of Western Europe. The state socialist countries lack private business firms, a capital market, independent trade unions and extensive feedback mechanisms. This has very important consequences. For example, the absence of extensive feedback mechanisms makes it much easier for Governments in the state socialist countries to persist with disastrous or unpopular policies.

Accordingly, the relevance of the experience of the state socialist countries for drawing positive lessons for Western Europe is problematical. Such policies require an institutional structure that does not exist. To try and apply them without the appropriate institutions and policies is not very promising. For example, the idea that incomes policy, state socialist style, can be applied in the very different institutional arrangements that we have here in Western Europe, seems doubtful (Ellman, 1980a).

O. CONCLUSIONS

1. The state socialist countries have a high share of investment in the national income. This has an opportunity cost in terms of consumption and also leads to a chronic state of investment tension and inefficiency. Nevertheless, it is an important factor contributing to full employment.

2. Transferring investment to the state has important consequences for the distribution of income and wealth.

3. State control of investment can play an important role in resolving regional problems.

4. It is not true that investment planning is sufficient to ensure that externalities are internalised.

5. In investment planning, as in other areas of life, it is important to distinguish between *intentions* and *results*. Investment planning may easily turn into purely paper planning with little effect on economic development.

Alternatively, it may turn into a process by which business firms impose their policies on the state and obtain financial benefits from the state. Even in the state socialist world, planning has only a limited influence on the course of economic life.

6. Stimulus for environment compatible and public sector investments may well be socially rational, but has little in common with investment planning East European style.

7. There is clearly much to be said for a reindustrialisation programme. It seems clear, however, that Japan would make a better model for this than Eastern Europe. This is because of its massive achievements combined with a situation and institutions more similar to the Netherlands, e.g. foreign trade dependence, private business firms, a capital market, independent trade unions and extensive feedback mechanisms.

8. An important lesson from the experience of Eastern Europe with economic planning, is that there are different decision-making processes, each with characteristic achievements and problems. With substantially different institutions, the Netherlands could easily ensure full employment, but this would have substantial costs in terms of inefficiency and bureaucratisation. There is no economic supermarket from which an optimal economic order can be constructed.

9. Government policies and actions can easily have an *adverse* effect on technical progress. Free movement of people and ideas, readiness to

import technology and a favourable attitude to multinational companies, can have important positive effects on technical progress. Technical progress depends, *inter alia*, on motivation, dispersal of initiatives, and an economic mechanism in which demand and competition play major roles. State control of the economy can easily have an adverse effect on all of these.

10. Close links with the world economy can play an important role in stimulating technical progress and preventing economic stagnation.

11. The popularity of 'investment planning' in certain quarters partly reflects ignorance of how it actually works. Economists familiar with the practice of investment planning show substantially less enthusiasm and much more awareness of its problems.

XIII. AGRICULTURAL PRODUCTIVITY UNDER SOCIALISM*

A. INTRODUCTION

The state socialist countries have made very considerable progress in increasing the gross value of agricultural output. Some data are set out in Tables XIII.1 and XIII.2. Table XIII.1 shows clearly that since the early 1950s the USSR has made enormous progress in raising the gross output of the chief agricultural products. Table XIII.2 shows clearly that since 1952 China has made substantial progress in raising gross agricultural output.

In the USSR, the sustained agricultural progress has led to a significant improvement in diet. This can be seen from Table XIII.3 which shows clearly the sharp improvement in the Soviet diet in the third quarter of the twentieth century. *Per capita* consumption of fruit and eggs more than trebled, of fish and meat more than doubled, of milk and milk products nearly doubled and of vegetables rose by two-thirds. At the same time, the consumption of potatoes halved and the consumption of bread fell. Nevertheless, even in 1976, *per capita* consumption of fruit, vegetables and meat was still significantly below the norm. Furthermore, the retail food market has continued to be marked by shortages and queues. This reflects the imbalance between money

* Originally published in *World Development* September/October 1981. I am grateful to C. Howe, W. Klatt, R. Knaack, M. Masuch, P. Nolan, A. Nove, G. Smith, E. Vermeer and K. Wädekin for helpful comments and discussion. I alone am responsible for errors. For reasons of space it has been impossible to go in detail into the questions discussed in this chapter. Hence some over-simplification and omissions are unavoidable.

incomes and food supplies, which can be explained by the disappointing level of agricultural production, wage drift, the official view that excess demand constitutes a stimulus to production, and fear of popular reactions to food price increases. In addition, since the mid-1970s meat output has stagnated and shortages worsened (see Chapter X).

Table XIII.1
Output of chief agricultural products in Russia/the USSR at selected dates
(million tonnes)

Years	Grain	Raw cotton	Meat (slaughter weight)	Milk
1909–1913 (average)	72·5	0·68	4·8	28·8
1924–1928 (average)	69·3	0·58	4·2	29·3
1951–1955 (average)	88·5	3·89	5·7	37·9
1976–1979 (average)	209·0	8·67	14·8	93·2

Note: Soviet grain output statistics are not comparable with those for most other countries. The Soviet statistics measure 'bunker' output rather than 'barn' output. The former exceeds the latter because it includes some moisture content of the grain, thrash and dirt admixtures, and losses during transport, handling and preliminary storage.
Source: *Narodnoe Khozyaistvo SSSR v 1979g* (Moscow: 1980), pp. 219–220.

For Marxists, however, the decisive area for the competition of the two systems is that of labour productivity. It is by breaking through to decisively higher levels of labour productivity that the superiority of socialism over capitalism will be demonstrated. So far, experience has been disappointing, as Table XIII.4 indicates. More than six decades after the October Revolution and more than five decades after the collectivisation of Soviet agriculture, overtaking and surpassing the leading capitalist country in labour productivity is still a dream for the distant future.

In China, although land productivity has risen substantially in the last 30 years, it still lags significantly behind Japan. The development of labour productivity too, both in industry and agriculture, has been disappointing. As Yang Jinbai and Li Xuenzeng (1980, pp. 186–187) have explained:

Table XIII.2
*Output of chief agricultural products in China at
selected dates (million tonnes)*

Year	Grain	Cotton	Pigs [stock (million)]
1952	163·9	1·3	89·8
1978	304·8	2·2	301·3

Note: 'Grain' includes soyabeans, potatoes in grain
equivalent, and is unhusked.
Source: *Social Sciences in China*, No. 2 (1980),
p. 184.

Table XIII.3
Improvements in the Soviet diet, 1950–76

	Per capita consumption in 1976	
	As % of 1950	As % of norm
Meat and fat	215	68
Milk and milk products	184	78
Eggs	348	72
Fish and fish products	263	101
Sugar	361	105
Vegetable oil	285	85
Fruit and berries	336	33
Vegetables and melons	169	59
Potatoes	49	123
Bread products (bread, flour, groats, pulse, macaroni)	82	128

Note: Soviet consumption figures, especially for meat, are non-
comparable with those for many other countries. The Soviet figures
give too favourable a picture of Soviet reality. The extent to which
the degree of non-comparability has varied over time (and hence the
extent to which Table XIII.3 gives an exaggerated picture of
improvements in the diet) is unknown to the writer.
Source: E. M. Agababyan and Ye. N. Yakovleva (eds) (1979),
Problemy Raspredeleniya i Rost Narodnogo Blagosostoyaniya
(Moscow), p. 142.

Table XIII.4

Labour productivity in the USSR relative to the USA (%)

	1950	1957	1965	1975
In industry	30–40	40–50	40–50	>55
In agriculture	20	20–25	20–25	20–25

Source: V. M. Kudrov, "Sovremennyi etap ekonomicheskogo sorevnovaniya dvukh mirovykh sistem", *Izvestiya Akademii Nauk SSSR: Seriya Ekonomicheskaya*, No. 4 (1976), p. 22.

Labour productivity in China's agriculture is too low. In 1978 the net value created by a Chinese peasant or farm worker, calculated at the current price level, averaged only 364·3 yuan, while that created by an industrial worker amounted to 2,809·2 yuan, or 7·7 times greater. If labour productivity worked out in terms of monetary value may not be accurate because of the price factor, the figures on grain output show that in 1978, while each producer in China reaped 1,036 kilograms, his counterpart in the United States brought in more than 50,000. Even if we take into account those industrial workers in the United States who rendered direct service to agriculture, numbering twice as many as the agricultural producers, the per capita output would still be much higher than ours. Moreover, labour productivity in China's agriculture fluctuated a great deal, showing a decrease in the sphere of grain production in 11 out of 30 post-liberation years. Agricultural labour productivity remains at roughly the same level as during the First Five-Year Plan period (1953–57). Over the last 20 years and more, China's agricultural production, which is predominantly grain production, has hardly improved its ability to take the burden of industry and the economy as a whole. The labour productivity in cash crop farming, forestry, animal husbandry and fishing also remains low.

B.   EXPLANATIONS OF LOW PRODUCTIVITY

1.   *Rationality Criteria*

Part of the explanation for this disappointing performance clearly lies in the different rationality criteria appropriate for a socialist state and private farmers. This is familiar from the literature on choice of techniques in less developed countries and on cost-benefit analysis. A capitalist firm is interested in its survival and profits. Costs borne by society as a whole are 'externalities'. A socialist state is concerned (or ought to be) with social costs and benefits. For a social state (like a peasant family) it is rational to employ labour till its marginal product is zero, whereas for a capitalist farmer it is only rational to employ labour till its marginal product equals the wage rate. For an individual capitalist enterprise, but not for a socialist state, the cost of maintaining the unemployed is an 'externality' (see Chapter XI). Hence, part of the explanation for the low labour productivity in agriculture under state socialism is the emphasis placed on work creation and the need to employ everyone. It is not a criticism of Chinese agriculture if the authorities prevent migration to the towns (to reduce urban unemployment) and organise work for all the rural inhabitants. Similarly, as Durgin (1978) has noted, part of the reason for the greater agricultural labour productivity in the USA than in the USSR is that whereas a Soviet collective farm is obliged to provide work for all its members, large US farms rely mainly on workers hired temporarily. Maintenance of the workers when they are not needed by the farm is an 'externality'. The unemployed farm workers, and the migrant farm workers, with their low living standards and poor working conditions, are the mirror image of the USA's high agricultural labour productivity.

2.   *Adverse Agricultural Environment*

Part of the explanation for the disappointing performance clearly lies in the economic environment. Agriculture in the USSR and China operates under adverse geographic and demographic conditions.

Only a small part of the USSR has the combination of soil, precipitation and temperature that is required for low-cost agriculture. The USSR has by far the world's largest and best soil resources. Nevertheless, in general where the soil is excellent the rainfall is inadequate, and where the rainfall is (barely) adequate the soil is usually poor. Only about 1% of Soviet farmland (mainly the eastern coast of the Black Sea) receives 28 in. or more precipitation a year. Much of the western USA and practically all the area east of Nebraska receives more than 28 in. Hence vast areas of the USSR are too dry for normal (non-irrigated) agriculture. Furthermore, because it is so far north and is only warm enough for a relatively short period, much Soviet arable land has only a short growing season.

China has to feed about a quarter of the world's population on the products of only 7% of the world's arable land. In addition, throughout the 1950s and 1960s the population grew at an average rate in excess of 2% p.a. The adverse and worsening land–labour ratio is a major burden for Chinese agriculture. Hence during the 1970s the authorities adopted vigorous birth control programmes.

3. Problems in System and Theory

Part of the explanation for the disappointing performance, however, lies in the economic order or economic system. The administrative economy ('socialist planning') operates in such a way as to generate substantial waste and inefficiency. On this there is a huge literature, with notable contributions by Kornai (1959, 1980), Brus (1972, 1975), Sik (1972) and Xue Muqiao (1981). In Ellman (1978) I argued that the fundamental cause of this inefficiency was theoretical—the inadequacy of Marxist-Leninist theory. As far as agriculture is concerned, the main theoretical inadequacies concern economies of scale, exaggerated expectations concerning the gains from abolishing private ownership, and the costs of the 'one-nation, one-factory' model. Although Marxist agricultural theory has been criticised since the time of Bernstein and David in the late nineteenth century (Klatt, 1971, pp. 67–68 and 464–465; Cliff, 1980, pp. 8–11), Marxist-Leninists have remained unmoved. Each new state socialist country has been surprised to discover that large-scale socialist agriculture suffers from serious problems.

(a) *Economies of scale*. These play an important role in Marxist-Leninist arguments about why peasant farming is not a viable way of organising agriculture and why socialist agriculture will overtake and surpass capitalist agriculture in productivity. Experience, however, has shown that agriculture is fundamentally different from industry in that organising workers in large productive units does not in general raise productivity. As Robinson (1964, p. 1) has explained:

> For the deployment of labour, a rather small scale is required. Workers are spread out over space so that discipline is hard to enforce; an incentive wage system is not easy to arrange or administer; there has to be great diffusion of managerial responsibility; every field is different, every day is different and quick decisions have to be taken. For getting work out of the workers a peasant family is hard to beat. Discipline and responsibility are imposed by the pressing incentive to secure the family livelihood.

This is the main explanation of the abundant evidence (Dorner, 1972, p. 120) that "output per unit of land is inversely related to farm size". As Lipton (1974, p. 289) has noted:

> Part of this relationship is spurious (because holding size is usually smaller on good soil), but much of it survives even in micro studies where the soil quality can be held constant. Small family farms can saturate the land with plenty of labour per acre, as there is little else for the labour to do (except perhaps at seasonal peaks). Large commercial farms must supervise labour and pay it the full market price, which is likely to rise if they buy too much of it. Another and more surprising fact is that, as Colin Clark has often emphasised, all the careful micro-work shows that *capital* per acre also increases as farm size declines.

In general, where labour is abundant relative to land, the efficient utilisation of scarce resources requires small, not large, units, a finding paradoxical from a Marxist-Leninist standpoint. Where there is a high labour–land ratio, the main production problem of agricultural development is to raise land productivity and not labour productivity. This explains the lesser gains in labour-abundant farming than in industry from organising labour in large units, where factories raise labour productivity by the division of labour and disciplining the workers. (The gains from the division of labour in agriculture are also limited by the sequential nature of much agricultural work.) Raising land productivity is largely a matter of the application of modern inputs such as artificial fertilisers. However, pre-war studies of the capital stock, including draft animals, in Chinese agriculture, showed that there was a certain minimum size below which the peasant could not afford to purchase or hire the means of production needed for high land productivity. Many farms were below this size. Hence mutual-aid arrangements were common, and so was the provision of means of production by land-owners to tenants; but even so many small farms did not have sufficient access to means of production to achieve high land productivity.

In addition, there are managerial diseconomies of scale in agriculture. The efficient large-scale organisation of labour requires efficient planning, administration and book-keeping work which is unnecessary under peasant or small-holder farming where each farmer organises his work himself. The extent of this managerial diseconomy of scale depends on two factors. First is the size of the organisation. The bigger it is, the more serious the problem. Second is the educational level of the farmers. An important cause of the adverse effects of organising Chinese agriculture into communes in 1958 was the large size of the work force per commune, in a society in which the majority of the farmers were completely illiterate. They were incapable of handling even the simplest book-keeping. Similarly in Tanzania, where the new villages created by the state in the mid-1970s were too large, the villagisation programme had an adverse effect on both labour and land productivity (Dumont and Mottin, 1980, pp. 171–172).

It is precisely because of agriculture's lesser economies of scale and the greater importance of diseconomies of scale that private agriculture has remained important in all the state socialist countries (Walker, 1965; Wädekin, 1973). (The only exceptions are the most advanced state socialist countries. In the German Democratic Republic (GDR) the private sector's contribution to output is now less than 10% and in Czechoslovakia it is slightly more than 10%). Where it has been abolished (as in China during the Great Leap Forward) or hampered (in the USSR in the late Khrushchev period or Poland in the mid-1970s) the results have always been adverse. It is because of these important lessons of experience that in contemporary China the Marxist idea of the superiority of state ownership over collective ownership and over private utilisation in agriculture has been questioned. The advantages of collective ownership and of individual and household economic activity have recently been officially recognised. As Yu Guangyuan (1980), the Vice President of the Chinese Academy of Social Sciences has argued:

> The state-owned economy may prove to be the most superior as far as big, modern industry is concerned, but in the vast countryside, socialist collective ownership is apparently superior to ownership by the state. Likewise, if we are to make good use of the labour power within families, individual economy as a supplementary economy plays a role neither the state-owned economy nor a collectively-owned economy can play. Thus, it is correct to say that small plots reserved for personal use, household sideline production and things like these have their own special superiority.

The former model commune of Dazhai, which had no private plots, has been extensively criticised. In fact, during 1980, considerable official attention in China was directed to the advantages of individual economic activity, both in the villages and in the towns, in generating employment, providing useful goods and services and being a healthy competitive stimulus for the state-owned economy (Zhou Jinghua, 1980). Similarly, in Vietnam in 1979, in the wake of the very disappointing development of agricultural productivity, the private sector was encouraged.

The great differences between agriculture and industry as far as economies of scale are concerned can be seen clearly by looking at the experience of the capitalist countries. Despite all the arguments of Marx, Kautsky and Lenin, agriculture in capitalist Europe has continued to be organised predominantly in small units. The family farm, where the farmer can exploit himself and his family, has proved remarkably competitive. The distribution of agricultural workers by number of workers per enterprise, differs radically from, say, engineering workers. Even in the USA, the country of agribusiness and large-scale capitalist farming, small units are much more important than in industry. The size distribution (both with respect to employment and output) of enterprises in the US farming industry differs radically from, say, the auto or steel industries.

Although, in the area of the efficient deployment of agricultural labour, the Marxist-Leninist thesis of the advantages of large-scale organisation is invalid where labour is abundant relative to land, there are important areas in which this thesis is correct; for example, transport, marketing (this was stressed by Kautsky) technical progress. Furthermore, when land is scarce, the efficient use of land of different qualities requires specialisation, which is incompatible with peasant farming in the strict sense of the term,* but specialisation is compatible with smallholder farming—small-scale farming whose output is destined for the market—and with large-scale capitalist farming. Also, the division of land into fragmented plots, and the use of land for boundary lines, are common sources of waste in agriculture when there is private ownership of land. In addition, as noted earlier, farms may be too small for high land productivity. Obviously investment in irrigation, water control and land reclamation may require very large-scale organisation, as in the irrigated areas of Soviet Central Asia or the river valleys of China or the USA. Hence it is understandable that in the irrigated cotton growing areas of Soviet Central Asia, which benefit both from large-scale water control and favourable prices, land productivity (but

---

* By 'peasant farming in the strict sense of the term' I understand subsistence farming (not for the market) by producers who do not hire labour.

not labour productivity) is high by international standards (Khan and Ghai, 1979).

The most appropriate farm size depends on the land–labour ratio, the product, the methods of production, the availability of modern inputs, the availability and cost of transport, and a variety of other factors. Economies of scale do exist in certain areas, and farms can be too small to maximise land, labour, capital, or combined input productivity; but a one-sided emphasis on economies of scale can have serious adverse effects on productivity.

(b) *Labour incentives.* Marxist theory has *exaggerated expectations concerning the gains from abolishing private ownership*. For a Marxist (Dobb, 1966, p. 39), "socialism has primarily to do with the way that capital and land (or the means of production) are *owned*". It was expected that once capitalist ownership, with its inevitable accompaniment of alienation, production for profit rather than for use, and class conflict, were swept away, labour productivity would rise rapidly. As a famous Marxist economist has quite rightly explained (Dobb, 1966, p. 56), "To anticipate this, and to take account of it in the structure and functioning of a planned economy, is *not* just wishful utopia-spinning— it is, indeed, a crucial article of faith of a socialist."

This "crucial article of faith of a socialist" suffers from a large number of limitations. For one thing, it pays inadequate attention to the costs involved in the transition from private ownership. The collectivisation of agriculture in the USSR was accompanied by the deportation of the best farmers from their villages ("the liquidation of the kulaks as a class") which naturally had an unfavourable effect on labour productivity.

For another, it pays too little attention to the fact that the socialisation of the means of production is a long *process* of which the formal nationalisation or collectivisation is only an initial step (Brus, 1975). An empirical study by the Soviet sociologist Arutyunyan (1971) showed that the majority of collective and state farmers in the farms sampled thought that they had no influence on the affairs of their work collective. This feeling of powerlessness increased as one descended the managerial and skill hierarchy. Nationalisation or collectivisation does not lead directly to a situation in which "every cook will govern" (Lenin). It leads to a situation in which the control of the means of production is exercised by a privileged bureaucracy, while the workers continue to feel (and to be) excluded from decision-making.* Hence, it is not true that on the morrow of the revolution (or collectivisation) the negative effects of capitalism on incentives are eliminated and labour productivity begins to rise rapidly. For labour productivity even to be maintained, let alone increased, an appropriate system of incentives is necessary.

To establish effective labour incentives for collectivist agriculture is a difficult but very important task. In the USSR, where collectivist agriculture was first established, labour was organised during the Stalin period on the basis of what Ellman (1979) termed 'quasi-feudal' relations of production. Medvedev and Medvedev (1977) termed them 'semi-feudal' and described the position of the peasantry as 'semi-serfdom'. The reason for this description is as follows. Work on the collective farms was enforced by coercion and paid very little. The livelihood of the farmers was gained from their private plots, the right to which depended on their performance of labour for the collective farm. The collective farmers were poverty stricken. (As late as the mid-1960s, the overwhelming majority of Soviet collective farmers lived in poverty.†) The peasants were tied to their land by the passport system. This system was very similar to that existing in mediaeval Western Europe and in pre-1861 Russia.

As is well known, serfdom is not a very good system for raising productivity. Neither was 'semi-serfdom'. Grain production in the USSR, the year Stalin died, was below the 1913 level, and grain production per head much below it. In 1953 meat production was also below the 1913 level. The stock of both cattle and sheep were below the 1928 level as was the *per capita* stock of pigs. In 1953 the entire Soviet population (except for a tiny élite) was only just above subsistence level, food was difficult to obtain, expensive, of poor quality, and (together with drink) it totally dominated the budget of urban families. The only exception to this dismal picture was cotton, the output of which in 1953 was more than five times that of 1913, partly as a result of

---

* For a discussion of this problem in Tanzania see Dumont and Mottin (1980, pp. 187–189). They conclude that in Tanzania, "A rushed and authoritarian villagisation has been implemented to *serve*, but also to *control* the peasants. It has also reduced agricultural output."

† McAuley (1979), p. 61. The measure of 'poverty' used by McAuley is a Soviet one, developed by Soviet specialists for Soviet conditions.

its favourable procurement price from the mid 1930s.

Since 1953 there has been a series of measures which, taken together, can be described (see Chapter IV) as a 'second emancipation'. (The first emancipation, of course, was in 1861 when serfdom was abolished. The need for a second emancipation was created, as explained earlier, by the regressive Stalinist policies.) These measures included the enormous increase in the real incomes of the rural population after 1953, the issue to them, beginning in 1976, of passports (which in principle means that they are no longer tied to the soil and have the same status as the urban population instead of being a separate estate), and the extension to them of a virtual wage system and of social security. The second emancipation was enormously significant for the USSR as a whole and for the rural population in particular and marked a major social advance for the USSR.*

The effect of this radical improvement was to end the situation in which the position of the rural population was much worse than that of the urban population and to diminish greatly the gap between conditions in the countryside and those in the towns. What is the actual effect of socialist planning on urban labour morale, enthusiasm and interest in the work done? The weight of the evidence points to the conclusion that under socialist planning labour morale, enthusiasm and interest in the work done are poor.† As Selucký (1979, p. 43) has noted, "While all the old forms of worker's alienation from his labour and from his product have not disappeared, new specific forms of alienation of the worker from his wage, from the plan and from the entire system have been brought about." This is particularly important in agriculture because of the difficulty of supervising labour in this sector. This results from the sequential nature of much agricultural work, the fact that it is spatially scattered, the heterogeneous nature of the resources (e.g. fields of different quality), and the erratic and seasonal nature of the natural inputs (e.g. precipitation and temperature). Moreover, there is no fixed or easily predictable relationship between inputs and outputs; the returns for work performed vary with the harvest. Two examples of the resulting problems are the apathetic attitude of the

---

* In China, the rural population is to this day still tied to the soil by administrative controls over movement, residence, employment and consumer goods.
† Ellman (1979a, pp. 171–173), Kornai (1980, Chapter 11).

labour force to the repair of agricultural machinery, and the chequered history of the link (*zveno*). They were discussed in Chapter 4 (pp. 66–67).

The absence of adequate labour incentives was also a serious problem for land reform in Chile. The Left parties made the classical Marxist mistake of assuming that with the abolition of private ownership the consciousness of the workers had been so transformed that material incentives could be neglected. As Lehmann (1974, p. 95) has noted, for this to have worked,

> there would have to be a high level of morally based co-operation among the *asentados* [co-operative farmers], in the absence of an effective material incentive. In practice, however, it was common to hear the argument that there is no point in a man working hard if another spends his time drinking. My interviews with *asentados* in 1969 show a very clear concern for a fair return to physical effort expended in work. Thus, where there is a lack of trust among co-operators they prefer to turn their energies to the family economy where such a return is more secure.

Also in Tanzania, in many cases the collective farming in the new villages established by the state in the mid-1970s was badly planned, badly organised and had a low return, and hence adversely affected labour productivity (Dumont and Mottin, 1980, p. 140).

Similarly in China, the system of distribution according to need introduced in 1958 when the communes were set up had to be abandoned rapidly because of its adverse effects on labour productivity. 'Why should we work hard if we will be fed anyway?' seems to have been a widespread thought. Hence the December 1958 Central Committee "Resolution on some questions concerning the People's Communes" argued that, "Any attempt to negate prematurely the principle of distribution according to work and replace it with the principle of distribution according to needs, that is, any attempts, when conditions are not mature, to enter communism by over-reaching ourselves . . . is undoubtedly a Utopian concept that cannot possibly succeed." In 1962, after the economic crisis of 1959–61 which was mainly caused by neglect of individual material incentives, diseconomies of scale and badly planned water control projects, the principle was established that production teams would be the basic unit of accounting. Each team was supposed to distribute among its members both 'basic grain' and 'workpoint grain', the former according to need and the latter according to work. The ratio between the two was supposed to be fixed by each team itself (Vermeer, 1979, p. 870). A careful analysis of China's experience with agricultural incentives in 1956–70 (Crook, 1970) emphasised the great importance for the successful collective agriculture of a well-designed, smoothly operating and stable incentive system. It is very understandable that the leadership which came to power in the wake of the Eleventh Congress (1977), and which is very concerned with the failure of Maoist policies to raise agricultural labour productivity, has raised procurement prices, encouraged private plots and household auxiliary production, criticised authoritarian behaviour of cadres, and in 1979–82 generally decollectivised (Nolan 1983, Watson 1983), in order to provide adequate incentives to raise labour productivity.

(c) *The costs of the 'one-nation, one-factory' model.* This is an important part of the explanation of the failure of labour productivity in socialist agriculture to overtake and surpass that in capitalist agriculture. The model seems to have been first explicitly formulated by Kautsky, but as Selucký (1979, p. 14) has rightly noted, "Though Marx was not its explicit author, he was certainly its spiritual father." As far as agriculture is concerned, the main costs of the model are the inefficiency of administrative (bureaucratic) methods and the dangers of simultaneously politicising agricultural decisions and eliminating feedback mechanisms.

A major negative aspect of collectivist agriculture in the state socialist countries is the use of administrative methods, such as instructions from above, rather than economic methods, such as price and tax policy, where the latter would be more efficient. The consequent growth of bureaucracy and decline of local initiative has been simply a dead loss to society. Not only does the use of administrative methods have a direct cost, but it may also have an adverse effect on those very things (e.g. marketed output) which it is the objective of the administrative methods to stimulate. As the Chinese economist Xue Muqiao has observed:

Up to now the systems of prescribed purchases, unified purchases and procurement quotas for grain and other main farm products are still in force and cannot be abolished for a while.* But we must not overlook the negative role they have played. In some places, where the amount of prescribed purchases and the procurement quotas are too high, the peasants who grow the crop cannot eat their fill and those who raise pigs do not have pork on their tables. Their flagging enthusiasm for production impaired the growth of agricultural production, which in turn made the shortage of supplies in the cities even more acute . . . According to our experience, when we purchased too much grain through the system of prescribed purchases, grain output in the following year went down immediately, conversely, when we purchased less, grain output in the following year went up as a matter of course. When our procurement quotas for meat and eggs were too high, these items became hard to get; when we relaxed or abolished the quota system, and made purchases at a price agreed on, the products would be in ample supply.†

A serious problem resulting from the replacement of market methods by administrative (bureaucratic) methods is that of production for plan rather than for use.‡ It is particularly serious in agriculture. Some causes and consequences of this situation were discussed in Chapter 4.

The result of the one-nation, one-factory model in a one-party system with strict censorship and an absence of independent social organisations is simultaneously to politicise all decisions and eliminate feedback mechanisms. This has had numerous adverse effects on agricultural productivity. The resulting problems are of two kinds, inefficiences resulting directly from counter-productive central policies, and inefficiencies resulting from unintended responses by local officials to central policies. Examples of the former range from Lysenkoism in Soviet genetics, to the economic crisis of 1959–61 in China, to the decline in Cuban agricultural labour productivity in the 1960s, the Chinese 1955–56 experience with the two-bladed, two-wheel plough, and the sudden increase in the area of double-cropped rice in China in 1956.

The fiasco of the two-bladed, two-wheel plough has been described

---

* 'Prescribed purchases' is a term for the grain procurement quotas. Each province, commune, brigade and team is obliged to sell a certain quantity of grain to the state. 'Unified purchases' is a term used for state cotton purchases. Teams must sell all their cotton output to the state, less that amount permitted to be retained for individual use (or sale) by the members of the team. 'Procurement quotas' refers to the quantities of pigs and eggs which the people who raise them have to sell to the state.

† *Beijing Review*, no. 43, 1979, p. 16.

‡ See, for example, Ellman (1973, pp. 51–53).

by Chao (1970, pp. 101–103) and Stavis (1978, pp. 67–68). As part of the collectivisation campaign in China it was decided to expand the production of the two-bladed, two-wheel plough. This decision was based on the Marxist idea that a social revolution required a technical revolution. Once the new plough was actually distributed on a large scale in southern China, serious problems were encountered. It sank into the mud of paddy fields and was too heavy and cumbersome to be used on the small plots of paddy or terraced fields. Generally two beasts were required to pull it, and Chinese draft animals were not accustomed to working in teams. After millions had been produced, production had to be discontinued in view of its defects. Substantial waste had been caused, not by 'rural idiots' but by the misguided policies of the central leadership.

An example of the second type of waste, that resulting from the unintended response of local officials to central policies, is provided by the Soviet 1959 experience with Ryazan methods (see page 62). What the Chinese term 'commandism', the arbitrary imposition of the will of officials on the farmers in response to political priorities or political campaigns emanating from higher up, has been a permanent problem for agriculture in the state socialist countries and a continuous hindrance to the growth of productivity.

The popularity of socialist agriculture in many non-socialist Third World countries does not in any way reflect its record in raising agricultural productivity, which has been profoundly disappointing. Partly it simply reflects ignorance of the actual situation. Partly, however, it reflects the effects of state socialist agriculture on *employment* and *distribution*. These topics are very important, but analysis of them is outside the scope of this chapter. It should be pointed out, however, that pursuit of these two goals may contradict the goal of raising productivity as indicated earlier with respect to employment. Similarly, it may be that the Chinese agricultural procurement system, while having an adverse effect on productivity has a favourable effect on distribution.

C. CONCLUSION

The growth of gross agricultural output under state socialism has been substantial. Nevertheless, the growth of agricultural productivity under state socialism has been very unsatisfactory from a Marxist-Leninist standpoint. After five decades of collectivised Soviet agriculture, and three decades after the Communist victory in the Chinese Civil War, overtaking the advanced capitalist countries in agricultural productivity is still in the distant future. Partly this results from the different rationality criteria appropriate for a socialist state and for private businesses. The unemployed are not an 'externality' for a socialist state. Partly it results from adverse factors, geographic and demographic, in the economic environment. Partly, however, it results from the inadequacy of Marxist theory, with its excessive stress on economies of scale, exaggerated expectations concerning the gains from abolishing private ownership, and failure to foresee the costs of the one-nation, one-factory model. These problems are not specific to agriculture but are general to socialist planning. They cause particular difficulties in agriculture because of some specific features of agriculture, e.g. the lesser importance of economies of scale, the greater difficulty of supervising spatially scattered labour and the need for initiative.

XIV. ECONOMIC REFORM IN CHINESE INDUSTRY*

A. INTRODUCTION

Economic policy in the post-Mao period has been characterised by a number of distinct periods. In April 1977 Chairman Hua issued a series of orders to prepare for a new leap forward within three years and at the first session of the Fifth National People's Congress in February 1978 he unveiled a very ambitious programme for the remaining eight years of the Ten Year Plan (1976–85), a kind of Mini Great Leap Forward. The emphasis was on the rapid development of heavy industry making use of extensive imports of technology. At a Central Committee meeting in December 1978 a radical change in policy was decided and much greater emphasis was given to agriculture. The new line was reflected in the speeches at the Second Session of the Fifth National People's Congress (June 1979) where Chairman Hua proclaimed a cooling-off period of three years, in which the economy had to readjust, to restructure, to consolidate and improve. The main focus was centred on readjustment (the establishment of macro-economic equilibrium) and restructuring (economic reforms). This policy was confirmed again and intensified during the Third Session (September 1980). Two months later, at the CC work-meeting of December 1980, emphasis was given to readjustment, and restructuring was downgraded, in view of the serious macro-economic problems facing the country. Hence in February

* Originally published in the *ACES Bulletin*, Summer 1981. The author is indebted to Wlodzimierz Brus, Erik Dirksen, Pat Ellman, Michael Ellman, Christopher Howe and Michael Masuch for valuable comments.

1981, at the Seventeenth Meeting of the Standing Committee of the Fifth National People's Congress, counter-reforms were announced and the economy was (partly) centralised again.

In this chapter an attempt is made to analyse the causes of these fluctuations in the economic policy of the Chinese leadership. We will see that economic policy in post-Mao China has basically followed the familiar East European economic and institutional cycle as described for example by Nuti (1979). The present leadership claims that counter-reforms are only temporary. It will be argued that this is far from self-evident.

B.   THE MINI GREAT LEAP FORWARD

In a speech at the Fourth National People's Congress (January 1975) Zhou Enlai outlined the principles of the coming Ten Year Plan (1976–85). These principles were a repetition of those he had stated in a speech at the Third National People's Congress (December 1964) on the eve of the coming Third Five Year Plan. (This plan was never elaborated or implemented because of the Cultural Revolution.) They were popularised as the 'Four Modernisations' (modernisation of agriculture, industry, defence, and science and technology). These principles were worked out by the State Council in a draft Ten Year Plan. Because this plan also included recommendations for strict regulation of the management of enterprises, it was rejected by the Leftists as being a 'revisionist document'. In 1976 the succession struggle led to enormous political unrest. This paralysed the economy, and affected economic development negatively. The goals of the draft Ten Year Plan for 1976 were not achieved; in 1976 there was scarcely any economic growth.

After the fall of the 'Gang of Four', the State Council produced a new version of the Ten Year Plan. The growth optimism, which is characteristic of the revised plan, was probably caused by a number of factors. First was the view that the economy had considerable reserves resulting from the elimination of the harmful 'Gang of Four' policies. This will have been confirmed by the enormous recovery of the economy in the second half of 1977. Secondly, the new leadership needed to issue its own economic platform. The revised plan was presented by Chairman Hua at the First Session of the Fifth National People's Congress

(February 1978). This ambitious plan, covering the remaining eight years of the Ten Year Plan, planned a yearly growth of agriculture of 4% and a yearly growth of industry of more than 10%. Moreover, it called for the construction of 120 large-scale industrial projects, of which 10 were iron and steel complexes.

A key role in socialist construction was assigned to foreign trade. Trade was to support agriculture and industry through the import of the necessary raw materials, technology and even complete factories. In 1976 and 1977 imports were reduced in order to restore the equilibrium of the balance of payments, but in 1978 the volume of trade increased, in comparison with 1977, by 30% (imports increased 41%, exports 21%).

By the end of 1978 there were some signs that the plan was quite unfeasible. According to Field (1979, p. 735), in the first half of 1978 industrial production increased by only 1·2% compared with the second half of 1977 and in the second half of 1978 by only 3·2% compared with the first half of 1978. (Industrial production in 1978 was still 13·5% higher than in 1977, but only because of the poor level of production in the first half of 1977.) In December 1978, the Central Committee discussed the main directions of economic policy. Attention was focused on the importance of a rapid growth of agricultural production. Procurement prices were raised and stress laid on the autonomy of agricultural units. The Central Committee concluded also that investments were too extensive, and that too large a share of investment was allocated to heavy industry, hindering agriculture and light industry; the national economy was unbalanced. This was worsened by imbalances in heavy industry itself. The production of oil, coal and electricity, as well as the transport system could not meet the demands of a fast-growing economy.

It is not surprising that in a period of disappointing economic growth, accompanied by a relatively high volume of investment, attention was focused more and more on the inefficient working of the economic system. Numerous articles, published at the time in the Chinese press, gave examples of this inefficient functioning. Gao Zhihua (1980, p. 7), for example, reported that by the end of June 1978 the stockpiles of goods and state supplies throughout China had reached such enormous amounts that they equalled the value of the national industrial output for the first half of the year. Hua Chiao-mu (1978, p. 22) complained that while labour productivity increased during the First Five Year Plan it had since stagnated. If it had continued to increase at the rate achieved in the First Five Year Plan, labour productivity in industry in 1977 would have been three times what it actually was. Others mentioned that investigations had shown that in general it has taken ten years on the average for the large and medium-sized capital construction projects to go into production, twice as long as the period required during the First Five Year Plan.*

Hence, the result of the failure of the Mini Great Leap Forward was to bring into question the efficiency of the traditional economic system.

C.   THE CHINESE CRITIQUE OF THE TRADITIONAL ECONOMIC SYSTEM

After 1949, the Chinese economy was modelled on Soviet experience. This applied both to the principles underlying its method of implementation (e.g. one-man mangement) and to the strategy. The share of investment in net material product was for a long time around 30–35%, while the share of heavy industry in total investment was more than 50% (Yang Jianbai and Li Xuezeng, 1980, pp. 189–194). With regard to the ownership of the means of production, in the 1950s emphasis was placed on a transition from individual ownership to collective ownership, from collectives on a small scale to collectives on a greater scale and from collective ownership to state ownership, both in town and country (Zhou Jianghua, 1980, p. 20).

Since 1949 the planning system has been changed several times. After November 1959, the majority of enterprises were placed under the responsibility of regional and local government. About 10% of enterprises were still administered by central government departments, although these enterprises provided more than 10% of the production and employment (Eckstein, 1977, p. 56). In fact, decentralisation mainly concerned decisions related to the use of existing capacity. Large-scale future developments remained the responsibility of the central authorities (Eckstein, 1977, p. 57). The division of power between the central authorities and the local authorities, that is to say

---

* *Beijing Review*, 13 October 1980, p. 18.

the division of power inside the 'super-structure', has changed frequently in the last twenty years. This is a reflection of a recurrent cycle in which "centralization leads to rigidity, rigidity leads to complaints, complaints lead to disorder, and disorder leads back to centralization" (Jiang Yiwei, 1980, p. 49).

The main topics which have been discussed during the Chinese criticism of the traditional planning system are: the functioning of the planning system, the sectoral development model (the share of investment in the national income and the sectoral allocation of investment), enterprise democracy, the use of material incentives and state ownership.

With regard to the *planning system*, the problems both of excessive centralisation and of excessive decentralisation have been widely discussed in the Chinese press. According to Jiang Yiwei (pp. 54–55), the reduction of the problem of economic reform to a problem of centralisation or decentralisation cannot lead to a fundamental solution. Only an economic reform which takes the view that the enterprise is the basic economic entity can be based on the 'objective laws of economic development', especially 'the law of value'. This is basically an argument for increasing the role of the market. According to Stalin, whose views always were an integral part of the Chinese orthodoxy, the role of the law of value in socialism is not important. It is restricted to the production of consumer goods. This point of view is not shared by a growing number of Chinese economists. The law of value should also, in their view, act as a regulator of production and investment. The already-mentioned Jiang Yiwei advocates that enterprises be made completely responsible for their profits and losses, which the government should be allowed to correct only by economic means. Others are less outspoken, but all advocate reforms emphasising cost calculation, the incorporation of new value categories in the calculation system, use of profit as the criterion for guiding and evaluating the work of the enterprises, relating profit to the value of capital employed instead of to the cost or price, a reform of the price system, improvement of the contract system and a strengthening of the position of the banking system.

The *sectoral development model* deals with two interlinked problems, namely the share of investment in national income and the sectoral allocation of investment. In most of the past thirty years the share of accumulation in net material product exceeded 30%. According to Wu

Jiang (1980, p. 17), this had not only an adverse effect on the standard of living, but also on the growth of the national income and state revenue. In years when the accumulation rate exceeded 30–35%, the growth rates of national income and state revenue fell. Hence, he advocates that private consumption should increase at the expense of investment. Some Chinese specialists think that a share of investment of 25% is the optimal one for China.* Also the share of heavy industry in investment (more than 50%) is regarded as too high. It must decrease in favour of investment in agriculture and light industry. Light industry has two advantages. First, compared with heavy industry it makes use of China's factor endowment (abundant labour and natural resources, limited capital and backward technology). It is also less energy intensive. Secondly, it provides resources for export (light industry provides 40% of China's foreign exchange earnings) and consumption (necessary for increasing labour productivity).

According to Marxist philosophy, socialism should be superior to capitalism on at least two counts. One is that the state, thanks to the public ownership of the means of production, is in a position to utilise the nation's manpower, material and financial resources in a planned way. It is, therefore, able to avoid the anarchy of the capitalist economy. Therefore, efficiency would be much higher than under capitalism. The other advantage is that, with the system of exploitation of man by man abolished and the working class as a whole now 'master of its own house', the people would be more creative and show more initiative, which would benefit the development of the entire national economy. Xue Muqiao (1980, p. 16) has argued that these two aspects of the superiority of socialism over capitalism contradict each other. In reality the enterprises are not governed by the workers, but by the state. Unified leadership is in the first place centralised. Hence, when one states that the working class is 'master of its own house', it chiefly means that political power is monopolised by a party which claims to represent the working class. Central command, in which the individual worker and the local authorities have to obey the orders of the state, prevents the development of any initiative from below. If, on the other hand, one-sided emphasis is laid on democratic management, thus weakening the unified leadership, it is possible to be caught once again in the

---

* *Beijing Review*, 5 May 1980.

pitfall of the anarchy of production. An economic reform in the form of a decentralisation of decision-making to the enterprises makes it possible to restore the identity of interests between worker (or work collectives) and the national economy as a whole which is lost in the traditional planning system and to find a solution for the problem of overcentralisation at the same time. As a part of the process of *democratisation of the enterprises* it has been advocated that cadres be elected (rather than appointed), that workers' congresses (works councils) be reactivated and that new life be breathed into the mass movements.

More emphasis has been laid by the post-Mao leadership on the use of *material incentives*. This is necessary, because "under the present and moral conditions in the historical period of socialism, a period of transition to communism, it is utopian fantasy to ask the working people to work for the public without any thought of themselves . . ." (Jiang Yiwei, 1980, p. 16). And Hua Chiao-mu (1978, p. 22) adds to these, that "in the historical period of socialism, when the principle 'to each according to his work' is implemented, there is an upswing in the national economy . . . when this principle is not implemented, the national economy fails to grow". In practice, the principle 'to each according to this work' connects the material interests of the workers to the success or failure of the enterprise. It stands for the increased use of bonuses and piece rates in order to increase labour productivity.

The critique of the traditional economic mechanism directs itself also to the other pillar of state socialist orthodoxy, namely the necessity of a high degree of *state ownership*. According to Yu Guangyuan (1980, p. 13), the basic Marxist approach to socialist ownership is to see which type can best promote the development of the productive forces. Therefore, the relations of production must adapt themselves to the level of the development of the productive forces. During a certain period of time it is possible for several different forms of ownership to coexist side by side. Each of these may show its own peculiar superior quality in certain sectors, in certain organisations of a given magnitude and so forth. Zhou Jinghua (1980) takes the same line. He also argues that at this state of development state ownership has some drawbacks. Not only are there only limited funds at the state's disposal, but it is also impossible for the state to take care of the needs of the public in various aspects of their daily life. Scattered or mobile service trades (including repair stores), some small-scale local transport, and the making of furniture operated by individuals can serve the public better than state-owned enterprises. State-owned enterprises are superior where big modern industry is concerned. The same can be said about agriculture, where state ownership, collective ownership and private utilisation all have their own special advantages (see Chapter 13 p. 205).

After surveying these critiques, the direction in which the economy—according to reform-minded Chinese economists—has to be transformed, is clear enough. The bureaucratised management by the state (central and local authorities included) has to be transformed. Regulation through planning should be combined with greater reliance on the market. This creates the possibility of extending the decision-making power of the enterprise and the ability of the workers and staff to participate in management, and secondly of expanding the role of the private sector. Moreover the planning strategy (emphasis on heavy industry) has to change.

D.   CONCRETE REFORMS

The policies adopted at the Second Session of the Fifth National People's Congress (June/July 1979) were based on this train of thought. The congress accepted the proposal of Chairman Hua to devote the three years beginning from 1979 to readjusting, restructuring, consolidating and improving the national economy. Hua defined *readjustment* as rectifying serious imbalances in the economy; *restructuring* as an overall reform of the structure of economic management in accordance with economic laws; *consolidating* as a resolute and effective shake-up in the existing enterprises, especially where management was in confusion; and *improvement* as raising as much as possible the levels of production, technology and management. These principles are not equal. The primary task is readjustment, supplemented by restructuring.*

The policy of readjustment of the economy aimed to correct the imbalanced sectoral developments of the country. The share of invest-

---

* *Beijing Review*, 4 February 1980, p. 16.

ment in material product of more than 36% in 1978 was considered to be too high.* In 1979, the authorities wanted to bring back that share to less than 28%. The sums released were intended to be used for an improvement in the living conditions in the towns and in the countryside. At the beginning of 1979 the prices of agriculture products were increased and agriculture taxes were reduced. This resulted in an increase of prices of agricultural products in the towns. As a consequence, the real wages of workers decreased, which was more than compensated by a rise in wages in the autumn of 1979. Because the prices of industrial products were intended to remain stable, the improvement of the position of the peasantry and workers had to be financed by the state with revenues which were expected to result from the increased production of consumer goods. Furthermore, in order to reduce the share of investment of heavy industry in favour of agriculture and light industry, a policy of "shortening the capital construction front" was launched. Some works were stopped or deferred in order to concentrate on finishing priority projects. Agriculture and light industry had to produce the goods which the farmers and workers wanted to buy with their increased incomes. This whole policy also influenced international trade. The import of machinery and technology, chiefly benefiting heavy industry, was curbed. In order to improve the balance of payments position, from June 1979 onwards foreign investment in the form of 'joint ventures' was permitted.

With regard to the policy of restructuring, from the end of 1978 onwards, experiments took place with forms of greater autonomy for the individual enterprises, new forms of concentration and co-operation were introduced and the role of the banking system was increased.

1. *Autonomy*

From October 1978 onwards experiments were conducted in an ever-increasing number of enterprises with forms of decentralised decision-making. By 1980 about 6600 enterprises were involved, 16% of the state-owned industrial enterprises that, however, produced more than 60% of the total value of production and accounted for 70% of total

---

* *People's Daily*, 20 October 1979, quoted in *Europe and China*, January 1980.

profits. In 1978 autonomy was organised by provincial decrees, as for example, in the 14-point experimental programme of the province Sichuan. Only in July 1979 was autonomy worked out on a national scale by the State Council in a document entitled "Measures for Expanding the Right of Self-Management of State-Owned Enterprises" and four other documents. Greater autonomy of the enterprises was achieved in various ways: they would be allowed, in the future, to spend a part of their profit and depreciation themselves; they would be allowed to develop some market-oriented behaviour independent of the local commercial departments; the labour relations inside the enterprise were rationalised and the decision-making process of the enterprise was democratised.

One of the first things that changed as a result of the movement towards more autonomy of the enterprises was the financial relationship between the enterprise and the state. Before the reform all income and expenditure was regulated by the state in a uniform way. For nearly all items, including items such as the necessary repairs of machines, not to mention an increase of the stock of fixed assets, the enterprise had to ask permission from the higher authorities. That meant that "something that can be done in several hours, remains undone for months. . . . Bureaucracy like this is highly incompatible with modernization which calls for great efficiency."[*] In order to solve this problem, the enterprises got more financial autonomy by means of a profit-sharing arrangement. There is not a uniform profit-sharing arrangement; every enterprise has its own. Some enterprises get a fixed percentage of the total profit (9% on average), others a fixed percentage of the above-plan profit (30–40%).[†] This is reflected in the huge dispersion of profit rates as a percentage of costs in various industries. The profit rates of petroleum, industrial equipment and coal are respectively 73, 29, and 0·7% (Ren Tao, 1980, p. 212). The part of profit and depreciation to be spent by the enterprises is paid to the enterprise fund. (Before the reform this was a fixed percentage of the wage fund.) The enterprise fund can be used for several purposes, including renewal of the stock

---

[*] *Beijing Review*, 26 October 1979, p. 17.
[†] The provincial regulations, which are used at this moment, are more profitable for the enterprises than the regulations determined by the State Council. Recently the Vice-Chairman of the State Council, Zhao Ziyang, has stated that for the time being the organisation of profit-sharing will be based on provincial regulations.

of fixed assets or an improvement and increase of the production assortment.

Since the reform, enterprises have become more flexible and able to develop more initiative with respect to the production and marketing of their products. In the past, the producers and consumers were cut off from each other. The producers did not know the needs of the consumers, and the consumers could not exert any influence on the production assortment. At the present time the enterprises are allowed—assuming they meet the eight targets of the state plan*— to regulate production and to develop additional production program- mes in the light of market demand. In 1979, the Congqing Iron and Steel Works, for example, sold by itself 130 000 tons of the 500 000 tons produced at fluctuating prices. The State Council also freed the trade organisations from the obligation to purchase the whole production of an enterprise. By this the State Council aimed to stimulate the enter- prises to improve the quality of their products. More freedom to sell intermediate products implies more freedom to buy the necessary inputs, which until now were delivered exclusively by the state. In the above mentioned city, Chongqing, the Zhongnan Rubber Plant itself negotiated the supply of 30% of its raw material by signing contracts with enterprises in other provinces (Lin Zili, 1980, p. 175). In addition the labour market is being reformed substantially. In the traditional 'iron rice bowl' system of labour force allocation, the labour depart- ments arbitrarily allocated people to various jobs. As a counterpart, there was virtually total job security. Nothing could happen to some- body's job, whether his work was satisfactory or not. The new system combines job placement by the labour departments with individuals finding jobs for themselves and individuals organising themselves on a voluntary basis to do the work they prefer. (The individual economy absorbed nearly half of the newly employed 20 million people, mostly youngsters, in the period 1978–1980.) Also the enterprises are now allowed to hire people directly.

With regard to the process of rationalisation of the labour relations in the enterprise, in 1978 Chairman Hua announced the disappearance of

---

* Referring to output, quality, variety, consumption of raw materials and energy resources, labour productivity, cost, profit and the rate of utilisation of circulating funds.

the Revolutionary Committees. From that moment onwards the enterprise was headed again by "the director under the unified leadership of the Party Committee". This conversion was announced both by the First and the Second Session of the Fifth National People's Congress. In most cases, this formal change stood only for a simple change of names.* Formally the "two-one-three system" is still operating, but in practice it is being phased out more and more. For example, in most enterprises the cadre participation in manual labour is made dependent on progress in the 'real' activities. Moreover, at present team discussions are minimised and, if possible, stripped of their political significance. The process of rationalisation is also illustrated by the practice of subdividing of the technical and economic norms among workshop, teams and individuals. Even the administrative and technical offices have their own targets to worry about. In the past, responsibility for the fulfilment of the eight state targets was placed entirely on the plant authorities. Now, those who fulfil or overfulfil their targets are rewarded, those who fail to do so get no reward, and those responsible for financial losses are penalised and their bonuses cancelled.

The reformers consider that the increase in the independence of the enterprises in fact means that more than in the past the workers and cadres can be 'masters in their own house'. Recently, on several occasions, there have been experiments with democratic methods of decision-making. First, this concerns the election of cadres by the workers. In Sichuan in 30 of the 100 enterprises participating in the experiments, the heads of the workshops and the leaders of the sections and teams were elected by the workers. In an exceptional case this also happened for the director. Two difficult problems have arisen, however. One concerns the cadres who have not been elected. Theoretically it is necessary to abandon the 'iron rice-bowl' concept according to which a cadre could only be promoted but not demoted. On the other hand, when a worker is elected a cadre, he is allowed to act as a cadre, but he will not receive the status of a cadre (Ren Tao, 1980, p. 215).

---

* For example, in the glassworks in Wuhu, which I visited in March 1979, all the members of the former Revolutionary Committee, including the chairman of the Party Committee (who was also the factory director), became members of the Party Committee.

Secondly, it concerns the workers' congress. At present the workers' congress plays only a limited role. For instance, it has no executive power over the main tasks of the enterprise nor has it the right to appoint, replace, award or punish the enterprise's leading members. In fact, it has only an advisory and supervisory right of raising criticisms and making suggestions. In some enterprises it has become a decision-making organ and deals with questions like the allocation of the enterprise bonus-share between collective welfare, individual bonuses and the improvement of production.

Thirdly, the mass movements have been reactivated. The Communist Youth League, the National Federation of Women, and especially the All-Chinese Federation of Trade Unions have responsibilities concerning welfare arrangements and personnel policies.

2. *Concentration and Co-operation*

In the last few years there have been experiments with new forms of concentration. At the end of 1978, for example, Beijing, Shanghai, Tianjin and Liaoning Province, the traditional economic centres, started to restructure their industries on a trial basis along the lines of specialisation and co-operation. Two more provinces, Sichuan and Jiangsu, joined the experiment the following year. The *Beijing Review* of April 7, 1980, provides some information about the restructuring of the machine-building industry in Beijing. The industry had 1283 plants, each belonging to a city district. The formerly universal plants have been transformed into specialised plants. Similar plants are joined in trusts, which in turn are subordinated to a specific municipal bureau. For instance, the 146 enterprises under the Bureau of Machine-Building formed 16 trusts, including an engineering machinery trust, a general machinery trust, a machine-tool trust, an electric machinery trust, etc.

Also some measures have been taken to integrate the processing industries of the traditional economic centres with the raw material producing enterprises. This takes several forms. Factories in industrially developed areas can provide technology, equipment and funds, in return for raw materials from raw material producing areas. Jointly run enterprises are created with investment by two geographically separated organisations, one providing technology and equipment, the other raw materials, labour and the site. There is also co-operation between technically advanced factories and technically less advanced factories. The former send technicians, the latter share resulting profits.

3.   The Banking System

In the past the enterprises needed permission from the central authorities in Beijing for every replacement and expansion investment. Once such permission was obtained, the Ministry of Finance provided the necessary funds as a grant. Since February 1979, decision-making about investment has been partly decentralised. For huge investment projects, the permission of Beijing is still necessary; for smaller projects only permission on a provincial level is required. To accompany this, in February 1979 the Bank of Construction and the Agricultural Bank were reorganised. In the 1960s both were integrated within the line organisation of the People's Bank. Currently they operate more or less as a 'department' of the Ministry of Finance. For huge projects they are an intermediary between the state and the enterprises; for the smaller projects they have specific decision-making authority (Worms, 1980, p. 177). With regard to circulating capital, all enterprises are obliged to keep an account with the People's Bank. All non-wage payments are transmitted through that account. In the past, at least the necessary initial capital was provided as a grant. At the present time, however, it is necessary to pay interest on it. For loans in excess of the quota, enterprises have to pay a higher rate of interest (7%) than for loans within the quota (4%) (Bennet, 1978, p. 141).

E.   CONSTRAINTS

There are three prerequisites for any successful economic reform, namely the reform must be embedded in a politically stable environment and the reform must be consistent, both in its micro aspect and in its macro aspect.

The first prerequisite for the success of an economic reform is that the reform is embedded in a politically stable and supportive environment. An in-depth, comprehensive reform that represents a sharp departure from the existing system requires a strong government and an equally strong bureaucratic apparatus which will have enough experience and confidence to prepare the proper grounds for the reform and enough patience to wait out an occasionally lengthy gestation period before the reform comes to fruition. These conditions were roughly fulfilled in Hungary, which explains the relative success of its economic reform compared with those in the other East European countries. The situation in China might be different. It is necessary to keep in mind that half of the current 38 million Party members joined the Party during the Cultural Revolution. Nowadays, they are permanently threatened by a political investigation. On the other hand, at present there is a continuous process of rehabilitation of old cadres who lost their positions during the Cultural Revolution. Of course, these two groups are opposed to each other, which irrevocably leads to personal animosity and the malfunctioning of many organisations. The history of the PRC has been marked not by political stability but by continuous political struggles. They are still continuing. A condition for political stability is 'socialist legality'. As a first step in this direction, a new Criminal Law was introduced in 1978. Furthermore, some participation of interest groups is necessary. For example, it is necessary to defuse working class opposition to price increases and labour mobility. In addition, participation can gradually overcome the feeling of being alienated, resulting in political disillusionment and apathy, crime and corruption. Such phenomena, which are widespread in present-day China, do not augur well for the reforms' chances of success. After all the political reversals of the last thirty years, there is less confidence in Marxism-Leninism and Mao Zedong thought. This is particularly true of the young people. Juvenile unemployment is enormous. This is caused partly by an illegal return to the cities of many youngsters who once were sent to the countryside as an outcome of the policy of *Shangshan Xiaxiang* (sending down). Also the increased criminality in the cities might be caused by the frustrations of those youngsters who cannot find a job, who have no accommodation of their own, who have difficulty in finding enough food and who are not allowed to marry. Recently, many of these people were sent to the reactivated 'reeducation through labour' camps without trial.* This clearly conflicts with the new criminal laws.

The problem of micro-economic consistency has been analysed by Wakar (1964, p. 621). He has pointed out that in any economic system the three elements of the stimulation system (the price system, the incentive system and the calculation system) have to form a harmonious whole. The various stimulation systems each have their own particular structure. For example, profit incentives require another method of price formulation and cost calculation than gross output incentives. The stimulation system should also form a consistent whole with the co-ordination mechanism. "To understand the role of this or that value relation (such as profit and prices), or this or that institution, it is necessary to know which ownership and allocation model it forms a part of" (quoted in Ellman, 1973, p. 107). These conditions are not met by the Chinese economic reform. That is admitted too. According to Lin Zili (1980, pp. 180–188), in the process of implementation of the economic reforms contradictions are bound to arise between the new economic relations and the old economic structure. For example, many enterprises complain that although they have more financial room for manoeuvre, they cannot get all the goods they need. The reason for this is that the state materials distribution departments and commercial agencies still have a big say in the supply of the means of production and the marketing of products. In order to make the profit rate an indicator of the overall work of an enterprise, working conditions have to be equalised as much as possible. To achieve this, the price structure has to be reconsidered: in the old price system the profit rates show too wide a dispersion. A price reform, however, strikes against provincial interests. For instance, an increase in the price of coal would benefit the province of Shanxi, but harm an industrial centre, such as Shanghai. On the other hand, the industrially developed provinces are favoured by the economic reform from the accumulation point of view. Because the less developed provinces are not yet able to accumulate sufficiently, they are pleading for a continuation of the central allocation of investment funds. The economic reform clearly shows the conflict—described by Kornai (1980)—between the conditions of economic efficiency and socialist ethical principles. The right of the enterprises to

---

* *Herald Tribune*, 3 June 1980.

attract or even dismiss labour at their own discretion conflicts with the principle of security, in this case job security. The actual situation is some kind of a compromise (see p. 225). In 1979, more than 100 enterprises in Beijing were closed down.★ These were enterprises which suffered losses over a long period because of poor management, too much consumption, or too much waste in their consumption of coke and raw materials. Unemployment in the cities, especially youth unemployment, has increased. The adverse effect of the readjustment policy on employment is countered only by stimulation of the private sector. At this moment in the Chinese press the question is discussed whether it would not be better to keep a part of the population (e.g. women) out of the labour force (Lin Zili, 1980, p. 193).

Successful economic reform requires macro-economic consistency, i.e. the macro-economic situation must be consistent with the reform's successful implementation. This implies, to use Kornai's (1972) terminology, that the central authorities pursue a policy of harmonious rather than rushed economic growth. Producer goods have to be readily available, otherwise the autonomy of enterprises is largely meaningless. With a tight balance some reshuffling of flows is unavoidable and previously signed contracts have to be abrogated (Keren, 1973, p. 571). Consumer goods have to be readily available, otherwise materials incentives are largely meaningless. Excessive investment and over-ambitious growth plans will maintain investment tension and the soft budget constraint render economic reform impossible. Considering China's macro-economic development from this standpoint, in 1979 the results were fair. Officially reported grain output (unhusked, including soybeans and potatoes, measured in grain equivalent) increased by 9% to 332 million tons and the industrial production increased by 8%. Industrial development was uneven. The energy sector lagged behind. Coal production increased by 2·8% and oil production by 2%. The process of adjustment, however, was slower than was expected. It is true, the share of agriculture and light industry in investment increased a little bit, but heavy industry still got the lion's share. Moreover, investment tension persisted. In 1979, only 9·7% of the projects under construction went into operation.† This imperfect adjustment was mainly caused by

---

★ *Beijing Review*, 4 August 1980.
† *Beijing Review*, 12 May 1980, p. 15.

a combination of insufficient control by the central authorities and the availability of funds and local desires to "build empires." Projects eliminated by the centre were continued, because the local authorities economised on other projects or supplied loans. According to the People's Daily, there are more than 30 channels through which financial resources may be obtained.* Kornai's (1980, Chapters 9 and 10) analysis of investment tension evidently applies as much to China as to Hungary.

The failure of light industry to increase its production quickly had serious effects. First, consumer goods production could not meet the increased purchasing power of the cities caused by the series of wage increases in 1978–80. The shortages of consumer goods were also increased by the use of part of the products of light industry for export. In order to give the people quick relief, the authorities eased the import control for goods brought in by overseas Chinese. (For a time, smuggling became easy and profitable for residents of Hong Kong and Macao.)† Secondly, in 1979 the government budget had a deficit (17 billion yuan on a total income of 110 billion yuan). Of course, the high military spending (the war with Vietnam) also had a big impact. This led to inflationary pressure which in 1979 resulted in an increase of state retail prices of 6%. Furthermore, some foodstuffs disappeared from state run shops and could often be found only at the new peasant free markets in the cities at high prices. The authorities tried to neutralise this floating purchasing power. On April 1 1979, they increased the interest rate on savings deposits from 2·7 to 3·3%. According to the authorities, the inflation was caused by 'profiteers', who had increased their prices in order to obtain more profit and bonuses. The authorities omitted to say that they themselves had created the conditions in which this could happen.

The economic picture of 1980 was roughly the same as that of 1979. The overall results were fair, but the readjustment process went slowly. The economy was still structurally unbalanced. Notwithstanding the bad weather, the overall grain output of 1980 was only 4·2% lower than the record harvest of 1979. However, a good or reasonable harvest overall is not enough to tide China over calamities in all provinces. In Hubei and Hebei provinces 43 million people have been affected by a

---

* *Financial Times*, 19 April 1980.
† *Far East Economic Review*, 27 July 1979, p. 24.

bad harvest resulting in a lowering of the grain rations. In the beginning of 1981 the Chinese government made an unprecedented appeal to the UN Disaster Relief Organization for help. The lower grain output of 1980 was also influenced by a new agriculture policy of sowing less acreage to grain, favouring the production of greater volume and variety of industrial and cash crops. In 1980, cash crops did well with a 23% rise in cotton and a 10% rise in sugar.

In 1980 industry did better (9% growth) than had been predicted at the Third Session (6% growth). Some progress had also been made with the readjustment policy: light industry increased by 18·4% and heavy industry by 1·4%. However, the energy sector lagged further behind: its output decreased by 2·9%. The unbalanced economy revealed itself again in the financial sphere. The budget deficit for 1980 turned out to be 12 billion yuan. This was below the 1979 deficit, but much more than the predicted budget deficit for 1980 of 8 billion yuan. Of this budget shortfall 63% was covered by printing new banknotes. This revelation was a shock. At the Third Session it was stated that the budget deficit would not threaten price stability, because the volume of currency in circulation had not been allowed to surge. According to official figures, average retail prices rose 6% in 1980 and for non-staple foodstuffs by as much as 13·8%. This time the officials did not blame the 'profiteers' but only themselves.

F. COUNTER-REFORMS

The outcomes of 1979 and 1980 made the February 1978 version of the 1976–85 plan completely worthless before the end of 1980. Therefore, at the Third Session it was announced that the Ten Year Plan had been scrapped in favour of a Five Year Plan for 1981–85, which could be incorporated into a new Ten Year Plan for 1981–90. This was a recognition of the fact that the state of imbalance in the national economy had not changed fundamentally. Especially the scale of capital construction had not been reduced as planned. Though the Central Government had already abandoned many of the plans announced by Chairman Hua at the First Session in 1978, provincial governments, basking in their new autonomy, declined to lower their sights. For 1980 as a whole provincial administrations spent two and one-half times their allotted capital construction budget (McDougall and Housego, 1981).

This was partly financed by a withholding of funds which should have been surrendered to the central government. A survey of Shanxi province at the end of 1980 found that out of 7049 enterprises liable to tax, 3180 had failed to surrender the tax due (Goodstadt, 1981, p. 74). It is clear that in this respect readjustment and restructuring were contradicting each other.

Shortly after the Third Session, fresh cutbacks of investment projects were announced. In October 1980 the proposed US-China Trade Center was cancelled. This was followed in December 1980 and January 1981 by the massive cancellation of Japanese and West German plant contracts for the Baoshan steel complex and the Nanjing chemical plant.

The continuing readjustment of China's national economy was decided at a working meeting of the Central Committee in December 1980 and made explicit at the Seventeenth Meeting of the Standing Committee of the Fifth National People's Congress (February 1981). At that meeting Deputy Premier Yao Yilin presented a new interim budget for 1981. Funds for capital construction were slashed and production targets for oil and coal were revised downward. At the same time, in order to keep the whole nation's finances and credit in balance, the management of the economy was centralised again.

The interim budget amount to a comprehensive revision of the budget presented to the Third Session in September 1980. First of all, some expenditures were savagely cut, especially capital construction and defence. The funds for capital construction were cut from about 50 billion yuan to about 36 billion yuan. Secondly, the budget deficit for 1981 is predicted to be about 5·3 billion yuan. The government will finance this deficit and a part of the 1980 deficit by issuing treasury bonds (4–5 billion yuan) and borrowing from the surpluses of local governments (around 8 billion yuan).* Third, in order to transfer resources from heavy industry to light industry (it should be noted that in the last quarter of 1980 total industrial output was actually lower than for the same period in 1979) (Goodstadt, 1981, p. 77) several production targets were revised downward. The steel production plan was reduced from 35 million to 33 million tons, oil from 106 to 100 million tons and coal from 350 million to 338 million tons.

---

* *Beijing Review*, 1981, No. 11, p. 18.

In order to make sure that the central readjustment policy would not be jeopardised by local initiative, from February 1981 onwards Beijing retreated (partly) from the financial and economic decentralisation adopted at the Second Session (June/July 1979). Not only would the number of enterprises involved with forms of decentralised decision-making not be expanded for the time being, but also their scope for autonomous decision-making was diminished. Eight fields of central-isation and unification were formulated.* Of course, one of the fields had to do with the decision-making about investments. All funds for capital construction were to be controlled by the State Planning Commission. The scale of construction and related investments in the provinces, autonomous regions and municipalities had to be examined by the State Planning Commission and approved by the State Council, and the capital construction of all ministries and commissions under the State Council had to be put under the unified management of the State Planning Commission. Moreover, the financial and taxation systems had to be centralised. From the viewpoint of centralisation, however, the most important measure was that all localities, departments and enterprises had to carry out fully plans for allocating important ma-terials, including important agricultural and sideline products and raw materials, which are prescribed by the state.

Characterising the described measures, it is clear that from Decem-ber 1980 onwards, readjustment is taken as the central task. Where the reforms contradict the readjustment, they have been postponed and put aside.

G. EVALUATION

The Chinese economic reforms, initiated at the end of 1978, are not unique. In the 1960s all state socialist countries experimented—with differing results—with comparable reforms. Considered theoretically, the Chinese discussions are simply a repetition of the East European and Soviet debates of the 1950s and 1960s. For example, the problem of commodity production and the law of value in socialism had been widely discussed, especially in Poland and the Soviet Union in the late

---

* *Beijing Review*, 1981, No. 11, p. 18.

fifties (Brus, 1973, Chapter 4). The concrete reforms of the planning system currently being advocated resemble very much the proposals of the Soviet reformers of the 1960s (Knaack, 1980, p. 405). In all countries experimenting with economic reform, the reform of the economic mechanism was accompanied by a policy of increasing the production of consumer goods and narrowing the gap between the growth of departments I and II.

Considered empirically, on the whole the first steps in economic reform in China are similar to those undertaken in Eastern Europe. An important difference, however, between for example Poland in the 1950s and China in the late 1970s, is the much lower level of economic development in the latter. At this moment, roughly 80% of China's population lives in the countryside. Therefore, compared with Eastern Europe, the success of any economic reform in China depends more heavily on the success of the agricultural reform, especially with respect to the emphasis on the individual economy. Also in China, on the eve of the economic reform, there was a greater reliance on administrative methods (e.g. the rationing of consumer goods, allocation of labour, strict control over residence and movement). Maoist China was more similar to the Soviet Union in 1940–56 or to England in World War II than to, say, Hungary in 1967. The introduction of a step-by-step reform in a hostile environment increases the chances of unexpected outcomes and of failure. Also China experimented before with an economic reform. In 1961, the central authorities launched an economic reform, called: "Readjustment, consolidation, filling out and raising standards." This meant cutting down over-ambitious targets in the plan and the magnitude of capital construction; consolidating the economic and technical foundations already in existence; strengthening the weak links in the national economy and exchanging the capacity of producing complete sets of equipment; increasing new varieties, raising the quality of products and striving for better economic results (Xue Muqiao, 1980, p. 19).

The reforms in East Europe, as in China, were reversed, not only for political reasons (China's economic reform of 1961 was reversed during the Cultural Revolution), but also for economic reasons (Brus, 1979, p. 263). For example, in Poland, contrary to what was intended, in the second half of 1958 investment increased sharply. This was caused by an increase of decentralised investment initiated by local enterprises under supervision of provinces, counties and towns, whose relative importance had greatly risen under the reform. This led to great imbalances, especially in the consumer goods markets, and produced inflationary pressures. Given these experiences, counter-reforms took place from 1959 onwards.

From a theoretical point of view, the experiences in East Europe and in post-Mao China followed basically the familiar economic and institutional cycle under state socialism as described, for example, by Nuti (1979, p. 256). The cycle works as follows. The measures of economic decentralisation do not go far enough. The hard budget constraint is not reintroduced. Hence the new system is not strong enough to overcome the built-in accumulation bias of the old system (it may even worsen it by relaxing central control). As a consequence, the economy remains in a state of strain and pressure on resources which does not give the economic decentralisation measures a chance to operate in a congenial environment: inflation and economic disruption are the result. The living standard of the population does not improve significantly, giving the opposition a weapon to end the decentralisation process. Central control, both economic and political, is tightened up again.

Finally we will deal with a last intriguing problem. The authorities claim that although the reform measures were slowed down, this did not indicate any change in orientation. On the contrary, it would provide the conditions for a renewed development of economic reforms. "Readjustment will create conditions for the national economy to develop in a better way. . . . A step backward today will mean greater advances in the days to come."*

Theoretically the Chinese authorities are right. Financial autonomy is meaningless when the real sphere is unable to provide the wanted goods. Indeed, economic reforms will end in failure when the financial and economic situation is not stable, when the macro-economic constraint is not fulfilled. This is not to say, however, that we can be sure that the moment the economy is balanced, the Chinese authorities will start again a new process of decentralising economic decision-making. The history of the economic reforms in the German Democratic Republic (GDR) might be illustrative in this respect. In the early 1963 the GDR was one of the first state socialist countries to draw conclusions for the shaping of its own economy from the Soviet Liberman discus-

---

* *Beijing Review*, 5 January 1981, p. 3.

sion in the summer and autumn of 1962. The New Economic System then introduced was an example of a comparatively profound economic reform, especially from the micro-economic consistency point of view. However, at the end of the 1960s the economy encountered difficulties. This was caused by Ulbricht's policy of accelerating economic growth, which caused imbalances (Keren, 1973, p. 581). Although the New Economic System was never officially denounced, at the end of 1970 and in 1971 the economy was centralised again (Leptin and Melzer, 1978, p. 98 onwards). Today the GDR is one of the most stable and prosperous economies of the CMEA countries. Although the need for a new economic reform can be argued again (Haase, 1980, p. 176). It will not, however, be implemented, mainly for political reasons.

Will this be the fate of the Chinese reforms too? The possibility for the Chinese economy to develop in a balanced and prosperous way will be determined to a great extent by the rate of development of agriculture and the energy sector and the possibility of forming a group of cadres capable of organising modern large-scale production. With respect to agriculture, it is already certain that the February 1978 400 million ton grain target for 1985 will not be met. This will affect industrial growth and employment unfavourably. This situation is eased a little bit because the rate of population growth has been reduced substantially. The immediate prospects of the energy sector too are not favourable. The major goals have been adjusted downwards. Therefore in order to obtain reasonable growth figures, it will be necessary to economise on the consumption of scarce resources. Hence, economic reforms, which have a positive effect on labour and capital productivity and the materials intensity of production are necessary from an economic point of view.

What are the political chances of a new economic reform in China in the future? Basically, this will be decided by the political élite. As in most state socialist countries—except Poland in 1956/7 and 1980/1—the reforms have been initiated from above. At this moment it is highly speculative to discuss the relative power of the different élite groups. More can be said about the support of the other social strata for a reform. According to Nove (1979, pp. 156–165), most of the strata in the Soviet Union were against the 1965 reform. What can be said about China? Certainly, the reform is in the interest of the managerial, technical and administrative personnel. No longer do they have to perform manual labour frequently and regularly. They can still be dismissed, but this no longer is seen as part of an ongoing class struggle. Security from arbitrary and unnerving political intimidation has increased (Andors, 1980, p. 53). The reform has negative aspects for the workers. The amount of supervision and control has increased. Also the stratification within the working class has increased, resulting in a more unequal distribution of income. The workers value job security highly. The transfer of surplus labour to where it is needed or the need to train or retrain as a consequence of the struggle for higher labour productivity might be inconsistent with this goal. These negative factors might be compensated by an increase of the standard of living. This is very important because since the Great Leap Forward the standard of living, especially in the cities, has hardly improved.* The position of the cadres is ambiguous too. The local officials dislike the reform, because a strengthening of the intermanagerial ties by co-operation will cross all kinds of regional boundaries. Only one-third of the cadres have technical or economical training. That means that the present emphasis on the use of economic criteria for management will have a negative impact on the position of a majority of the cadres, who already are under the threat of political investigations. On the other hand, the present leadership seems to favour a normal career for cadres. Maybe 'Socialist Legality' can end the situation in which most cadres, sooner or later, are 'unmasked'. On the whole there might be a slumbering conflict between economic liberalism and the supremacy of the Party apparatus.

This conflict will arise once more the moment the economy is balanced again. What will be the outcome? We know for sure that in the other state socialist countries the reforms, once abolished, never returned. On the other hand, the political situation in China is rather unique. The leadership of today is not the heir of orthodoxy, but the victim of orthodoxy which makes their claim more reliable that the current emphasis on readjustment is only temporary. What is clear is that the evolution of the Chinese economic mechanism depends, *inter alia*, on the future course of political events.

---

* According to Wu Zhengkun, *Beijing Review*, 23 March 1981, p. 16, the real wages of workers and staff members in units owned by the whole people in 1978 were 4·46% less as compared with 1957. We have to bear in mind, however, that in 1957 each worker supported 3·2 persons as against 1·8 persons in 1980. This reflects a higher rate of female participation in 1980 as compared with 1957. Therefore, the increase in the *per capita* income of workers' families from 186 yuan in 1957 to 395 yuan in 1980 has been made possible by doubling the daily tasks of women.

H.   CONCLUSION

Economic policy in the post-Mao period was characterised by sharp fluctuations. During the first Session of the Fifth National People's Congress, Chairman Hua unveiled a very ambitious program for the next eight years of the Ten Year Plan 1976–85. Given the fact that in those periods in which the Maoist policies dominated, industrial production collapsed, it was believed that the moment the planning system was freed from the Maoist alternative, the economy would recover automatically. The expected boom did not materialise. Logically enough, the idea developed that the source of the economic problems might be the economic system itself.

The theoretical criticisms of the economic system centred on the problems of the planning system, the sectoral development model (the share of investment in the national income and the sectoral allocation of investment), material incentives, enterprise democracy, and state ownership.

From October 1978 onwards in a great number of enterprises experiments were conducted with forms of autonomy. This had to do with the creation of a profit-sharing arrangement, the notion that enterprises develop some initiative with respect to the production and marketing of their products, the rationalisation of labour relations and experimentation with democratic methods of decision-making. In the new relationship between the state and the enterprises the role of the banking system was increased. The Bank of Construction and the Agricultural Bank obtained new significance in the economy. In order to obtain more specialisation and co-operation, trusts were formed and some processing industries were integrated in different ways with the raw material producing enterprises. Attempts were made to restore equilibrium to the unbalanced sectoral development.

The results of the economic reforms were mixed. The position of agriculture seems to have improved. The position of the workers, however, was ambiguous. Money wages increased, but the amount of supervision and control increased too. Furthermore the system of job security was threatened. The position of the majority of the cadres was worsened by the reform too. The readjustment went slower than was planned for: there were serious inflation and unemployment problems. These were mainly caused by the non-fulfilment of the prerequisites for the success of every economic reform, especially the prerequisite of macro-economic consistency. Therefore, in order to balance the economy from February 1981 onwards, counter-reforms took place.

The leadership claims, however, that the current emphasis on readjustment is only temporary. The reliability of that claim depends on the success of the agricultural reform and the outcome of the slumbering conflict between economic liberalism and the supremacy of the Party bureaucrats.

XV.   *ODNOWA* IN STATISTICS*

An important aspect of the *odnowa* (renewal) movement which swept through Poland in 1980–81 is the improvement in official statistics to which it has led and is leading. Under strong social pressure, notably from the trade union Solidarity, it has been officially accepted that in the past official statistics often gave too favourable a picture of the economic situation. In an article published in January 1981 the former President of the Central Statistical Office gave a number of cases where the government had deliberately falsified figures to mislead the public. They included exaggerating the number of dwellings completed in a year by including also in it dwellings expected to be completed in the first quarter of the following year, deliberately giving a lower figure for investment than the actual investment costs, or falsely publishing a higher figure for coal exports in a year than actually exported in the year by also including exports in January of the following year.†

A working group of the Central Statistical Office is preparing proposals for improvement and the May 1981 number of the journal of the Central Statistical Office printed ten papers on this subject. T. Walczak, the vice-president of the Central Statistical Office distinguished three sources of statistical error. They were deliberate falsification of the figures, enforced from outside the Central Statistical Office; problems in the reporting system; and methodological difficulties.‡ The first fruits of the new statistical candour can be found in the 1981 edition of

* Originally published in *Soviet Studies*, January 1982. We are grateful to W. Brus, M. Kaser, R. Ramer and K. E. Wädekin for helpful comments on, and discussion of, an earlier version.
† S. Kuzinski, "Prawdy i nieprawdy o statystyce", *Polityka*, no. 3, 17 January 1981.
‡ *Wiadomosci Statystyczne*, vol. 25, no. 5, May 1981, pp. 1–5.

the concise statistical handbook (*Maly rocznik statystyczny*, Warsaw, 1981). Interesting and useful novelties in it include data on work conditions (e.g. industrial fatalities), the cost of living by social groups, investment efficiency, meat distribution, internal exports, the money stock, and employment and wages in the state and judicial apparatus.

Data on work conditions are given in three tables (pp. 52–53): one of them is set out in Table XV.1.

Table XV.1
Work accidents in socialised sector

		In absolute numbers		
	Total	*Fatalities*	*Causing inability to work*	
				more then 28
			4–28 days	*days*
1970		176 544	1 282	118 380	56 882
1975		213 062	1 307	142 189	69 566
1978		196 526	1 408	129 375	65 743
1979		194 806	1 463	127 241	66 102
of which (in 1979)					
Industry		104 383	572	70 098	33 713
Construction		23 962	257	14 439	9 266
Agriculture		15 434	126	9 345	5 963
Forestry		3 065	39	1 820	1 206
Transport and communications		17 337	263	10 684	6 390
Trade		13 482	66	9 222	4 194
Public services		5 294	54	3 394	1 846
		Per thousand persons employed			
1970		17·42	0·13	11·68	5·61
1975		17·49	0·11	11·67	5·71
1978		15·72	0·11	10·35	5·26
1979		15·60	0·12	10·19	5·29
of which (in 1979)					
Industry		21·00	0·12	14·10	6·78
Construction		18·16	0·20	10·94	7·02
Agriculture		16·89	0·13	10·23	6·53
Forestry		21·75	0·28	12·92	8·55
Transport and communications		15·54	0·23	9·58	5·73
Trade		11·92	0·06	8·15	3·71
Public services		13·79	0·04	8·84	4·91

Source: *Maly rocznik statystyczny 1981*, Warsaw, 1981, p. 53.

Table XV.1 shows that, measured in fatalities per thousand persons employed, the Polish socialised sector became safer in the early 1970s and marginally less safe in the late 1970s. Curiously, with the classification used in the handbook (in which mining is included with manufacturing in industry), the most dangerous sector is forestry. Perhaps future publications will distinguish between coal mining, other mining and quarrying, and manufacturing. By international standards, measuring in terms of fatalities per thousand persons employed and relying on the statistics published in the ILO *1980 Yearbook of Labour Statistics* (chapter 7), the Polish economy appears to be less safe than a very safe country such as the UK, but much more safe than a high risk country such as Turkey. Data similar to those in Table XV.1 were published in the statistical annuals for 1970 and 1971, but thereafter publication of data on this sensitive topic ceased. The data published in the 1970 and 1971 annuals were actually better than those in the 1981 concise handbook, since the former also gave a breakdown of industry into sectors and in addition gave data on the causes of the accidents.

Cost of living indices by social group are set out in Table XV.2. The type of data presented in Table XV.2 is in principle interesting both analytically and for policy purposes. Analytically, they make it obvious that food price increases (largely absent in the early 1970s but present in 1980) bear disproportionately heavily on pensioners. From a policy point of view the data direct attention to the need for money income increases in compensation for food price increases to be differentiated by socio-economic group. Unfortunately, the shortages and repressed inflation in Poland which characterised both years make the meaning of the data in Table XV.2 problematic.

Some important information on investment efficiency is set out in Table XV.3 Table XV.3 shows vividly the bad and worsening situation in the late 1970s with respect to the efficiency of the implementation of investment projects. Comparing 1980 with 1975, although the value of investment projects completed fell sharply, the cumulative cost of uncompleted projects rose enormously and there was a large increase in the estimated cost of completing projects already started. At the end of 1980 the cost of completing all the projects already started was almost six times the value of the projects actually finished in 1980. These future commitments were in excess of half the net material product.

In view of the crucial importance of meat in present day Poland, it is

Table XV.2
Cost of living by social groups

	1975 (1970 = 100)	1980 (1979 = 100)
Employee households	112·6	109·1
of whom		
full time employees	112·6	109·1
worker-peasants	112·7	108·7
Peasant households	112·3	108·2
Pensioners and recipients of transfer payments	108·4	110·0

Source: *Maly rocznik statystyczny*, p. 71.

Table XV.3
Investment in the socialised sector
(milliards of zlotys, current prices, stocks at 31 December)

	1975	1979	1980
Past, present and anticipated future expenditure on investments in progress during year	1352·3	2199·7	2258·0
of which			
started in same year	393·8	378·2	224·0
Investment projects completed	276·9	348·3	220·0
Cumulative cost of investment projects under construction or not yet in operation	360·7	664·8	788·0
of which			
machinery	27·2	45·3	53·2
imports	17·6	31·8	32·6
Anticipated expenditure to complete already started projects	714·7	1186·6	1250·0

Source: *Maly rocznik statystyczny*, p. 89.

Table XV.4
Production and distribution of meat, fat and offal

	Thousands of tonnes				Per person (kg)		
	1970	1975	1979	1980	1970	1975	1980
Output of living animals for slaughter, in meat equivalent	2186·7	3067·0	3264·5	3147·0	67·2	90·1	88·5
Live exports, in meat equivalent	19·0	22·1	77·2	68·6	0·6	0·6	1·9

Table XV.4 – *cont.*

| | Thousands of tonnes | | | | Per person (kg) | | |
	1970	1975	1979	1980	1970	1975	1980
Balancing item	52·7	86·5	14·6	8·7	1·6	2·5	0·3
Slaughterings (meat, fat and offal)	2115·0	2958·4	3172·7	3069·7	65·0	87·0	86·3
of which							
by industry	1480·3	2476·2	2720·3	2608·5	45·5	72·8	73·3
by households	634·7	482·2	452·4	461·2	19·5	14·2	13·0
Loss of weight due to cooling	34·2	42·2	42·3	40·3	1·0	1·2	1·1
Production (i.e. slaughterings less loss)	2080·8	2916·2	3130·4	3029·4	64·0	85·7	85·2
of which							
meat	1698·6	2405·5	2622·4	2560·4	52·2	70·7	72·0
of which							
beef	412·2	593·7	655·6	626·9	12·7	17·5	17·6
pigmeat	1033·8	1461·5	1470·7	1417·0	31·8	43·0	39·8
poultry	115·2	234·8	396·7	419·3	3·5	6·9	11·8
other	137·4	115·5	99·4	97·2	4·2	3·4	2·8
offal	142·3	177·2	183·5	176·3	4·4	5·2	5·0
fat	239·9	333·5	324·5	292·7	7·4	9·8	8·2
Additional fat after slaughtering	36·2	41·5	36·9	34·0	1·1	1·2	0·9
Losses in slaughter and processing	63·1	136·9	121·7	111·6	1·9	4·0	3·1
of which							
fat intended for industrial purposes	34·3	86·9	64·4	51·8	1·1	2·6	1·5
meat lost in processing	7·8	12·4	18·4	18·1	0·2	0·4	0·5
Exports	148·1	220·4	191·1	180·1	4·6	6·5	5·1
Imports	77·3	15·5	9·1	60·3	2·4	0·5	1·7
Stockbuilding (+ is a decrease − is an increase)	+7·1	+56·0	+2·6	+89·8	+0·2	+1·6	+2·5
Consumption (meat, fat and offal)	1990·2	2671·9	2866·2	2921·8	61·2	78·5	82·1
of which							
meat and offal	1724·4	2393·3	2574·4	2633·6	53·0	70·3	74·0
from state supplies	1175·4	1963·8	2171·5	2220·7	36·1	57·7	62·4
from household slaughterings	549·0	429·5	402·9	412·9	16·9	12·6	11·6
of which							
meat	1583·6	2224·7	2395·0	2461·2	48·7	65·4	69·2
of which							
beef	410·0	527·5	604·4	666·4	12·6	15·5	18·7
pigmeat	950·9	1389·8	1339·3	1319·8	29·2	40·9	37·1
poultry	112·5	212·9	379·9	399·8	3·5	6·3	11·2
other	110·2	94·5	71·4	75·2	3·4	2·8	2·2
offal	140·8	168·6	179·4	172·4	4·3	5·0	4·8
slaughter fat	265·8	278·6	291·8	288·2	8·2	8·2	8·1
of which							
from state supplies	181·2	228·4	244·8	242·7	5·6	6·7	6·8
from household slaughterings	84·6	50·2	47·0	45·5	2·6	1·5	1·3

Source: *Mały rocznik statystyczny*, pp. 153, 154 and 23.

understandable to find detailed information on its use in the handbook, and this is set out in Table XV.4.

Table XV.4 shows that Poland was a meat exporting country throughout this period, exporting both live animals and meat. It also shows that meat consumption *per capita* increased significantly in the period 1970–80 (from 48·7 kg in 1970 to 69·2 kg in 1980). Most of this increase in consumption took place in the first half of the 1970s. Indeed, if only beef and pigmeat is considered, *per capita* meat consumption actually fell in 1975–80. In 1975–80 the *per capita* production and consumption of pigmeat fell. In the 1970s there was a significant decline in household slaughterings. The *per capita* consumption of poultry increased rapidly in 1970–80. The table also shows (and this is the main new information in it) that the commonly quoted figures for Polish meat consumption *per capita* (53·0 kg in 1970 and 74·0 kg in 1980) are too high since they include offal. This seems to be the first time in official statistics that offal has been subtracted from meat. From Table XV.4 it can also be seen that a significant (but declining) proportion of Poland's meat consumption comes from animals slaughtered by households. It is unclear how accurate the data on this are.

In Table XV.5 some data are set out on 'internal exports' (i.e. domestic sales by the state for hard currency).

Table XV.5
Internal exports (million US dollars, current prices)

	Total			of which, imports		
	1975	1979	1980	1975	1979	1980
Total	169·8	329·4	455·7	63·6	122·1	183·6
of which						
Food	6·1	11·1	15·7	4·4	7·5	14·4
Alcoholic drinks	23·5	87·2	100·6	4·1	12·3	14·9
Clothing materials	26·5	23·7	28·9	16·9	8·3	14·6
Clothes	25·0	54·1	90·0	21·3	48·9	84·2
Cars and spare parts	62·5	98·7	152·7	—	13·1	18·8
Machinery and agricultural equipment	2·4	7·6	11·6	—	—	—
Construction materials	4·2	4·8	8·8	—	—	—

Source: *Maly rocznik statystyczny*, p. 202.

Table XV.5 gives precise data on a system of queue jumping (for example for domestically produced cars) organised by the authorities for those fortunate enough to have hard currency. A similar table was published in the 1976 edition of the handbook, but only in zlotys. Using the end-1980 black market exchange rate, in 1980 the internal exports included in Table XV.5 had a value of roughly 7% of total state retail trade. In each year, there is a discrepancy between the items specified in Table XV.5 and the total given in the table. It may be that this difference is accounted for by flats, the hard currency sale of which is known to be significant.* Alternatively, it may be that the discrepancy consists of sundry minor items and that flats are altogether excluded from Table XV.5.

Under conditions of severe repressed inflation and rising open inflation, data on the money stock in the hands of the population are obviously important, and these are set out in Table XV.6.

Table XV.6
Stock of money in hands of the population
(milliards of zlotys at 31 December)

	1960	1970	1975	1979	1980
TOTAL	41·3	170·9	435·0	674·6	765·7
of which					
Savings deposits	16·2	114·8	302·8	456·6	492·8
Current accounts	—	2·6	4·4	6·	6·9
Cash	25·1	53·5	127·7	211·0	266·0
Ratio of total money stock in hands of the population to personal incomes	0·16	0·33	0·45	0·46	0·47
Ratio of cash to personal incomes	0·09	0·10	0·13	0·14	0·16

Sources: *Maly rocznik statystyczny*, pp. 274 and 64; *Rocznik Statystyczny 1970*, Warsaw, 1970, p. 79.

Table XV.6 shows clearly the rapid increase in 1960–80 in the money stock in the hands of the population, both absolutely and relative to personal incomes. The main relative increase was in 1960–75. It also shows how, since 1970, the cash element has risen both relative to personal incomes and to the total money stock in the hands of the population. Table XV.6 understates the liquidity of the population since it excludes notes and bank deposits in hard currency.

In response to demands for details of the pay and perks of officials in the state and repressive apparatus, the handbook contains information

---

* W. Brus, "Na marginesie 'Uwag o sytaucji gospodarczej kraju'". *Aneks*, no. 20, 1979, p. 45.

about employment and wages in the state administration and judicial apparatus (p. 284). Since the table does not distinguish between high officials and humble clerks and janitors, has no information about non-monetary perks, and excludes the police and state security organs (this may explain the discrepancy between the data on p. 284 and those on p. 40), it is a very half-hearted response.

Publication by the central statistical authorities of more of the data which they already have available, as was done in the 1981 concise statistical handbook, is only part of the long and difficult task of improving the quality of published economic statistics. It is also necessary to alter the old planning and management system. This created a situation in which economic units were economically motivated to distort the data they provided to the statistical agencies and there were no really independent agencies gathering their own data or checking the data gathered by the state organs.

CONCLUSION

As part of the renewal process in contemporary Poland, the authorities have recognised, under pressure from the independent trade union Solidarity, that in the past the state sometimes published false statistics to mislead the public about the economic situation. In addition, the authorities have commenced the publication of additional statistics on a number of topics, ranging from industrial accidents via investment efficiency to the production and distribution of meat, which provide important new information about economic and social developments in Poland. This is a useful part of the wider process of improving the quality of Polish economic statistics.

CAPITALISM

XVI. NATURAL GAS, RESTRUCTURING AND RE-INDUSTRIALISATION: THE DUTCH EXPERIENCE OF INDUSTRIAL POLICY*

A. INTRODUCTION

The Netherlands is a small, densely populated, highly developed country, dependent on foreign trade, with one of the highest living standards and best developed welfare states in the whole world. Its Gross National product (GNP) per head of the population is among the twenty highest in the world and its social indicators are also among the best in the world. According to *World Tables 1976* (World Bank, 1976, p. 496), its *per capita* GNP—in a list which includes countries such as Kuwait, United Arab Emirates and Qatar—was the sixteenth highest in the world. Its 1970 death rate for children from 1 to 4 was bettered by only three countries—Sweden, Iceland and Finland—in the whole world and was only 1/14 of that in Mexico (World Bank, 1976, p. 521). Intolerance, chauvinism and authoritarianism are all conspicuous by their absence. Its traditional tolerance towards minorities, openness to the outside world and very small penalties for infringing the laws, are all noteworthy. It is a member of Benelux, the EEC, NATO and the UN,

* Originally published as chapter 6 of T. Barker and V. Brailovsky (eds) (1981), *Oil or Industry?* Academic Press, London and New York. This book was based on the proceedings of a conference held in Oaxaca, Mexico in 1980. The author is grateful to J. van der Meulen, J. de Beus and the participants in the Oaxaca conference, for helpful comments and discussion.

and sympathetic to the needs of the South in South–North dialogues. Its most populous city, Amsterdam, can reasonably claim to be the birthplace of capitalism. Its second most populous city, Rotterdam, is one the world's great ports. It is also the home of a number of giant multinationals. It is a former imperial power, and the experiences of its former colonies, such as Surinam, South Africa and Indonesia, are examples of the seamy side of European imperialism. Plantation slavery, racialism and ruthless exploitation were important features of Dutch colonialism.

B.   ECONOMIC STRUCTURE

The Netherlands is a country in which most of the working population is engaged in services. Although the country is a net agricultural exporter (and a beneficiary of the EEC's Common Agricultural Policy), the proportion of the working population in agriculture is very small, and the proportion in the secondary sector has been falling steadily since the mid-1960s. Some relevant data are set out in Table XVI.1.

Table XVI.1 shows a number of important things. Firstly, in the past

Table XVI.1
The sectoral distribution of the Dutch labour force 1849–1977

Year	Total labour force (thousands)	Primary sector (%)	Secondary sector (including construction and utilities) (%)	Tertiary sector (including Government) (%)	Per capita income (1963 = 100)
1849	c.1100	44	26	30	c. 20
1859	c.1200	38·3	28·9	32·8	c. 22
1889	1653	31·8	32·2	36·0	32
1909	2259	28·4	32·7	37·9	50
1920	2719	23·5	35·7	39·7	50
1930	3179	20·6	36·5	41·8	64
1947	3866	19·3	36·9	42·4	59
1965	4502	8·6	41·9	49·5	105
1977	4658	6·2	32·4	61·1	160

Source: *Sectorstructuurbeleid: Mogelijkheden en beperkingen*, Wetenschappelijke Raad voor het Regeringsbeleid, The Hague, 1980, p. 52.

130 years the Netherlands has experienced a major process of de-agriculturalisation. Whereas 130 years ago almost half the labour force was engaged in agriculture, today only about 1/20 is engaged in this sector. This decline has resulted from the increase in the availability of jobs in other sectors and the steady mechanisation of agriculture.

Nevertheless, the Netherlands, like the USA, Canada, Australia, New Zealand and Denmark, is an advanced agricultural *exporting* country. It imports grain and exports livestock products and flowers. The latter are also exported indirectly via the tourists who come to watch them growing in the fields. De-agriculturalisation has brought only benefits to the country. It has reduced the amount of back-breaking manual labour that has to be done, allowed the labour force to work in more attractive occupations, and not been at the expense of the balance of payments. The country has an efficient agricultural, food-processing and food distribution sector, adequate for its needs.

Secondly, it has experienced a continuous process of serviceisation. The tertiary sector, which already in the middle of the nineteenth century employed almost one third of the labour force, now employs almost two thirds. In part this is a general trend in economic development, which has been much discussed by Colin Clark and others. In part it has particularly Dutch features deriving from the country's location and its welfare state.

The Netherlands is situated on the mouth of the Rhine and on the edge of the North Sea. It has easy river communications with Germany and easy sea communications with England, France and Scandinavia. Since the seventeenth century (the 'Golden Age' of the Netherlands) it has been a major trading country. In the seventeenth century, trade with the Baltic was of exceptional importance for the Dutch economy. Today trade with the other EEC countries is enormously important. For centuries the commercial service sector has been a major positive contributor to the balance of payments. Today the port of Rotterdam, the airport at Schiphol and the shipping companies, airlines, trading companies, construction firms, banks and insurance companies are major sources of foreign exchange earnings.

The expansion of the Dutch welfare state has led to a major expansion of employment in education, medical care, social services and government. The high standards of education, medical care, recreational and cultural facilities and public transport and the virtual absence of poverty are important consequences.

Thirdly, the country has experienced two major phases of industrialisation, in 1859–1920 and in 1947–65, but since 1965 has experienced rapid de-industrialisation. Nevertheless, incomes and employment have continued to rise, the former rapidly and the latter slowly.
This de-industrialisation is not just relative but also absolute, as Table
XVI.2 makes clear. In the fifteen years 1965 to 1980 industrial employment fell by about 30% and this trend is still continuing.

C.   THE ENERGY BALANCE

In the late 1950s a very large deposit of natural gas was discovered in the
north of the country. Development began in 1963. Since then some
small additional deposits of gas have been found, both onshore and

Table XVI.2

Number of employees in industry (annual average in millions of man years)

1963	1965	1966	1968	1970	1976	1977	1978	1979	1980[a]
1·2	1·33	1·23	1·20	1·20	1·04	1·02	0·98	0·96	0·94

Due to classification changes the figures are not fully comparable.
[a] Estimate
Source: For 1965, 1970, 1976 and 1977 the 1979 edition of *Statistisch zakboek*, The
Hague, for 1963, 1966 and 1968 the 1969 edition, and for 1978, 1979 and 1980 *Centraal
Economisch Plan 1980*, The Hague, 1980, p. 153.

Table XVI.3

Dutch net international trade in energy

Year	Millions of tonnes of oil equivalent	Billions of current guilders
1974	4·7	−2·5
1975	14·4	−0·6
1976	12·7	−1·1
1977	13·2	0·4
1978	6·6	0·3
1979	4·3	−1·2
1985	−13·6[a]	not available
2000	−87·7[a]	not available

[a] Estimate.
Sources: *Centraal Economisch Plan 1980*, The Hague, 1980,
p. 70; *Nederland na de Gasbel*, SMO, Scheveningen, 1979,
p. 32.

offshore. During the 1970s the country became a significant natural gas exporter (Ellman, 1977). In 1976, which was the peak year for natural gas exports in physical terms, they were about 51 billion cubic metres or about 44 million tonnes of oil equivalent (toe). A country which had been a traditional energy *importer* became an energy *exporter*. Some data are set out in Table XVI.3.

Measured in physical terms the country was a net energy exporter (although minor by international standards) in the mid-1970s but soon rapidly reverted to being a net importer. Measured in prices, the country was never really a significant net energy exporter but its natural gas exports did protect its balance of payments in the 1970s from the adverse swing in the terms of trade experienced by energy-importing countries. The reason why the Netherlands was a net energy exporter when measured in toe in all the years 1974–79, but a net energy importer when measured in prices in four of those six years, was because the price of natural gas relative to oil was less favourable than the coefficients used to convert natural gas to toe.

Table XVI.3 summarises a situation in which natural gas exports, although they peaked in 1976 in physical terms, will remain significant throughout the 1980s but will be increasingly outweighed by coal and especially oil imports. This is shown in more detail in Table XVI.4.

Table XVI.4
Dutch international trade in energy, by fuel (millions of toe)

Fuel	1977			1985			2000		
	Exports	*Imports*	*Balance*	*Exports*	*Imports*	*Balance*	*Exports*	*Imports*	*Balance*
Coal	0·5	4·0	−3·5	0·5	7·6	−7·1	0·5	20·7	−20·2
Oil	44·1	68·0	−23·9	52·3	87·8	−35·5	87·5	144·4	−56·9
Gas	40·8	0·3	40·5	35·4	6·4	29·0	0·0	7·6	−7·6
total	85·4	72·3	13·1	88·2	101·8	−13·6	88·0	172·7	−84·7

Source: *Nederland na de Gasbel*, SMO, Scheveningen, 1979, p. 32.

D. ECONOMIC EFFECTS OF NATURAL GAS EXPORTS

The initial impact of cheap domestic energy production on the economy seemed wholly favourable. It removed the balance of payments constraint and provided abundant cheap energy. Both these factors had a favourable impact on the growth of the economy in the late 1960s and early 1970s. In this period the Netherlands had one of the highest growth rates in Western Europe, with rising investment, large real wage increases and a high increase in labour productivity. More generally, domestic energy riches increased the country's freedom of action in domestic economic policy and in foreign policy. Nevertheless, increased output, higher prices, and a longer time span have shown that these domestic energy riches also have a negative side. In the long run the four main domestic effects of Dutch natural gas production have been on:

(1) the income of the state budget,
(2) the balance of payments,
(3) the exchange rate and
(4) the structure of the economy.

There has also been a significant external effect. Exports to the Netherlands have had a useful positive effect on output and employment in the other EEC countries, Japan and the newly industrialising countries.

1. *Income of the State Budget*

During the 1970s the income derived by the state, in effect rent, from the production of natural gas, became a significant contribution to the state budget. Of the net receipts from the sale, both external and internal, the state derives about 80% and the oil companies which found the gas (Shell and Exxon in the case of the huge onshore deposit) the balance. For an account of the various channels through which the state share is derived see Koops *et al.* (1978, p. 394). Some data on the significance of this source of revenue are set out in Table XVI.5.

Table XVI.5 shows clearly that since the oil and gas price explosion of 1973/4 state revenues from gas have risen sharply and are now a very significant income item in the state budget. This new source of income is one of the factors which has permitted the growth of public expenditures, notably transfer payments. The share of central and local government and social security expenditures in the national income has risen from 34% in 1964 to 50% in 1979, with a particularly steep rise (from 42% to 48%) in 1973–75. In 1979 the number of those whose income came from transfer payments was 79% of the number whose income came from the market sector.

Table XVI.5.
Natural gas and the state budget

Year	Central government income from natural gas sales	
	as % of the total income of the central government	as % of the national income
1974	4·4	1·4
1975	8·6	2·8
1976	11·0	3·6
1977	11·0	3·8
1978	9·9	3·4
1979	8·8	3·1
1980	11·3	4·2
1981	14·5	5·5

Source: *Miljoenennota 1981*, The Hague, 1980, p. 20.

The declining gas output (it peaked in 1976), combined with low economic growth, the substantial public sector deficit (currently about 7% of the national income), the decline of the market sector (employment in which fell on average 1·25% per annum in 1972–78), the volume and indexing of transfer payments, a well organised labour force, and an independent-minded Central Bank determined not to permit monetary financing of the budget, together make the outlook for the state budget bleak. Substantial government revenues from natural gas will continue to accrue throughout the 1980s. As exports fall (in physical terms) and prices rise, however, they will increasingly have the character of an indirect tax which impoverishes the domestic population, rather than a rent deriving from low production costs and largely paid by foreign consumers.

2.   Balance of Payments

In the late 1960s and early 1970s the rapid growth of domestic energy production relaxed the balance of payments constraint and hence stimulated economic growth. During the mid-1970s, the balance of payments on current account seemed to be in structural surplus. In 1977 the present author rashly referred to the "permanent current account surplus" (Ellman, 1977, p. 282). In fact the surplus only lasted from 1972 to 1977, and both in 1978 and 1979 the current account was in deficit. The contribution of natural gas exports and import substitution

Table XVI.6

Natural gas and the balance of payments on current account (in current prices)

Year	Current account balance		Direct effect of natural gas exports and import substitution	
	billions of guilders	% of net national income	billions of guilders	% of net national income
1970	−1·7	−1·6	1·5	1·4
1971	−0·4	−0·3	2·3	1·9
1972	4·3	3·2	2·7	2·0
1973	6·7	4·3	3·7	2·4
1974	6·0	3·4	8·9	5·1
1975	5·2	2·7	10·6	5·6
1976	7·6	3·5	12·9	6·0
1977	2·3	1·0	14·1	5·9
1978	−1·9	−0·8	12·6	4·9
1979	−4·0	−1·5	14·6	5·3

Source: *Rapport over het Nederlandse concurrentievermogen*, CED, SER, The Hague, 1980, mimeo version, p. 2.

to the balance of payments in the 1970s was very substantial. Some data are set out in Table XVI.6.

The substantial current account surplus of the mid-1970s was used for overseas investment. The Netherlands is, for example, one of the largest overseas investors in the USA. Such investments were encouraged by the Central Bank in order to provide income when the gas exports declined and to prevent excessive appreciation of the currency. As far as the return on such investments is concerned, up till now it is probable that the average rate of return has been less than that which would have been achieved by leaving the gas in the ground. As far as preventing excessive appreciation is concerned, Brouwer (1979, p. 299) has argued on the basis of the Dutch experience that capital exports are not an effective method for preventing appreciation. There seems, for the Netherlands in the 1970s, to have been little connection between the basic balance (current account + capital account) and the exchange rate, but a much stronger link between the current account alone and the exchange rate. Nevertheless, from a long-term point of view, transforming the gas into overseas assets was better than transforming it into competitive imports (which would have reduced employment and reduced income in the future) or domestic consumption (which could not have been sustained and hence would have generated future inflation and unemployment).

In 1976, when the natural gas effect reached a peak as a percentage of the national income (although this may be exceeded in 1980 and 1981 due to sharp price increases), it amounted to about 13% of total visible exports and almost a quarter of manufactured exports. This substantial source of extra purchasing power over foreign goods brought with it two direct dangers. They concerned its effect on imports and on what would happen when it began to decline. The extra income generated by the natural gas sector, in a small open economy such as the Dutch, generated substantial extra imports. These extra imports are generally reckoned to be about one half to two-thirds of the direct effect of the natural gas. In so far as these imports consisted of competitive imports which replaced domestic production, they reduced employment and future income. Furthermore, now that the volume of gas exports is declining, there is a structural adverse shift in the balance of payments (from energy exporter to importer). This was underlined in a gloomy 1980 report on *Dutch Competitiveness* by the Government's Council of Economic Experts. This worsening of the balance of payments position is an important reason why average real incomes are expected to fall in 1980, after many years of steady increases. The prospects for real income growth in the 1980s are poor, since substantial resources will be required to offset the worsening of the energy balance.

3.   *Exchange Rate*

During the 1970s the guilder, which is closely linked to the German mark both informally and formally in the snake and the EMS, was a strong currency. In 1970–79 it appreciated relative to all currencies except the Swiss franc and the German mark. Some data are set out in Table XVI.7.

The effect of the appreciation of the guilder, combined with the modest increase in domestic money wages and the increasing cost of the social security system, has been to raise costs relative to those of other countries, squeeze profits in exporting and import-competing sectors, stimulate imports and discourage employment in internationally competitive sectors, and impose rapid structural change on the economy (one aspect of which is de-industrialisation). Labour costs in the

Table XVI.7
Changes in the value of the guilder 1971–78 (% changes over previous year)

	1971	1972	1973	1974	1975	1976	1977	1978	Cumulative
Relative to suppliers	1·0	1·5	3·0	4·5	2·0	1·0	4·0	5·5	24·5
Relative to competitors in foreign markets	1·5	2·5	5·5	6·0	2·5	1·5	6·5	3·5	33·5

Source: *Plaats en toekomst van de Nederlandse industrie*, WRR, The Hague, 1980, p. 41.

Table XVI.8
Labour costs in manufacturing industry in 1979 (German marks per hour)

Country	Total labour costs per hour	Average hourly wage	Social costs per hour
Belgium	21·53	12·41	9·12
Sweden	21·36	12·95	8·41
Netherlands	21·18	12·07	9·11
West Germany	21·14	12·46	8·68
Switzerland	20·62	14·22	6·40
Denmark	20·29	16·80	3·49
USA	16·95	12·24	4·71
Italy	15·25	7·33	7·92
Canada	15·05	11·71	3·34
France	15·05	8·41	6·64
Austria	14·14	7·56	6·58
Japan	11·77	9·69	2·08
UK	10·20	7·85	2·35
Spain	10·16	6·39	3·77
Ireland	8·98	6·96	2·02
Greece	6·25	4·11	2·14

Source: *Financial Times*, 12 August 1980, p. 14.

Netherlands are now virtually the highest in the world and substantially above those in the USA, as indicated in Table XVI.8.

Table XVI.8 shows clearly that the fact that labour costs are higher in the Netherlands than in the USA does not benefit the workers (whose wages are lower than wages in the USA) but the beneficiaries of the social security system (pensioners, children, the sick, unemployed and unfit for work).

4. Economic Structure

The high level of costs in the Netherlands (partly resulting from the high exchange rate induced by natural gas) has been an important factor accelerating structural change. In Section B some data were presented about the de-industrialisation process at work since the mid-1960s. In Table XVI.9 some more detailed information is given about structural change.

Table XVI.9
Output by sector 1970–78, based on gross value added in 1970 market prices

	Changes in % per annum		Shares %		
	1970–73	1974–78	1970	1973	1978
1. Agriculture	5·1	2·1	7·0	7·0	7·1
2. Dairy and meat processing	4·8	1·0	0·4	0·4	0·4
3. Other food processing	4·0	2·4	3·0	2·9	2·9
4. Drink and tobacco	7·8	3·2	2·4	2·5	2·6
5. Textiles	−1·5	−4·6	1·4	1·1	0·8
6. Clothing and leather goods	−6·4	−7·3	1·0	0·7	0·4
7. Paper and printing	1·8	4·1	2·7	2·4	2·6
8. Woodworking and building materials	4·5	−0·5	2·7	2·6	2·3
9. Chemicals	10·5	2·8	4·7	5·6	5·6
10. Metal manufacture	6·6	−1·0	1·6	1·7	1·4
11. Oil refining	10·3	−2·0	2·1	2·2	1·8
12. Mechanical engineering	4·4	0·8	5·5	5·1	4·7
13. Electrical engineering	7·4	2·5	3·9	3·9	3·9
14. Vehicles and ships	5·1	−3·2	2·0	2·0	1·5
15. Industry—(2–14 inclusive)	5·6	1·0	33·4	33·1	30·9
16. Mining	18·8	2·8	1·9	2·8	2·8
17. Public utilities	12·4	4·2	2·7	3·3	3·5
18. Construction	1·5	−0·8	8·5	7·5	6·6
19. International services	5·8	4·0	24·8	24·9	26·8
20. Domestic (i.e. internal) services	4·8	3·4	21·7	21·5	22·4
21. Total business sector	5·5	2·5	100	100	100

Source: *Plaats en toekomst van de Nederlandse industrie*, WRR, The Hague, 1980, p. 42.

During the 1970s the textile and clothing industries virtually disappeared; metal manufacturing, mechanical engineering, vehicles and ships, construction and building materials, all declined; and a continuous process of serviceisation took place.

The market force which generates rapid structural change is the dispersion of profit (or loss) rates. During the 1970s the labour-intensive internationally competitive sector of the economy (e.g. shipbuilding) experienced low profits or losses. Given the exchange rate and the burden of the social security system, it is impossible to make standard ships, televisions or calculators, let alone clothes or shoes, at prices competitive with South Korea or Taiwan.

In view of the fact that the Netherlands is a very open, capitalist, economy, much of its industrial capacity has migrated to cheap labour countries, as multinationals have switched production in accordance with market forces. A good example of the present situation is provided by Philips, the famous electrical and electronics company, which is the biggest private sector employer in the country. Less than one-third of its employees are now in the Netherlands and their numbers are falling steadily. Its financial health depends entirely on its overseas operations, its domestic operations being roughly at the break-even level.

What the labour force mainly notices about structural change is the growth of unemployment. Ten years ago this was virtually non-existent. At the present time, officially measured unemployment is 'only' about 6% of the labour force. Dutch official unemployment statistics, however, are a by-product of the social security and political systems. They do not purport to measure all those without jobs who want them, but only those officially registered as unemployed. To be included in this category one must be registered, not older than 64, already without a job, and immediately available for employment for more than 25 hours per week. Hence those seeking part-time work, those officially categorised as unemployable (*niet bemiddelbaar*), people who are not registered (e.g. married women not eligible for unemployment benefits), foreigners, etc. are excluded from the official 'unemployment' statistics (Haaster and Salverda, 1977). Many of the unemployed appear in the official statistics not as 'unemployed' but as 'unfit for work'. This category, and the income from the state which goes with it, was originally mainly a generalisation of benefits for invalids and victims of industrial accidents and diseases, but expanded rapidly in the 1970s. Now firms who want to replace their older workers with stronger, younger ones normally seek to have the older ones officially certified as 'unfit for work'. This is a 'humane' way of firing them. The number of those officially 'unfit for work' is currently more than double the number of those 'unemployed'. (Many of the 'unfit for work' are genuine invalids, victims of work accidents, etc. and should *not* be treated as disguised unemployed.)*

E.   DEPLETION AND PRICE POLICY

1.   *Depletion Policy*

In the late 1960s when the first export contracts were signed, the world was still in the era of abundant cheap energy. It was thought that the way to maximise the benefits of the gas discovery was to sell as much gas as possible as quickly as possible. In this way the present discounted value of the income stream would be maximised. Since the huge energy price increases of 1973/74 opinion has changed radically. Domestic gas is now seen as an enormously valuable asset which should be conserved as long as possible. The further price increases of 1979 have reinforced this view. Consequently, for some years now, the Dutch have been pursuing a very cautious depletion policy. The peaking of exports and output in 1976 (in physical units), and the fact that the country will probably be a net energy importer from 1981 onwards (in toe—it already is in prices), are not *technical* necessities but *policy* decisions.

In order to conserve domestic gas supplies, the Dutch have been busy arranging substantial energy imports. Already in 1979 about 7% of Dutch domestic gas consumption was met by imports (from Norway). Negotiations are under way for additional imports from Norway. Contracts have been signed with Nigeria for deliveries of liquefied natural gas beginning in 1984/5 and negotiations with the USSR for gas imports equivalent to about 10% of current domestic consumption are under way. Substantial coal imports from Poland have also been arranged. Odell (1979) has argued that this is a perverse policy which creates the very energy shortage it is trying to avoid. Considered from

---

* The official method of measuring 'unemployment' has been altered since this chapter was first published. The new method produces figures in excess of those generated by the standardised OECD method.

the standpoint of the industrialised world as a whole, this is true. Nevertheless, for an individual small country such as the Netherlands, the current cautious depletion policy makes excellent sense. It insulates the country against possible future shocks with respect to the price or physical availability of energy imports and reduces the economic disruption and de-industrialisation facilitated by temporary foreign exchange and government revenue windfalls.

2.   Price Policy

Before 1974 the existence of abundant cheap energy had a very favour-able effect on the growth of the energy-intensive industries (e.g. chemicals, metallurgy, paper and horticulture). It is generally reckoned that this factor added about a quarter to the rate of growth of labour productivity in the Dutch business sector in the early 1970s. Since 1974 an orthodox policy has been pursued of raising internal prices in line with world market prices. Indeed, because it is easier to raise domestic prices than alter international agreements, domestic prices have often been above export prices (which may be termed an 'ultra-orthodox' policy). Thus the main favourable effect of the natural gas on output and employment has been ended by the government which had adopted an ultra-orthodox neo-classical position.

F.   INDUSTRY POLICY

As pointed out in Section B, in 1947–65 the Netherlands experienced a process of industrialisation with a significant increase in industrial employment and a rapid growth in industrial output. This process was wholeheartedly supported by the state. The government looked to industry as a source of employment, exports and income to replace the lost Empire. In 1949–63 the Ministry of Economic Affairs issued eight White Papers on industrialisation and vigorously stimulated industrial growth. An important aspect of the industrialisation policy was a successful incomes policy which held labour costs relatively low. This lasted till 1962. (1963 was the first year of free collective bargaining and 1964 saw a wages explosion.) Another important aspect was the attraction of foreign (mainly US) capital. Exports were stimulated by devaluation (in 1949), the incomes policy, export credits, and rapidly expanding demand in West Germany and the world as a whole.

In the late 1960s it seemed to many observers as if the economy could run itself very well without government intervention. Public debate increasingly focused on income distribution, aid to developing countries and the environment. The report of the Club of Rome had an enormous impact in small, densely populated, highly industrialised Netherlands.

During the 1970s it became increasingly obvious that the economy could *not* be left to itself. The authorities became increasingly concerned about unemployment, public expenditure and its financing, the balance of payments, and the decline of the market sector. Their concern about unemployment and industrial decline took the form of efforts to reduce the rate of growth of public spending, attempts to keep down the growth of labour costs, and industrial 'restructuring'.

'Restructuring' of industries is a term that dates from the mid-1960s. It was used in connection with government financial assistance in easing the closing down of the coal mining industry in that period. Given the level of energy prices then prevailing, and the expectation that this would persist, the coal mines were uneconomic. There was no possible way of producing coal at a price competitive with the prevailing level of oil prices. To ease the closing of the mines the government provided money to finance early retirement of former miners, the provision of alternative employment in the coal mining area, and the conversion of the state-owned mining company (DSM) into a chemical company. The decision to close the mines was undoubtedly implemented in a relatively equitable, harmonious and socially just manner. This type of policy, cushioning the social effects of industrial change with public money, was called 'restructuring'.

In the 1970s restructuring expanded and became more extensive. From 1974 it embraced the following (Teulings, 1978, pp. 21–22; *Financiele*, 1977, pp. 28–45):

(1) grants for research into industrial structure and for consultancy work;
(2) credit guarantees, whereby public agencies either provide finance directly or guarantee private sector loans;
(3) investment grants;
(4) closing-down grants;

(5) loans on favourable conditions;
(6) grants for training and retraining;
(7) bringing in NEHEM (see later); and
(8) grants for firms that transfer appropriate activities to less developed countries or which suffer from imports from these countries.

NEHEM (The Netherlands Restructuring Company) was established in 1972 and is a public agency which exists to promote restructuring. It is analogous to the former Industrial Reorganisation Corporation (IRC) and National Enterprise Board (NEB) in Britain and the Bundeskartelamt in West Germany. In fact it was originally inspired by the example of the IRC. Similarly, there are a number of regional development organisations which use public money to stimulate development or to retard decline in less developed regions of the country.

Restructuring in the Netherlands does *not* mean the state imposing its will on a firm or industry in a planned way. It means the state providing money for policies agreed between representatives of employers and workers. As a Dutch specialist on industrial organisation has accurately explained (de Jong, 1980, p. 44),

> the Dutch Government—and this is confirmed by the most recent White Paper on structural policy—has never imposed her will on the social partners, but listens to their ideas and then comes to a compromise decision that does not go much further than that which is acceptable to all. The Government does not steer, impose or dictate, but registers the balance and helps to look for a precarious balance.

In the Netherlands this type of decision-making is often referred to as 'negotiations democracy' (van den Doel, 1979). In the UK it is known as 'concerted action' (by those who support it) or 'corporatism' (by those who criticise it). A similar system exists also in West Germany and Austria. This style of decision-making, and the results which emerge from it, have been much criticised in the Netherlands but reflect fundamental features of the society (strong trade unions, powerful business firms, a multiplicity of political parties and proportional representation) and are unlikely to change quickly.

Negotiations democracy has had an important impact on restructuring. For example, the NEHEM, with its board made up of civil servants, employers' representatives and workers' representatives, and powerless to impose its will, was a typical example of negotiations democracy. At the present time NEHEM is generally regarded as a failure, as an organisation which has failed to carry out successful restructuring. As Inja (1980, p. 117) has observed,

> In the Netherlands a form of structural policy has been carried out. If one examines the activities of, and the developments within, the NEHEM, however, it is impossible to speak of a successful policy. On the contrary; in the six years of the existence NEHEM has never been able to bring even one restructuring scheme to an entirely satisfactory conclusion.

Besides being ineffective, restructuring policy has also been inefficient. It has provided substantial assistance for concerns with no survival prospects. This is understandable, since in practice it is not long-term market prospects but short-term unemployment prospects that play a dominant role in obtaining state finance. Its main positive achievement has been a social one, in cushioning the adverse social effects of rapid structural change.

During the 1970s, the prevailing view in the Netherlands about the decline of industry and the continuous serviceisation of the economy was that it was a normal and healthy development. Following Colin Clark and Daniel Bell it was argued (e.g. Kwee, 1979; Lambooy, 1979) that countries first industrialise and then develop into post-industrial societies. Hence, there was nothing to worry about. Government policy in the economic field should largely confine itself to an innovation policy aimed at stimulating knowledge-intensive sectors, e.g. computer software, biotechnology, micro-electronics etc.

In 1980 an official advisory organ of the government, the Netherlands Scientific Council of Government Policy (which very roughly corresponds to the Central Policy Review Staff in the UK) produced a Report which advocated a government-backed programme of reindustrialisation (WRR, 1980). It argued that the process of industrial decline had created a serious problem for the economy and should be arrested. It was partly based on the British discussion of de-industrialisation (Blackaby, 1979). This report received very extensive publicity. The initial reaction of Ministers was favourable, but at the time of writing the definitive Government reaction to the Report had not yet been published. In the public discussion, opinions expressed about the Report ranged from enthusiastic acceptance of it, via scepticism of its feasibility, to rejection of re-industrialisation as a policy goal (van den Doel, 1980).

In the 1981 Budget the Government announced that the extra

revenue to be received from abroad by reasons of the increase in natural gas export prices would be used to strengthen industry. This would be done, *inter alia*, by reducing company taxation and increasing investment subsidies. These proposals, and public acceptance of them, partly reflected the impact of the Report (with its emphasis on industrial decline and the need to reverse it) on Dutch political debate.

G. SUMMARY

For a short time in the 1970s, the Netherlands, traditionally an energy importer, became a net energy exporter. Its natural gas exports, non-existent in 1965, had reached 51 billion cubic metres per annum by 1976. During the 1970s, partly as a result of the natural gas revenues, the guilder was a strong currency and the relative volume of transfer payments rose sharply.

Since 1965 the Netherlands has experienced a rapid process of de-industrialisation. It currently suffers from serious economic problems. The government experiences these as the state budgetary deficit and the balance of payments deficit; the population as declining real incomes and unemployment; and the business world as losses or low profits in internationally competitive labour-intensive sectors. The natural gas production and exports have contributed to these problems by increasing competitive imports, raising domestic costs (via the exchange rate and the social security system whose rapid expansion was facilitated by natural gas revenues), squeezing profits in internationally competitive sectors (via the exchange rate and the domestic cost level) and substituting, for exports which employ labour to produce them (e.g. industry and services), exports (natural gas) which require virtually no labour.

As far as the natural gas itself is concerned, the government has pursued since 1973/74 a cautious depletion policy and an ultra-orthodox price policy. The latter has prevented industry obtaining direct benefits from the negligible production costs of the country's energy riches. As far as industry is concerned, the government has pursued a policy of restructuring. This has cushioned change and prevented de-industrialisation having social consequences that are too harmful. Economically it has been ineffective and inefficient. At the present time a policy of state-sponsored re-industrialisation is being discussed.

With the exception of the sensible depletion policy (and to some extent the accumulation of overseas assets), the Dutch experience is mainly an example of how *not* to use the temporary revenues from energy exports if one wants to help employment and the healthy long-term development of an economy.

H.   CONCLUSION

Substantial production and exports of oil and gas can have favourable effects on an economy, by relaxing the balance of payments constraint, allowing additional imports of technically advanced investment goods and of complementary goods, providing cheap energy, and favourably influencing labour productivity (via their effect on investment and real wages). They can also have harmful effects on an economy, especially on employment and industry. They can do this by generating additional competitive imports, raising domestic costs, squeezing profits and substituting non-labour-intensive exports for more labour-intensive exports. More generally, they can facilitate and enforce structural changes which make the provision of employment and, when energy exports begin to decline, also income, increasingly difficult.

The policy problem created by this situation is to try to capture the potential favourable effects and avoid the potential harmful effects. This involves transforming temporary resources into resources which yield a permanent stream of income and employment, e.g. domestic industry, a highly skilled labour force and overseas investments. As far as Mexico is concerned, the Dutch experience emphasises the importance of going slow on production and exports, pursuing a very conservative depletion policy and using the resources obtained to expand industry and agriculture. It supports the arguments of Brailovsky (Barker and Brailovsky, 1981, chapter 5) and, as far as the UK is concerned, Barker (Barker and Brailovsky, 1981, chapter 3) and Noreng (Barker and Brailovsky, 1981, chapter 3). Present policies threaten to transfer much of the employment benefit from oil and gas production to those countries which expand their exports to Mexico and the UK.

As far as the world economy is concerned, the level of production in a single country is one of the factors which, via its influence on the global supply and demand situation, contributes to determining the size and distribution of the rent currently being generated in the energy sector of the world economy. If other countries, e.g. OPEC, are prepared to maintain rising real prices by production reductions, then a rapid expansion of production by a non-OPEC country enables that country to enjoy a rentier existence while the production lasts. This may result in the kind of internal conflict in the country common in rentier families (as happened in Iran) or it may enable discontent to be bought off (as happened in the Netherlands). It may also eventually condemn that country to the typical fate of the ex-rentier—inability to earn his/her own living when the source of the unearned income ceases.

XVII. DOBB AND THE CRISIS*

A. INTRODUCTION

Maurice Dobb (1900–1976) was one of the leading Marxist economists of the twentieth century. In a hostile environment he kept alive the tradition of Marxist political economy. He both expounded Marx's own work and analysed contemporary problems. His work formed a bridge between academic economics (he was for many years a member of the Economics Faculty of Cambridge University) and Marxism. His academic work combined historical, analytical and policy elements. He was not only an academic but also a practitioner of the Marxist idea of the unity of theory and practice. He was an active and loyal member of the CPGB (Communist Party of Great Britain) from 1921 till his death, and devoted much of his time to adult education. During the 1920s and 1930s he took a leading part in the work of the National Council of Labour Colleges, which was the main organisation for Marxist education in the trade unions. He wrote extensively for its journal *Plebs*. Personally, he was an English gentleman and an efficient correspondent. The long letters in his distinctive and legible handwriting are familiar to all his former students and colleagues.

Dobb's scientific work was in five areas, the critique of Western academic orthodoxy, the transition from feudalism to capitalism, the exposition of Marxism, the Soviet economy and development economics. He did, however, also analyse the crisis, from both a theoretical and a policy perspective.

---

* Originally published, in Dutch, in *Intermediair*, 10 July 1981, as part of a series about the views of prominent economists on economic crises. I am grateful to J. de Beus, J. Eatwell, M. Masuch, G. Reuten and M. Sint for useful criticism.

B.   CRISIS THEORY

Unlike those economists for whom the crisis is caused by extraneous shocks such as sunspots or OPEC, for Dobb, as for all Marxists, the crisis is an integral part of capitalist dynamics. As he explained in the chapter on economic crises of *Political Economy and Capitalism* (1937),

> Marx clearly regarded crises, not as incidental departures from a predetermined equilibrium, not as fickle wanderings from an established path of development to which there would be a submissive return, but rather as themselves a dominant form of development which forged and shaped the development of capitalist society. To study crisis was *ipso facto* to study the dynamics of the system; and this study could only be properly undertaken as part of an examination of the forms of movement of class relations (the class struggle) and of the class revenues which were their market expression.

Furthermore, for Dobb the crisis is not purely the unnecessary and irrational phenomenon 'observed' by Keynesians and other who think that a crisis-free development of a capitalist economy is both desirable and possible. For Dobb the crisis plays an essential role in capitalist development. Since in a capitalist economy *ex ante* co-ordination (i.e. planning) is impossible, the socially necessary co-ordination can only be provided *ex post* by the crisis, which thus plays an essential role in this mode of production. "A crisis appears as catharsis as well as retribution: as the sole mechanism by which, in this economy, equilibrium can be enforced, once it has been extensively broken".

This view of the crisis, as a necessary feature of the capitalist mode of production, which plays an essential role within it and reveals one of its key contradictions (between the social nature of the production process and the dispersed decision-making and lack of *ex ante* co-ordination characteristic of capitalism) differs radically from the Keynesian, monetarist and neo-classical perspectives. For a Keynesian, crises can always be overcome (and even prevented) by wise government policies. For a monetarist, crises can always be avoided by sensible monetary policies. For a neo-classical, crisis can always be overcome by cutting wages (and transfer payments and government expenditure generally). For a Marxist, such as Dobb, crises (under capitalism) are unavoidable They are necessary for this mode of production, helping to discipline the workers and restructure capital. Unemployment forces the workers to submit to the dictates of capital, reducing their wage demands and their opposition to changes in the labour process. Bankruptcies lead to a scrapping of surplus capacity (caused by the over-investment typical of the boom) and a concentration of capacity and finance in the hands of strong dynamic firms that can take advantage of the next upswing. Crises are also one of the phenomena that indicate that capitalism is a wasteful, inefficient and irrational mode of production which will be swept away by the working class and replaced by socialism. Under socialism, society will be rationally organised and socially irrational phenomena typical of capitalist crises such as massive unemployment and idle capacity will not exist.

The Marxist analysis stresses the positive role of the crisis under capitalism in reducing wage demands and worker resistance to changes in the labour process, weeding out uncompetitive firms and strengthening efficient ones. This Marxist analysis is also shared by some politicians with non-Marxist political aims. A good example of this is the Thatcher regime in the UK (and possibly also the new Reagan regime in the USA). The Thatcherites have deliberately deepened the British recession by maintaining a high exchange rate and high interest rates. This is intended to produce 'realism' in the trade unions and efficiency in industry. The fact that the Marxist analysis of the positive role of the crisis under capitalism is accepted by politicians with entirely non-Marxist political objectives is important. It suggests that the Marxist theory of the crisis has an important scientific element and that Marxist criticism of the Keynesian notion of perpetual crisis free growth under capitalism contains important elements of the truth.

Although he repeated, systematised and expounded the Marxist analysis of crises, Dobb did not develop it. In this respect he compares unfavourably with the famous Polish Marxist economist Kalecki. Kalecki was an outstanding analyst of *contemporary* capitalism, working out much of modern macro-economics in the 1930s, explaining why it would not lead to permanent full employment even before full employment had been officially adopted as a Government policy goal, and analysing price formation, distribution and growth in a fresh and lively way. Kalecki's work was a major advance in understanding economic crisis, something which cannot be said about Dobb's work.

How did Dobb react to the existence and importance of economic crisis under state socialism? As far as I am aware, neither the Soviet economic crisis of 1931–33, the Soviet stagnation of 1938 nor the Chinese economic crisis of 1959–61 found any reflection in his theoretical work. In recent years a considerable volume of writing has accumulated about the crisis under state socialism (Bajt, 1971; Brus, 1973; Eckstein, 1975; Davies, 1976; Ellman, 1980) but Dobb made no contribution to it. It is noteworthy that another leading English-speaking Marxist economist, Paul Sweezy, soon after Dobb's death, was forced to change his ideas substantially under the influence of developments in the state socialist countries (Sweezy, 1977, 1979).

C. CRISIS POLICY

As far as crisis policy is concerned, Dobb considered that within a capitalist framework, crisis policy is futile. The elimination of crises requires the elimination of capitalism. As Stalin put it in a 1934 talk with the English writer H. G. Wells which was approvingly cited by Dobb in an essay of 1950

> If capitalism could adapt production, not to the acquisition of maximum profits, but to the systematic improvement of the material conditions of the mass of the people . . . there would be no crisis. But then, also, capitalism would not be capitalism. To abolish crises, capitalism must be abolished.

Keynesian policy prescriptions rest to a considerable extent on the motion of a socially neutral state which can and will solve efficiently the problems of society. For Dobb such notions were both wrong and harmful. As he put it in his 1950 essay,

> Once economic theory is allowed to employ the *deus ex machina* of an impartial, classless state, actuated by social purposes and ironing out the conflicts of actual economic society, all manner of attractive miracles can be demonstrated, even without the aid of algebra. One might dismiss such attempts as harmless pastimes, were it not that ideas play a role in history, and can not only disseminate the opium of false hopes, but in the cold war of today weave dangerous illusions about the grim realities of present-day capitalism.

In the current Dutch situation, Dobb would have considered that policies to resolve the crisis by neo-classical (public expenditure cuts and wage cuts), Keynesian (public expenditure increases and incomes policy) or monetarist methods (steady low growth of the money supply), were all doomed to failure. In his view, all such policies re-flect a failure to comprehend the nature and dynamics of the capitalist economic system. Full employment, he would have argued, requires a socialist planned economy. (This question is discussed at length in Chapter 11.) Hence, policies which would actually resolve the crisis have to be analysed in the context of 'the transition to socialism'. For an example of such an analysis see *Britain's economic crisis* (Spokesman Pamphlet no. 44, Nottingham, England, 1974).

Accordingly, Dobb would *not* have regarded a programme such as G. Reuten, B. Thio, R. de Klerk and C. van Ewijk, *Economisch beleid uit de klem* (Amsterdam, 1980; for a summary see *Intermediair*, 10 October 1980) as a basis for an effective anti-crisis *economic* policy. It assumes a benevolent Keynesian-type state, ignores the need for balance of payments equilibrium, and has nothing in it about a transition to socialism. He would have treated it primarily as a piece of agitation, a *political document* aimed at rallying a broad united front under the leadership of the CPN (Communist Party of the Netherlands) against the monopolists, the Government and the leadership of the PvdA (Labour Party) and the trade unions. As such, depending on current CP policy, he might well have approved of it.

D. THE CRITIQUE OF WESTERN ACADEMIC ORTHODOXY

When Dobb studied economics (1919–24) and became a lecturer (1924), English academic economics was entirely dominated by neo-classical orthodoxy. Students were taught about the central importance in economic progress of the entrepreneur, about the role of prices and competition in attaining and maintaining an efficient economic system. As Dobb (1924) wrote in a youthful essay,

> From the standpoint of the economist, therefore, the economic world is a complex of price-relations—of persons striving to satisfy certain wants and coming constantly into conflict with obstacles to that satisfaction. In the centre of this chaos stands the capitalist undertaker (i.e. entrepreneur). The to-be or not-to-be of a productive enterprise is in his hands; the distribution of resources between competing uses is under his control; and he regulates his actions by movements of prices, indicative of movements of market demand. The undertaker, therefore, is the nerve-centre of the organism, infinitely delicate. On his state of mind depends the efficiency of the whole. All the technical inventions in the world would avail little if this co-ordinating mechanism ceased to function.

Hence, the need for the undertaker is conditioned by the highly complex differentiation of modern society. The payment to evoke this activity is a "necessary" cost in the sense that it is imposed, not by a particular system of politico-legal regulations, but by the division of labour and ultimately by nature. The more clearly the price index finds expression and the more imperatively the profit principle exacts obedience, the more efficiently is the undertaker likely to fulfil the economic maxim.

Dobb, like all Marxists, regarded this as a myth, which ignored the central role of *capital*, its origin, use and victims. Dobb persistently challenged Western academic economics, its scientific nature, explanatory power and policy relevance.

For Dobb, as for all Marxists, Western academic economics is not a *science* which explains important aspects of reality, but an *ideology* which attempts to conceal important aspects of reality in the interest of a dominant and parasitic ruling group. Western academic economists are generally prepared to admit that the 'vision' of an economist, his approach to a problem and his selection of relevant facts, inevitably contains an ideological element. They generally claim, however, that their *analysis* is a value-free scientific work entirely uncontaminated by ideological elements. For example, for Hennipman and his followers, Paretian welfare economics, which many writers have accused of having normative elements, is in fact a value-free positive science. For Dobb, all such arguments were entirely unacceptable. Considering such an argument put forward by Schumpeter, who distinguished between an inevitably ideological vision and a neutral analysis, Dobb (1973, p. 35) wrote that,

> the distinction that Schumpeter tried to draw between Economics as pure analysis and as Vision of the economic process into which ideological slant and colouring inevitably enter cannot be sustained, unless the former is restricted to the formal framework, simply, of economic statement, and not to economic theory as substantial statement about the real relations of economic society; since into the formulation of the latter, and into the very act of judgement of its degree of realism, historical intuition, social perspective and vision cannot fail to enter. For this reason it is possible to characterize and classify economic theories, even the most abstract, according to the manner in which they depict the structure and roots of economic society, and according to the significance of so depicting it for historical judgement and contemporary social practice.

In a class-divided society, Dobb argued, there can be no neutral, value-free, scientific economics. What purports to be the latter is actually an ideology which attempts to hide the fact that capitalism is a mode of production based on exploitation.

Dobb does not seem to have explicitly discussed anywhere the question of the scientific status of Marxism itself in the light of the theory of ideology. If every theory inevitably has an ideological element, does this mean that Marxism too is non-scientific? Is Marxism too merely an ideology, reflecting the interests of a different class but having no more scientific status than 'bourgeois economics'? The famous Polish economist Lange (1963, chapter 7), following the official Soviet textbook of political economy, and echoing Lukacs, 'solved' this problem by an 'epistemological wager on the working class'. According to this conception, Marxism is a science because it expresses the interests of a class (the working class) which has an interest in discovering the truth about capitalism. Acceptance of this idea requires prior acceptance of the scientific nature and truth of the Marxist theory of capitalist society. How can this theory be scientific if "ideological slant and colouring" inevitably enter all social theories? Are its main propositions (e.g. the division of capitalist society into two classes defined by reference to ownership of the means of production, the growing polarisation of capitalist society, the impoverishment of the workers) true? Are there not important true propositions (e.g. the role in revolutions of students and peasants; the role in social evolution of war, the national question and age and sex differences; the growth in working-class living standards that capitalism can bring about) which are ignored or denied by the Marxist theory of capitalist society? Is not Marxism, with its advocacy of a society in which there is no scarcity and in which everyone agrees with everyone else, not a science but a Utopia?

Stress on the ideological elements in social thought opens up the dangerous path actually trodden in the USSR in which genuine scientific work is denounced as 'bourgeois' and charlatanry (such as Lysenkoism) is proclaimed to be scientific. It is partly because of this adverse experience that an outstanding contemporary writer on scientific methodology such as Lakatos (1978) stresses the internal factors in the development of scientific ideas and pours scorn on 'externalist rubbish.'

It is disappointing that in a book published in 1973 which is explicitly concerned with the relationship between ideology and economic theory and which sums up the author's arguments in this area over half a century, none of these questions are seriously discussed. Neither

Mannheim nor Lakatos appear in the book and Lange's analysis is simply referred to in a footnote. Within mainstream Anglo-Saxon economics it was a refreshing and useful book, an up-to-date version of Myrdal's well known book *The Political Element in the Development of Economic Theory*. It combined the raising of fundamental epistemological questions with knowledge of the most recent debates in economic theory and knowledge of the history of economic thought. Dobb's stress on the social conditioning of economic thought seems to me entirely sensible and important. I have myself applied it both to the Soviet discussion of mathematical economics (Ellman, 1973) and to the Tinbergian theory of convergence (Chapter 18). Nevertheless, from a wider perspective which includes the international discussion of ideology, current discussions of scientific methodology and the experiences of the state socialist countries, the limitations of the book are more noticeable. There is no analysis in it of the status of Marxism itself in the light of the theory of ideology. There is no discussion of the 'epistemological wager on the working class'. The fundamental questions, posed above, which the theory of ideology raises *for Marxism*, remained unanswered.

For Dobb, Western academic economics, because of its unscientific nature, had no explanatory power. It could not have, since it abstracted from the essential aspects of economic life and focused on formal aspects of the exchange process. In a famous paper on *"The Trend of Modern Economics"* (1937) he argued that the propositions of Western economics "can surely be precious little guide to the 'laws of motion of capitalist society'—or, indeed, to any of the other matters on which they are intended to pass an economic judgement". Although in his academic writings he paid extensive attention to Western economics (mainly to criticise it and draw attention to its limitations and inadequacies) when he wanted to analyse real problems he looked to Marxist theory and Soviet practice for illumination. An interesting and important example of the implications of Dobb's position concerns the theory and practice of wage determination. Dobb (1929) criticised the theory that wages are determined by the marginal product of labour, with its corollaries that government intervention in wage determination is harmful, unemployment is caused by excessive wages, and that if there is unemployment it is wages that have to be reduced. In his theoretical writing he stressed the role of bargaining and of property income as a residual. In his practical activity as a teacher and Communist he strove to strengthen the position of workers in wage bargaining. The theoretical criticism of the marginal productivity theory of distribution in the last thirty years, and the stress laid by contemporary writers on the activity of the labour movement (both industrial and political) as a factor in raising living standards, are striking evidence in support of his position.

For Dobb, to look to Western academic economics for relevant policy ideas was a waste of time. How could an unscientific, apologetic theory throw any light on the urgent problems of unemployment, poverty and the degradation of the workers?

The standard statements of Dobb's critique of Western economics are to be found in his 1924 essay on "The Entrepreneur Myth", his 1937 essay on "The Trend of Modern Economics", his 1950 essay on "Full Employment and Capitalism" and his 1973 book on *Theories of Value and Distribution since Adam Smith*. In additon he collaborated closely with P. Sraffa in laying the basis for what has come to be called the 'neo-Ricardian', 'Cambridge' or 'Anglo-Italian' critique of neo-classical economics. He worked with Sraffa on the latter's famous ten volume edition of the *Works and Correspondence of David Ricardo*, contributing several editorial notes and introductions.

A serious problem for Dobb's position was created by the rise of the Soviet school of mathematical economists in the 1960s. Kantorovich and his school criticised Marxism-Leninism (as set out for example in Stalin's booklet *Economic Problems of Socialism in the USSR* and in the official Soviet textbooks of political economy) and introduced into Soviet economics many ideas which Dobb had devoted years to criticising. These included, the usefulness of prices as guides to efficiency, the importance of scarcity and of the efficient allocation of resources, the value of mathematical maximising techniques for all modes of production, the concept of opportunity costs, and the importance and practical usefulness of the notion of an 'optimum'. He dealt with these issues in his 1969 book *Welfare Economics and the Economics of Socialism*. In this he conceded two important principles of welfare economics (that, in general, the free choice of consumers enables them to get the most satisfaction from the money available to them, and that it is important and possible to allocate inputs in such a way as to maximise production). To criticise the market he was reduced to repeating the academic welfare economics arguments about the distribution of income and externalities. That, under the influence of Soviet discussion, Dobb was forced to recognise the relevance and usefulness of that despised

Western academic economics that he had spent so long criticising, was a deeply ironical phenomenon. It illustrated and reflected the crisis (in the Kuhnian sense) of Marxism-Leninism (Sweezy 1979; Althusser 1977, 1978) to which Dobb had so long been a faithful adherent.

E.   THE TRANSITION FROM FEUDALISM
TO CAPITALISM

The central idea of Marxist political economy, which distinguishes it decisively from Western academic economics, is that of a *mode of production*. The existence of distinct modes of production, governed by distinct economic laws, is a central thesis of Marxist political economy. Although Marx devoted most of his efforts to discovering the laws of motion of *capitalist* society, he also devoted some attention to the origins of that society, to the transition from feudalism to capitalism. Marx objected to contemporary accounts of how 'previous' accumulation had come into being. He suggested that for the vulgar economists of his time it played about the same role in economics as original sin in theology. "In times long gone by", he wrote in *Capital*, vol. 1, chapter 26, "there were two sorts of people: the diligent, intelligent, and above all, frugal elite: the other, lazy rascals, spending their substance, and more, in riotous living . . . Thus it came to pass that the former sort accumulated wealth, and the latter sort had nothing to sell except their own skins". Marx attacked this notion and argued that the essence of Smith's 'previous' accumulation was actually "the historical process of divorcing the producer from the means of production" commonly by force, e.g. the English enclosures and the Scottish clearances. The "epoch-making" moments in the history of original accumulation are those when "great masses of men are suddenly and forcibly torn from their means of subsistence, and hurled as free and 'unattached' proletarians on the labour market". In the development of the capitalist economy, Marx argued, the "expropriation of the agricultural producer, of the peasant, from the soil, is the basis of the whole process".

   Despite this eloquent and suggestive *hint*, Marx did not develop an articulated *theory* of the transition from feudalism to capitalism. Dobb attempted to fill this lacuna. Being an Englishman embedded in the English empirical tradition, he naturally tried to combine detailed historical research with the theory of historical materialism. A major result was his book *Studies in the Development of Capitalism* (1946). Dobb's work was an important contribution to an extensive international debate, of which Anderson's two 1974 books, *Passages from Antiquity to Feudalism* and *Lineages of the Absolutist State* and Wallerstein's *The Modern World System* (1974) are well known recent contributions.

Dobb's book is a powerful statement of the proposition that the problem of economic development must be approached historically, that any theory of economic development must be constructed in historically specific terms. Dobb thus follows Marx in rejecting any attempt to grasp economic transformations in terms of transhistorical economic laws based on such postulates as profit and utility maximisation and methodological individualism. It follows from the Marxist position that attempts to analyse all human societies with the tools of neo-classical economics are absurd and bound to be a failure. Stone age peoples, classical antiquity and feudalism cannot be understood in terms of scarcity, profit and utility maximisation and methodological individualism. It also follows that socialism, understood as a society in which human motivation and behaviour is radically different from that under capitalism, is possible. It also follows that much of Western development economics is absurd, since it focuses on minor issues and fails to analyse the key issue, the transition from one mode of production to another.

Although Dobb's *methodological* position is a powerful one, his *historical* position is a dubious one, as numerous authors have pointed out. Did there really exist a feudal ruling class in England in 1640? If Dobb did not satisfactorily resolve such questions, he at any rate raised them and contributed to a lively and fruitful debate among historians and historical materialists.

F.   EXPOSITION OF MARXISM

At the present time, Marx is generally recognised as a major figure in the history of economic thought on a par with Adam Smith, Ricardo, Marshall, Walras, Schumpeter and Keynes. For example, the famous (and non-Marxist) Japanese mathematical economist Morishima in his book *Marx's Economics: A Dual Theory of Value and Growth* (1973) treats Marx as a major economist. He developed a macro-dynamic model and is one of the contributors to the Marx – v. Neumann model. The recently rediscovered factor–price frontier is in fact one of his tools. All in all, there are ample grounds, according to Morishima, "to recommend Marx as a purely academic economist for one of the very few chairs with the highest authority". Similarly Heertje (1973) and Schouten (1957) take Marx seriously as an important economist. Such a recognition of Marx's role in the development of the subject is quite recent. For most of Dobb's life Western academic economics dealt with Marx either by ignoring him or by treating him as a minor, and muddle-headed, figure. Dobb was one of the very few economists in the Anglo-Saxon world in the 1920s, 30s, 40s, 50s and 60s (others were Meek and Sweezy) who took Marx seriously, expounded his ideas, and defended his work from criticism (often of a very superficial and ill-informed kind). A valuable feature of Dobb's exposition of Marx was that Dobb was very familiar with Western academic economics and hence was able to present Marxism in a way comprehensible to Western academic economists.

G. THE SOVIET ECONOMY

Like all Communists, Dobb had a keen interest in the October Revolution and its aftermath. In his case this took the shape of study of, and research into, the development of the Soviet economy. He learned Russian, visited the USSR several times, and was the author of a well known economic history of the USSR, numerous articles about the USSR and Soviet economic thought, and a stream of popular writing about the USSR. Most of his writing in this area, notably his popular writing during the Stalin era, had an apologetic rather than scientific character. In a well known and vivid passage in the Afterword to the second German edition of *Capital* Marx wrote of bourgeois political economy after 1830 that

> It was henceforth no longer a question whether this theorem or that was true, but whether it was useful to capital or harmful, expedient or inexpedient, politically dangerous or not. In place of disinterested enquirers there were hired prize-fighters; in place of genuine scientific research, the bad conscience and evil intention of apologetic.

The same could be said, *mutatis mutandis*, about much of Dobb's work on the USSR. His repetition of Stalin's view about War Communism; his failure to analyse the extent to which the grain crisis of the 1920s was actually caused by the policies of the Soviet government (with respect to prices, taxes and statistics); his defence of the Stalinist economic model, of the emphasis on heavy industry and of the necessity of collectivisation; his failure to analyse shortages and investment tension; and his silence about the victims of collectivisation, the mass arrests of 1937–38, the Gulag Archipelago and the extensive use of informers; are all deeply disturbing by contemporary standards. They have to be seen, however, against the background of the hysterical anti-Sovietism common in England and the lack of serious research of the Soviet economy for many years after the October Revolution.

Dobb's first full realisation that state socialism is not a conflict-free utopia seems to have been in response to the massive workers' demonstration in Poznan (Poland) in 1956. He witnessed this personally (he was a member of a group of British economists at the Poznan fair) and it made a deep impression on him. This impression cannot be seen from his academic writings, but was evident in his political activity and popular writing. As he himself put it in some biographical notes written in 1965 for a Polish colleague and published in his (1978), after Poznan

> He participated actively in the intense discussions later in the year in British communist and left-wing circles around the events in Hungary; and at the 1957 Congress of the British CP (to which he was a delegate from Cambridge) he made a speech seconding an amendment to the main resolution—an amendment to state that "dogmatism" (in place of "revisionism" was the main danger to be combatted (the amendment was defeated). He also supported some other minority resolutions and amendments (in this reflecting the opinions of the branches on whose behalf he was a delegate).

From 1956 onwards he struggled, within the CPGB, for a more realistic attitude to the state socialist countries. After the 22nd Congress*, a CPGB journal retrospectively defended the silence of 'progressives' in

---

* The twenty-second Congress of the Soviet Communist Party was held in 1961. At this Congress Stalin's policies were publicly attacked and numerous examples were publicly given about the repressions of the 1930s. A resolution was adopted at the Congress to remove Stalin's body from the Lenin Mausoleum on Red Square. This Congress marked the high point of destalinisation in the USSR.

the 1930s about the mass Soviet repression and terror of that period. It put forward the familiar argument of solidarity. It was argued that

> for the international movement the only choice at the time could be: either solidarity with the socialist revolution under fire, including recognition of the right of a revolutionary régime to determine what emergency measures it requires for its maintenance; or to join the clamour of the anti-Soviet counter-revolutionary chorus.

Dobb (1962) publicly criticised this article and argued for a realistic understanding of Soviet history. From the 1968 Soviet invasion of Czechoslovakia (which, like the CPGB as a whole, he opposed) onwards, he publicly recognised the *political* nature of economic reform in the USSR and Eastern Europe. A good example of the impact of reality on his popular writing is his 1970 booklet *Socialist Planning: Some Problems*.

As one of the founders of empirical research on the Soviet economy and as someone who was able to keep research on the Soviet economy apart from the propaganda needs of Western governments, Dobb was an important and significant figure. As a contributor to the political economy of socialism, however, he must be judged a failure. His work compares unfavourably with respect to depth, quality, originality and insight, to that of economists such as Brus and Kalecki (Poland) or Kornai (Hungary). The main reasons for this seem to have been his distance from events, his sense of solidarity, and his voluntary acceptance of what is known in English as 'commitment' and in Russian, with special reference to the Soviet Communist Party, as *partiinost'*. This is the view that all activities have to be judged by the extent to which they help or hinder the current political line of the movement one supports. For Dobb, this was the USSR and the CPGB. Such an attitude can be harmful for scientific work, as Dobb's apologetics and failure to contribute to the political economy of socialism, clearly show.

H.   DEVELOPMENT ECONOMICS

Dobb's interest in what subsequently came to be known as development economics largely dates from his 1951 visit to India. This gave rise to a stream of publications culminating in his 1960 book *An Essay on Economic Growth and Planning*. His writings in development economics were largely concerned with arguing, in effect, that developing countries should follow the Soviet economic model. This was in fact done in the Chinese Five Year Plan and the Indian Second Five Year Plan. Both these countries subsequently reacted against the Soviet model in view of its failure to contribute to the difficult employment problem and to raising the living standards of the rural population, and of its neglect of the key sectors of agriculture and foreign trade. In development economics Dobb was an apologist for a type of policy diffusion that is quite unattractive for independent states. His stress on the desirability and possibility of industrialisation was valuable, but he failed to provide a balanced appreciation of the lessons of Soviet experience.

I. CONCLUSION

Dobb was one of the leading Marxist economists of the twentieth century. He expounded and defended Marxist ideas, and engaged in adult education and political action, in a hostile environment. His work was influential, widely read and lasting. For five decades he held high and passed on to new generations the banner of criticism of neo-classical economics, social concern and economic rationality achieved by *ex ante* co-ordination (i.e. planning).

As far as the crisis is concerned, Dobb shared Stalin's view that to talk about policies for ameliorating the situation under capitalist conditions is a harmful illusion. Under capitalism, the crisis plays an essential role. It is *through* the crisis that dynamic equilibrium is maintained. Crises are necessary, in the wasteful and irrational capitalist system, to discipline the workers and restructure capital. This view is shared by the Thatcher administration. The only way to eliminate crises, in his view, was to eliminate capitalism. The existence of economic crises under state socialism raises fundamental problems for his position.

Dobb's scientific work was in five fields, the critique of Western academic orthodoxy, the transition from feudalism to capitalism, the exposition of Marxism, the Soviet economy and development economics. His work was strikingly novel and original for an English academic economist. Viewed in a broader perspective, against the traditions of other disciplines and other countries, the international Marxist movement and developments in the USSR, his work is less impressive. After the 1956 upheaval in Poland, the 1968 Soviet invasion of Czechoslovakia, and the twentieth and twenty-second congresses, Dobb began to reflect on the real (as opposed to the mythical) development of state socialism. He stressed the need for political struggle to achieve economic progress in those countries and took a progressive position in the debates inside the CPGB.

RELATIONS BETWEEN
THE SYSTEMS

XVIII. AGAINST CONVERGENCE*

A. INTRODUCTION

The purpose of this chapter is to criticise the convergence theory. It will be argued that while this theory has both positive and negative features, the latter are important and lead to a failure to understand the evolution of the world economy.

The convergence theory was originally advocated in his (1961) by the famous Dutch economist Tinbergen, the first Director of the Dutch Central Planning Office. It basically argued that a movement was taking place away from the polar opposites of communist and free (referred to in the rest of this chapter as 'state socialist' and 'capitalist') economies as each system adopted elements of the other. Tinbergen's convergence theory was an extension to the world economy of the harmony model of economic and social development. Where "old fashioned", "outdated" writers saw conflict and struggle as the key concepts in international (and domestic) economic development, Tinbergen saw harmony and possibilities of co-operation. Tinbergen's argument fitted in well with the arguments of sociologists such as Kerr (1973) according to which

* Originally published in English in the *Cambridge Journal of Economics*, September 1980, and in Dutch, with a few modifications, in the *Tijdschrift voor Politieke Ekonomie*, September 1980. The present version mainly follows the latter text. A criticism of the paper, together with a rejoinder by the author, were published in the *Cambridge Journal of Economics*, December 1981. The original paper was accompanied by the following note: Earlier versions of this paper were given as a lecture, circulated as a Research Memorandum, and presented as seminars at Amsterdam and Groningen Universities and the London School of Economics. I am grateful to E. Dirksen, S. Gomulka, J. van den Doel, J. J. Klant, R. Knaack, the referees of the *Cambridge Journal of Economics* and the editors of the *Tijdschrift voor Politieke Ekonomie* for helpful comments.

industrialisation leads to a broadly similar type of industrial society in all countries. Both arguments to some extent reflected the great post-war boom in the capitalist world and the impact this made on observers in both capitalist and state socialist countries. For example, the long period of full employment in the capitalist world made emphasis on unemployment as a fundamental *difference* between the systems, seem out of date for many years.

The convergence theory gave rise to a wide international discussion, which is summarised in Lauterbach (1976) and Spulber and Horowitz (1976). In view of the huge international literature on the subject, this chapter cannot deal with all the arguments that have been put forward. It concentrates on the theory originated by Tinbergen (1961) and modified by his pupil van den Doel (1971) and pays much less attention to the theory of technobureaucratic convergence as discussed by Brzezinski and Huntington (1965, pp. 10–11), Meyer (1970) and Baum (1977). The main difference between the two variants of the convergence theory concerns their theoretical base. The Tinbergen–van den Doel variant is based on ideas drawn from welfare economics, the technobureaucratic theory on ideas drawn from sociology. The former is the main focus of attention in this chapter both because the author is an economist not a sociologist and for reasons of space.

There are huge and growing number of facts which 'confirm' the convergence theory. Some of these were cited by Tinbergen in his paper. Otherwise have become more apparent in recent years. These range from the similar problems of educational planning in the two systems to the common application of agri-business, from a common concern with pollution to the common introduction of management information and control systems and the common development of multinational concerns. This list could be multiplied almost without end. Nevertheless, as all good Popperians know, the existence of confirmations is not decisive for the scientific standing of a theory.

In my view, the convergence theory has played a positive role in discussion, both scientific and political. From a scientific point of view, its emphasis on the similarities of the rival systems has been fruitful and is one of the basic elements in contemporary analysis of comparative economic systems (Pryor, 1973; Montias, 1976). Contemporary analysis of comparative economic systems, which uses common ideas (e.g. systems theory) to examine common problems (e.g. incentives) in the rival economic systems, would be impossible if the rival systems were divided by an unbridgeable chasm. Hence, the convergence discussion, with its criticism of the 'unbridgeable chasm' played an important role in making the contemporary analysis possible. From a political point of view, its emphasis on similarities rather than differences, which was and is opposed by the orthodox on both sides, played a healthy role in reducing Cold War hysteria.

B. CRITICISM OF THE ORIGINAL CONVERGENCE THEORY

Despite the above-mentioned positive features, the original convergence theory also had five important negative features. They are, incorrect observations, important differences, divergence, changed geographical relationship, and the importance of struggle.

1. *Incorrect Observations*

Many of the 'observations' made in the light of the theory are wrong. A good example of this is provided by the Kosygin reform of the 1960s in the USSR. This actually consisted of a number of detailed changes in the planning system designed to raise efficiency and change the distribution of income. Many observers, blinded by the convergence theory, 'saw' instead a radical reform making a substantial move towards a market economy. This interpretation could not stand close study of the Soviet experience (see Chapter 5).

2. *Important Differences*

The convergence theory focuses attention on *similarities* between the systems. Writers who adopted this standpoint paid less attention to *differences* between them. These, however, are of great importance and persistence. Important differences between the systems include, the existence and importance in the capitalist world of the capital market and property income, unemployment, insecurity of employment, continuous inflation, and rapid invention and production of revolutionary new goods (Kornai, 1971). The capital market is very important both for firms, their survival and growth, and also in determining the wealth of individuals (Thurow, 1976). Similarly, there are significant differences between the two systems in the allocation of labour (Nove, 1964; Garnsey, 1975; Pryor, 1977), with the state socialist countries having higher participation rates and a lower proportion of the labour force engaged in distribution. The smaller proportion of the population and of the labour force engaged in distribution under state socialism is a deliberate policy by governments which stress the crucial importance in economic growth of manufacturing industry and strive to minimise the allocation of labour to 'non-productive' sectors.* In addition, there are significant differences between the two systems in the area of distribution. The state socialist countries appear to have a significantly more equal distribution of income than comparable capitalist countries and also lack large private fortunes. Moreover, the state socialist countries tend to be supply constrained, the capitalist economies demand constrained. This has important implications for the investment goods, consumer goods, and labour, markets, for technical progress and for the foreign trade and external financial policies of these economies. For example, whereas investment in the state socialist world is normally characterised by investment tension, that is shortages of materials and workers and long construction periods, in the capitalist world investment is often insufficient to maintain full employment. Furthermore, there are very important differences between the systems in what are sometimes called 'non-material goods' (e.g. the output of the media, politics, religion and tourism; science and education; literature and the arts) arising from the political differences between state socialism and capitalism and the intellectual and cultural diversity of the advanced capitalist countries.

The technobureaucratic convergence theory is clearly right in some respects. The efficient operation of modern industry does require good time-keeping, multi-shift working in some cases and an ever-increasing technical division of labour. On the other hand, the theory tends to belittle the important differences between modern industrial societies, of which some examples were given in the previous paragraph. More generally, empirical evidence suggests that the social division of labour is not uniquely determined by technology. The work of the group of

---

* Pryor also found, and clearly this is closely related to the finding about the allocation of labour to distribution, that there was a significant inter-system difference in shopping time, with considerably more time required for shopping in state socialist countries (especially in Poland) than in comparable capitalist countries.

sociologists who compared industrial plants in Israel, Yugoslavia, Austria, Italy and the United States (Tannenbaum, 1974), Gallie's (1978) comparison of oil refineries in Britain and France, and Dore's (1974) comparison of British and Japanese industry, demonstrate clearly that widely different social arrangements may be associated with the same modern industrial technology. The empirical evidence suggests that the situation is that the efficient use of modern technology requires some uniformities but also permits a range of diversity, and that efficiency is not the sole goal of industrial societies.

3.   *Divergence*

The convergence theory ignores the extent of *divergence*. It is easy to make out a case for the two economic systems being further apart today than fifty-five years ago, during NEP. At that time the USSR had an extensive private sector, unemployment, price–market relations played a key role in the economy and there was no central economic planning. Similarly, comparing the UK and the USSR, it is easy to see that their economic systems, quite similar during World War II (both had rationing of consumer goods, state allocation of labour, state control of production, prices, foreign trade and foreign exchange), have since become more dissimilar. Furthermore, the end of the great post World War II boom in the capitalist world has re-emphasised important differences between the systems (e.g. full employment and job security in the state socialist countries) previously masked by the boom.

4.   *Changed Geographical Relationship*

The convergence theory fails to deal with changes in the geographical relations between the two systems. Since Tinbergen's article appeared, a number of third world countries (e.g. Cuba, Ethiopia, Angola, Kampuchea, South Vietnam, Mozambique, South Yemen) have adopted state socialist institutions. Significant groups in these countries evidently see important differences between the systems and regard state socialism as superior.* What is attractive about state socialism in much of the third world is not only Adler-Karlsson's three Es (employ-

---

* For an exposition of this point of view see Adler-Karlsson (1976, pp. 113–123).

ment, equality and essentials) but also the rapidity of economic development in the state socialist world and the fact that this development was along a path quite different from that taken and recommended by the capitalist countries. At the same time, some advanced state socialist countries have made (e.g. the NEM in Hungary and subsequent liberalisation), or attempted to make (e.g. Hungary in 1956, Czechoslovakia in 1968 and Poland in 1980–81), radical changes in their institutions. Similarly, supporters of state socialism in the advanced capitalist countries ('Eurocommunists') have abandoned significant parts of their old beliefs. Why is state socialism on the retreat in Europe and on the advance in the third world? What has to be explained is not that the two systems are getting closer, but that one is attractive in the third world and the other in the first world.

5.   *Importance of Conflict*

The convergence theory, like harmony thought in general, neglects the importance in social evolution of struggle and conflict. In international affairs this means to neglect the importance of war, armed conflict and revolution, and to emphasise the possibility and desirability of co-operation. In this respect the convergence theory is infected with utopian thinking (Carr, 1939) and neglects important and central, but disagreeable, factors in social evolution. In realist thought (both Marxist and conservative) war plays a major role in deciding the fate of mankind. Since the present divisions of the world economy are mainly the result of revolutions and wars, this is a serious consideration.

C.   THE MODIFIED CONVERGENCE THEORY OF VAN DEN DOEL: AN EXPOSITION

The convergence theory, as formulated by Tinbergen, was strongly opposed by officialdom in Eastern Europe and by many Sovietologists. This opposition largely rested on the second of the five objections made above, i.e. the important differences remaining between the systems.*

---

* This is essentially the main point in *Sovremennye* (1970), a standard Soviet criticism of the convergence theory. It is interesting to note that rejection of the convergence theory is one of those things that the authorities in Eastern Europe have in common with their opponents. See for example Rakovski (1978, chapter 4).

In an effort to overcome this opposition, a student of Tinbergen's reformulated it in his doctoral thesis (van den Doel, 1971). He hoped (van den Doel, 1971, p. 208)

> that this modified version of Tinbergen's convergence thesis will meet with a more positive reception by Eastern European economists and Western sovietologists than was the case with the original version, because it is believed that the modification does more justice to the exclusive character of the Soviet aims and to the Soviet policy in the past 25 years.

The modified convergence theory was based on four assumptions. First, that there exists an optimal economic system whose properties can be discovered by studying and developing standard welfare economics (Tinbergen, 1964, 1967). Secondly, that the actual systems function in similar environments. Thirdly, over time actual economies tend to move closer to the optimum. Fourthly, different economic systems have different objectives. (This was van den Doel's key modification of Tinbergen's theory.) The conclusion drawn from these assumptions was that in some respects the two systems are bound to move closer (since, for example, externalities and increasing returns mean that some centralisation is optimal for both systems), but in other respects important differences will remain as long as the objectives of the systems are different. Each system evolves towards an optimal economic order, but the optima are different because the objectives of the systems are different. This theory of *partial convergence* is illustrated in Fig. 18.1.

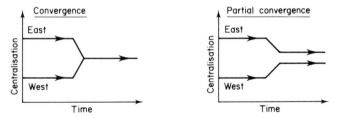

Fig. 18.1 Convergence and partial convergence. Source: J. van den Doel, *Konvergentie en Evolutie* (Assen, Netherlands, 1971), p. 193.

The modified convergence theory modified the Tinbergian in three respects, which concern its scope, empirical corroboration and theoretical base. As for as its scope is concerned, it focused attention on concentration and centralisation of economic decision-making as key features of an economic order, and did not consider all the many and varied phenomena discussed by other writers on convergence. Empirically, it analysed the factual material on the development of the US and Soviet economies in 1945–70. On this basis it argued that the Tinbergian version of the theory must be considered refuted and the modified version corroborated.* It also led to a prediction (that the evolution of the two economies in 1970–95 would be along the lines observed for the period 1945–70) the non-observance of which would be a refutation of the modified theory. This empirical analysis was a healthy application of Popperion methodology (although postponement of the possibility of refutation for twenty-five years clearly has conventionalist elements).

Theoretically, van den Doel linked up the convergence theory with theoretical welfare economics by locating it in the Tinbergian theory of the optimal economic order (as had already been done by Tinbergen himself). Instead of being merely an *ad hoc* inductive generalisation about developments in the world economy, it became a deduction from the principles of welfare economics. In this way, it not only asserted something about the development of the world economy, but also validated the importance, relevance and scientific status of welfare economics. For example, it was argued that decentralisation is desirable for the production of all goods the production of which is not under conditions of increasing returns, have no significant external effects, are not merit goods nor (in Soviet-type economies) plan priority sectors. This is demonstrated by welfare theory and corroborated by the actual experience of an economic system which rejects welfare economics and attempts to base its economic life on entirely different principles. Hence welfare economics is not a mere ideology, nor dependent on controversial value judgements, but a true, positive science.† That there are

---

* Another Tinbergian theory which has serious weaknesses in his theory of development planning. See Killick (1976).

† Van den Doel's idea that Partian welfare economics is a value-free, positive science was borrowed from his predecessor in the chair of welfare economics at Amsterdam University, P. Hennipman. It is argued in Hennipman (1976). It is undoubtedly a logically coherent point of view. It deals with the widespread criticism of welfare economics by retreating from the broad arena occupied by many welfare economists to a more restricted domain. This retreat raises two problems.

substantial economic propositions that are always true irrespective of socio-economic institutions and which are not the ideological expression of class interests, is an important and interesting fact. It was both important and healthy to stress this at a time when the opposite was being widely proclaimed.

The dynamics of the alleged convergence process, according to Tinbergen and van den Doel, are explained by each society's efforts to overcome inefficiencies. Since there is an optimal economic order which is the same for all societies (Tinbergen) or similar for all societies (van den Doel), and all societies function in similar environments, then efforts to reduce waste automatically generate convergence. This is analogous to the argument that since imperfect competition is inefficient, all societies will converge on perfect competition (for the production of private goods for which external effects, increasing returns to scale and indivisibilities are not significant). The three crucial assumptions in this dynamic process are the existence of an optimal economic order, the dominant role in social evolution of the search for efficiency, and the similarity of environments.

First, the area outside the Hennipman conception of welfare economics, that of recommending or condemning economic policies and evaluating economic institutions, is in fact an important one which many economists want to occupy. Moreover, it is not true that it is sharply delimited from economic science. As Blaug (1976, p. 175) has noted, the thesis that normative, as opposed to methodological, value judgements are not subject to rational discourse, is untenable. Maintaining it simply denies welfare economics of a potentially fruitful area of analysis. For the beginning of such an analysis see Sen (1970) pp. 58–64. See also Ward (1972). In addition, economists, because of their knowledge of economics, are better qualified for it that non-economists.

Secondly, is the restricted domain occupied by welfare economics in the Hennipman interpretation so small as to be trivial? Judging by the attention paid to it in their writing (e.g. van den Doel, 1978) it would seem that the Hennipman school regard the study of Pareto-optimal allocations as not only positive but also non-trivial. This can only be so if we make the hidden assumption (it is not made explicitly in their writings as far as I can see) that static allocative efficiency is either a widely shared goal or quantitatively important or both. What is the evidence for these assumptions? As far as I am aware, all the evidence suggests that they are false. This may well be an example of the phenomenon discussed by Lakatos (1976, pp. 43–47) by which criticism shows that an argument depends on an assumption which is both hidden and false.

D. THE MODIFIED CONVERGENCE THEORY OF
VAN DEN DOEL: A CRITIQUE

In spite of its positive features, it seems to me that the modified convergence theory has a large number of important weaknesses. These are considered in the following sections.

1. *The Optimal Economic Order*

The concept of an 'optimal' economic order is an application to the economy as a whole of the elementary mathematics of optimisation. It is vulnerable to a number of well known criticisms (Pasinetti, 1965; Kornai, 1971; Simon, 1976; Schon, 1971; Dunn, 1971; Loasby, 1976; Petrakov, 1976). They concern its conception of *rationality* and of *the environment* in which decisions are made.

As far as *rationality* is concerned, it is assumed that there exists an objective function and that rational behaviour consists of its maximisation. Both assumptions are of an *a priori* nature and are not confirmed by empirical observations. Kornai (1971) has pointed out, on the basis of his observation of, and participation in, the formulation of national economic plans, that national economic planning is not a process of maximising a national economic objective function. Rather it is a process of interaction between the aspirations of politicians and what is technically feasible as calculated by economists, leading to the adoption of plans which are consistent (but may be unfeasible) and satisfactory. In the same vein Petrakov (1976) has argued that the conception of national economic planning as the maximisation of an exogenous objective function is inappropriate. This conception, in his opinion, is an illegitimate extension to a complex, indeterminate, uncertain, social system of an idea appropriate to some problems of operations research. Similarly, Loasby (1976) has pointed out that business decision-making uses multiple objectives which are only loosely related to reach satisfactory decisions. As numerous authors have pointed out, human rationality is a learning process not a maximising one.

As far as *the environment* is concerned, the maximising model assumes that it is one in which the choice set is given and completely known, computational techniques are adequate to produce an optimal solution in the time available at negligible cost, and the multiplication of decision makers is insignificant. In fact, the decision-making environment is normally characterised by partial ignorance, inadequate techniques for data processing and complexity. Hence, the search for optimal solutions is often not feasible. In 'developing' Tinbergen's theory, van den Doel retreated from Tinbergen's work on target planning (Tinbergen, 1952), which as Simon (1976, p. 138) has noted was a pioneering example of satisficing, to his later work within the traditional maximising framework.

It is important to note that rejection of the notion of an 'optimal' economic order undermines the dynamic process which, as explained above, is generating the alleged convergence (or partial convergence). The existence of an optimal economic order is one of the three crucial assumptions necessary for the process.

2. *The Rational Actor Fallacy*

The generalisation of the notion of maximising behaviour from the individual (for whom it was originally developed) to society as a whole, generates what has come to be called the 'rational actor' fallacy (Allison, 1971). This is the notion that a collective, such as a nation, can usefully be treated as if it were an individual maximising some objective/s. A clear statement of this position was made by van den Doel (1977 p. 124) in one of his applications of his theory. "When I speak of 'the' aims of the Chinese People's Republic, I am making use of a holistic concept of a single indivisible Chinese society." It is well known from contemporary writing on decision making (Allison, 1971; Lindblom, 1965; Steinbruner, 1974) that this can generate serious failures of understanding. Society is not a single actor seeking to maximise its goals. Depending on the problem one is interested in, one can make use of one or more of the various models developed in the decision-making literature, e.g. the organisational conflict, bureaucratic politics, cybernetics, etc. For the analysis of many economic and social questions it makes most sense to see society not as a rational actor seeking to maximise some goals, but as an arena in which different interests fight it out for supremacy. Hence society stumbles from one imperfect compromise to another.

The disadvantages of the rational actor model relative to the conflict model can be seen clearly by contrasting van den Doel's rational actor model of Chinese economic development (van den Doel, 1977) with Lampton's analysis (1974, 1977) of Chinese economic policy. According to van den Doel, China is evolving to its own optimum. This optimistic diagnosis and prediction ignores the extent to which econo-mic policies have been *reversed* in China. For example, consider the industrial planning and management system. Although there have been important elements of continuity, there have also been significant changes. The Soviet system was copied in the early 1950s and aban-doned in the late 1950s. In the early 1960s industrial management emphasised the importance of production and recognised the import-ance of material incentives, qualified engineers and authority in main-taining and increasing it. During and after the Cultural Revolution there was less piecework and individual cash bonuses, devolution of initiatives to provinces and lower-level authorities and emphasis on horizontal integration of the economy and local self-sufficiency, a reduction in the number of ministries and other central bodies, despe-cialisation of production, attacks on rules and regulations and manage-rial authority, attacks on cadres and formation of revolutionary com-mittees, and stress on workers' control. After the downfall of the 'Gang of Four' in 1976 there was renewed stress on the need for discipline, authority, hierarchy, specialisation and centralisation, and on the importance of production, its profitability, quality and quantity. How does this fit into the gradual optimisation scenario? It easily fits into the perpetual conflict one. Each stage in policy was characterised by a different dominant group of decision makers.

On the other hand, study of the politics of China's medical policies led Lampton (1974, p. 11) to formulate the hypothesis that

China's leaders (in the health sphere) have been limited in their selection of policy alternatives by a dearth of trained manpower and money, by fragmentation of authority (both functionally and by organisational level), by cooptation and professionalization of subordinates, by external (e.g. international) pressures, by leader-mass linkages, by elite strife, and by the unanticipated result of previous policies. In the process of attempting to overcome these limitations, political bargaining and co-alition formation occurs. This suggests that "rational decision making" approaches, which view policy as the result of a detached assessment of the "best" policy in terms of preferred values, are inapplicable. Public policies in China are often compromises among several constituencies, each of which tries to maximise realization of its values.

This hypothesis enabled Lampton to make sense of the fluctuating medical policies pursued (for example with respect to traditional medicine, provision of curative care in rural areas, and professional-isation) in the People's Republic of China.

3. *Outcomes as Revealed Preferences?*

Van den Doel derives from neo-classical consumer demand theory the idea that observed outcomes enable inferences to be drawn about the preferences of decision makers. This is a doubtful assumption for two reasons. First, it ignores the implementation process. What is actually done may be very different from what the decision makers prefer as a result of élite politics, bureaucratic inertia, organisational conflict and ignorance. Secondly, it treats the preference set of the decision makers as very large. The differences, in this subjectivist conception, between the economic policies pursued in the USA, USSR and PRC mainly reflect the different objectives of the decision makers. This ignores the extent to which the goals of decision makers are constrained by objective facts, notably technical progress, the position of the country concerned in the world economy and international politics.

4. *Progress?*

Van den Doel shares the optimistic world view of the Enlightenment, preserved in the ideology of the socialist movement, that the world is gradually getting better. Thus not only *is* there an optimum, but we are actually moving *closer* towards it. This ignores the possibility both of retrogression and of stasis. Take for example the problem of unemployment in the advanced capitalist countries. It is easy to see that in this area we have regressed in the past decade. Ten years ago the problem was thought to have been eliminated. In ten years time it may be worse. A good example of stasis is provided by Poland. As far as radical economic reform is concerned, that country is at about the same stage as it was about twenty years ago. The balance of internal and external forces is such that the country cannot abandon talk about economic reform but cannot implement one either.

5. *Efficiency and Economic Evolution*

The idea of the role of efficiency in economic life which Tinbergen and van den Doel borrowed from welfare economics is a vulnerable one for a whole number of reasons. Factors other than economic efficiency may be very important in determining social evolution (this, of course, was recognised by Tinbergen, but de-emphasised). Despite Keynes's well

known remark, *interests* are important in economic policy. As Dobb
(1937, p. 337) so eloquently argued:

> The struggle of mankind to-day is as much—nay, more—a struggle to
> unseat a powerful interest whereby to banish the 'mean and malignant'
> system which this interest upholds, as it was in the days when classical
> Political Economy launched its influential attacks, with unrestrained
> partisanship, upon the monopolistic system of its day. When interest
> obstructs reason, to preach reason is vain unless it [is] preach[ed] to
> dethrone interest.

Kowalik (1978, p. 150) has noted that this argument is also relevant
under state socialism. I have given an example of its relevance to the
organisation of agricultural labour in Chapter 4, pp. 66–67 above.

For many years, numerous economists in the state socialist countries
have criticised the inefficiency of the administrative economy, but
radical reform has been rare and in the USSR largely absent. An
important reason for this is the interest in the present system of those
who gain from it. As a character in Zinoviev (1978, pp. 152–153) has
correctly noted:

> Just count up how many we have of ministers, deputy ministers, heads of
> chief administrations and trusts, directors, secretaries of regional and
> district party committees, academicians, writers, officers and generals,
> etc etc down to policemen, heads of sectors, university departments,
> housing administrations, warehouses, shops etc etc. This system is their
> system.

In addition, inertia is very important in economic policy. Inertia and
interest may well be closely linked, as Dobb (1970, pp. 68–69) noted
apropos of economic reform in Eastern Europe:

> the centralised system will have bred attitudes and habits and work of its
> own, together with a structure of relationships between administrative
> levels that may exercise a strongly conservative resistance to change and
> to the adoption and cultivation of new attitudes, relationships and
> methods. The old centralised mechanism will have reared a generation of
> planners and administrators, even of managers of enterprises, who
> having grown up with it and with its methods are practiced in this and
> nothing else. They may well also have also a vested interest in its
> continuance, especially if any privileges, economic or social, attaching to
> position or to function, are involved. In course of time built-in resistance
> to other methods and to change come into being.

Furthermore, the most efficient institution or policy for solving this or that problem (e.g. de-industrialisation) may not be known. (Naturally Tinbergen recognised this, but he treated it as a problem for his research programme rather than as something which reduced the explanatory power of this theory.) Both Van Eijk (1979, p. 525) and Allsopp and Joshi (1980, p. 103) have pointed out, with reference to macro-economic policy in the Netherlands and the UK respectively, that the notion of applying an indubitably efficient policy is simply not applicable. No-one today can be sure what is an efficient policy.

Moreover, there may be important complementarities between policies or institutions so that substantial gains in efficiency in one area cannot be obtained without substantial costs in terms of inefficiencies elsewhere. An example of the importance of these complementarities is full employment policy. Full employment is a major achievement of state socialism (see chapter 11). It is combined, however, with major problems of labour inflexibility, work morale and lack of effort and interest by workers. It may sound strange to many readers, but it is an important fact that in 1978–79 there took place extensive public and press discussions both in Poland and China about the problems generated by security of employment and full employment and the difficulty of combining them with adequate effort. For many economists and administrators in the state socialist countries, security of employment and full employment, while recognised to be achievements from a social point of view, are considered to be serious problems from an efficiency point of view. For example, in a letter published in the Polish weekly *Polityka*, 30 September 1978, some Polish managers criticised the low level of work discipline and worker effort in their country and suggested as a remedy reintroducing some unemployment. The idea was to use the threat—and reality—of unemployment as a means of disciplining the workers, of making them work harder and more conscientiously.* The importance of the complementary nature of economic control mechanisms has been emphasised by Kornai (1979, pp. 17–18) in a vivid and striking passage cited on p. 191. There Kornai argued that economic systems exhibit important complementarities and that arbitrarily picking out positive features of a system without automatically also selecting

---

* For a German translation of this letter, and of some of the reactions to it, see *Osteuropa-Archiv*, 1979, pp. A 571–A 583.

the negative features was impossible. Hence the idea of gradually raising efficiency by gradually increasing the positive aspects of an economic system and gradually reducing the negative aspects is often unfeasible. The holistic nature of an economic system may render it impossible. To express the same thought another way, fixed coefficients may apply not just to production processes but also to economic systems as a whole.

As a result of the complementary nature of economic institutions or policies, an institution or policy which forms part of an efficient system may not be an improvement if introduced on its own into an inefficient system. A well known practical example of this is provided by economic reform in Eastern Europe. It was long ago argued by Kornai, and has since been amply demonstrated, that a substantial gain of efficiency on the administrative economy requires the introduction of a whole package of measures, which are well thought out and carefully related to each other. A theoretical exposition of this point, developed quite independently of the process of institutional change under state socialism, is the (welfare theoretical) theory of the second best.

The four factors discussed above (interests, inertia, ignorance and the complementarity of efficient policies or institutions) are all important. Taken together, they severely constrain the applicability of the second of the key assumptions of the alleged dynamic convergence process (the dominant role in social evolution of the search for efficiency).

6. *Similarity of Environments*

The similarity of environments is an important hidden assumption in the work of van den Doel. He tends to discuss the efficiency of economic policy measures without sufficient attention to the fact that efficiency is always relative to given resources and constraints. These resources and constraints may differ profoundly from country to country, and hence policies efficient in one country may be inefficient in another. For example, the policy which he has advocated of expanding the public sector so as to reduce inefficiency (i.e. unemployment) makes a certain sense in the Netherlands with its efficient public services and not too serious bureaucratisation. In Italy, on the other hand, with its largely parasitic public sector, such a policy would be profoundly inefficient.

7. *Communism*

In his discussion of Soviet goals, van den Doel (1971, chapter 4) follows the dominant Anglo-Saxon tradition, much criticised by P. C. Roberts, of relegating the higher stage of Communism to mere theology, of no practical importance. This seems rather doubtful, at any rate in this extreme formulation. Take for example the OGAS.* The possibility of undertaking this project has been created by the scientific-technical revolution, it is partially similar to work being undertaken throughout the world, and its desirability is obviously much influenced by what are seen as undesirable social consequences of economic reform (i.e. unemployment, inequality, inflation, end of strictly hierarchical society). Nevertheless, it would hardly have been embarked upon and such resources invested in it, were it not that the prevailing image of the type of planned economy that will prevail under Communism is one that envisages (Liberman, 1970, p. 74) "the management from the centre of an all embracing extremely detailed nomenclature of commodities".

8. *Weaknesses Shared with the Original Theory*

The modified theory shares the weaknesses of the original theory (incorrect observations, important differences, divergence, changed geographical relationship, importance of conflict). The importance of the fifth weakness of the original theory for van den Doel's modified theory can been seen very easily by considering van den Doel's analysis, in his (1971) Chapter 4, of Soviet goals. The fact that Soviet goals are largely relative to the position of the leading countries, as a result of the conflicts that characterise international affairs, is not mentioned at all, although it is of great importance. Soviet economic history can scarcely

---

* The OGAS is a Soviet acronym which literally means 'Nation-wide automated system for the gathering and processing of information for accounting, planning and control of the national economy'. For an analysis of the OGAS see Cave (1980).

be understood without the concept of 'overtaking and surpassing', especially in the crucial military field, a goal forced on the country by its position in the world economy and the state of international politics. Military factors are of great importance in influencing the Soviet economic mechanism. This was explained by Stalin in a famous speech of 1931 and repeated by Lange in his famous description of the administrative economy as "a *sui generis* war economy". For harmony theorists, however, these are disagreeable facts which they would prefer not to think about. Similarly, the changes in the Chinese economic mechanism in recent years can scarcely be understood without remembering that modernisation of the armed forces is one of the 'four modernisations'.

E.   IDEOLOGY AND CONVERGENCE

Ad hominem arguments are always a little disreputable, and quite rightly, since they throw no light on the *truth* of a theory. Nevertheless, economics is not physics, and despite Lakatosite jibes about 'externalist rubbish', the social background to a theory in economics can throw considerable light on why it is developed and maintained. In my view, the convergence theory, considered not as a scientific theory to explain systemic change, but as a psychological and sociological phenomenon which itself requires explanation, has to be considered part of the ideology of Social Democracy in general and of the Dutch Labour Party (PvdA) in particular. From this point of view it has three advantages. First, it is an anti Cold War doctrine. Social Democratic parties do not like the Cold War very much. The resources devoted to arms have an opportunity cost in terms of social programmes. The hysteria it generates is not suitable for rational discussion of reforms. Ideologically, it strengthens liberalism (in the Friedmanite sense). The convergence theory questions the view that the two sides are divided by an unbridgeable chasm and hence reduces the importance of Cold War considerations.*

---

* Similarly, the Swedish writer Adler-Karlsson, who is not a convergence theorist but who is also a Social Democrat, in his (1976, p. 71) peddles the illusion that we are witnessing a transition "from military to economic confrontation". As I pointed out in a review of this book (*De Economist*, 1978, no. 2, p. 278) "it is not true as he suggests by his subtitle on p. 71 that military confrontation has been replaced by economic confrontation. Military preparations in all quarters are continuing at a rapid rate."

Secondly, it is a 'progressive' doctrine. It concerns itself not just with the current situation but with developmental trends. It turns out that in both systems not only are differences being reduced but that the situation is getting better.

Thirdly, it contains arguments which provide an effective rebuttal to Marxist critics of Social Democracy. (The PvdA was formed in 1946 from various groups, Marxist and non-Marxist, and its leadership has traditionally had to face criticism from Marxists.) When criticised by a Marxist for breaching proletarian unity, a spokesman for the PvdA familiar with the modified convergence theory can always say, "We would love to cooperate with you, but unfortunately this is not possible so long as our *goals* are different. You, for example, are opposed to all income from property whereas we think that only large property incomes are undesirable. As soon as you adopt our goals, then cooperation will be possible."

It is not an accident that both Tinbergen and van den Doel are prominent members of the PvdA (the latter being for a time a member of the lower house) and that someone (J. Pronk) who worked with Tinbergen for a while on this theory in the 1960s (Linneman *et al.*, 1970) subsequently became a PvdA Minister.

F. SUMMARY

The original convergence theory is an inductive generalisation about the world economy. It has both positive and negative features. Five of the latter are particularly important. The modified convergence theory deduced modified convergence from unproblematic background knowledge. The modified theory has one advantage over the original theory (the abandonment of the idea that the two systems will converge). It also has, however, a number of additional weaknesses, arising from the fact that the 'unproblematic background knowledge' from which the modified theory is deduced is actually very problematic. The dynamics of the alleged convergence (or partial convergence) rest on three assumptions, all of which are vulnerable to criticism. Besides internalist criticism of the truth of the convergence theory, an externalist hypothesis was presented to explain the psychological and sociological questions of why the theory is believed and what its social function is. The chapter considered mainly the convergence theory of Tinbergen and his school and neglected other variants, e.g. the technobureaucratic convergence theory.

REFERENCES

Adam, J. (1973). "The Incentive System in the USSR: the Abortive Reform of 1965". *Industrial and Labour Relations Review*, October.

Adler-Karlsson, G. (1976). *The Political Economy of East-West-South Co-operation*. Vienna and New York: Springer.

Allison, G. (1971). *Essence of Decisions*. Boston: Little, Brown.

Allsopp, C. and Joshi, V. (1980). "Alternative Strategies for the UK". *National Institute Economic Review*, no. 91, February.

Althusser, L. (1977) Talk at a Venice conference. Published in French in Il Manifesto. *Pouvoir et opposition*, Paris: 1978.

Althusser, L. (1978). "De krisis van het marxisme". *Te elfder ure*, no. 24.

Amann, R., Cooper, J. M. and Davies, R. W. (eds) (1977). *The Technological Level of Soviet Industry*. New Haven: Yale University Press.

Ames, E. (1965). *Soviet Economic Processes*. Homewood, Ill.: Richard Irwin.

Anchishkin, I. A. (1977). *Ekonomischeskie usloviya rosta blagosostoyaniya sovetskogo naroda*. Moscow: Nauka.

Andors, S. (1980). "The Political and Organizational Implications of China's New Economic Policies, 1976–1970". *Bulletin of Concerned Asian Scholars*, vol. 12, no. 2.

Arutyunyan, Yu. V. (1973). "The Distribution of Decisionmaking among the Rural Population of the USSR". *Social Stratification and Mobility in the USSR* (M. Yanowitch and W. A. Fisher, eds). New York: International Arts and Sciences Press.

Bachurin, A. V. (1973). *Planovo-ekonomicheskie metody upravleniya*. Moscow: Ekonomika.

Bajt, A. (1971). "Investment Cycles in European Socialist Economies: A Review Article". *Journal of Economic Literature*, no. 1.

Barker, T. and Brailovsky, V. (eds) (1981). *Oil or Industry?* London and New York: Academic Press.

Barsov, A. A. (1968). "Sel'skoe khozyaistvo i istochniki sotsialisticheskogo nakoplenie v gods pervoi pyatletki (1928–1932)". *Istoriya SSSR*, no. 3.

Barsov, A. A. (1969). *Balans stoimostnykh obmenov mezhdu gorodom i derevnei*. Moscow: Nauka. The main statistical source used by Barsov is *Materialy* (1932).

Barsov, A. A. (1974). "Nep i vyravnivanie ekonomicheskikh otnoshenii mezhdu gorodom i derevnei". *Novaya ekonomicheskaya politika: Voprosy teorii i istorii*. Moscow: Nauka.

Bauer, T. (1978). "Investment Cycles in Planned Economies". *Acta Oeconomica* vol. 21, no. 3.

Baum, R. (1977). "Diabolus ex machina: Technological Development and Social Change in Chinese Industry". *Technology and Communist Culture*. (F. J. Fleron, ed.). New York: Praeger.

Bazarova, G. V. (1968). *Pribyl' v ekonomicheskom stimulirovanii proizvodstva*. Moscow: Nauka.

Becker, A. S. (1972). "National Income Accounting in the USSR". *Soviet Economic Statistics* (V. G. Treml and J. P. Hardt, eds). Durham, North Carolina: Duke University Press.

Bek, A. (1971). *Novoe naznachenie*. Frankfurt: Posev.

Bennett, G. (ed.) 1979). *China's Finance and Trade. A Policy Reader*. London: Macmillan.

Bergson, A. (1961). *The Real National Income of Soviet Russia since 1928*. Cambridge, Mass.: Harvard University Press.

Bergson, A. (1981). "Can the Soviet slowdown be reversed?". *Challenge*, November/December.

Berliner, J. (1976). *The Innovation Decision in Soviet Industry*. Cambridge, Mass.: Harvard University Press.

Berri, L. Ya. (ed.) (1977). *Planning a Socialist Economy*. Moscow: Progress.

Blackaby, F. (ed.) (1979). *De-industrialisation*. London: Heinemann.

Blaug, M. (1976). "Kuhn versus Lakatos". *Method and Appraisal in Economics* (S. J. Latsis, ed.). Cambridge: Cambridge University Press.

Bornstein, M. (1972). "Soviet Price Statistics". *Soviet Economic Statistics* (V. G. Treml and J. P. Hardt, eds). Durham, North Carolina: Duke University Press.

Brezinski, Z. K. and Huntington, S. (1965). *Political Power USA/USSR*. New York: Viking.

Brody, A. (1980). "On the Discussion about Measurement—A Rejoinder". *Acta Oeconomica*, vol. 25, nos 1–2.

Broekmeyer, M. J. (1976). *Het wetenschapsbedrijf in de Sovjet-Unie*. The Hague: Nederlands Instituut voor vredesvraagstukken.

Broekmeyer, M. J. (1978). "De particuliere landbouw in de USSR". *Internationale Spectator*, October.

Bronson, D. and Severin, B. (1966). "Recent Trends in Consumption and Disposable Money Income in the USSR". *New Directions in the Soviet Economy*: US Government Printing Office.

Brouwer, M. (1979). "Het aardgas en onze economie, zegen of vloek". *Samenleving en onderzoek* (J. J. Klant et al., eds). Leiden and Antwerp: Stenfert Kroese.

Brouwer, M. and de Jong, H. (1978). "Herstructurering, werkgelegenheid en internationalisatie". *Herstructurering van de industrie* (A. W. M. Teulings, ed.). Alphen a/d Rijn: Samson.

Brus, W. (1972). *The Market in a Socialist Economy*. London: Routledge and Kegan Paul.

Brus, W. (1973). *The Economics and Politics of Socialism*. London: Routledge and Kegan Paul.

Brus, W. (1975). *Socialist Ownership and Political System*. London: Routledge and Kegan Paul.

Brus, W. (1979). "The Eastern European Reforms: What Happened to Them? *Soviet Studies*, April.

Brus, W. (1981). "Les conséquences économiques du stalinisme". *Revue européene des Sciences sociales et Cahiers Vilfredo Pareto*, vol. XIX, nr. 57.

Bush, K. (1973). "Resource Allocation Policy: Capital Investment". *Soviet Economic Prospects for the Seventies*. (Joint Economic Committee US Congress, Washington DC).

Bychek, N. R. & Chistyakov, M. I. (1977). *Metodologiya razrabotki pyatletnogo plana*. Moscow: Ekonomika.

Carr, E. H. (1939). *The 20 Years' Crisis*. London: Macmillan.

Carr, E. H. (1961). *What is History?* London: Macmillan.

Carr, E. H. and Davies, R. W. (1969). *Foundations of a Planned Economy*, vol. 1, part 1. London: Macmillan.

Carr, E. H. and Davies, R. W. (1969). *Foundation of a Planned Economy*, vol. one II. London: Macmillan.

Cave, M. (1980. *Computers and Economic Planning*. Cambridge: Cambridge University Press.

Chao, K. (1970). *Agricultural Production in Communist China 1949–1965*. Madison, Wisconsin: University of Wisconsin Press.

Chapman, J. G. (1983). "Earnings distribution in the USSR, 1968–1976". *Soviet Studies* vol XXXV no. 3 July.

Clarke, R. A. (1972). *Soviet Economic Facts 1917–1970*. London: Macmillan.

Cliff, T. (1980). *Marxism and the Collectivisation of Agriculture*. London: Socialist Workers' Party.

Cohen, S. F. (1974). *Bukharin and the Bolshevik Revolution*. London: Wildwood House.

Cooper, J. (1970). *Innovation for Innovation in Soviet industry*. CREES discussion paper B 11. Birmingham University.

Cornwall, J. (1977). *Modern Capitalism*. London: Martin Robertson.

Crook, F. W. (1970). *An Analysis of Work-payment Systems used in Chinese Mainland Agriculture, 1956 to 1970*. Unpublished Ph.D. dissertation, Fletcher School, Tufts University.

CIA, (1974). *Potential Implications of Trends in World Population, Food Production, and Climate*, Washington DC.

CIA, (1976). *USSR: The Impact of Recent Climate Change on Grain Production*. Research Aid. Washington DC.

Dando, W. A. (1976). "Man-made Famines". *Ecology of Food and Nutrition*, vol. 4.

David, E. (1903). *Socialismus und Landwirtschaft*. Berlin: Verlag der socialist. Monatshefte, 2nd. ed. Leipzig 1922.

Davies, R. W. (1976). "The Soviet Economic Crisis of 1931–1933." Mimeo Discussion Paper, CREES Birmingham, England.

Davies, R. W. & Wheatcroft, S. eds (1985). *Materials to the balance of the Soviet economy*. Cambridge: Cambridge University Press.

Davis, C. and Feshbach, M. (1980). *Rising Infant Mortality in the USSR in the 1970's*. Washington DC: US Department of Commerce.

Davis, C. M. (1979). *The Economics of the Soviet Health System: An Analytical and Historical Study, 1921–1978*. Unpublished PhD Thesis, Cambridge.

Deutscher, I. (1950). *Soviet Trade Unions*. London: Royal Institute of International Affairs.

Deutscher, I. (1963). *The Prophet Outcast*. London: Oxford University Press.

Differentsirovannyi balans dokhodov i potrebleniya naseleniya (1977). Moscow: Nauka.

Dirksen, E. (1981). "The Control of Inflation? Errors in the Interpretation of CPE Data". *Economica*, August.

Dobb, M. (1924). "The Entrepreneur Myth." *Economica*, no. 10. Reprinted in Dobb, *On Economic Theory and Socialism* (1955). London: Routledge and Kegan Paul.

Dobb, M. (1929). "A Sceptical View of the Theory of Wages." *Economic Journal*, December.

Dobb, M. (1937). *Political Economy and Capitalism*. London: Routledge and Kegan Paul.

Dobb, M. (1962). "Communication". *Labour Monthly*, January.

Dobb, M. (1966). *Argument on Socialism*. London: Lawrence and Wishart.

Dobb, M. (1970). *Socialist Planning: Some Problems*. London: Lawrence and Wishart.

Dobb, M. (1973). *Theories of Value and Distribution since Adam Smith*. Cambridge: Cambridge University Press.

Dobb, M. (1978). "Random Biographical Notes." *Cambridge Journal of Economics*, vol. 2, no. 2.

Doel, J. van den (1971). *Konvergentie en Evolutie*. Assen: van Gorcum.

Doel, J. van den (1977). "Carry out the Revolution and Increase Production". *De Economist*, vol. 125, no. 2.

Doel, J. van den (1978). *Demokratie en welvaartstheorie*. 2nd. ed. Alphen a/d Rijn: Samson.

Doel, J. van den (1979). *Democracy and Welfare Economics*. Cambridge: Cambridge University Press.

Doel, H. van den (1980). "Evolutie en Structuur". *Economische Statistische Berichten*, no. 3266.

Domar, E. (1974). "On the Optimal Compensation of a Socialist Manager". *Quarterly Journal of Economics*, February.

Dore, R. P. (1973). *British Factory–Japanese Factory*. London: Allen and Unwin.

Dorner, P. (1972). *Land Reform and Economic Development*. London: Penguin.

Driehuis, W. and van den Doel, J. (1979). "Werkloosheid en economische orde". Geschriften van de vereniging voor arbeidsrecht 2. *Werkloosheid: recht of beleid?* Alphen a/d Rijn: Samson.

Driehuis, W. and van der Zwan, A. eds (1978). *De voorbereiding van het economische belaid kritische bezien.* Leiden: Stenfert Kroese.

Dumont, R. and Mottin, M. F. (1980). *L'Afrique Etranglée.* Paris: Ed. du Seuil.

Dunn, E. S. (1971). *Economic and Social development: A Process of Social Learning.* Baltimore: The Johns Hopkins Press.

Durgin, F. A., Jr. (1978). "The Inefficiency of Soviet Agriculture versus the Efficiency of US Agriculture." *The ACES Bulletin,* vol. 20, nos 3–4.

Eckstein, A. (1975). *China's Economic Development.* Ann Arbor: University of Michigan Press.

Eckstein, A. (1977). *China's Economic Revolution.* Cambridge: Cambridge University Press.

Economic Survey of Europe in 1976. Part II. *The Five Year Plans for 1976–1980 in Eastern Europe and the Soviet Union.* UN: Geneva and New York. 1977.

Eijk, C. J. van (1979). "Ontwikkelingen in de voorbereiding van de nederlandse economische politiek". *Maandschrift Economie,* no. 12.

Ellman, M. (1971). *Soviet Planning Today.* Cambridge: Cambridge University Press.

Ellman, M. (1973). *Planning Problems in the USSR: The Contribution of Mathematical Methods to their Solution.* Cambridge: Cambridge University Press.

Ellman, M. (1975). "Did the Agricultural Surplus provide the Resources for the Increase in Investment in the USSR during the First Five Year Plan?". *Economic Journal,* December.

Ellman, M. (1977). "Report from Holland: The Economics of North Sea Hydrocarbons". *Cambridge Journal of Economics,* September.

Ellman, M. (1978). "The fundamental problem of socialist planning". *Oxford Economic Papers,* July.

Ellman, M. (1979). *Socialist Planning.* Cambridge: Cambridge University Press.

Ellman, M. (1979a). *Full Employment—Lessons from State Socialism.* Leiden & Antwerp: Stenfert Kroese. Reprinted in *De Economist* 1979, no. 4.

Ellman, M. (1979b). "De gevolgen van de collectivisatie voor de landbouw in de USSR, 1929–1979. *Internationale Spectator,* no. 10.

Ellman, M. (1979c). "Full Employment—Lessons from State Socialism". *De Economist,* no. 4.

Ellman, M. (1980). "De ekonomische krisis in de Sovjet-Unie". *Ost Europa Verkenningen,* no. 48, April. English version: *Critique,* no. 12, 1980.

Ellman, M. (1980a). "What are the conditions for a viable incomes policy?— The Soviet experience". *Reverse Sovietology* (S. Markowski, ed.). London: Forthcoming.

Erlich, A. (1950). "Preobrazhenski and the economics of Soviet industrialisation". *Quarterly Journal of Economics*, vol. LXIV, no. 1. February.

Europe and China (1980). January

Faber, B. L. (ed.) (1976). *The Social Structure of Eastern Europe*. New York: Praeger.

Fallenbuchl, Z. M. (1967). "Collectivisation and Economic Development". *Canadian Journal of Economics and Political Sciences*, vol. XXXIII, no. 1, February.

Fehér, F., Heller, A. and Márkus, G. (1983). *Dictatorship over needs*. Oxford: Basil Blackwell.

Feinstein, C. H. (ed.) (1967). *Socialism, Capitalism and Economic Growth*. Cambridge: Cambridge University Press.

Field, R. M. (1979). "A Slowdown in Chinese Industry". *The China Quarterly*, December.

Filtzer, D. (1978). "Preobrazhensky and the Problem of the Soviet Transition". *Critique 9*.

Financiele (1977). "Financiele aspecten van herstructurering". *Herstructurering Deel III*, Rotterdam: Department of Finance and Investment Erasmus Universiteit, mimeo.

Finansy SSSR (1975). no. 6.

Fitzgerald, E. V. K. (1982). "Planned Accumulation and Income Distribution in the Small Peripheral Economy". (Mimeo). To be published in *Readings in capitalist and non-capitalist development strategies* (K. Martin ed.). London: 1985.

Fleron, F. J. (ed.) (1977). *Technology and Communist Culture*. New York: Praeger.

Friedman, M. (1969). *The Optimum Quantity of Money and Other Essays*. Chicago: Aldine.

Friedman, M. (1975). *Unemployment versus Inflation?* London: Institute of Economic Affairs.

Friedman, M. (1977). *Inflation and Unemployment*. London: Institute of Economic Affairs.

Friss, I. (1971). "On Long Term National Economic Planning". *Economic laws, policy, planning* (I. Friss, ed.). Budapest: Akadémiai Kiadó.

Furth *et al* (1978). Furth, D., Heertje, A. & R. J. v.d. Veen, "On Marx's theory of unemployment". *Oxford Economic Papers* vol XXX.

Galenson, W. (1955). *Labour Productivity in Soviet and American Industry*. New York: Columbia University Press.

Gallie, D. (1978). *In Search of the New Working Class*. Cambridge: Cambridge University Press.

Gao Zhihua (1980). "What is the Best Economic Set-Up for China?" *Social Sciences in China*, vol. 1. no. 1.

Garnsey, E. (1975). "Occupational structure in industrialised society: some notes on the convergence thesis in the light of Soviet experience". *Sociology*, vol. 9, no. 3.

Garnsey, E. (1982). "Capital accumulation and the division of labour in the Soviet Union". *Cambridge Journal of Economics* March.

Garvy, G. (1975). "Stabilization Policy and Monetary Equilibrium". Milan: CESES.

Garvy, G. (1977). *Money, Financial Flows, and Credit in the Soviet Union.* Cambridge, Mass.: Ballinger.

Gomulka, S. (1971). *Inventive activity, diffusion and the stages of economic growth* Aarhus, Denmark: Institute of Economics, Aarhus University.

Goodstadt, L. (1981). "The Great Chinese Economic Retreat". *Euromoney*, April.

Haase, H. (1980). "GDR: Prospects for the 1980s" (NATO colloquium 1980). *Economic Reforms in Eastern Europe and Prospects for the 1980s.* Oxford: Pergamon.

Haaster, D. van and Salverda, W. (1977). "Verborgen werkloosheid". *Tijdschrift voor Politieke Ekonomie*, no. 1.

Hafkamp, W. A. and Reuten, G. A. (eds) (1980). *Investeringsplanning als remedie tegen werkloosheid.* Alphen a/d Rijn: Samson.

Halm, G. N. (1960). *Wirtschaftsysteme. Eine vergleichende Darstellung.* Berlin.

Hanson, P. (forthcoming). "Job Security". *Reverse Sovietology.* London.

Hanson, P. (1980). "International technology transfer from the West to USSR". *Soviet Economy in a New Perspective* (JEC, US Congress). Washington DC: US Government Printing Office.

Hanson, P. (1981). "Economic Constraints on Soviet Policies in the 1980s". *International Affairs*, winter 1980–81.

Hanson, P. and Hill, M. R (1979). "Soviet Assimilation of Western Technology: A Survey of UK Exporters' Experience". *Soviet Economy in a Time of Change.* JEC, US Congress), Washington DC.

Hare, P. (1979). "Investment in Hungary: the Planners' Nightmare". Paper presented to the 1979 conference of the National Association for Soviet and East European Studies, Cambridge.

Harrison, M. (1978). "The Soviet Economy in the 1920s and 1930s". *Capital and Class*, vol. 5.

Harrison, M. (1980). "Why did NEP fail?" *Economics of Planning*, vol. 16, no. 2.

Harrison, M. (1983). "Why was NEP abandoned?" *Studies in the Soviet Rural Economy* (R. C. Stuart, ed.): Allanhold Osmon and Co: forthcoming.

Hayden, E. W. (1976). *Technology Transfer to East Europe. US Corporate Experience.* New York: Praeger.

Heertje, A. (1973). *Economie en technische ontwikkeling.* Leiden: Stenfert Kroese.

Heertje, A. (1979). "Economie, technische ontwikkeling en economie". *Innovatie.* (Preadviezen van de Vereniging voor de Staathuishoudkunde 1979). Leiden and Antwerp: Stenfert Kroese.

Henderson and Quandt (1958). *Microeconomic Theory.* New York: McGraw-Hill.

Hennipman, P. (1976). "Pareto Optimality: Value Judgement or Analytical tool?" *Relevance and precision. From quantitative analysis to economic policy. (The P. de Wolff festschrift).* Alphen a/d Rijn: Samson.

Hillege, J. W. (1979). "Overheidsbeleid gericht op industriele vernieuwing". *Innovatie* (Preadviezen van de Vereniging voor Staathuishoudkunde 1979). Leiden and Antwerp: Stenfert Kroese.

Hirszowicz, M. (1980). *The Bureaucratic Leviathan*. Oxford: Martin Robertson.

Hodgman, D. R. (1964). *Soviet Industrial Production 1928–1951*. Cambridge, Mass.: Harvard University Press.

Holzman, F. D. (1960). "Soviet Inflationary Pressures, 1928–1957: Causes and Cures. *Quarterly Journal of Economics*, vol. 74.

Horvat, B. (1958). "The Optimum Rate of Investment". *Economic Journal*.

Horvat, B. (1965). "The Optimum Rate of Investment Reconsidered" *Economic Journal*.

Hough, J. F. (1969). *The Soviet Prefects: The local Party Organs in Industrial Decision Making*. Cambridge, Mass.: Harvard University Press.

Hough, J. F. (1976). "The Man and the System". *Problems of Communism*, 25.

Hough, J. F. (1977). *The Soviet and Social Science Theory*. Cambridge, Mass.: Harvard University Press.

Hua Chiao-mu (1978). "Observe Economic Laws, Speed Up the Four Modernizations". *Beijing Review*, nos 45, 46, 47.

Hunter, H. (1973). "The Overambitious Soviet First Five Year Plan". *Slavic Review*, vol. 32, no. 2.

Hunter, H. (1981a). "Modelling Structural Change using early Soviet data". *Journal of Development Economics*, vol. 9.

Hunter, H. (1981b). "Soviet agriculture, 1928–1940, with and without collectivisation". (Mimeo).

Inja. C. (1980). "Sectorstructuurbeleid: Instituties en instrumenten". *Sectorstructuurbeleid: Mogelijkheden en beperkingen*. WRR, The Hague: Staatsuitgeverij.

Innovatie (1970). *Innovatie* (Preadviezen van de Vereniging voor de Staatshuishoudkunde). Leiden and Antwerp: Stenfert Kroese.

Innovatienota (1979). *Innovatie*. The Hague: Staatsuitgeverij.

Ishikawa, S. (1967). *Economic Development in Asian Perspective*. Tokyo: Institute of Economic Research, Hitotsubashi University.

Janossy, F. (1971). *The End of the Economic Miracle*. New York: International Arts and Sciences Press.

Jasny, N. (1949). *The Socialized Agriculture of the USSR*. Stanford: Stanford University Press.

Jiang Yiwei (1980). "The Theory of an Enterprise Based Economy". *Social Sciences in China*, vol. 1, no. 1.

Jong, H. W. de (1979). "Geleid beleid?" *Economisch Statistische Berichten*, 19-9-'79.

Jong, H. W. de (1980). "Het Nederlands structuurbeleid: "De zichtbare vinger aan de onzichtbare hand". *Sectorstructuurbeleid: Mogelijkheden en beperkingen*. The Hague: Staatsuitgeverij.

Kahan, A. (1964). "The Collective Farm System in Russia: Some Aspects of its Contribution to Soviet Economic Development". *Agriculture in Economic Development* (C. Eicher and L. Witt, eds). New York: McGraw-Hill.

Kaldor, N. (1976). "Inflation and recession in the world economy". *Economic Journal*, December.

Kalecki, M. (1970). "Theories of Growth in Different Social Systems". *Scientia*, CV.

Kalecki, M. (1972). *Selected Essays on the Economic Growth of the Socialist and the Mixed Economy*. Cambridge: Cambridge University Press.

Kaser, M. (1961). "A survey of the national accounts of Eastern Europe". *Income and Wealth*, vol. IX.

Katz, A. L. (1973). *The Unusual Summer of 1972*. (Translation by L. A. Hutchinson of book published by Gidrometizdat, Leningrad.)

Kautsky, K. (1899). *Die Agrarfrage*. Stuttgart: Dietz.

Kawakami, T. (1979). "The Crisis of the Capitalist World: A Marxist View". *Cambridge Journal of Economics*, vol. 3, no. 2, June.

Keren, M. (1973). "The New Economic System in the GDR: An Obituary". *Soviet Studies*, April.

Kerr, C. *et al.* (ed.) (1973). *Industrialism and Industrial Man*. London: Penguin.

Kerr, C. (1983). *The future of industrial societies*. Cambridge Mass.: Harvard University Press.

Khan, A. R and Ghai, D. (1979). *Collective Agriculture and Rural Development in Soviet Central Asia*. London: Macmillan.

Khozyaistvennaya reforma i problemy realizatsii (1968). Moscow: Ekonomika.

Killick, T. (1976). "The Possibilities of Development Planning". *Oxford Economic Papers*, vol. 28, no. 2, July.

Klatt, W. (1971). "Comment" and "Successes and failures of communist farming". *Agrarian Policies and Problems in Communist and Non-Communist Countries* (W. A. D. Jackson, ed.). Seattle: University of Washington Press.

Klatt, W. (1976). "Reflections on the 1975 Harvest". *Soviet Studies*, October.

Klein, L. (1978). "The Supply Side". *American Economic Review*, vol. 68, no. 1, March.

Knaack, R. (1980). "The Role of Profit in the Soviet Economy". *De Economist*, vol. 128, no. 3.

Knaack, R. (1982). "China's nieuwe tien goboden". *Economisch Statistische Berichten*, 26 May.

Knaus, W. A. (1981). *Inside Russian Medicine: An American Doctor's First Report*. New York: Everest House.

Komarov, B. (1978). *Unichtozhenie prirody*. Frankfurt: Posev.

Konrad, G. and Szelenyi, I. (1979). *The Intellectuals on the Road to Class Power*. Brighton: Harvester.

Koops, J. G., Olthof, J. D. and Stoppelenburg, D. A. (1978). "Baten van het Nederlandse aardgas: nu en in de toekomst". *Economisch Statistische Berichten*, no. 3150.

Kornai, J. (1959). *Overcentralization in Economic Administration*. Oxford: Oxford University Press.

Kornai, J. (1970). "A General Descriptive Model of Planning Process". *Economics of Planning*, nos 1–2.

Kornai, J. (1971). *Anti-equilibrium*. Amsterdam and London: North-Holland.

Kornai, J. (1972). *Rush versus Harmonic Growth*. Amsterdam: North-Holland.

Kornai, J. (1979). *The Dilemmas of a Socialist Economy: The Hungarian Experience*. Dublin: Economic and Social Research Institute. Reprinted in *Cambridge Journal of Economics*, 1980, no. 2.

Kornai, J. (1980). *Economics of Shortage*. Amsterdam: North-Holland.

Kornai, J. (1983). Convergence theory and historical reality, *Society and Labour* (Tokyo) vol 30 December.

Korzec, M. (1978). "De inkomensrevoluties in de Soviet-Unie en China". *Intermediair*, December 22.

Kovalev, L. A. and Lapeta, D. D. (1971). *Effectivnost' khozyaistvennoi reformy v promyshlennosti*. Minsk: BNIINTI.

Kowalik, T. (1978). "The Institutional Framework of Dobb's Economics, *Cambridge Journal of Economics*, vol. 2, no. 2.

Koz'bor, E. I. and Chevkassov, N. G. (1969). *Plata za proizvodstvennye fondy v evropeiskikh sotsialisticheskikh stranakh*. Moscow: Ekonomika.

Kozyrev, V. M. (1972). *Renta, tsena khozraschet v neft'yanoi prommyshlennosti*. Moscow: Ekonomika.

Kwee, S. L. (1979). "Nederland op weg naar een post-industriele samenleving? *Nederland op weg naar een postindustriele samenleving?* (S. L. Kwee, J. G. Lambooy, J. Buit and M. de Smidt, eds). Assen: Van Gorcum.

Kyn, O. (1974). "On international comparisons in artificial prices." (Mimeo, Vienna Institute for International Economic Comparisons).

Lakatos, I. (1976). *Proofs and Refutations*. Cambridge: Cambridge University Press.

Lakatos, I. (1978). *The Methodology of Scientific Research Programmes*. Cambridge: Cambridge University Press.

Lambooy, J. G. (1979). "Enkele sociaal-economische aspecten van de post-industriele maatschappij". *Nederland op weg naar een post-industriele samenleving?* (S. L. Kwee, J. C. Lambooy, J. Buit and M. de Smidt, eds). Assen: Van Gorcum.

Lampton, D. M. (1974). *Health, Conflict and the Chinese Political System*. Ann Harbour: Center for Chinese Studies, University of Michigan Michigan Papers in Chinese Studies, no. 18.

Lampton, D. M. (1977). *The Politics of Medicine in China*, Folkestone: Dawson.

Lane, D. (1976). *The Socialist Industrial State*, London: Allen and Unwin.

Lange, O. (1963). *Political Economy*, vol. 1. Oxford: Pergamon.

Lauterbach, A. (1976). "The 'convergence' controversy revisited". *Kyklos*, vol. 29, fasc. 4.

Lee, W. T. (1979). "USSR gross national product in established prices, 1955–1975". *Jahrbuch der Wirtschaft Osteuropas*. Band 8. Munich and Vienna: Günter Olzog.

Lehmann, D. (1974). "Agrarian reform in Chile, 1965–1972. An essay in contradictions". *Agrarian Reform and Agrarian Reformism* (D. Lehmann, ed). London: Faber and Faber.

Leptin, G. and Melzer, M. (1978). *Economic Reform in East German Industry.* Oxford: Oxford University Press.

Lewin, M. (1974). "'Taking grain': Soviet Policies of Agricultural Procurements before the War". *Essays in Honour of E. H. Carr* (C. Abramsky, ed.). London: Macmillan.

Liberman, E. G. (1950). *Khozyaistvennyi raschet mashinostroitel'nogo zavoda.* Moscow: Ekonomika.

Liberman, E. G. (1970). *Ekonomicheskie metody povysheniva effektivnosti proizvodstva.* Moscow: Ekonomika.

Liberman, E. G. (1972). *Economics Methods and the Effectiveness of Production.* New York: International Arts and Sciences Press.

Liberman, Ya. G. (1968). "Optimal'noe upravlenie ekonomiki i effektivnost' material'nogo stimulirovaniya". *Ekonomika i matematicheskie methody,* no. 5.

Lin Zili (1980). "Initial Reform in China's Economic Structure". *Social Sciences In China,* vol. 1, no. 3.

Lindblom, C. E. (1965). *The Intelligence of Democracy.* New York: Macmillan.

Linneman, H., Pronk, J. P. and Tinbergen, J. (1970). "Convergence of economic systems in East and West". *The Soviet economy* (M. Bronstein and D. R. Fusfeld, eds). Homewood, Ill.: Richard Irwin.

Lipton, M. (1974). "Towards a Theory of Land Reform". *Agrarian Reform and Reformism* (D. Lehmann, ed.). London: Faber and Faber.

Loasby, B. J. (1976). *Choice, Complexity and Ignorance.* Cambridge: Cambridge, University Press.

Lowenhardt, J. (1975). "De vonk en de fakkel. Prive-initiatief in de sovjet-wetenschap". *Internationale Spectator,* 1975, no. 1.

Makhaisky, J. W. (1905). *Umstvennyi rabochii* (3 parts, Geneva 1904 and 1905, under pseudonym A. Volsky, previously circulated in Russia in hectographed form).

Malafeev, A. N. (1964). *Istoriya tsenoobrazovaniya v SSSR (1917–1963 gg).* Moscow: Mysl'.

Markowski, S. (ed.) forthcoming. *Reverse Sovietology.* London.

Marx, K. (1961). *Capital,* vol. I. Moscow: Foreign Languages publishing House.

Materialy (1932). *Materialy po balansu narodnogo khozyaistva za 1928 i 1929 i 1930 gg* (A. I. Petrov, ed.). Moscow: TsUNKhU SSSR. A copy of this book is at the Centre for Russian and East European Studies, Birmingham University (CREES).

Matthews, M. (1978). *Privilege in the Soviet Union.* London: Allen and Unwin.

Maynard, G. (1963). *Economic Development and the Price Level.* London: Macmillan.

McAuley A. (1982). "Sources of Earnings Inequality". *Soviet Studies,* July.

McAuley A. (1979). *Economic welfare in the Soviet Union*. Madison, Wisc. and Hemel Hempstead: University of Winconsin Press.

McAuley, A. (1981). *Women's Work and Wages in the Soviet Union*. London: Allen and Unwin.

McDougall, C. and Housego, D. (1981). "China's Perplexing Economic U-Turn". *Financial Times*, 2 March 1981.

Medvedev, R. A. and Medvedev, Zh. A. (1977). *Khrushchev: The Years in Power*. Oxford: Oxford University Press.

Mesa-Lago, C. (1968). *Unemployment in Socialist Countries: Soviet Union, East Europe, China and Cuba*. Unpublished Ph.D. Dissertation, Cornell University.

Meyer, A. G. (1970). "Theories of Convergence". *Change in Communist systems* (C. Johnson, ed.). Stanford: Stanford University Press.

Michels, R. (1962). *Political Parties*, an English translation of his classic 1911 study, New York.

Millar, J. R. (1970). "Soviet Rapid Development and the Agricultural Surplus Hypothesis". *Soviet Studies*, vol. 22.

Millar, J. R. (1971). "The Agricultural Surplus Hypothesis: A reply to Alec Nove". *Soviet Studies*, vol. 23.

Millar, J. R. (1974). "Mass Collectivisation and the Contribution of Agriculture to the First Five Year Plan". *Slavic Review*, December.

Millar, J. R. (1976). "What's Wrong with the Standard Story". *Problems of Communism*. July–August.

Millar, J. R. (1977). "The Prospects for Soviet Agriculture". *Problems of Communism*.

Millar, J. R. (1978). "A note on primitive accumulation in Marx and Preobrazhensky". *Soviet Studies*, July.

Montias, J. (1976). *The Structure of Economic Systems*. New Haven: Yale University Press.

Morishima, H. (1973). *Marx's Economics: A Dual Theory of Value and Growth*. Cambridge:

Morton, H. W. (1979). "The Soviet Quest for Better Housing—an Impossible Dream?" *Soviet Economy in a Time of Change*, vol. 1. Washington D.C.: Joint Economic Committee, US Congress.

Mouly, J. (1977). "Employment: A Concept in Need of Renovation". *International Labour Review*, vol. CXVI.

Naidenov, V. and Radina, Yu. (1974). "Analiz napryazhennosti planov". *Planovoe khozyaistvo*, no. 3.

Nickum, J. E. (1978). "Labour Accumulation in China and its Role since the Cultural Revolution". *Cambridge Journal of Economics*, no. 3.

Nolan, P. (1983). De-collectivisation of agriculture in China, 1979–82, *Cambridge Journal of Economics* vol 7. no 3/4 Sept/Dec.

Nove, A. (1964). *Was Stalin Really Necessary?* London: Allen and Unwin.

Nove, A. (1969). *An Economic History of the USSR*. London, Allen Lane.

Nove, A. (1971a). "The Agricultural Surplus Hypothesis: A Comment on James R. Millar's Article". *Soviet Studies*, vol. 22.

Nove, A. (1971b). "A Reply to the Reply". *Soviet Studies*, vol. 23.

Nove, A. (1977). *The Soviet Economic System*. London: Allen and Unwin.

Nove, A. (1979). *Political Economy and Soviet Socialism*. London: Allen and Unwin.

Nove, A. (1982). "Income distribution in the USSR". *Soviet Studies*, April.

Nuti, M. (1979). "The Contradictions of Socialist Economies: A Marxian Interpretation". *The Socialist Register 1979* (R. Miliband and J. Saville, eds). London: Merlin.

Odell, P. R. (1979). "Een kritische beschouwing van de uitgangspunten van het nederlandse energiebeleid". *Economisch Statistische Berichten*, no. 3205.

Osiatynski, J. (1973). "On the Price Bias in Comparative Analysis of Planned and Market Economies". (Mimeo, Vienna Institute for International Economic Comparisons.)

Osipov, G. V. (ed.) (1972). *Informatsionnyi byulleten*, no. 73. Moscow: Institut Konkretnykh Sotsial'nykh Issledovanii AN SSSR.

Paine, S. (1976). "Balanced Development: Maoist Conception and Chinese Practice". *World Development*, no. 4.

Pasinetti, L. L. (1965). "A New Theoretical Approach to the Problems of Economic Growth". *The Econometric Approach to Development Planning*. Amsterdam: North-Holland.

Perakh, M. (1977). "Utilization of Western technological advances in Soviet industry". *East-West technological cooperation*. Brussels: NATO.

Petrakov, N. Ya. (1976). "Mekhanizm funktsionirovaniya sotsialisticheskoi ekonomiki i problema narodnokhozyaistvennogo kriteriya optimal' nosti". *Ekonomika i matematicheskie metody*, no. 5.

Pickersgill, J. (1977). "Soviet Inflation: Causes and Consequences". *Soviet Union/Union Sovietique*, 4.

Planovyi (1981). *Planovyi differentsirovannyi balans dokhodov i potrebleniya naseleniya*. Moscow.

Pokazateli (1980). *Pokazateli sotsial'nogo razvitiya i planirovaniya*. Moscow: Nauka.

Poltorygin, V. (1969). "Naprazhennyi plan predpriyatiya i khozyaistvennaya reforma. *Planirovanie i khozyzistvennaya reforma* (M. Z. Bor and V. K. Poltorygin, eds). Moscow: Mysl'.

Portes, R. (1971). "The control of inflation: Lessons from East European experience". *Economica*, vol. 44.

Portes, R. (1978). "Inflation under Central Planning". *The Political Economy of Inflation* (J. H. Goldthorpe and F. Hirsch, eds). Oxford: Martin Robertson.

Portes, R. and Winter, D. (1977). "The Supply of Consumption Goods in Centrally Planned Economics". *Journal of Comparative Economics*, vol. 1.

Portes, R. and Winter, D. (1978). "The Demand for Money and for Consumption Goods in Centrally Planned Economies". *Review of Economics and Statistics*, vol. 60.

Portes, R. & Winter, D. (1980). "Disequilibrium Estimates for Consumption

Goods Markets in Centrally Planned Economies". *Review of Economic Studies*, vol. 47.

Potrebnosti, dokhody, potreblenie. (1979). Moscow: Nauka.

Preobrazhensky, E. (1965). *The New Economics*, 2nd edn. Oxford: Oxford University Press.

Pryor, F. L. (1973). *Property and Industrial Organisation in Communist and Capitalist Nations.* Bloomington, Ind.: Indiana University Press.

Pryor, F. L. (1973). "Some Costs and Benefits of Markets: An Empirical Study". *Quarterly Journal of Economics*, February.

PK (1979). *Partijkrant (Ledenblad van de Partij van de Arbeid).* no. 1, November.

Rabkina, N. E. and Rimashevskaya, N. M. (1978). "Raspredelitel'nie otnosheniya i sotsia'noe razvitie". *Ekonomika i organizatsiya promyshlennogo proizvodstva*, no. 5.

Rakovski, M. (1978). *Towards an East European Marxism*, London: Allison and Busby.

Rapport van de Commissie Economische Deskundigen (1978) The Hague: SER.

Ren Tao, Sun Huzying and Liu Jinglin (1980). "Investigation Report: Enterprises in Sichuan Province Acquire Greater Independence". *Social Sciences in China*, vol. 1, no. 1.

Robinson, J. (1964). "Chinese Agricultural Communes". *Coexistence*, May.

Robinson, J. (1975, 1976). *Economic management in China*, London.

Robinson, J. (1977). "Employment and the Choice of Technique". *Society and Change.* (K. S. Krishnaswamy, A. Mitra, J. G. Patel, K. N. Raj and M. N. Srinivas, eds). Bombay: Oxford University Press.

Rowthorn, R. (1965). "The Trap of an Incomes Policy". *New Left Review*, no. 34.

Rowthorn, R. (1977). "Conflict, Inflation and Money". *Cambridge Journal of Economics*, no. 3.

Rzhanitsyna, A. S. (1979). Chapter in *Problemy raspredeleniya i rost narodnogo blagosostoyaniva.* Moscow: Nauka.

Samuelson, P. (1948). *Foundations of Economic Analysis.* Cambridge, Mass.: Harvard University Press.

Sanderson, F. H. (1954). *Methods of Crop Forecasting.* Harvard: Harvard University Press.

Sarychev, V. G. (ed.) (1970). *Problemy vnutrennogo rynka pri sotsializme.* Leningrad: Leningrad Institute of Soviet trade, *Trudy* vol. 35.

Schon, D. A. (1971). *Beyond the Stable State: Public and Private Learning in a Changing Society.* London: Maurice Temple Smith.

Schouten, D. (1957). *Exacte Economie.* Leiden: Stenfert Kroese.

Schroeder, G. and Severin, B. (1976). "Soviet Consumption and Income Policies in Perspective". *Soviet Economy in a New Perspective.* Washington: US Government Printing Office.

Schroeder, G. E. (1972). "An Appraisal of Soviet Wage and Income Statistics". *Soviet Economic Statistics* (V. G. Treml and J. P. Hardt, eds). Durham, North Carolina: Duke University Press.

Schroeder, G. E. (1973). "Recent Developments in Soviet Planning and Incentives". *Soviet Economic Prospects for the Seventies*. (Joint Economic Committee US Congress, Washington DC).

Sectornota (1979). *Voortgangsnota Economisch Structuurbeleid*. The Hague: Staatsuitgeverij.

Selectieve groei (1976). (*Economische structuurnota*). The Hague: Staatsuitgeverij.

Selucky, R. (1972). *Economic Reforms in Eastern Europe*. New York: Praeger.

Selucky, R. (1979). *Marxism, Socialism, Freedom*. London: Macmillan.

Sen, A. (1975). *Employment, Technology and Development*. Oxford: Clarendon Press.

Sen, A. K. (1970). *Collective Choice and Social Welfare*. San Francisco: Holden-Day.

Sen, A. K. (1977). "Starvation and Exchange Entitlements: A General Approach and its Application to the Great Bengal Famine." *Cambridge Journal of Economics*, vol. 1, no. 1.

Sergeev, S. S. (ed). (1972). *Kapital'nye vlozheniya v sel'skoe khozyaistvo: planirovanie i effektivnost'*. Moscow:

Severin, B. S. (1979). "USSR: The all-union and Moscow collective farm market price indexes". *The ACES Bulletin*, vol. XXI, no. 1, spring.

Shaffer, H. G. (ed.) (1977). *Soviet agriculture*. New York: Praeger.

Shanin, T. (1972). *The Awkward Class*. Oxford: Clarendon Press.

Sik, O. (1972). *Czechoslovakia, The Bureaucratic Economy*. New York: International Arts and Sciences Press.

Simatupang, B. (1981). "Polish Agriculture in the 1970s and the Prospects for the early 1980s". *European Review of Agricultural economics*, no. 4.

Simms, Jr. J. Y. (1982). "The Crop Failure of 1891". *Slavic Review*, summer.

Simon, H. A. (1976). "From Substantive to Procedural Rationality". *Method and Appraisal in Economics* (ed. S. Latsis, ed.). Cambridge: Cambridge University Press.

Singleton, F. (ed.) *Environmental Misuse in the Soviet Union*. New York: Praeger.

Sinha, R. P. (1975). "Chinese Agriculture: A Quantitative Look". *Journal of Development Studies*, vol. 11.

Sitnin, V. V. (1969). *Problemy pribyli i khozyaistvennogo rascheta v promsyshlennosti*. Moscow: Finansy.

Skilling, H. G. and Griffiths, F. (1971). *Interest Groups in Soviet Politics*. Princeton: Princeton University Press.

Slama, J. and Vogel, H. (1977). "Technology Advances in CMEA Countries". *East-West Technological Co-operation*. Brussels: NATO.

Soos, K. A. (1978). "Some General Problems of the Hungarian Investment System". *Acta Oeconomica*, vol. 21, no. 3.

Sovershenstvovanie (1970). *Sovershenstvovanie gosudarstvennoi statistiki na sovremennom etape*. Moscow: Statistika (Materialy vsesoyuznogo soveshchaniya statistikov.)

Sovremennye (1970). *Sovremennye burzhuaznye teorii o sliyanii kapitalizma i sotsializma*. Moscow: Nauka.

Spulber, N. and Horowitz, I. (1976). *Quantitative Economic Policy and Planning*. New York: Norton.

Stavis, B. (1979). *The Politics of Agricultural Mechanization in China*. Ithaca: Cornell University Press.

Steinbruner, J. D. (1974). *The Cybernetic Theory of Decisions*. Princeton: Princeton University Press.

Stone, R. (1970). "A Comparison of the SNA and MPS". *Mathematical Models of the Economy and Other Essays*, Chapter XIII. London: Chapman and Hall.

Sutton, A. C. (1973). *Western Technology and Soviet Economic Development 1945 to 1965*. Stanford, Calif.: Hoover Institute Press.

Sweezy, P. (1977). *American Economic Review*. Papers and Proceedings, February.

Sweezy, P. (1979). "A Crisis in Marxian theory". *Monthly Review*, June.

Swianiewicz, S. (1965). *Forced Labour and Economic Development*. Oxford: Oxford University Press.

Szelenyi, I. (1972). "Housing System and Social Structure". *The Sociological Review Monograph*, vol. XVII, February. Repr. *The Social Structure of Eastern Europe* (B. L. Faber, ed). New York, 1976.

Szelenyi, I. (1979). "The Position of the Intelligentsia in the Class Structure of State Socialist Societies". *Critique* 10/11.

Szymanski, A. (1979). *Is the Red Flag Flying?* London: Zed Press.

Tannenbaum, A. S. *et al.* (eds) (1974). *Hierarchy in Organisations*. San Francisco: Jossey-Bass.

Tarling, R and Wilkinson, F. (1977). "The Social Contract: Post-War Incomes Policies and their Inflationary Impact". *Cambridge Journal of Economics*, no. 4.

Teulings, A. W. M. (ed.) (1978). *Herstructurering van de Industrie*. Alphen a/d Rijn: Samson.

Thurow, L. C. (1976). *Generating Inequality*. London: Macmillan.

Ticktin, H. (1973). "Towards a Political Economy of the USSR". *Critique* 1.

Tinbergen, J. (1961). "Do Communist and Free Economies show a Converging Pattern?" *Soviet Studies*, vol. 12, no. 4.

Tinbergen, J. (1964). "The Significance of Welfare Economics for Socialism". *On Political Economy and Econometrics*. Essays in honour of Oskar Lange. Warsaw: PWN.

Tinbergen, J. (1967). "Some Suggestions for a Modern Theory of the Optimum Regime." *Socialism, Capitalism and Economic Growth* (C. H. Feinstein, ed.). Cambridge: Cambridge University Press.

Treml, G. (1968). "The Politics of 'Libermanism'". *Soviet Studies*, vol. 19, no. 4, April.

Trezise, P. H. (1976). *Rebuilding grain reserves*. Washington DC: Brookings Institute.

Trotsky, L. (1923). *Dvenadtsatyi s"ezd rossiiskoi Kommunisticheskoi partii (bol'shevikov)*, pp. 315 and 321. Moscow: Krasnaya Nov.

Trotsky, L. (1927). *Sochineniya*, vol. 21, pp. 301–3. Moscow: Gosudarstvennoe Izdatel'stvo. This is part of a speech delivered in 1922.

Trud (1968). *Trud v SSSR*. Moscow: Statistika.

Tucker, R. C. (ed.) (1977). *Stalinism: Essays in Historical Interpretation*. New York: Norton.

Turner, H. A. (1972). "Can Wages be Planned?" *The Crisis in Planning* (M. Faber and D. Seers, eds). London: Chatto and Windus.

Vainshtein, A. L. (1967). "Dinamika narodnogo dokhoda SSSR i ego osnovnykh komponentov". *Ekonomika i matematicheskie metody*, vol. 3, no. 1.

Vainshtein, A. L. (1969). *Narodnyi dokhod Rossii i SSSR*. Moscow: Nauka.

Vasil'eva, N. A. (1973). "Fond pooshchreniya i napryazhennost' planovykh zadanii". *Ekonomicheskie problemy sovershenstvovaniya upravleniya promyshlennym predpriyatiem* (R. G. Karagedov, G. V. Grenbek and V. A. Grigor'ev, eds). Novosibirsk: Nauka.

Vermeer, E. G. (1979). "Social welfare provisions and the limits of inequality in contemporary China". *Asian Survey*, September.

Volkonsky, V. A. (1981). *Problemy sovershenstvovaniya khozyaistvennogo mekhanizma*. Moscow: Nauka.

Voslensky, M. (1980). *La nomenklatura* (transl. from German original). Paris: Belfond.

Vyas, A. (1974). "Real Wages in the Soviet Economy (1928–1937)". Birmingham Ph.D.

Vyas, A. (1979). "Primary Accumulation in the USSR Revisited". *Cambridge Journal of Economics*, vol. 3, no. 2, June.

Wädekin, K. E. (1973). *The Private Sector in Soviet Agriculture*. Berkeley: University of California Press.

Wagstaff, H. R. (1972). "The Economic Surplus of Agriculture in the United Kingdom". *Journal of Agricultural Economics*, vol. 23, no. 3.

Wakar, A. (1964). "Prices, Incentives, and Calculation Methods". *On Political Economy and Econometrics*. Warsaw: PWN.

Walker, K. R. (1965). *Planning in Chinese Agriculture*. London: Cass.

Ward, B. (1972). *What's Wrong with Economics?* New York: Basic.

Watson, A. (1983). "China looks for shoes that fit", *World Development*, August.

Weitzman, M. L. (1975). "The New Soviet Incentive Model". *The Bell Journal of Economics*. vol. 7, no. 1.

Wheatcroft, S. (1974a). "The Reliability of Russian Prewar Grain Output Statistics". *Soviet Studies*, April.

Wheatcroft, S. (1974b). "Views on Grain Output, Agricultural Reality and Planning in the Soviet Union in the 1920s". Unpublished thesis, Birmingham.

Wheatcroft, S. (1977). "Grain Production Statistics in the USSR in the 1920s and 1930s". Mimeo, Birmingham.

Wheatcroft, S., Davies, R. W. and Cooper, J. M. (1982). "Soviet Industrialisation Reconsidered: Some Preliminary Conclusions about Economic Developments between 1926 and 1941". Mimeo, Birmingham.

Wheelwright, E. L. and B. McFarlane (1971). *The Chinese Road to Socialism.* New York.

Whyte III, L. T. (1977). "Deviance, Modernization, Rations and Household Registers in Urban China". *Deviance and Social Control in Chinese Society.* (A. Wilson, S. L. Greenblatt and R. W. Wilson, eds). New York: Praeger.

Wiles, P. (1962). *The Political Economy of Communism.* Oxford: Blackwell.

Wiles, P. (1972). "Soviet Unemployment on US Definitions". *Soviet Studies,* vol. 23.

Wiles, P. (1974). *Distribution of Income: East and West.* Amsterdam: North-Holland.

World Bank (1976). *World Tables.* Baltimore and London.

Worms, C. (1980). "Het financiewezen in de Volksrepubliek China". *De Chinese economie* (M. Ellman, ed.). Leiden/Antwerp: Stenfert Kroese.

Worswick, G. D. N. (ed.) (1976). *The Concept and Measurement of Involuntary Unemployment.* London: Allen and Unwin.

Wu Jiang (1980). "On the Basic Economic Law of Socialism". *Beijing Review,* 13 October 1980.

WRR (1980). *Plaats en toekomst van de Nederlandse industrie.* The Hague: Staatsuitgeverij.

Xue Muqiao (1980). "On Reforming the Economic Management System". *Beijing Review,* nos. 5, 12, 14.

Xue Muqiao (1981). *China's Socialist Economy.* Beijing: Foreign Languages Press.

Yang Jianbai and Li Xuezeng (1980). "The Relations between Agriculture, Light Industry and Heavy Industry in China". *Social Sciences in China,* no. 2.

Yanowitch, M. (1963). "The Soviet Income Revolution". *Slavic Review,* pp. 683–397.

Yu Guangyuan (1980). "The basic approach to socialist ownership". *Beijing Review,* no. 49.

Zhou Jinghua (1980). "Discussions about Individual Economy". *Beijing Review,* no. 45.

Zielinski, J. (1973). *Economic Reforms in Polish industry.* London: Oxford University Press.

Zinoviev, A. (1978). *Svetloe Budushchee.* Lausanne: L'Age d'Homme.

Zurawicki, L. (1979). *Multinational enterprises in the West and East.* Alphen a/d Rijn and Germantown, Maryland: Sijthoff and Noordhoff.

INDEX